Adolescent Online Social Communication and Behavior:
Relationship Formation on the Internet

Robert Zheng
University of Utah, USA

Jason Burrow–Sanchez
University of Utah, USA

Clifford Drew
University of Utah, USA

INFORMATION SCIENCE REFERENCE

Hershey · New York

Director of Editorial Content:	Kristin Klinger
Senior Managing Editor:	Jamie Snavely
Assistant Managing Editor:	Michael Brehm
Publishing Assistant:	Sean Woznicki
Typesetter:	Jamie Snavely, Sean Woznicki
Cover Design:	Lisa Tosheff
Printed at:	Yurchak Printing Inc.

Published in the United States of America by
Information Science Reference (an imprint of IGI Global)
701 E. Chocolate Avenue
Hershey PA 17033
Tel: 717-533-8845
Fax: 717-533-8661
E-mail: cust@igi-global.com
Web site: http://www.igi-global.com/reference

Library of Congress Cataloging-in-Publication Data

Adolescent online social communication and behavior : relationship formation
on the Internet / Robert Zheng, Jason Burrow-Sanchez, and Clifford Drew,
editors.
      p. cm.
  Includes bibliographical references and index.
  Summary: "This edited volume addresses the pressing need to establish a
unified theoretical framework for adolescent online social communication
research,specifically, identify the role and function of the Internet in
adolescent social communication behavior, dynamic relationships among such
things as adolescent social-psychological needs, personality, and social norms
in online communication, and theories with practices in adolescent online
social communication"--Provided by publisher.
  ISBN 978-1-60566-926-7 (hardcover) -- ISBN 978-1-60566-927-4 (ebook) 1.
Internet and teenagers--Psychological aspects. 2. Online social networks--
Psychological aspects. I. Zheng, Robert. II. Burrow-Sanchez, Jason J. III.
Drew, Clifford J., 1943-
  HQ799.2.I5A36 2010
  302.23'1--dc22
                          2009021594

British Cataloguing in Publication Data
A Cataloguing in Publication record for this book is available from the British Library.

All work contributed to this book is new, previously-unpublished material. The views expressed in this book are those of the authors, but not necessarily of the publisher.

Table of Contents

Section 1
Emerging Conceptual and Theoretical Perspectives

Robert Z. Zheng, University of Utah, USA
Jason J. Burrow-Sanchez, University of Utah, USA
Stephanie Donnelly, University of Miami, USA
Megan E. Call, University of Utah, USA
Clifford J. Drew, University of Utah, USA

Gustavo S. Mesch, University of Haifa, Israel

Laura Widyanto, Nottingham Trent University, UK
Mark Griffiths, Nottingham Trent University, UK

Susan M. Miller, Kent State University, USA
Kenneth L. Miller, Youngstown State University, USA
Christine Allison, Kent State University, USA

Detailed Table of Contents

Section 1
Emerging Conceptual and Theoretical Perspectives

Section 1 presents a theoretical perspective on adolescent online social communication. It explores various issues from theoretical framework for adolescent online communication research to adolescent online social relationship, to online behavior such as Internet addiction, to adolescent developmental needs, and finally to a theoretical perspective on adolescent sexual identity development in the Internet

Chapter 1

Robert Z. Zheng, University of Utah, USA
Jason J. Burrow-Sanchez, University of Utah, USA
Stephanie Donnelly, University of Miami, USA
Megan E. Call, University of Utah, USA
Clifford J. Drew, University of Utah, USA

This chapter presents a conceptual framework for research exploring teen online communication. It brings attention to the influences of related elements such as social and individual factors on adolescent needs and behaviors in online communication. The proposed conceptual framework posits that adolescent online behaviors are linked to their needs pertaining to developmental, social-psychological, and cognitive demands. While adolescent needs are influenced by the social and individual factors, such influences also impose indirect impact on adolescent online behaviors. This framework provides a comprehensive picture of teen online communication in terms of the components involved in such communication. Suggestions for future studies are outlined with regard to the validation and implementation of the proposed framework.

Chapter 2

As the Internet has been adopted and integrated in the daily lives of an increasing number of young adolescents in western countries, scholars and commentators are debating and speculating on the impact of these new media on the activities, social relationships and worldview of the young generation. The communication environment has become more and more complex, as youth combine the use of electronic mail, open forums, chat rooms, instant messenger and social networking sites. In this chapter the author argues that the use of different social applications, partially define the structure and content of social communication and association. Discussions were made on the motivations for the use of each social application and the impact of the use on the type, size and quality of social ties that are maintained and created.

Chapter 3

It has been alleged by some academics that excessive Internet use can be pathological and addictive. This chapter reviews what is known from the empirical literature on "Internet addiction" and its derivatives (e.g., Internet Addiction Disorder, Pathological Internet Use etc.) and assesses to what extent it exists. The chapter briefly overviews (i) the history and concept of Internet addiction, (ii) research on (adolescent and adult) Internet addiction, (iii) the attraction of the online world to adolescents, (iv) Internet users in their own words, an (v) an examination of online versus offline identity. The authors have demonstrated that research into adolescent Internet addiction is a relatively little studied phenomenon and argued that a further research in this area is needed.

This chapter explores the formation of online relationships in the dual contexts of adolescent cognitive and psycho-social development and characteristics of Internet communication technologies. Research revealed that teens use the Internet to support existing, offline relationships and that such use is associated with closer relationships. For those who form online relationships, these are viewed as close or even romantic in nature. However, when compared along various dimensions, online relationships demonstrate weaker ties than do offline relationships. In general, extroverted teens are more likely to form online relationships, although, if that is their purpose, so do introverted teens. Forming online relationships may rest with the teen's awareness of how to present him or herself given the anonymity of the cue-free Internet environment.

Chapter 5

Bryant Paul, Indiana University, USA
Lelia Samson, Indiana University, USA

This chapter considers the potential role of the Internet in the process of adolescent sexual identity construction. It starts by providing evidence of the ever-increasing role the Internet is playing in the lives of adolescents and by considering the potential impact such a technology is likely to have given the transitional nature of the adolescent brain. A consideration of theoretical approaches for understanding the role the Internet is likely to play in individuals' sexual self-identity development is then undertaken. A review of the specific role Internet communication technologies have come to play in the process of adolescent sexual socialization is then carried out. The authors argue that future research addressing the role of the Internet in the process of adolescent sexual socialization and identity development must consider both the specific structure of the adolescent brain and the unique nature of the Internet as a source of information and an opportunity for social networking.

Section 2
Current Legal Perspectives and Future Legal Needs

Section 2 presents an important aspect in the research on adolescent online social communication. That is, the legal perspectives and the legal needs related to current and future practice and research. This section consists of two chapters contributed by authors who have considerable practical experiences and who have conducted substantial research on this issue.

Chapter 6

Larry L. Burriss, Middle Tennessee State University, USA

The chapter offers a discussion on the legal aspects related to adolescents and social networking sites such as Second Life. The author identified aspects related to what is protected and what is not in the ever-expanding CyberVillage which include (a) speech that occurs in school and deals with public policy and does not cause substantial disruption, is protected, (b) expressions that occur in the school building itself, or as part of an officially-sanctioned off-school-property function, whether part of the curriculum or not, and is disruptive or runs counter to the school's basic educational mission, is not protected, (c) speech that is "merely" offensive, and is created off-campus, is probably protected, even if the message is later distributed in the school, and (d) expression that causes or has the potential to cause serious disruption, or that can be considered a "true threat," is not protected. Given the current legal climate, the author proposed that it is critical that schools develop written policies regarding the role of the school in education for civility, free speech, disruption, threats and proper computer use, and how computer use relates to these areas.

Chapter 7

This chapter first reviews The Children's Internet Protection Act (CIPA; 2000) as well as other existing regulations in protecting children on the Internet, followed by an empirical study showing the evidence that CIPA is associated with a decrease in high school students' Internet use at school but does not appear to have a beneficial effect on their knowledge of Internet safety or opportunities for Internet safety education. Recommendations were made regarding assessing the real impact of CIPA as well other Internet safety regulations on young Internet users.

Section 3
Recent Research Findings, Educational Perspectives and Practical Applications

Section 3 consists of seven chapters covering a wide range of topics from effects of motives for Internet use, to adolescent fear in online environment, to risk factors affecting adolescent online social communication, and so forth. The researchers discussed various issues through unique lenses which revealed with considerable depth and breadth the causality and relationship of adolescent online social communication.

Chapter 8

The advent of new media technologies has dramatically changed both the nature and number of social compensation and mood management devices available to most youngsters. Although previous research has examined how the Internet has become an important resource for information and entertainment, little research has focused on the ways in which individuals use the Internet for social communication and support. In particular, how personality traits, such as perception of aloneness and age identity gratifications, together with motives for Internet use impact Internet habits and perceived social support are much-neglected areas of research. This chapter investigates how differences in these constructs among adolescents and children influence their online social behavior (such as use of instant messaging, online games, and participating in forums).

Chapter 9

The chapter focused on the interactions between the social networks of young adolescents and their computer usage. Particular attention was devoted to determining whether heavy computer use tended to isolate adolescent users. The findings challenged the common attributions of prevalent danger, that heavy youthful computer users would experience social isolation. The author concluded that the interpersonal lives and computer activities of early adolescents reciprocally reinforced patterns of behavior that lowered the likelihood of risk behaviors to a significantly greater degree than did direct parental involvement. Recommendations to responsible adults were offered to re-focus energies and efforts in directions that would support appropriate computer use and promote pro-social behaviors of online adolescents.

Chapter 10

    Megan E. Call, University of Utah, USA
    Jason J. Burrow-Sanchez, University of Utah, USA

The Internet is widely used among adolescents. Although the Internet is a beneficial tool for youth, some children and adolescents are at risk for being victimized online. Media reports portraying online predators and their victims have received increasing publicity. However, some information in these stories can be inaccurate or misleading. Therefore, it is important that mental health professionals and parents receive accurate information about online victimization in order to protect youth from harm. The purpose of this chapter is to provide research-based information on adolescent Internet use and the risk factors associated with online victimization. Further, recommendations for increasing protective factors are provided as a means to keep youth safe while using the Internet.

Chapter 11

    Sharmila Pixy Ferris, William Paterson University, USA

In this chapter the author explores Millenials' participation in the public good, investigating whether they use social networking for social responsibility. Millenials, the wired, connected generation for whom social networking is an essential aspect of life, are often criticized for their lack of social responsibility. Social networking, as new media uniquely a part of Millenials' wired and connected lifestyles, has the potential to "transform citizenship." To investigate Millenials' social networking and social responsibility, a Webnography was conducted. Findings go against conventional wisdom as the author found that Millenials use social networking to take social and political action, engage in social entrepreneurship, and conduct charitable solicitation and donation.

Chapter 12

    Ikuko Aoyama, Baylor University, USA
    Tony L. Talbert, Baylor University, USA

Cyberbullying is a growing phenomenon among adolescents, teens, and young adults who either perpetrate and/or are the recipients of harassing and threatening behaviors through the use of technologies such as emails, Internet communities and social networking Web sites, chat rooms, and cell phones. The incidences of cyberbullying have increased predominantly among students who are residents of technologically advanced countries throughout North America, Europe, and Asia. This chapter presents the characteristics and theoretical frameworks that define and contextualize cyberbullying including the international prevalence and related statistics, backgrounds and profiles of perpetrators, and adults' roles. It also provides educators and parents with prevention and intervention strategies to address cyberbullying among youth.

Maja Pivec, University of Applied Sciences, Austria
Paul Pivec, Deakin University, Australia

Many academics have stated that the perceived decline in education is attributed to the change in the students themselves; that students today think differently, process information differently, and get bored with traditional schooling techniques; they are the digital generation. While it is agreed that technology such as electronic games provide a wealth of opportunities and are strong advocates of the use of these methods, there is not enough evidence to show that the digital generation learns any differently than previous generations, or children who have never been exposed to computing of any kind. This chapter discusses the role of media and students. Suggestions are made about how the creative mind can be captivated in both traditional and digital teaching environments.

Muhammet Demirbilek, Suleyman Demirel University, Turkey
Berna Mutlu, University of Florida, USA

Information and communication technologies (ICT) have become an inevitable part of adolescents' daily life and have caused macro and micro changes that are shaping the societies in which adolescents of the future will live. As a two-way real time communication tool, chat rooms are one of the most popular forms of ICT in adolescents' daily life. Adolescents use ICT for meaningful communication and social interaction with their peers and relatives. The chapter offers a detailed discussion on issues related to chat rooms as a two-way real time communication tool frequently used by adolescents with an emphasis on the effects of chat rooms on adolescents' second language development.

Preface

Adolescent use of social online media such as blogs, chat rooms and text messaging has dramatically increased over the past decade largely due to the accessibility of such technology. For example, a recent report by Pew foundation (Pewinternet.org, 2007) indicated that approximately 64% of adolescents ages 12 to 17 engaged in at least some type of online social networking, up from 57% of online teens in 2004; however, about 47% of teens reported posting photos where others can see them and 89% of those who posted photos said that people comment on the images at least "some of the time." Posting personally identifiable information on the Internet is a general public concern and the news media indicates that online social communication may pose more threats than benefits to adolescents (Isakson, 2007; NBC Dateline, 2006; PBS Frontline, 2008). Echoing the growing concerns of the media, academia has been exploring the issues related to this emerging social phenomenon. So far, research on online teen social communication has been in separate directions, ranging from identifying adolescent cognitive development characteristics (Greenfield, 2004; Greenfield & Subrahmanyan, 2003), to personality and individual differences (Amichai-Hamburger, Wainapel, & Fox, 2002; Anolli, Villani, & Riva, 2005; McKenna & Bargh, 2000), to social communication (Dietz-Uhler & Bishop-Clark, 2005; Eastin, 2005), and to media characteristics (Hrastinski & Keller, 2007). There has been a failure to provide a coherent and well organized compendium of adolescent online communication research until now.

We believe that the key to a better understanding of adolescent online communication behavior is first to develop a unified theoretical framework on this topic (Zheng, Burrow-Sanchez, Donnelly, Call, & Drew, 2010). A unified theoretical framework of adolescent online social communication research will provide more guidance to the public in understanding teen online social communication behavior as well as generating new research in this area. This edited volume is significant in that it presents, for the first time, a systematic approach to the study of adolescent online social communication undergirded by a unified theoretical framework.

THE CONTRIBUTION OF THIS BOOK

This edited volume addresses the pressing need to establish a unified theoretical framework for adolescent online social communication research which has been lacking until now. More specifically, this volume serves to (a) identify the role and function of the Internet in adolescent social communication behavior, (b) bring together top researchers in the field who discuss the dynamic relationships among such things as adolescent social-psychological needs, personality, and social norms in online communication, and (c) bridge the theories with practices in adolescent online social communication by offering practical guidance to the public on this issue. In order to meet these objectives, we have taken an interdisciplinary approach that has drawn on the knowledge and research of educators across the globe with an emphasis on diverse aspects of adolescent online social communication such as social and cognitive development, communication characteristics and mode of communication. This volume, thus, moves beyond traditional disciplinary and geographical boundaries and provides important and useful information to researchers, educators and practitioners on adolescent online social communication.

THE ORGANIZATION OF THIS BOOK

The foci of this edited volume are to (a) understand the theoretical aspects of adolescent online social communication, (b) identify the mechanism that supports and regulates adolescent online social communication, and finally (c) provide important evidence on successful development and implementation of adolescent online social environment. Of fourteen excellent contributing chapters, three distinct themes have emerged. They include *emerging conceptual and theoretical perspectives*; *current legal perspectives and future legal needs*; and *recent research findings, educational perspectives, and practical application*. A discussion of the themes and relevant sections follows.

Section 1 presents a theoretical perspective on adolescent online social communication. It explores various issues from theoretical framework for adolescent online communication research to adolescent online social relationship, to online behavior such as Internet addiction, to adolescent developmental needs, and finally to a theoretical perspective on adolescent sexual identity development in the Internet.

In **Chapter 1**, Robert Z. Zheng, Jason J. Burrow-Sanchez, Megan E. Call, and Clifford J. Drew, of University of Utah, and Stephanie Donnelly, of University of Miami, explore a conceptual framework for research on teen online communication. It brings attention to the influences of related elements such as social and individual factors on adolescent needs and behaviors in online communication. The authors proposed that adolescent online behaviors are linked to their needs pertaining to developmental, social-psychological, and cognitive demands. While adolescent needs are influenced by the social and individual factors, such influences also impose indirect impact on adolescent online behaviors. This framework provides a comprehensive picture of teen online communication in terms of the components involved in such communication.

In **Chapter 2**, Gustavo S. Mesch, of the University of Haifa in Israel, discussed the motivations for the use of each social application and the impact of the use on the type, size and quality of social ties that are maintained and created. Drawing from multiple perspectives in adolescent online communication including social relationships and worldview of the young generation as well as the multiple venues of social communication such as the use of electronic mail, open forums, chat rooms, Instant Messenger and social networking sites, the author delved deep into the issue pertaining to the impact of these new media on adolescent social activities in an online environment. The author concluded that the communication environment has become more and more complex, further research should be conducted to understand the use of different social applications, the structure and content of social communication and the behavioral and psychological association with those applications and content.

In **Chapter 3**, Laura Widyanto and Mark Griffiths, Nottingham Trent University of UK, provided an extended discussion on the pathological and addictive nature of the Internet. The authors reviewed the history and concept of Internet addiction and the research on Internet addiction. They made several important conclusions about the current research in adolescent Internet addiction. Finally, the authors proposed directions for future research by identifying key areas related to adolescent Internet addiction.

Chapter 4 raises an important issue related to the formation of online relationships in the dual contexts of adolescent cognitive and psycho-social development and characteristics of Internet communication technologies. Susan M. Miller, Kent State University; Kenneth L. Miller, Youngstown State University, and Christine Allison, Kent State University, reviewed the literature on how teens use the Internet to support existing, offline relationships. Their discussion was then extended to online communication where adolescents' online behaviors were distinguished by their psychological and personal traits. The authors concluded that forming online relationships may rest with the teen's awareness of how to present him or herself given the unique cue-free Internet environment.

Bryant Paul and Lelia Samson, of Indiana University, presented in **Chapter 5** a new perspective on adolescent online social communication and relationship formation by considering the potential role of the Internet in the process of adolescent sexual identity construction. The authors asserted that the Internet is likely to play a critical role in individuals' sexual self-identity development in the millennia age. The authors then reviewed the specific role Internet communication technologies have come to play in the process of adolescent sexual socialization and argued that future research addressing the role of the Internet in the process of adolescent sexual socialization and identity development must consider both the specific structure of the adolescent brain and the unique nature of the Internet as a source of information and an opportunity for social networking.

Section 2 presents an important aspect in the research on adolescent online social communication. That is, the legal perspectives and the legal needs related to current and future practice and research. This section consists of two chapters contributed by authors who have considerable practical experiences and who have conducted substantial research on this issue.

Chapter 6 offers a discussion on the legal aspects related to adolescents and social networking sites such as Second Life. Larry L. Burriss, of Middle Tennessee State University, identified aspects on what is protected and what is not in the ever-expanding CyberVillage in relation to speech, expressions, and other cyber related behavior. Given the current legal climate, the author proposed that it is critical that schools develop written policies regarding the role of the school in education for civility, free speech, disruption, threats and proper computer use, and how computer use relates to these areas.

In **Chapter 7**, Zheng Yan, of State University of New York at Albany, reviewed The Children's Internet Protection Act (CIPA; 2000) as well as other existing regulations in protecting children on the Internet, followed by an empirical study showing the evidence that CIPA is associated with a decrease in high school students' Internet use at school but does not appear to have a beneficial effect on their knowledge of Internet safety or opportunities for Internet safety education. Recommendations were made regarding assessing the real impact of CIPA as well other Internet safety regulations on young Internet users.

Section 3 consists of seven chapters covering a wide range of topics from effects of motives for Internet use, to adolescent fear in online environment, to risk factors affecting adolescent online social communication, and so forth. The researchers discussed various issues through unique lenses which revealed with considerable depth and breadth the causality and relationship of adolescent online social communication.

In **Chapter 8**, Louis Leung, of the Chinese University of Hong Kong, focused on the ways in which individuals use the Internet for social communication and support. In particular, how personality traits, such as perception of *aloneness* and *age identity gratifications,* together with *motives for Internet use* impact Internet habits and behavior. The author investigated how differences in the above constructs among adolescents and children influence their online social behavior such as use of instant messaging, online games, and participating in forums.

In **Chapter 9**, Myron Orleans, of California State University at Fullerton, focused on the interactions between the social networks of young adolescents and their computer usage. Particular attention was devoted to determining whether heavy computer use tended to isolate adolescent users. The findings challenged the common attributions of prevalent danger, that heavy youthful computer users would experience social isolation. The author concluded that the interpersonal lives and computer activities of early adolescents reciprocally reinforced patterns of behavior that lowered the likelihood of risk behaviors to a significantly greater degree than did direct parental involvement.

Taking a different perspective Megan E. Call and Jason J. Burrow-Sanchez, of University of Utah, identified in **Chapter 10** risk factors involved in adolescent online social communication. The authors claimed that although the Internet is a beneficial tool for youth, some children and adolescents are at risk for being victimized online. They further pointed out that media reports portraying online predators and their victims can be inaccurate or misleading. Therefore, it is important that mental health professionals and parents receive accurate information about online victimization in order to protect youth from harm. The chapter provides research-based information on adolescent Internet use and the risk factors associated with online victimization. Further, recommendations for increasing protective factors are provided as a means to keep youth safe while using the Internet.

Chapter 11 explores Millenials' participation in the public good, investigating whether they use social networking for social responsibility. Sharmila Pixy Ferris, of William Paterson University, described social networking, as new media uniquely a part of Millenials' wired and connected lifestyles, has the potential to "transform citizenship." Using a Webnography approach, the author investigated Millenials' social networking and social responsibility. Findings go against conventional wisdom as the author found that Millenials use social networking to take social and political action, engage in social entrepreneurship, and conduct charitable solicitation and donation.

In **Chapter 12**, Ikuko Aoyama and Tony L. Talbert, of Baylor University, investigated cyberbullying among adolescents, teens, and young adults who either perpetrate and/or are the recipients of harassing and threatening behaviors through the use of technologies such as emails, Internet communities and social networking Web sites, chat rooms, and cell phones. This chapter presents the characteristics and theoretical frameworks that define and contextualize cyberbullying including the international prevalence and related statistics, backgrounds and profiles of perpetrators, and adults' roles. It also provides educators and parents with prevention and intervention strategies to address cyberbullying among youth.

Maja Pivec, of University of Applied Sciences in Austria, and Paul Pivec, of Deakin University in Australia, took a unique perspective by examining the relationship between electronic games and adolescent online social communication. **Chapter 13** discusses the role of media and students. The authors claimed that while it is agreed that technology such as electronic games provide a wealth of opportunities for digital generation learners, there is not enough evidence to show that the digital generation learns any differently than previous generations, or children who have never been exposed to computing of any kind. Finally, the authors concluded that the creative mind can be captivated in both traditional and digital teaching environments.

Finally, **Chapter 14** describes how information and communication technologies (ICT) are shaping the societies in which adolescents of the future will live. Muhammet Demirbilek, of the University of Wisconsin, and Berna Mutlu, of the University of Florida, elaborated on the functionalities of chat rooms for social communication and relationship formation. The chapter offers a detailed discussion on issues related to chat rooms as a two-way real time communication tool frequently used by adolescents. Emphases were made on the effects of chat rooms on adolescents' second language development.

REFERENCES

Amichai-Hamburger, Y., Wainapel, G., & Fox, S. (2002). "On the Internet no one knows I'm an introvert": Extroversion, neuroticism, and Internet interaction. *CyberPsychology & Behavior, 5*(2), 125-128.

Anolli, L., Villani, D., & Riva, G. (2005). Personality of people using chat: An online research. *CyberPsychology & Behavior, 8*(1), 89-95.

Isakson, C. (2007). *Caught on the Web*. Retrieved February 5, 2008, from http://www.eddigest.com

Dietz-Uhler, B., & Bishop-Clark, C. (2005). Formation of and adherence to a self-disclosure norm in an online chat. *CyberPsychology & Behavior, 8*(2), 114-120.

Eastin, M. S. (2005). Teen Internet use: Relating social perceptions and cognitive models to behavior. *CyberPsychology & Behavior, 8*(1), 62-75.

Greenfield, P. (2004). Developmental considerations for determining appropriate Internet use guidelines for children and adolescents. *Applied Developmental Psychology, 25*, 751-762.

Greenfield, P., & Subrahmanyan, K. (2003). Online discourse in a teen chatroom: New codes and new modes of coherence in a visual medium. *Developmental Psychology, 24*, 713-738.

Hrastinski, S., & Keller, C. (2007). Computer-mediated communication in education: A review of recent research. *Educational Media International, 44*, 61-77.

McKenna, K., & Bargh, J. (2000). Plan 9 from cyberspace: The implications of the Internet for personality and social psychology. *Personality and Social Psychology Review, 4*(1), 57-75.

NBC Dateline. (2006, April). *Most teens say they've met strangers online*. Retrieved February 5, 2008, from http://www.msnbc.msn.com/id/12502825

PBS Frontline. (2008, January). *Growing up online*. Retrieved February 5, 2008, from http://www.washingtonpost.com/wp-dyn/content/discussion/2008/01/17/ DI2008011702141.html

Pewinternet.org. (2007). *Reports: Family, friends and community*. Retrieved February 5, 2008, from http://www.pewinternet.org/ppf/r/230/report_display.asp

Zheng, R., Burrow-Sanchez, J., Donnelly, S., Call, M., & Drew, C. (2010). Toward an integrated conceptual framework of research in teen online communication. In R. Zheng, J. Burrow-Sanchez, & C. Drew (Eds.), *Adolescent online social communication and behavior: Relationship formation on the Internet*. Hershey, PA: Information Science Reference.

Acknowledgment

We wish to express our appreciation to colleagues who contributed chapters to this volume. The success of any edited book is a function of the quality of the individual authors. This volume represents the collective wisdom of many who voluntarily spent hundreds of hours putting together a series of chapters that provide excellent overview of the theories and practice in adolescent online social communication.

Our appreciation also goes to our reviewers who provide insightful input and suggestions. I thank all of our authors for their own expert assistance. I would also like to thank the following reviewers in particularly for their hard work, generous donation of their time, and their attention to detail:

Deanna Blackwell, University of Utah
Megan Call, University of Utah
Richard Hoffman, University of Utah
Melda N. Yildiz, William Paterson University

A special note of acknowledgment is given to Kristin M. Klinger and Julia Mosemann, editors at IGI Global, whose expertise and generous support make this project a great success. We would also like to thank the publishing team at IGI Global who has demonstrated the highest level of professionalism and integrity.

Finally, we would like to acknowledge the support from the Utah State Commission on Criminal and Juvenile Justice and the Center for the Advancement of Technology in Education (CATE) at University of Utah.

Robert Z. Zheng
Jason J. Burrow-Sanchez
Clifford J. Drew

April 2009

Section 1
Emerging Conceptual and Theoretical Perspectives

Chapter 1
Toward an Integrated Conceptual Framework of Research in Teen Online Communication

Robert Z. Zheng
University of Utah, USA

Jason J. Burrow-Sanchez
University of Utah, USA

Stephanie Donnelly
University of Miami, USA

Megan E. Call
University of Utah, USA

Clifford J. Drew
University of Utah, USA

ABSTRACT

This article presents a conceptual framework for research exploring teen online communication. It brings attention to the influences of related elements such as social and individual factors on adolescent needs and behaviors in online communication. The proposed conceptual framework posits that adolescent online behaviors are linked to their needs pertaining to developmental, social-psychological, and cognitive demands. While adolescent needs are influenced by the social and individual factors, such influences also impose indirect impact on adolescent online behaviors. This framework provides a comprehensive picture of teen online communication in terms of the components involved in such communication. Suggestions for future studies are outlined with regard to the validation and implementation of the proposed framework.

DOI: 10.4018/978-1-60566-926-7.ch001

INTRODUCTION

Research on adolescent online communication has grown rapidly in the past decade ranging from developmental identity to individual differences, and from behaviors in chatrooms to communication patterns on the Internet (Anolli, Villani & Riva, 2005; Greenfield, 2004; Gross, 2004; Livingstone, 2002; Valkenburg & Pater, 2007). Along the way, several researchers have provided major conceptual and practical insights into our understanding of how cognitive, psychological, social, and biological influences have affected adolescent online communication behaviors (Eastin, 2005; Sheeks & Birchmeier, 2007; Whitlock, Powers & Eckenrode, 2006). The key to deepening our understanding of adolescent online communication behavior is to synthesize existing conceptual frameworks to create new, eclectic models that capture the dynamics of teen online communication. These new models must incorporate relevant historical frameworks while simultaneously presenting new theoretical perspectives that address the interaction of the multiple domains of teen online communication within a contemporary context. Current theories explain teen online behaviors based on developmental models (Greenfield, 2004; Subrahmanyan, Smahel & Greenfield, 2006) or from the perspective of personality traits (Anolli et al., 2005; Widyanto & McMurran, 2004) or social relationship (Peter, Valkenburg & Schouten, 2006; Sheeks & Birchmeier, 2007; Valkenburg & Peter, 2007). However, a comprehensive model that examines the relationship of adolescent development and online behavior needs to be set forth. If there is to be an indepth and more accurate understanding of adolescent online behaviors, researchers must account for the factors that influence teen behaviors in online communication such as adolescent developmental needs, individual differences, and social environments. This paper explores the multifaceted aspects of adolescent online communication by identifying adolescent developmental needs, and related social and individual factors. An integrated conceptual framework will be proposed that examines the relationship of various components including adolescent cognitive, developmental and social needs as well as individual and environmental factors in teen online communication.

A REVIEW OF RESEARCH ON TEEN ONLINE COMMUNICATION

Past research has been primarily focused on the relationship between media effects and teen behaviors (Bushman & Anderson, 2001; Hrastinski & Keller, 2007; Rubin, 2002). For example, Suoninen (2001) explored the media effects on adolescent social communication and concluded that media play an important part in adolescent "identity work when young people build their own personal spheres of life" (p. 218). Groebel (2001) examined youth media behavior such as aggressiveness using the Internet by focusing on media effects involved in teen online communication. Greenfield and Yan (2006) argue that the existing research should go beyond "media effects" to examine how adolescent developmental needs relate to online communication. Buckingham (2004) made a similar statement by asserting that media studies including the study of the Internet "need to move beyond a determinist view of the effects media technology on children … to consider these new media and communication technologies within the context of broader changes in children's culture" (p. 108). Lloyd (2002) points out that mass media constructs must become integrated into a broader understanding of adolescent psychological functioning.

Investigation of teen online communication has shown that adolescents vary significantly in their online communication behaviors (Anolli et al., 2005; Gross, 2004; McKenna, Green & Gleason, 2002). While some adolescents are proactive in communicating with their peers, others are less involved. Some try to develop positive relationships by forming online collaboration. Others alienate themselves from their peers by displaying aggressiveness in online chatrooms. Recently, researchers have proposed several theoretical models to explicate the variability of adolescent online behaviors that include developmental needs (Greenfield, 2004; Subrahmanyan et al., 2006), self-efficacy (Eastin, 2005; Lin, 2006; Livingstone, Bober & Helsper, 2005; Valkenburg, Peter & Schouten, 2006), and social communication (Peter et al., 2006; McKenna et al., 2002).

Developmental Identity Formation and Online Communication

Some developmental theorists (e.g., Greenfield, 2004; Lloyd, 2002; Subrahmanyan et al., 2006) have concluded that teen online behavior such as aggressiveness and online addiction are related to adolescents' developmental needs. According to Greenfield (2004), constructing and developing personal identity is a major task facing adolescents, which can be resolved in one of two directions, one being adaptive (successful) and the other maladaptive (unsuccessful). Erikson (1968) describes this as an identity crisis which may affect an individual to face future challenges in life. Evidence has shown that failure to resolve identity crisis can lead to aggressiveness in language or physical behavior due to frustration and confusion in constructing a successful identity. Subrahmanyan et al. (2006) found a high level of aggressiveness in teen online communication such as using racial slurs and sexually explicit language in chatrooms. They concluded that such aggressiveness was caused by a developmental identity crisis where failure to successfully construct personal identity leads to a high level of anxiety which consequently generates some undesirable behaviors in a less restrictive environment like the Internet. Developmental identity formation theory explains, to some extent, teen behaviors in online communication; however, it focuses primarily on adolescent adjustment to the environment in terms of personal

identity construction. Research suggests that the study of personal identity in adolescents should be placed in a larger context where the influences of social and individual factors are considered (Baker, Victor & Chambers, 2004; van Aken, van Lieshout & Scholte, 1998).

Social Identity

Interpreting adolescent developmental needs merely from the perspective of biological needs limits our understanding of the social influence on adolescent development. According to Tajfel and Turner (1986), social identity is concerned with when and why individuals identify with, and behave as part of, social groups, adopting shared attitudes with outsiders. Social identity is operationally defined as social validation, expression, self-clarification, social control, and relationship development (Tajfel, 1978; Tajfel & Turner, 1986). There are two important concepts related to social identity: reciprocity and deindividualization. Dietz-Uhler and Bishop-Clark (2005) point out that reciprocity plays a critical role in forming social identity within a community. For example, social validation and relationship development are built on mutual trust which is often shown in the form of self-disclosure in online or off-line settings. The initial self-disclosure is likely to elicit a self-disclosure from the partner because participants are aware of reciprocity.

In contrast to reciprocity, deindividualization emphasizes group salience in the formation of social identity. Spears and Lea (1992) assert that members of a social community are often compelled to adhere to the norms of the group when the social identity is moderately salient. For example, if one of the norms of a group is self-disclosure, then group members are increasingly likely to disclose information about themselves to other group members. Both reciprocity and deindividualization are important concepts in understanding adolescents' social identity and developmental identity in teen online communication since adolescent development is characterized by a process of increasing social awareness with a constant effort of adjusting to social norms on the part of individuals (Waterman & Archer, 1990).

Online Social Communication

Social communication theories such as social inhibition theory (McKenna et al., 2002; Peter et al., 2006; Sheeks & Birchmeier, 2007) and social penetration theory (Dietz-Uhler and Bishop-Clark, 2005; Valkenburg & Peter, 2007) have significantly influenced the research on adolescent online communication. Social inhibition theory asserts that social communication can be inhibited by "gating features" such as physical appearance, communication skills, stuttering, and shyness (McKenna et al., 2002). These features can prevent people from developing positive social relationships with others because of the strong impact they have upon first impressions which influence the subsequent development of friendship. McKenna et al. point out that the effects of gating features become mitigated on the Internet because "such features are not initially in evidence and thus do not stop potential relationships from getting off the ground" (p. 11). Based on the unique features of the Internet, McKenna et al. propose a stimulation hypothesis to explain how people form online relationships. According to their hypothesis, the formation of relationship between strangers is facilitated by reduced cues and self-disclosure which stimulate the closeness of friendship (also see Peter et al., 2006; Sheeks & Birchmeier, 2007). However, research about online communication has revealed that reduced cues and self-disclosure facilitate not only the formation of relationships among strangers but also relationship maintenance among existing friends (Peter, Valkenburg & Schouten, 2005; Valkenburg & Peter, 2007). The stimulation hypothesis has been used to explain reduced cues and self-disclosure as stimuli to bring people close together in online community.

Contrary to social inhibition theory, social penetration theory posits that breadth (content area of communication) and depth (intimacy level of communication) are important determinants of relationship maintenance. Valkenburg and Peter (2007) assert that perceived breadth and depth about online social communication by adolescents can lead to closeness among friends in an online communication environment. They further argue that adolescents discuss a wider range of topics online than offline because the breadth in the content area of communication as perceived by adolescents facilitates a relaxed online communication which induced higher level of intimacy.

Individual Differences

A significant body of work has attempted to describe the relationship between individual differences and adolescent online communication (Anolli et al., 2005; Chak & Leung, 2004; Madell & Muncer, 2006; Sheeks & Birchmeier, 2007). Researchers are particularly interested in finding out how personality traits such as introversion/ extroversion, neuroticism, and psychoticism affect adolescents' behaviors in online communication (Anolli et al., 2005; Chak & Leung, 2004; Madell & Muncer, 2006). Research on introversion and extroversion is polarized in terms of the impact each has on adolescent online communication. Some researchers argue that since extroverted people are "social, needing to have people to talk to, and disliking reading or studying by him- or herself" (Bianchi & Phillips, 2005, p. 41), the Internet which has no time and geographic limitation thus becomes an ideal place for them to establish their social network. Researchers in this school (e.g., Amichai-Hamburger, 2002; Bianchi & Phillip, 2005; Valkenburg & Peter, 2007) support the rich-get-richer hypothesis that extroverted people may benefit from the online social environment by becoming more socially involved in online communication. They also note that extroverted people could become addicted to online communication due to its flexibility, ease of control, and synchronous multiple connections among participants. Other researchers (e.g., Anolli et al., 2005), however, have not found strong correlation between extroversion and adolescent online behaviors. In Anolli et al.'s study, extroverted participants actually used chat significantly less than introverted ones, a finding that was in contrast to what has been found in Bianchi and Phillips's study.

Contrary to the assumptions that the extroversion causes people to become addicted to the Internet communication, researchers (e.g., Madell & Muncer, 2006; Mesch, 2001; Widyanto & McMurran, 2004) who studied the relationship between introversion and online behaviors found that Internet communication appeals to introverted people and may partially explain why people become addicted to online chat. They argue that introverted people are usually socially shy and often have difficulty developing relationships with others in face-to-face settings, particularly when such relationship development is affected by "gating features" such as stuttering. Mesch (2001) surveyed Israeli youth (*n* = 927) about their online social behavior and found that the lower an individual's level of attachment to close friends and the less prosocial attitudes he/she expressed, the higher was the likelihood of his/her being a frequent Internet user. Chak and Leung (2004) explain that because of the perceived control of online communication, introverted people are more likely to go to the Internet to meet their social and intimacy needs. With all the affordances of the Internet, that is, anonymity, flexibility, multiple interaction, and so forth, socially anxious or lonely people can be socially compensated by communicating online with others without being overly conscious about who they are or what they say, and at the same time feel that their self-image is safeguarded (Peter et al., 2005; Valkenburg et al., 2006). This group (Peter et al., 2005; Valkenburg et al., 2006) support the stimulation hypothesis, arguing that reduced visual

and auditory cues via the Internet can alleviate the social anxiety that introverted people experience and thus stimulate them to develop more positive relationships online.

Like the debate on introversion versus extroversion, research on the effects of neuroticism and psychoticism on web use has shown mixed results. Psychoticism, according to Eysenck and Eysenck (1964), refers to people who are impulsive, hostile, and creative whereas neuroticism includes those who are shy, anxious and depressed. Anolli et al. (2005) studied the impact of neuroticism on individuals' online behavior and found a significant correlation between neuroticism and age in terms of online chatting, with similar findings for psychoticism. Conversely, studies by Bianchi and Phillips (2005) and Madell and Muncer (2006) found that neuroticism was negatively related to web usage such as online chat since neurotic people are often overly sensitive and resistant to sensitive talks posted anonymously (also see McKenna & Bargh, 2000). Both studies excluded neuroticism as a factor for influencing individuals' behaviors in online communication.

Self-Efficacy

Perspectives on adolescent online communication concur regarding the necessity for including self-efficacy in the study of adolescent online behavior. According to Bandura (1993), self-efficacy is the most central or pervasive variable that influences learners' behavioral performance. Several models have been proposed to explain the role of self-efficacy in teen online communication. In this paper, we examine models related to self-efficacy in online learning including Lin's (2006) behavioral intention model, Eastin's (2005) expectation model, and Livingstone et al.'s (2005) model on self-efficacy and online interaction. Based on the theory of planned behavior (TPB), Lin's model of self-efficacy describes the relationship among self-efficacy, perceived behavioral control, and behavioral intention in online communication. In this model self-efficacy is seen to be one of the factors that affect perceived behavioral control which further influences behavioral intention. The significance of this model is that it identifies the motives behind the intention with self-efficacy being one of the prominent motives for teen online communication.

Differing from Lin's behavioral intention model, Eastin (2005) proposes that positive self-efficacy influences positive expectations. Eastin's model identifies social group success, prior experience, and parental success as factors that affect teen's self-efficacy in online communication. Among those factors, social group success and prior experience are considered to be particularly important because teens' self-confidence and self-esteem, two important concepts in self-efficacy, are influenced by their perception of the group as a successful community and their prior experience related to online communication. Another important factor that influences teen self-efficacy is the concept of locus of control (Sheeks & Birchmeier, 2007; Widyanto & McMurran, 2004). The features of the Internet provide adolescents, especially those having an introverted personality, with an internal locus of control regarding online social communication which they often do not have in offline communication. The feeling of being able to control internally enhances teens' self-efficacy and leads to positive expectations about online communication.

The third model proposed by Livingstone et al. (2005) documented the relationship among individual/social factors, self-efficacy, and online interaction. Using path analysis the model provides a comprehensive picture of how individual/social variables affect self-efficacy which in turn determines the level of interaction in an online environment. According to Livingstone et al., factors like age, gender, social-economic status, years of online experience, and so forth can significantly influence an individual's self-efficacy and subsequently his/her interaction with others in online communication.

Taken together, adolescent identity needs accompanied by their growing biological needs, environmental factors such as gating features, individual differences and self-efficacy constitute, among other variables, key factors that significantly influence adolescent online behavior. Nevertheless, previous research has been focused on individual areas that limit our understanding of how those factors interact and influence each other to impact adolescents' overall behavior in online environments. The following section introduces a unified theoretical framework for research on adolescent online behavior with an attempt to address the gap in existing research.

TOWARD AN INTEGRATED CONCEPTUAL FRAMEWORK

The proposed framework is based on previous research and was created by identifying factors that play a key role in adolescent online behavior. However, it differs from previous research in that it examines these factors within a unified theoretical framework that recognizes the reciprocal relationship among those factors and the dynamic role of individual factors in influencing overall adolescent online behavior. Commenting on the emerging research agenda relating to the online behavior of children, Livingstone (2003) accentuates three aspects that need to be carefully considered in research. They are (1) the effects of online communication on the change of social networks and peer culture, (2) the role of identity, and (3) the impact of online communication on local networks and children's relationships. Two important factors are clearly associated with children's behavior in online environment: social (e.g., social networks, peer culture, local networks, children's relationship, etc.) and individual (e.g., identity) factors. However, we believe there is a third factor that influences children's online behavior: environmental (e.g., synchronous/asynchronous communication, anonymity, etc.).

Social Factors

There are multiple social factors that affect an individual's behavior but three most identified are social norms (Dietz-Uhler & Bishop-Clark, 2005; McKenna et al., 2002; Spears & Lea, 1992; Waterman & Archer, 1990), policies by the government, districts or schools that determine what is allowed and what is not allowed in online communication (Jordan, 2008) and community support including parents' attitudes and perceptions (Livingstone, 2002). These factors can be critical in terms of adolescents' behavior toward each other in online communication.

Individual Factors

As discussed previously, individual factors can significantly leverage how adolescents behave in an online environment. These factors include identity awareness (Greenfield, 2004; Subrahmanyan et al., 2006), self-efficacy (Eastin, 2005; Lin, 2006; Livingstone et al., 2005), personality traits (Anolli et al., 2005; Bianchi & Phillip, 2005; Madell & Muncer, 2006), social anxiety (Valkenburg & Peter, 2007) and demographic factors such as age, gender, years of online experience (Livingstone et al., 2005). These factors are perceived to have significant impacts on adolescents' behavior and have thus been widely studied.

Environmental Factors

Because of the criticism on media effects studies (Buckingham, 2006; Greenfield & Yan, 2006; Lloyd, 2002), researchers are cautious about drawing conclusions with respect to the influence of environmental factors on adolescents' behavior in online communication. Environmental factors refer to the unique features in online environment such as anonymity, anytime and anyway accessibility, communication mode (e.g., synchronous/asynchronous) and so forth. These factors can indirectly affect adolescents' behavior such as self-revelation and civic participation in online communication.

Adolescent Online Behavior

Adolescent online behavior refers to how individuals behave themselves or within a group in online environments. In general two kinds of behavior exist: positive and negative behaviors. Negative behaviors reflect an adverse consequence toward self or others. They include behaviors such as aggressiveness, bullying and self-denigration. Positive behaviors refer to those that positively impact self and online community and include things such as active collaboration, civic participation and role modeling that foster a congenial atmosphere in online communication. A summary of the above factors and online behavior is presented in Table 1.

Relationship among the Factors

Evidence from literature indicates that social factors may influence individual factors in online communication. For example, community support can significantly influence self-efficacy in online communication (Eastin, 2005). In addition, factors within a specific category can influence each other. For example, age and gender can affect self-efficacy, both of which are individual factors (Table 1). Finally, there is a strong relationship between environmental factors and individual factors. The anonymity in online environment is correlated with personality types (e.g., introversion and extroversion) in terms of online communication (Anolli et al., 2005; Madell & Muncer, 2006).

Relationship between Factors and Online Behavior

So far, research has shown that social, individual, and environmental factors influence adolescents' behavior at various levels in online communication (Anolli et al., 2005; Livingstone et al., 2005; Mad-

Table 1. Factors and behavior relevant to online communication

Social Factors	Individual Factors	Environmental Factors	Online Behavior
Community support Policies Social norms Etc.	Age Gender Identity awareness Personality traits (introversion vs. extroversion, neuroticism, psychoticism) Self-efficacy Social anxiety Etc.	Anonymity Ubiquitous accessibility (anywhere, anytime access) Communication mode (synchronous vs. asynchronous) Non-linear information access Etc.	Aggressiveness Bullying Online addiction Self-denigration Self-disclosure Self-revelation Active collaboration Civic participation Role modeling Helping others Etc.

ell & Muncer, 2006; Valkenburg & Peter, 2007). However, there is a missing link in this entire picture. That is, the above factors influence but may not cause the behavior to occur. To illustrate, community support may not necessarily lead to adolescent civic participation unless he/she has a desire or need to do so. Similarly, self-efficacy will not automatically trigger positive behavior unless the self-efficacy is fueled by a need to perform well in online communication. Following the same logic, environmental factors like anonymity will not cause the adolescent to self-disclose unless there is a desire or need to do so. Obviously, behavior, including online behavior, is caused by human needs to act meaningfully in life.

Research suggests that human needs (i.e., biological, social and cognitive needs) cause what is called the behavioral action to occur (Deci & Ryan, 2000; Greenfield, 2004; Staub & Pearlman, 2002). Based on the human needs-actions paradigm, we propose a theoretical framework for research in adolescent online behavior (Figure 1).

According to Greenfield (2004), adolescent developmental/biological needs are the key to understand teens' behavior in online communication. The developmental theory posits that adolescent development is characterized by a growing awareness of sexuality and the need for personal identity. A lack of fulfillment of these needs can lead to serious problems in social relationship with others, which causes undesirable behaviors

to occur. Subrahmanyan et al. (2006) assert that research on the Internet should link to the construct of adolescent development. Differing from Greenfield and her associates (Greenfield, 2004; Subrahmanyan et al., 2006), Deci & Ryan (2000) explored the relationship between social needs and behavior. Central to Deci and Ryan's theory is the concept of social connection within a group. It is believed that human need for relatedness (i.e., the urge for social connection) leads to gregarious efforts in forming interpersonal relationships and group membership. Finally, cognitive needs are believed to have causal relationship with behavior (Staub & Pearlman, 2002). Staub and Pearlman argue that cognitive needs such as the need to comprehend the reality and the world reflect human's basic need to survive. Failing to meet such needs can lead to a less-than-optimal level of functioning in life. In short, the above discussion reaffirms the needs-actions paradigm in adolescent online behavior research. Despite the fact that each need is supported by its own individual construct, it is suggested that these needs be examined under an umbrella construct called adolescent needs in which researchers are able to observe the distinct but connected links among these individual needs.

If adolescent needs are the causal factor to behavior, then social, individual and environmental factors are presumed to play supporting roles in this framework. This presumption is supported by

Figure 1. The theoretical framework for research in adolescent online behavior

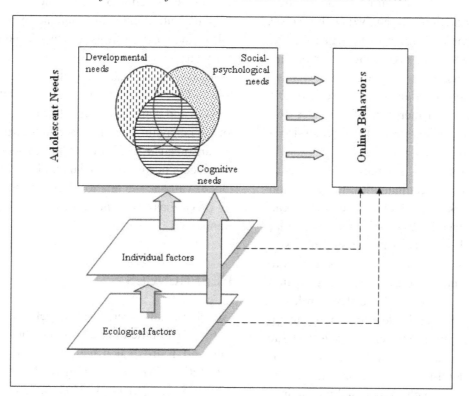

the logic argument we made earlier that it is the human needs not the social or individual factors that directly cause human behavior to occur. In this framework, social factors, individual factors and environmental factors are seen to support human needs and at the same time exert indirect influences on adolescent online behavior. For example, social and individual factors such as community support, identity awareness and self-efficacy can affect adolescents' social and development needs in terms of searching for self-identify and a desire for social connectedness. These factors can indirectly influence adolescent online behavior as an increase in community support could create a supporting environment for active online collaboration.

Application and Challenges

The framework can help researchers and practitioners to identify the complexity of adolescent online behavior by analyzing adolescent needs as well as the influences of social, individual and environmental factors. The framework holds promises for several areas of research and practice. For example, school teachers can apply this framework to their classroom teaching. Especially with the increasing use of social communication tools such as blogs in teaching (Boling, Castek, & Zawilinski, 2008; Glass & Spiegelman, 2007-2008), understanding the roles of adolescent needs and various social, individual and environmental factors in their online behavior is critical to the success of integrating blogs in teaching and learning. The framework is also helpful to researchers and school counselors who try to explain such adolescent behaviors as online bullying, self-disclosure, self-denigration and online addiction. By analyzing the causal factors in terms of adolescent needs as well as influencing factors such as individual personality and social norms, researchers are able to identify the role that each factor plays in adolescent online communication and therefore offer advice and suggestions to teachers and other professional practitioners.

Notwithstanding its strength and benefits to research and practice communities, the application of the framework has some challenges. First, it can be a daunting task for those who are not familiar observing multiple factors in a single study setting. Second, it poses tremendous challenges to researchers in terms of the research design within which so many variables play different roles simultaneously in an online learning environment. Third, related to the second challenge is the issue of measurement since variables are at various levels and under different constructs that may be difficult to draw conclusions based on findings which are intricately diverse.

CONCLUSION

The existing research on teen online communication differs significantly in topics, constructs, and theories. The proposed conceptual framework brings the existing research within an integrated conceptual framework that enables researchers and practitioners to understand the dynamic roles of various factors which influence adolescent online behavior. Based on the needs-actions paradigm, the proposed framework emphasizes the causal role of adolescent needs which include cognitive, developmental, and social needs in adolescent online behavior. Meanwhile, it points out the direct relationship between social, individual, and environmental factors and adolescent needs as well the indirect relationship of these factors with adolescent online behavior. The significance of the framework is that it helps clarify the relationships among various components in adolescent online communication and brings to attention the distinct role of these components in affecting adolescent online behavior.

Future research should focus on both qualitative and quantitative measures to understand the breadth and depth of issues related to adolescent online behavior. It is suggested that further studies are needed to examine the connectivity of adolescent needs with social and individual factors to validate the relationships and functionality of various components demonstrated in this framework.

REFERENCES

Amichai-Hamburger, Y., Wainapel, Y. G., & Fox, S. (2002). On the Internet no one knows I'm an introvert: Extroversion, neuroticism, and Internet interaction. *Cyberpsychology & Behavior*, *5*(2), 125–128. doi:10.1089/109493102753770507

Anolli, L., Villani, D., & Riva, G. (2005). Personality of people using chat: An online research. *Cyberpsychology & Behavior*, *8*(1), 89–95. doi:10.1089/cpb.2005.8.89

Baker, S. T., Victor, J. B., & Chambers, A. L. (2004). Adolescent personality: A five-factor model construct validation. *Assessment*, *11*(4), 303–315. doi:10.1177/1073191104269871

Bandura, A. (1993). Perceived self-efficacy in cognitive development and functioning . *Educational Psychologist*, *28*, 117–148. doi:10.1207/s15326985ep2802_3

Bianchi, A., & Phillips, J. G. (2005). Psychological predictors of problem mobile phone use. *Cyberpsychology & Behavior*, *8*(1), 39–51. doi:10.1089/cpb.2005.8.39

Boling, E., Castek, J., & Zawilinski, L. (2008). Collaborative literacy: Blogs and Internet projects. *The Reading Teacher*, *61*(6), 504–506. doi:10.1598/RT.61.6.10

Buckingham, D. (2004). New media, new childhoods? Children's changing cultural environment in the age of digital technology. In M. J. Kehily (Ed.), *An introduction to childhood studies* (pp. 108-122). Maidenhead, UK: Open University Press.

Bushman, B. J., & Anderson, C. A. (2001). Media violence and the American public: Scientific fact versus media misinformation. *The American Psychologist*, *56*, 477–489. doi:10.1037/0003-066X.56.6-7.477

Chak, K., & Leung, L. (2004). Shyness and locus of control as predictors of Internet addiction and Internet use. *Cyberpsychology & Behavior*, *7*(5), 559–570.

Deci, E. L., & Ryan, R. M. (2000). The "what" and "why" of goal pursuits: Human needs and the self-determination of behavior. *Psychological Inquiry*, *11*, 227–268. doi:10.1207/S15327965PLI1104_01

Dietz-Uhler, B., & Bishop-Clark, C. (2005). Formation of and adherence to a self-disclosure norm in an online chat. *Cyberpsychology & Behavior*, *8*(2), 114–120. doi:10.1089/cpb.2005.8.114

Eastin, M. S. (2005). Teen Internet use: Relating social perceptions and cognitive models to behavior. *Cyberpsychology & Behavior*, *8*(1), 62–75. doi:10.1089/cpb.2005.8.62

Erikson, E. H. (1968). *Identity: Youth and crisis*. New York: Norton.

Eysenck, H. Y., & Eysenck, S. B. G. (1964). *Manual of the Eysenck personality inventory*. San Diego, CA: Educational and Industrial Testing Service.

Glass, R., & Spiegelman, M. (2007-2008). Incorporating blogs into the syllabus: Making their space a learning space. *Journal of Educational Technology Systems*, *36*(2), 145–155. doi:10.2190/ET.36.2.c

Greenfield, P. (2004). Developmental considerations for determining appropriate Internet use guidelines for children and adolescents. *Applied Developmental Psychology*, *25*, 751–762. doi:10.1016/j.appdev.2004.09.008

Greenfield, P., & Yan, Z. (2006). Children, adolescents, and the Internet: A new field of inquiry in developmental psychology. *Developmental Psychology*, *42*, 391–394. doi:10.1037/0012-1649.42.3.391

Groebel, J. (2001). Media violence in cross-cultural perspective: A global study on children's media behavior and some educational implications. In D. G. Singer & J. L. Singer (Eds.), *Handbook of children and the media* (pp. 255-268). Thousand Oaks, CA: Sage.

Gross, E. F. (2004). Adolescent Internet use: What we expect, what teens report. *Applied Developmental Psychology*, *25*, 633–649. doi:10.1016/j.appdev.2004.09.005

Hrastinski, S., & Keller, C. (2007). Computer-mediated communication in education: A review of recent research. *Educational Media International*, *44*, 61–77. doi:10.1080/09523980600922746

Jordan, A. B. (2008). Childrens media policy. *The Future of Children*, *18*(1), 235–253. doi:10.1353/foc.0.0003

Lin, H. F. (2006). Understanding behavioral intention to participate in virtual communities. *Cyberpsychology & Behavior*, *9*(5), 540–547. doi:10.1089/cpb.2006.9.540

Livingstone, S. (2002). *Young people and new media*. Thousand Oaks, CA: Sage.

Livingstone, S. (2003). Children's use of the Internet: Reflections on the emerging research agenda. *New Media & Society, 5*(2), 147–166. doi:10.1177/1461444803005002001

Livingstone, S., Bober, M., & Helsper, E. J. (2005). Active participation or just more information? Young peoples take up of opportunities to act and interact on the Internet. *Information Communication and Society, 8*(3), 287–314. doi:10.1080/13691180500259103

Lloyd, B. T. (2002). A conceptual framework for examining adolescent identity, media influence, and social development. *Review of General Psychology, 6*, 73–91. doi:10.1037/1089-2680.6.1.73

Madell, D., & Muncer, S. J. (2006). Internet communication: An activity that appeals to shy and socially phobic people? *Cyberpsychology & Behavior, 9*(5), 618–622. doi:10.1089/cpb.2006.9.618

Madell, D., & Muncer, S. J. (2007). Control over social interactions: An important reason for young peoples use of the Internet and mobile phones for communication? *Cyberpsychology & Behavior, 10*(1), 137–140. doi:10.1089/cpb.2006.9980

McKenna, K., & Bargh, J. (2000). Plan 9 from cyberspace: The implications of the Internet for personality and social psychology. *Personality and Social Psychology Review, 4*(1), 57–75. doi:10.1207/S15327957PSPR0401_6

McKenna, K., Green, A. S., & Gleason, M. E. (2002). Relationship formation on the Internet: Whats the big attraction? *The Journal of Social Issues, 58*(1), 9–31. doi:10.1111/1540-4560.00246

Mesch, G. S. (2001). Social relationships and Internet use among adolescents in Israel. *Social Science Quarterly, 82*(2), 329–339. doi:10.1111/0038-4941.00026

Peter, J., Valkenburg, P., & Schouten, A. P. (2005). Developing a model of adolescent friendship formation on the Internet. *Cyberpsychology & Behavior, 8*(5), 423–430. doi:10.1089/cpb.2005.8.423

Peter, J., Valkenburg, P., & Schouten, A. P. (2006). Characteristics and motives of adolescents talking with strangers on the Internet. *Cyberpsychology & Behavior, 9*(5), 526–530. doi:10.1089/cpb.2006.9.526

Rubin, A. M. (2002). The uses-and-gratifications perspectives of media effects, In J. Bryant & D. Zillmann (Eds.), *Media effects: Advances in theory and research* (pp. 525-548). Mahwah, NJ: Laurence Erlbaum.

Sheeks, M. S., & Birchmeier, Z. P. (2007). Shyness, sociability, and the use of computer-mediated communication in relationship development. *Cyberpsychology & Behavior, 10*(1), 64–70. doi:10.1089/cpb.2006.9991

Spears, R., & Lea, M. (1992). Social influences and the influence of the "social" in computer-mediated communication. In M. Lee (Ed.), *Contexts in computer-mediated communication* (pp. 30-65). London: Harvester Wheatsheaf.

Staub, E., & Pearlman, L. (2002). *Understanding basic psychological needs*. Retrieved August 20, 2008, from http://www.heal-reconcile-rwanda.org/lec_needs.htm

Subrahmanyan, K., Smahel, D., & Greenfield, P. (2006). Connecting developmental constructions to the Internet: Identity presentation and sexual exploration on online teen chatrooms. *Developmental Psychology, 42*, 395–406. doi:10.1037/0012-1649.42.3.395

Suoninen, A. (2001). The role of media in peer group relations, In S. Livingstone & M. Bovill (Eds.), *Children and their changing media environment* (pp. 201-219). Mahwah, NJ: Laurence Erlbaum.

Tajfel, H. (1978). Social categorization, social identity, and social comparison. In H. Tajfel (Ed.), *Differentiation between social groups: Studies in the social psychology of inter-group relations* (pp. 61-76). London: Academic Press.

Tajfel, H., & Turner, J. C. (1986). The social identity theory of intergroup behavior. In S. Worschel & W. C. Austin (Eds.), *Psychology of intergroup relations* (pp. 7-24). Chicago: Nelson-Hall.

Valkenburg, P., Peter, J., & Schouten, A. P. (2006). Friend networking sites and their relationship to adolescents well-being and social self-esteem. *Cyberpsychology & Behavior, 9*(5), 584–590. doi:10.1089/cpb.2006.9.584

Valkenburg, P. M., & Peter, J. (2007). Preadolescents and adolescents online communication and their closeness to friends. *Developmental Psychology, 43,* 267–277. doi:10.1037/0012-1649.43.2.267

van Aken, M. A. G., van Lieshout, C. F. M., & Scholte, R. H. J. (1998). *The social relationships and adjustment of the various personality types and subtypes.* Paper presented at the 7th Biennial Meeting of the Society for Research on Adolescence, San Diego, CA.

Waterman, A. S., & Archer, S. L. (1990). A life-span perspective on identity formation: Developments in form, function, and process. In P. B. Baltes, D. L. Featherman, & R. M. Lerner (Eds.), *Life-span development and behavior* (pp. 29-57). Hillsdale, NJ: Laurence Erlbaum.

Whitlock, J. L., Powers, J. L., & Eckenrode, J. (2006). The virtual cutting edge: The Internet and adolescent self-injury. *Developmental Psychology, 42,* 407–417. doi:10.1037/0012-1649.42.3.407

Widyanto, L., & McMurran, M. (2004). The psychological properties of the Internet addiction test. *Cyberpsychology & Behavior, 7*(4), 443–450. doi:10.1089/cpb.2004.7.443

Chapter 2
Internet Affordances and Teens' Social Communication:
From Diversification to Bonding

Gustavo S. Mesch
University of Haifa, Israel

ABSTRACT

As the Internet has been adopted and integrated in the daily lives of an increasing number of young adolescents in western countries, scholars and commentators are debating and speculating on the impact of these new media on the activities, social relationships and worldview of the young generation. The communication environment has become more and more complex, as youth combine the use of electronic mail, open forums, chat rooms, instant messenger and social networking sites. In this chapter the author argues that the use of different social applications, partially define the structure and content of social communication and association. In this chapter the author reviews the literature on the motivations for the use of each social application and the impact of the use on the type, size and quality of social ties that are maintained and created.

INTRODUCTION

The incorporation of social software into everyday life is redefining the social networks of youth. Fast and interactive online communication supports the formation, maintenance and expansion of social networks. As information and communication technologies are developing a rapidly advancing history of technological innovations, the past, present and future of youth associations and communication

are indistinguishable from the various technologies that were and are available. From electronic mail and newsgroups, from open forums to open chat rooms, from Instant Messenger to social networking sites, the prevailing technologies partially define the structure and content of social communication and association. Furthermore, young people's communication environment has become increasingly complex, as the different technologies listed above are used simultaneously.

The purpose of this chapter is to investigate the motivations for the use of each technology and the

DOI: 10.4018/978-1-60566-926-7.ch002

impact of this use on the social circle of adolescents. In particular the analysis will address a number of issues. First, whether different motivations shape the use of email, chat rooms, instant messenger and social networking sites. Second, the effect of the use of each technology on the size and quality of social ties that are maintained or created. Third, the effect of media choices on adolescents' access to social support, sociability and social capital.

Our understanding of teens' use of social media is dominated by several tensions that will be addressed in this chapter. One tension concerns the impact of social media on young persons' social circles and the extent that social media isolate teens from their friends or liberate them from the constraints of place and social similarity. A second tension refers to the extent that the effect of social media diversifies social networks or expands social bonding with known individuals. The third tension is the extent that social media replace strong ties by weak ties. The main argument of the chapter is that our understanding of the impacts of social media will benefit from a grasp of the specific characteristics of each social software and the motivations for its use. Thus, social media effects are dependent on both the teen motivations and the tool that is used.

YOUNG PEOPLE'S COMMUNICATION ENVIRONMENT

In the last 10 years the communication environment of youth has changed as more and more teens have gained access to computer-mediated communication and cellular phones. A recent study in the USA found that 63 percent of all teens avail of cell phones, and access to the Internet is almost universal. Most of the use is for social purposes, as 93 percent send and receive emails, 68 percent send and receive instant messages, 55 percent have a profile in a social networking site, 28 percent have created or work in an online journal (blog)

and 18 percent visit chat rooms (Lenhart & Madden, 2007). In Canada, a recent study shows that 77 percent send and receive instant messages, 74 percent send and receive electronic mail, 24 percent visit chat rooms and 19 percent have created or work in an online journal (Media Awareness Group, 2005). In Europe figures vary according to country, but the trend in the use of social applications is similar. For example in the UK 81 percent send and received email, 78 percent send and receive instant messages and 20 percent participate in chat rooms. In Italy the percentages are lower: as 59 percent of the youth send and receive email, 49 percent send and receive instant messages and 33 percent participate in chat rooms (MediAppro, 2005). The distinguishing characteristic of these data is that the use of the different applications varies, and as the communication partners differ according to the application being used, variation in the outcomes can be expected.

Online communication, then, is frequent among youth in the Western world. But unlike the early years of online communication, the existence of different applications now calls for a reevaluation of the unique affordances of each one and the theoretical frameworks that are relevant to the understanding of online communication and relationship formation and maintenance in adolescence. Before we turn to this topic the importance of the latter subject will be addressed.

YOUTH AND FRIENDSHIP FORMATION AND DEVELOPMENT

Adolescence is an important developmental stage, during which social relationships outside the family expand; their quality has been linked to various behavioral outcomes (Giordano, 2003). Social interaction with peers provides a forum for learning and refining socio-emotional skills needed for enduring relationships. Through interactions with peers, adolescents learn how to cooperate, to take different perspectives, and to satisfy growing needs for intimacy (Rubin, Bukowski & Parker, 1998; Crosnoe, 2000). Youth who report having friends are more confident, more altruistic, and less aggressive, and demonstrate greater school involvement and work orientation. For adolescents, personal relationships are a type of social support. Those with more supportive friendships were shown to have higher self-esteem, to suffer depression or other emotional disorders less often, and to be better adjusted to school than youth with less supportive friendships (Hartup, 1996; Collins & Larsen, 1999; Beraman & Moody, 2003).

The literature on personal relations has long been concerned with the quality of the ties that bind individuals. One way to measure this quality is by the strength of these ties (Marsden & Campbell, 1984). A tie's strength is usually assessed by a combination of factors such as perceived closeness, intimacy and trust. Weaker ties are evinced in more casual relationships and in sparser exchanges; they typify relationships of those who enjoy fewer kinds of support. Strong ties exist in relationships on a high level of intimacy, involving more self-disclosure, shared activities, emotional as well as instrumental exchanges, and long-term interaction (Marsden & Campbell, 1984; Haythornthwaite, 2002).

ONLINE RELATIONSHIP FORMATION AND MAINTENANCE

Studies on the quality of online relationships are divided in their conclusions regarding the type and qualities of social ties that are created and maintained through the Internet (Cummings, Buttler & Kraut, 2002; Mesch & Talmud, 2006). I use the term affordance to describe the potential for action, the perceived capacity of individuals to create and maintain different kinds of relationships. Some internet supported social applications are less used and some more, certain applications afford the creation of new social ties, based on shared interests and motives, others maintain, support and expand existing social ties.

Early conceptualizations, assuming the technological determinism of the Internet, described the weakness of electronic media in supporting social ties (McKenna, et al, 2002). The term, technological determinism, is used to refer to the common assumption that new technologies and new media channels of communication shape and constrain the content and type of messages that are exchanged. The "reduced social cues perspective" is based on the observation that computer-mediated communication (CMC) allows the exchange of fewer cues than face-to-face environments and suggests that CMC is less appropriate for the support of emotional exchanges or the conveyance of complex information and a sense of social presence. This early perspective that technology is the sole determinant of the nature of social ties is quite skeptical of the ability of CMC to support strong ties. Moreover, precisely because CMC provides access to a wider audience of individuals who may share interests and hobbies, it has been suggested that the reduced social cues environment on which CMC is based is more suited to supporting weak ties by reducing the risks associated with contacting unknown others (Sproull & Kiesler, 1986).

Social constructivists, by contrast, argue that some features of online communication, such as anonymity, isolation, lack of "gating features", and ease of finding others with the same interests, make it easier for individuals to form strong ties (McKenna et al., 2002). The formation of close interpersonal relationships requires the establishment of trust, that is, a sense that intimate information disclosed in interpersonal exchanges is not widely disseminated and is not used to ridicule friends. The relative anonymity of the Internet reduces the risk of such disclosure, especially intimate information, because such intimate information can be shared without fear of embarrassment resulting from disclosing intimate information to members of the close-knit, often transient, face-to-face social circle (McKenna et. al, 2002).

Consistent with this argument, some studies have shown that people often disclose intimate information about themselves online (McKenna et al., 2002; Joinson, 2001). The high levels of self-disclosure in CMC interactions have proved to be related to anonymity (Joinson, 2001). Individuals who disclosed personal and intimate information over the Internet reported greater closeness to their online friends (McKenna et al., 2002).

Empirical evidence for these perspectives is mixed. A few studies report that the quality of online social interactions and relationships is lower than that of face-to-face interactions. In other words, off-line friends are perceived as closer because the frequency of communication with face-to-face friends is higher than with online friends (Mesch & Talmud, 2006).

The mixed results might be the result of a lack of distinction of the different types of communication technologies and the user's motivation for its use. The perspectives of reduced social cues and of social constructivism were both developed at a time when online communication was mainly through electronic mail, forums and chat rooms. Also, a small percentage of the young population had access to the Internet so the most common relationship formation was with strangers.

In the existing youth communication ecology, adolescents' communicate with each other through chat rooms, instant messenger, email and social networking sites. In such an environment the technological affordances of each technology and its differential use have to be clarified. Different motivations probably lead to the use of different channels and to different social outcomes. Accordingly, the observed mixed results might be the result of confounding the motivation for, with the social outcomes of, the use of different technologies. In the following pages we elaborate the affordances of a number of technologies and review knowledge on the motivation for their use and the results in terms of sociability.

Forums and Chat Rooms

Forums and chat rooms are spaces of interaction in which users maintain their anonymity by using nicknames and interact with others who might not be known, and may reside in a different city, state or country. Individuals join forums and chat discussions according to the topic around which the platform is defined. The defining characteristics of the developing social interaction are the existence of this common topic and similarity in social status (age group, marital status) or location (city or state). As the context of the interaction is based on mutual emotional or intellectual interests, much of the interaction is with unknown individuals who share a concern, hobbies, or other interests.

When presenting the results of surveys in various countries at the beginning of the chapter, it was shown that the percentage of youth who participate in chat rooms and forums is lower than that of youth who communicate through e-mail, Instant Messenger and social networking sites. Thus, motivations for the use of different platforms most probably differ among adolescents. Some have suggested that participation in this type of communication is more likely among youngsters who are introvert and shy (Amichai-Hamburger & Ben Artzi, 2003). By the social constructivist approach, some characteristics of online communication in these channels might facilitate relationship formation for these individuals. By the stimulation hypothesis, the relative anonymity, lack of gating features for relationship formation, and shared specialized interests are conducive to the development of closeness, intimacy and the disclosure of the inner self to others faster than in face-to-face relationships (Valkenburg & Jochen, 2007). This effect is more likely to be found for individuals who are introvert, shy and lack social support in their peer group (McKenna et al., 2002). According to the stimulation hypothesis, online communication in forums and chat rooms will probably lead to an increase of the size of an adolescent's social network.

From a sociological viewpoint, Mesch (2007) has argued that an important motivation for participation in online communities (forums and chat rooms) is social diversification. Societies are characterized by varying levels of social segregation. In societies that reward individuals differentially according to income, prestige, ethnicity and power, stratification systems result in a differential ability of individuals to gain access to jobs and residential locations. As a result, individual social associations tend to be with individuals of similar social characteristics such as age, gender, marital status, ethnicity, religion, and nationality. Studies on the formation, development, maintenance, and dissolution of close social relationships have emphasized the importance of network homophily (McPherson, Smith-Lovin & Cook, 2002). Social similarity in the social network is the result of the opportunity structure for interaction that emerges from the social structuring of activities in society. Feld (1981) used the concept of foci of activity, defining them as "social, psychological, legal or physical objects around which joint activities are organized." Whether they are formal (school) or informal (regular hangouts), large (neighborhood) or small (household), foci of activity systematically constrain choices of friends. From this perspective, association with others is the result of a two-step process: foci of activity place individuals in proximity (for example, they provide opportunities for frequent meetings), which causes individuals to reveal themselves to each other. Specifically, people tend to choose their friends from the set of people available through these foci.

The Internet as a focus of activity becomes an institutional arrangement that brings individuals together in repeated interactions around the focal activities. In this sense, as many societies are ethnically and racially segregated, chat rooms and forums provide a space of interaction in which teens are exposed to others of different ethnic origin and can discuss different family practices and different perspectives on history, and can interact with others based on common interests and topics without the barrier that race and ethnicity imposes in everyday life (Tynes, 2007). A study that compared racial and ethnically related comments and stereotypes in two youth chat rooms found reference to these primordial categories in the discussions, but the number of racial remarks online seemed lower than in everyday life. Furthermore, a more positive approach and openness to members of other ethnic groups was found in chat rooms in which the discussion was moderated (Subrahmanyan & Greenfield, 2008). These studies indicate support for the diversification perspective, and for the view that chat rooms and forums organized around specific topics and interests tend to support the development of friendship across ethnic and racial lines; this is an important development in highly residentially segregated societies.

As the diversification perspective assumes exposure to members of other groups is conducive to a reduction in network homophilly. A study on the outgroup orientation of different ethnic groups in chat rooms found that the more opportunities European Americans had to interact with different ethnic groups, the more open they became over time to the diverse groups. Furthermore, an increase in the number of levels of contact proved associated with building cross-race friendships online. These findings imply that social interaction in chat rooms may increase levels of intergroup interaction and reduce network homophilly (Tynes Giang & Thompson, 2005). In another study in Israel, adolescents' participating in online chat rooms and forums were compared with the ones that did not have access to the Internet. The results show that online youth report networks that are more heterogeneous in terms of gender and age than the ones that have not access online (Mesch & Talmud, 2007).

Consequently, an important motivation for individuals to form online relationships is to diversify their social network and identify other individuals who share their interests, concerns, or problems, but who are not part of their social circle. Online social formation is thus not a general need, as not all individuals are involved in this activity; nor is it only the result of insufficient relationships with family or friends but also the need to find other individuals with similar interests, not available in the social network because of its deterministic similarity. Diversification of social ties, rather than a need for company and lack of social skills motivates online relationship formation.

Another important motivation for participation in online communities (such as forums and chat rooms) is identity exploration. The relative anonymity in virtual spaces allows youth to engage in experimentation in their self presentation, that is, individual attempts to convey information on the image of the self and its identities to others. Studies on youth have presented evidence on this use as almost a quarter of adolescents who used chat rooms or email reported that they presented themselves differently from what they were in real life. A recent study found that 50 percent of the young participants stated that they had engaged in Internet-based identity experiments. The foremost motive for these experiments was to investigate how others reacted, to overcome shyness, and to facilitate relationship formation. Age, gender and introversion were significant predictors of frequency of identity exploration. Younger adolescents experimented more often than older ones. Girls engaged in identity self exploration (how others react) and boys were more concerned to overcome shyness. Introverts were more likely to engage in identity experiments than extraverts (Valkenburg, Shouteen & Peter, 2005).

Participation in chat rooms and forums is often motivated by the need for specific and round-the-clock social support. Online support groups differ in the degree of involvement of professionals. Some have a professional moderator, others lack any moderator. But the common characteristics are that members are youth with a shared condition such as hearing impairment, diabetes, recovery from cancer, sexual abuse, or pregnancy, who assemble to cope with their condition through sharing knowledge and providing mutual support (Mesch, 2006).

This type of communities attracts interest mainly because social support is deemed to require the exchange of verbal and non-verbal messages conveying emotion, information, and advice on reducing uncertainty or stress associated with the condition. Social support is exchanged through computer-mediated communication in relatively large networks of individuals who do not know each other and do not communicate face to face. Also, non-geographic computer-mediated social support communities develop among strangers whose primary connection is sharing a concern over a source of personal discomfort. Social support online is available day and night. As the Internet is a global communication technology the likelihood of finding social support when needed, at any time of the day, is high. An important characteristic of online social support communities is that a very narrow and specific topic is defined, and this attracts individuals who when joining tend to identity themselves as having the particular problem or concern.

An obvious advantage for online social support is its avoidance of the embarrassment that ordinarily follows the voicing of personal and intimate problems in face-to-face relations. Online social support also facilitates interaction management, namely taking time to elaborate and write thoughts online (Walther & Boyd, 2002). These three characteristics, shared identity, anonymity, and interaction management, provide an ideal context for social support (Turner, Grube & Myers, 2001; Walther & Boyd, 2002).

A young person might be motivated to join an online social support group because he or she suffers from an embarrassing or socially stigmatized condition. Because of their anxiety and uncertainties, individuals are impelled by the force of social comparison to seek out others with the same condition. But they prefer to do so online by virtue of the anonymity provided by participation in Internet groups (Bargh & McKenna, 2004). As to the advantages of participation in online social support communities, McKay, Glasgow, Feil et al. (2002) found that social support by this means in a group of patients with diabetes led to improvements in dietary control similar to those experienced by members of conventional social support groups.

Others have argued that the motivation for participation in virtual social support communities is the lack of real-world social support. According to this view, in face-to-face communities social support is often hard to come by, particularly when the concern or personal condition is relatively uncommon and culturally devalued (Cummings, Sproull, & Kiessler, 2002). Furthermore, social support is often sought from others with the same condition and who have experienced the difficulties associated with changes in daily life (Loader, Muncer, Burrows, Pleace & Nettleton, 2002; Preece & Ghozati, 2001). For some teens online social support is important as they can discuss personal problems. Peer advice and support help teens navigate romantic relationships and sexual health issues; these are the most frequent topics of conversation in teen chat rooms and forums (Tynes, 2007; Suzuki & Calzo, 2004).

In sum, regarding the tensions described at the beginning of the chapter the studies reviewed on forums and chat rooms carry several implications for adolescents' social life. The use of these communication channels seems to have an effect on the size and composition of social ties. On the one hand, participation in forums and chat rooms enlarges the social network, providing access to a significant, large number of new potential social ties that can provide diverse resources, from emotional support to access to information and exposure to others of a different background. Participation in these online communities provides opportunities for the practice of social skills and identity experimentation, and in the long term fur-

nishes opportunities for network diversification. On the other hand, online social participation has some costs, at least in the short term. It comes at the price of a decrease in intensity of communication, in perceived closeness and in intimacy with the face-to-face peer group. The time invested in the formation of online ties is at the expense of involvement with existing friends and peer group. So the end result, for this type of communication, is a trade of strong ties for weak ties. But this seems to be a short-term effect: as time goes by, online ties have the potential to become close ties providing social support and companionship and moving from online to face-to-face communication (Mesch & Talmud, 2006).

FROM DIVERSIFICATION TO BONDING: INSTANT MESSAGING AND SOCIAL NETWORKING

Instant messaging and social networking sites differ from other online communication channels in a variety of characteristics. The adoption of the technology is social, as it results from a group of friends settling on a particular IM or social networking system. IM is adopted because of peer pressure that helps to create a critical mass of users in a social group. Today, for adolescents to be part of a peer group they must engage in perpetual communication online after school hours. Those who do not, cannot be part of the peer group. Not being online or not having an IM user name means exclusion from most of the daily social interaction. Using IM requires having an active list of buddies and being on a friends' list by the authorization of peers. In that sense, the use of IM with strangers is uncommon as its appeal is mainly to existing friends.

While chat rooms and forums are technologies that link individuals around a shared topic of interest and concern, Instant Messenger, text messaging and social networking sites are technologies that link teens who have some knowledge of each other and belong to the same social circle or to the social circle of their friends.

Compared with other communication channels such as email, forums and chat rooms, IM has unique features. It is synchronous communication, mostly one-to-one or one-to-many. IM chatters enjoy real-time conversations and have a short spell to think before replying. Users are aware of other users' online presence, and can choose to communicate to others and communicate their status (online, offline, away or busy). The application allows multitasking, namely to perform other tasks and chat at the same time. A blocking mechanism allows users to remove themselves from another user's list or remove a friend from the list. At the same time, users are not able to communicate with others who are not enrolled with the same provider.

Young people's use of instant and text messaging might be motivated by the need to belong to, maintain, and develop an existing social circle. In recent years a number of studies have confirmed this argument. A study of late adolescents that investigated motivations for IM use based themselves on the uses and gratifications framework. Participants named four main motivations for IM use. One was social entertainment, in which the user conducted IM communication to spend spare time, and to stay in touch with friends. A second, less frequent motivation was task accomplishment, that is, to learn from others how to do things, generate ideas, and make decisions. A third motivation was social attention, in particular mitigation of loneliness and getting support and affection from peers. The least frequent motivation named by the participants was meeting new people (Flanagin, 2006).

A study on motivation for and effects of participation in chat rooms and Instant Messenger sessions investigated in a sample of pre-adolescents whether online communication reduced perceived closeness to friends or stimulated closeness to existing friends. Online communication using IM proved to exert a positive effect on perceived close-

ness to friends. This effect was mainly because IM communication is conducted with friends who are known and represent and additional channel of communication that reinforces existing ties (Valkenburg & Peter, 2007). Another study of pre-adolescents (7th graders) probed the role of IM in their social life. Participants reported using the application for more frequent social interaction with their friends, gossip, and romantic communication. The most frequent motive, given by 92 percent of the respondents, was hanging out with a friend after school hours. Participants described their IM partners as long-standing friends and peers, first met at school. The study investigated the association between IM use and psychological well-being. Participants who reported feeling lonely at school on a daily basis were found more likely to have chat rooms sessions with individuals they met online and did not know face to face. Teens who felt well connected with their school friends tend to use IM to seek out additional opportunities of social interaction with them after school hours, mostly as a continuation of conversations that started during school hours (Gross, Juvonen & Gable, 2002).

A longitudinal study on the effect of different Internet activities on the quality of close adolescent relationships (best friendship and romantic relationships) among adolescents found that using the Internet for entertainment had a different effect on social ties from using social software. The type of Internet activity proved to have an influence on relationship quality a year later. Use of IM was positively associated with different aspects of romantic relationships and best friendship quality. In contrast, visiting chat rooms was negatively related to best friendship quality. Using the Internet for games and for general entertainment predicted decrease in relationship quality with best friends and romantic partners. As most communication through IM is with existing friends, these findings indicate that this type of communication maintains and improves positive aspects of best friendship and romantic ties such as trust and communication, and does not increase negative aspects such as alienation and conflict. Conversely, visiting chat rooms was related to increased alienation and conflict and decreased intimacy and companionship with best friends. Visiting chat rooms is communication mostly with strangers, and it is at the expense of time with close friends; this creates emotional distance and probably conflict with existing friends (Blais, Craig, Pepler, & Connolly, 2008).

A new but fast growing communication channels is SMS or short message service (SMS) that allows for short text messages to be sent from one cell phone to another cell phone or from the Web to another cell phone. Youth use SMS primarily to stay connected with their existing social network. The cell phone numbers of the personal social network are kept in the cell phone memory. Youth often send messages to their existing friends, to express their thoughts and feelings. SMS allow to youth to communicate with their friends, even when they are not able to conduct a phone conversation because of the presence of parents or others around.

Studies have shown that this is used for "microcoordination", a concept that refers to the instrumental use of mobile phones to coordinate in real time by allowing adjustment and readjustment in real time of the time and place of meeting (Ling & Yitri, 2002). Rather than setting a fixed time and place, youth use SMS to converge in real time on a common location. Other studies have investigated with whom teenagers communicate using SMS. From these we learn that SMS is often used for communication with parents and peers. It is rare that SMS is used to communicate with strangers (Grinter & Eldrige, 2001; Ling, 2004).

It is interesting to note that both SMS and IM are used to support an important developmental task of adolescence: the creation of a sense of autonomy. SMS messages allow teenagers to work within the constraints imposed upon them, such as their inability to drive and consequent reliance on public or parental transportation and

the need to balance school and parental requirements on one hand with their social desires on the other. SMS is a channel that allows teenagers to stay in touch and communicate when doing homework and when being between family and extracurricular activities (Ito, 2001). For teenagers in traditional groups that constrain cross-sex meetings without adult control, IM serves to communicate with friends of the opposite sex without the knowledge and control of parents and siblings (Mesch & Talmud, 2007). In a study of Arab and Jewish Israelis, Mesch and Talmud (2007) found that Arab youngsters blended their IM use in with other computer work. If a parent or sibling approached, IM use was rendered temporarily invisible through window management, namely minimizing or hiding the chat window. Yet studies have found some differences in the use of SMS and IM. Often teenagers kept the phone engaged all the time and even responded to messages while they were meeting with others.

Two different types of Instant Messenger users were found: continuous and sporadic. The continuous mode involved running the IM software for lengthy periods, regardless of its use for chat or of its being in the background while other activities went on. The software was minimized but never closed, and text was added over the course of hours or days. Every teenager who used the IM in this way had a computer in their room and access to Internet connection. A second group preferred intensive sessions, setting a time of the day to chat with their close friends. These users usually did not have constant access to the computer, and arranged for conversations to be held during the hours when they did. As to the purpose, IM and SMS were found similar in that they were used to plan events, discuss homework, and exchange experiences. While event-planning with SMS involved sending messages to revise and update existing plans, such as informing that the bus was late, event-planning with IM referred to a place and time that once agreed remained fixed (Ling & Yttri, 2002).

Some caution is necessary in study of the use of Instant Messenger, SMS and social networking sites. The buddy list usually contains a very large number of contacts, including family, close friends and distant contacts. These applications are often used like phone books, encompassing all possible contacts. In fact, most adolescents contact regularly just close friends, but the length of the list of buddies often serves as an indication of popularity, and is displayed to the peer group (Taylor & Harper, 2003). It is not uncommon for the cell phone to be left purposely lying on the table, so friends can see the list.

An additional tension in the potential outcomes of the use of online communication that needs to be addressed the tension between social diversification and social bonding. At the center of the diversification approach is a conceptualization of ICT's (Information and communication technologies) as a space of activity and social interaction. The Internet is not only about communication with existing ties. Although it is true that many adolescents use the Internet as another channel of communication with existing relationships, the innovative aspect of the Internet is to provide opportunities for activities that induce social interaction, providing a space for expansion and diversification of social relationships. Playing interactive games is more than playing games in a group of online members, and as in any game groups are formed, interaction is recurrent, and names and phone numbers are exchanged. Among adolescents, proximity is important for friendship formation because it establishes the boundaries within which they choose friends. Every individual occupies several separate but overlapping social worlds, each a potential sphere for association. A key location for meeting and making friends is school, where adolescents spend a large part of their waking hours. But other settings may be important as well. Adolescents spend their free time in neighborhood hangouts that they frequent after school. In shopping malls, video arcades, and movie theaters, usually in the neighborhood

or nearby, groups of adolescents get to know others who live in the same neighborhood but do not attend the same school (Cotterell, 1996). Unlike other groups that are geographically more mobile and exposed to more diverse foci of activity, adolescents lack geographic mobility and are trapped in social relationships that involve individuals similar to them. Thus, certain technologies might support expansion of social relationships, including access to information, knowledge and skills that teens cannot access due to residential segregation.

Still, diversification is very likely to take place together with social bonding. The use of technologies that require previous knowledge, and even belonging to the same social circle, can be used to coordinate group activities, continue conversations that started at school, to express personal and intimate concerns, and to provide social support. In that sense, these technologies can support the development of peer group cohesion and the formation of a sense of togetherness for those who are part of the social circle. At the same time, they might exclude others who lack access to the technologies and those who are not accepted in the group.

Clarification of the intricate interaction of motivations for the use of different technologies with the type of social circle involved in their use is central to an understanding of the effects of information and communication technologies on the size, composition, and nature of the social relationships that characterize adolescence in the information age. We now attempt to illumine this crucial issue by reviewing and integrating knowledge from published empirical studies.

A number of studies support our position that online communication and its effects on network size, composition, and strength should be differential. The use of different channels leads to different results. For example, a longitudinal study of 884 adolescents on the effect of Internet use for social purposes (chat rooms and Instant Messenger) and for entertainment purposes found that Internet activity influenced later relationship quality with the best friend and romantic partner (Blais, et al, 2008). IM use was positively associated with most aspects of romantic relationship and best friendship quality. In contrast, visiting chat rooms was negatively related to best friendship quality. Using the internet to play games and for general entertainment predicted decreases in relationship quality (Blais et al., 2008). Another study on the use of Instant Messenger in Canada and Israel found that in both countries youth used this application to stay in touch with their romantic partner and best friends, and much less to contact individuals who were met online (Mesch, Quas-Han and Talmud, 2008). These studies indicate that when used to connect with members of the peer group, IM promotes rather than hinders intimacy, with frequent IM conversations encouraging the desire to meet face-to-face with friends (Hu, Yifeng & Smith, 2004). The main uses of IM are for socializing, event-planning, task accomplishment, and meeting new people (Grinter & Pallen, 2002; Flanagin, 2006). Thus, IM has a positive effect when used with known friends. Conversely, visiting chat rooms expands the size of young people's networks and provides complementary social support; but this apparently is at the expense of intimacy with known friends and results in a perception of increased alienation and conflict and decreased intimacy and companionship with face-to-face friends. These two different activities clearly serve different functions.

Social networking sites are those that allow users to present information about themselves (such as age, gender, location, education and interests). Users are encouraged to link to known and likeminded others whose profile exists in the site, or invite known and likeminded individuals to join the site, establish and maintain contact with other users, post content, create a personal blog, and participate in online groups (Boyd & Ellison, 2007). The use of social networking sites appeals to the young population. A recent comparative study of social networking use in Europe and North America discovered a relationship between age and use. While 54 percent of those aged 16-24 had a profile, the percentage decreased to 26 percent in the group aged 25-34, to 12 percent in the group aged 35-44, and to 7 percent in the group aged 45-54 (Ofcom, 2008).

In fact, social networking sites appeal to a large number of users because they integrate in a single site capabilities that previously required moving from site to site. Examples of such capabilities are displaying a personal profile, sending and receiving messages of site members, participating in online communities and posts, and exchanging multimedia content (music, short movies, artwork and pictures).

Most sites encourage users to construct accurate representations of themselves, but is difficult to know to what extent individuals do so. Some people tend to provide limited information about themselves, while others, tend to disclose intimate information. Using the information about themselves, their e-mail contacts and the contacts of known others, users are able to build a network of connections. These connections may be actual offline friends or acquaintances, or people they only know or have met online, and with whom they have no other link.

As to user motivations, in a recent study in the USA of the Pew and American Life Project, 91 percent of all social networking teens said they used the sites to stay in touch with friends they saw frequently while 82 percent used them to stay in touch with friends they rarely saw in person; 72 percent used the sites to make plans with their friends. Only 49 percent used them to make new friends (Lenhart & Meiden, 2007). In the UK the findings were similar in that although users reported massive numbers of individuals as "friends", the actual number of close friends was approximately the same as that of face-to-face friends (Smith, 2007). The research found that although the sites allowed contact with hundreds of acquaintances, people tend to have around five close friends and 90 percent of the contacts were people they had met face to face. Only 10 percent were contacts made with total strangers (Smith, 2007). The comparative Ofcom study found that on average only 17 percent of respondents with profile in social networking sites used the site to talk with people they did not know (Ofcom, 2008).

As to the social outcomes of the use of social networking sites, a few studies evaluated the extent that social networking sites facilitate increasing contacts with individuals belonging to a different social group or to the same social group of the user. They indicate that youngsters' use of social networking sites results in an increase in social bonding, that is, contact with family and friends who reside in a different city or country and keeping in touch with friends who are met on a daily basis. Social networking sites facilitate updating others about the user's activities and planning social and entertainment events with members of the peer group. The number of individuals on the contact list is often used as an indication of social standing, the extent of being socially involved with others. Far fewer are reports of making contact with others based on shared interests or hobbies (Ellison, Steinfeld & Lampe, 2006).

CONCLUSION

This chapter reviewed current studies on young people's use of different types of social media. The main object was to take a close look at the possible sources of contradictory findings reported on the effect of online communication on adolescent social ties. From this review a number of important conclusions are drawn, which should illuminate future research. The most important conclusion is that the new social media have important implications for the understanding of adolescence. Youth face a media environment and conduct their social interactions using multiple channels of communication. Adolescents that have not access to the Internet very rapidly

find themselves at a disadvantage, with the risk of being excluded from the most significant social activities of the peer group and access to information. At the theoretical level, theories of youth friendship formation and adolescence need to incorporate this emerging digital divide that affects the opportunities and impact of digitally based exclusion in peer groups.

Second, for adolescents that do have access, different motivations shape their choices of technologies and the different choices have different outcomes. The need to expand the social network and to diversify entail greater use of forums and chat rooms, which results in diversification and increase of network size; but this is at the expense of closeness to face-to-face friends, at least in the short run. The need to be highly involved with the face-to-face peer group and to increase belonging drives the use of IM, SMS and social networking sites, resulting in a higher perceived closeness to members of the peer group, and greater ability to coordinate joint activities. Theories of computer mediated communication that have focused on online communication among strangers need to be expanded to account for this rapid movement from online to offline and from offline to online.

Adolescent research should incorporate more the study of the differential use of social media and their differential effects on young people's social networks. In particular, we must expand our understanding of the characteristics of adolescents who use diverse combinations of social media, what the motivations for these different combinations are, and what are the developmental outcomes.

DIRECTIONS FOR FUTURE RESEARCH

For youth establishing social connections is an important developmental activity. In this chapter the link between social media and the formation, development and maintenance of social ties has been reviewed. There is a need to study the effect of contextual factors on this process. Most social media is acquired through the action of existing social networks and choices of different applications might be affected by the actions of the peer group. Future research should explore the process of technology adoption by peers and how preferences are made to use Instant Messenger or Social Networking Sites.

The expansion of youth social ties is conducted in the context of belonging to a family and attending school. Until recently, the family and school had an important influence in the choice of friends. The school restricted the individuals to whom youth are exposed on a daily basis and parents' try to exercise control on children's friends. How these institutions are adopting to the potential expansion of youth social networks, and the potential change in their structure needs to direct future research.

Finally, much of our discussion has focused on the positive characteristics of social networks, namely access to information, to sociability, companionship and social support. Future studies should direct their focus to potential negative effects of social networks such as cyber bullying and harassment. In particular, how variations in the use of different applications are associated with these behaviors.

REFERENCES

Amichai-Hamburger, Y., & Ben Artzi, E. (2003). Loneliness and Internet use. *Computers in Human Behavior*, *19*, 71–80. doi:10.1016/S0747-5632(02)00014-6

Bargh, J. A., & McKenna, K. Y. A. (2004). The Internet and social life. *Annual Review of Psychology*, *55*, 573–590. doi:10.1146/annurev.psych.55.090902.141922

Bargh, J. A., McKenna, K. Y. A., & Fitzsimons, G. M. (2002). "Can you see the real me?" Activation and expression of the "true self" on the Internet. *The Journal of Social Issues*, *58*, 33–48. doi:10.1111/1540-4560.00247

Beraman, P. S., & Moody, J. (2004). Adolescents' suicidability. *American Journal of Public Health*, *94*, 89–95. doi:10.2105/AJPH.94.1.89

Blais, J. J., Craig, W. M., Pepler, D., & Connolly, J. (2008). Adolescents online: The importance of Internet activity choices to salient relationships. *Journal of Youth and Adolescence*, *37*, 522–536. doi:10.1007/s10964-007-9262-7

Boyd, D. M., & Ellison, N. B. (2007). Social network sites: Definition, history, and scholarship. *Journal of Computer-Mediated Communication*, *13*(1), article 11. Retrieved from http://jcmc.indiana.edu/vol13/issue1/boyd.ellison.html

Collins, W. A., & Laursen, B. (1999). *Relationships as developmental contexts*. Mahwah, NJ: Lawrence Erlbaum Associates, Inc.

Crosnoe, R. (2000). Friendships in childhood and adolescence: The life course and new directions. *Social Psychology Quarterly*, *63*, 377–391. doi:10.2307/2695847

Cummings, J. N., Butler, B., & Kraut, R. (2002). The quality of online social relationships. *Communications of the ACM*, *45*, 103–108. doi:10.1145/514236.514242

Cummings, J. N., Sproull, L., & Kiesler, S. B. (2002). Beyond hearing, where real world and online support meets. *Group Dynamics*, *5*, 78–88. doi:10.1037/1089-2699.6.1.78

Ellison, N. B., Steinfield, C., & Lampe, C. (2007). The benefits of Facebook "friends": Social capital and college students' use of online social network sites. *Journal of Computer-Mediated Communication*, *12*(4), article 1. Retrieved from http://jcmc.indiana.edu/vol12/issue4/ellison.html

European Commision. (2006). *The appropriation of New Media*. Brussels, Belgium: Mediappro.

Feld, S. (1981). The focused organization of social ties. *American Journal of Sociology, 86*, 1015–1035. doi:10.1086/227352

Flanagin, A. (2006). IM online: Instant messaging use among college students. *Communication Research Reports, 22*(3), 175–187. doi:10.1080/00036810500206966

Giordano, P. C. (2003). Relationships in adolescence. *Annual Review of Sociology, 29*, 257–281. doi:10.1146/annurev.soc.29.010202.100047

Grinter, R. E., & Palen, L. (2002). *Instant messaging in teen life*. Paper presented at the CSCW'02, New Orleans, Louisiana.

Grinter, R. E., Palen, L., & Eldridge, M. (2006). Chatting with teenagers: Considering the place of chat technologies in teen life. *ACM Transactions on Computer-Human Interaction, 13*(4), 423–447. doi:10.1145/1188816.1188817

Gross, E. F., Juvonen, J., & Gable, S. L. (2002). Internet use and well being in adolescence. *The Journal of Social Issues, 58*, 75–90. doi:10.1111/1540-4560.00249

Hartup, W. W. (1997). The company they keep: Friendships and their developmental significance. *Annual Progress in Child Psychiatry and Child Development*, 63-78.

Haythornthwaite, C. (2002). Strong, weak, and latent ties and the impact of new media. *The Information Society, 18*, 385–402. doi:10.1080/01972240290108195

Hu, Y., Wood, J. F., Smith, V., & Westbrook, N. (2004). Friendship through IM: Examining the relationship between instant messaging and intimacy. *Journal of Computer Mediated Communication, 10*(6). Retrieved from http://jcmc.indiana.edu/vol10/hu.html

Lenhart, A., & Madden, M. (2007). *Social networking sites and teens: An overview*. Washington, DC: Pew Internet and American Life Project.

Ling, R. (2004). *The mobile connection: The cell phone's impact on society*. San Francisco: Elsevier.

Ling, R., & Ytri, B. (2002). Hyper-coordination via mobile phone in Norway. In J. E. Katz & M. Aakhus (Eds.), *Perpetual contact: Mobile communication, private talk, public performance* (pp. 139-169). Cambridge, UK: Cambridge University Press.

Loader, B. D., Muncer, S., Burrows, R., Pleace, N., & Nettleton, S. (2002). Medicine on line? Computer mediated social support and advice for people with diabetes. *International Journal of Social Welfare, 11*, 53–65. doi:10.1111/1468-2397.00196

Mardsen, P., & Campbell, K. E. (1984). Measuring tie strength. *Social Forces, 63*, 482–494. doi:10.2307/2579058

McKay, H. G., Glasgow, R. E., Feil, E. G., Boles, S. M., & Barreta, M. (2002). Internet-based diabetes self-management and support: Initial outcomes from the diabetes network project. *Rehabilitation Psychology, 47*, 31–48. doi:10.1037/0090-5550.47.1.31

McPherson, M., Smith-Lovin, L., & Cook, J. M. (2002). Birds of a feather: Homophily in social networks. *Annual Review of Sociology, 27*, 415–444. doi:10.1146/annurev.soc.27.1.415

Media Awareness Group. (2005). *Young Canadians in a wired world*. Canada: Erin Research Inc.

Mesch, G. (2006). Online communities. In R. Cnaan & C. Milofsky (Eds.), *Handbook of community and community organization*. New York: Springer.

Mesch, G. S. (2007) Social diversification: A perspective for the study of social networks of adolescents offline and online. In N. Kutscher & H. U. Otto (Eds.), *Grenzenlose cyberwelt* (pp. 105-121). Heidelberg, Germany: Verlag für Sozialwiseenschaften.

Mesch, G. S., & Talmud, I. (2006). The quality of online and offline relationships, the role of multiplexity and duration. *The Information Society, 22*(3), 137–149. doi:10.1080/01972240600677805

Mesch, G. S., & Talmud, I. (2007). Similarity and the quality of online and offline social relationships among adolescents in Israel. *Journal of Research on Adolescence, 17*(2), 455–466. doi:10.1111/j.1532-7795.2007.00529.x

Preece, J. J., & Ghozati, K. (2001). Observations and explorations in empathy online. In R. Rice & J. E. Katz (Eds.), *The Internet and health communication: Experience and expectations* (pp. 237-260). Thousand Oaks, CA: Sage.

Rubin, K. H., Bukowski, W. M., & Parker, J. G. (1998). Peer interactions, relationships and groups. In N. Eisenberg (Ed.), *Handbook of child psychology: Social, emotional and personality development* (pp. 619-700). New York: Wiley.

Smith, L. (2007). Online networkers who click to 1000 friends. *The Times*. Retrieved September 20, from http://www.thetimes.co.uk/tol/news/science/article2416229

Sproull, L., & Kiesler, S. (1986). Reducing social context cues: Electronic email in organizational communications. *Management Science, 32*, 1492–1512. doi:10.1287/mnsc.32.11.1492

Subrahmanyam, K., & Greenfield, P. (2008). Online communication and adolescent relationships. *The Future of Children, 18*(1), 119–146. doi:10.1353/foc.0.0006

Suzuki, L., & Calzo, J. (2004). The search for peer advice in cyberspace: An examination of online teen bulletin boards about health and sexuality. *Journal of Applied Developmental Psychology, 25*, 685–698. doi:10.1016/j.appdev.2004.09.002

Taylor, A. S., & Harper, R. (2003). The gift of the gab? A design oriented sociology of young people's use of mobiles. *Computer Supported Cooperative Work . International Journal (Toronto, Ont.), 12*(4), 267–296.

Turner, J. W., Grube, J. A., & Meyers, J. (2001). Developing an optimal match within online communities: An exploration of CMC support communities and traditional support. *The Journal of Communication*, 231–251. doi:10.1111/j.1460-2466.2001.tb02879.x

Tynes, B. M. (2007). Internet safety gone wild? Sacrifing the educational and psychosocial benefits of online social environments. *Journal of Adolescent Research, 22*, 575–584. doi:10.1177/0743558407303979

Tynes, B. M., Giang, M. T., & Thompson, G. N. (2005). Ethnic identity, intergroup contact and outgroup orientation among diverse groups of adolescents on the Internet. *Cyberpsychology & Behavior, 11*(4), 459–465. doi:10.1089/cpb.2007.0085

Valkenburg, P., & Jochen, P. (2007). Preadolescents' and adolescents' online communication and their closeness to friends. *Child Development, 43*, 267–277.

Valkenburg, P., Schoutten, A., & Peter, J. (2005). Adolescents' identity experiments on the Internet. *New Media & Society, 7*(3), 383–401. doi:10.1177/1461444805052282

Walther, J. B., & Boyd, S. (2002). Attraction to computer-mediated social support. In C.A. Lin & D. Atkin (Eds.), *Communication technology and society: Audience adoption and uses* (pp. 153-188). Cresskill, NJ: Hampton Press.

Chapter 3
Unravelling the Web:
Adolescents and Internet Addiction

Laura Widyanto
Nottingham Trent University, UK

Mark Griffiths
Nottingham Trent University, UK

ABSTRACT

It has been alleged by some academics that excessive Internet use can be pathological and addictive. This chapter reviews what is known from the empirical literature on "Internet addiction" and its derivatives (e.g., Internet Addiction Disorder, Pathological Internet Use etc.) and assesses to what extent it exists. The chapter briefly overviews (i) the history and concept of Internet addiction, (ii) research on (adolescent and adult) Internet addiction, (iii) the attraction of the online world to adolescents, (iv) Internet users in their own words, an (v) an examination of online versus offline identity. The chapter has demonstrated that research into adolescent Internet addiction is a relatively little studied phenomenon although most effects found among adult users are thought to occur among adolescents too. In conclusion it would appear that if Internet addiction does indeed exist, it affects only a relatively small percentage of the online population and there is very little evidence that it is problematic among adolescents.

THE HISTORY AND CONCEPT OF INTERNET ADDICTION

The notion of 'Internet addiction' is not an entirely original one. The more general term 'computer addiction' had emerged even when the development of the Internet was still in its early stages. An example of the acceptance of this concept can be found in two court cases whereby the defence was found 'not guilty by reason of computer addiction' (Surratt, 1999). One of these cases took place in London in 1993, where Paul Bedworth was accused of hacking-related crime. He refused to plead guilty as he claimed to be addicted to the computer and because of that, was unable to form the necessary intent. His psychological assessment stated that he spent unnaturally long hours in the computer laboratories and that any of his activities involving computers took precedence over anything else. An expert witness in addictive behaviour con-

DOI: 10.4018/978-1-60566-926-7.ch003

cluded *"He's completely hooked on computing... The child, whose best friend is a computer rather than a person, is not going to function normally in society. We need to be able to predict how he will behave and what treatments will restore him to normal health"* (Gold, 1993).

Shortly after the Bedworth case was concluded, psychiatrist Ivan Goldberg, in an attempt to force the psychiatric community to re-think the usefulness of creating and labelling new 'disorders', made up a set of diagnostic criteria for Internet Addiction Disorder (IAD). He modelled the set after the Diagnostic and Statistical Manual (DSM) criteria for substance use (American Psychiatric Association, 1994). Goldberg also started an online support group called the Internet Addiction Support Group (IASG) for individuals who were suffering from this new affliction. Instead of realising that Goldberg's criteria was a ruse, popular press journalists seized this idea of a new disorder, and reports of the extent of problems the Internet was causing some individuals soon began to emerge. The first significant publication of IAD was on March 1995 in the *New York Times* entitled *"The Lure and Addiction of Life On Line"* (O'Neill, 1995). While it did not cite any scientific research or use the IAD label, the article claimed that a growing number of individuals were starting to spend so much time on the Internet that it had begun to interfere with some aspects of their lives.

A steady stream of similar articles began to appear, and these articles sparked off the interests of many academics and mental health professionals, one of whom was Kimberley Young. Due to her work, and assisted by the media, the label of IAD had spread throughout online community. For example, Hamilton and Kalb (1995) focused an article in *Newsweek* on Young's work and her estimate that 2% to 3% of online users were addicted to the Internet. Although they pointed out that Goldberg's IASG was intended as a joke, they cited many more sites dedicated to Internet addicts such as 'Webaholics' and 'Interneters

Anonymous'. They also quoted various respondents who were self-labelled as addicts. What they did not realise was that many of the WWW pages they cited as proof of IAD were nothing more than parodies, created by online users to mock the idea.

Some academics had alleged that excessive Internet use can be pathological and addictive and that it comes under the more generic label of "technological addiction" (e.g. Griffiths, 1996a; 1998). Technological addictions are operationally defined as non-chemical (behavioural) addictions that involve human-machine interaction. They can either be passive (e.g., television) or active (e.g., computer games), and usually contain inducing and reinforcing features which may contribute to the promotion of addictive tendencies (Griffiths, 1995). Technological addictions can be viewed as a subset of behavioural addictions (Marks, 1990) and feature core components of addiction (i.e., salience, mood modification, tolerance, withdrawal, conflict and relapse (see Griffiths, 2005).

- Salience – where the specific activity becomes the most important thing in a person's life; dominating their thoughts, feelings and behaviour.
- Mood Modification – where the person reports the subjective feeling as a result of that particular activity (e.g., they experience a 'buzz' or a 'high').
- Tolerance – where an increasing amount of the activity becomes essential to arouse the same level of effect it had previously.
- Withdrawal symptoms – where unpleasant feelings are observed in the absence or cutting back of the activity (e.g., moodiness, irritability, etc.).
- Conflict – which refers to the conflict between the addict and the people around him/her, as well as within him/herself.
- Relapse and reinstatement – where the behaviour would be repeated even after long abstinence.

In terms of excessive Internet usage, some studies have shown that individuals have displayed similar symptoms to those described above (Young, 1996; Griffiths, 2000a). Young (1998) stated that in behaviour-oriented addiction, individuals are addicted to what they do and the feelings they experience while engaging in it. A part of the problem in defining addiction is the fact that the cut-off point to separate normal from addictive habit is arbitrary. Therefore, the problems it caused in life become the 'measuring-tape'. In other words, the extent of damage to an individual's life reflects the level of the individual's involvement in an activity.

In terms of Internet usage, Young (1998) reported some serious incidents wherein the users' activities online disrupt their real life severely, to the extent that they abandon their real life in favour of online lives. For instance, there was a report of a father who forgot to pick up his daughter because he was too busy participating on an online forum; an employee who was fired because of her excessive Internet usage from the office computer; a recovering alcoholic who was using the Internet so much, he found himself lying to his wife; and a college student whose grades suffered immensely because of her involvement with her new online friends. It should also be noted that most of the research carried out in this area has concentrated on adult rather than adolescent samples (Griffiths, 2008) although there are research papers that feature both adult and adolescent accounts of Internet addiction (Griffiths, 2000).

Young and Rodgers (1996) further reported that addictive Internet use could be associated with decline of academic and work performance, marital discord as well as a decrease of social activities. Psychologists are now becoming more circumspect of the extent of the problem that might be caused by this excess usage of the Internet. There are numerous help outlets available for people who feel they are addicted to the Internet, or friends and families of the addict. Somewhat ironically, most of these are available online (Centre for Online Addiction, Cyberwidow, Computer Addiction Services at McLean Hospital, etc.). In addition, a preliminary draft of the DSM-V includes a section defining some forms of "Cyber Disorders" (Zenhausen, 1995), signifying the growing awareness and recognition of the problem. Having overviewed the history of the origins of Internet addiction, the next section examines whether Internet addiction really exists. And if it does exist, are adolescents more susceptible?

ADOLESCENTS AND INTERNET ADDICTION

Yellowlees and Marks (2007) point out that there is growing evidence to suggest that some individuals' problematic Internet use is only related to certain online activities. Similarly, Griffiths (1999) had argued that most of the individuals who use the Internet excessively are not addicted to the Internet itself, but use it as a medium to fuel other addictions (i.e., addictions on the Internet rather than to the Internet). He gave the example of a gambling addict who chose to engage in online gambling, as well as a gaming addict who plays online, stressing that the Internet is just the place where they conduct their chosen behaviour. In contrast, he also acknowledged that there are some case studies that appear to report an addiction to the Internet itself (Young, 1996b; Griffiths, 2000b). Most of these individuals use functions of the Internet that are not available in any other medium, such as chat rooms or various role playing games. However, it can be argued that even in these cases, it may be misleading to call it 'Internet Addiction'. It would perhaps be more informative to investigate if there were certain types of function that users are using more excessively than others.

It could be argued that compared to adults, adolescents live their lives under a different set of parameters, limits and possibilities and that such individuals deserve special consideration. A number of writings have highlighted the danger that IAD may pose to adolescents and young adults (e.g., students) as a population group (Griffiths, 2008). This population is deemed to be at risk given the accessibility of the Internet and the flexibility of their schedules (Moore, 1995; Neimz, Griffiths & Banyard, 2005). Such logic is also applicable to adolescents. Scherer (1997) studied 531 students at the University of Texas at Austin, and 381 students who used the Internet at least once per week were further investigated. Based on the criteria that paralleled chemical dependencies, 49 of these students (13%) were classified as "Internet dependent". Within the 'Dependents' group, 71% were men and 29% were women. 'Dependent' users averaged 11 hours per week online as opposed to the average of eight hours per week for 'Non-Dependents'. Furthermore, 'Dependents' were three times more likely to use interactive synchronous applications. Again, the weakness of this study appears to stem from the imbalance between male and female participants. Furthermore, 'Dependents' averaged 11 hours per week online, which worked out to be slightly more than an hour a day. This amount of time could hardly be called excessive, despite the significant difference with 'Non-Dependents' (Griffiths, 1998).

Morahan-Martin and Schumacher (1997) conducted a similar online study. Pathological Internet Use (PIU) was measured by a 13-item questionnaire assessing problems due to Internet use (e.g., academic, work, and relationship problems, tolerance symptoms, and mood-altering use of the Internet). Those who answered 'yes' to four or more of the 13-item questionnaire were defined as pathological Internet users, while those who answered 'yes' to between one and three items were considered as users with limited problems. Two hundred and seventy seven undergraduate Internet users were recruited and 27.2% reported no symptoms, 64.7% were in the limited problems category, and 8.1% were classed as pathological users category. Pathological Internet users were more likely to be male and to use technologically sophisticated sites. However, no gender differences were found in IRC use. On average, they spent 8.5 hours per week online. It was also found that 'pathological users' scored higher on the UCLA Loneliness Scale, and they used the Internet to meet new people, for emotional support, play interactive games, and they were more socially disinhibited online. As with Scherer's study, the average of 8.5 hours per week online seemed slightly low compared to other findings, although the authors argued that it was indicative of problems surfacing in relatively short periods of being online. Moreover, the items used to measure dependency in this study were similar to items used in Brenner's (1997) study of Internet addiction that were criticized by Griffiths (1998) as not really measuring addiction.

Anderson (1999) reported a slightly lower percentage (9.8%) of dependent student users, most of which were those majoring in hard sciences. The DSM-IV substance-dependence criteria were used to classify participants into 'Dependents' and 'Non-Dependents'. Those endorsing more than three of the seven criteria were classified as being 'Dependent'. Of the 106 Dependents, 93 were males, and they averaged 229 minutes per day compared to Non-Dependents who averaged 73 minutes per day. Anderson collected data from a mixture of colleges in the US and Europe, which yielded 1302 responses (649 males, 647 females, 6 without gender information) using pen-and-paper questionnaires. On average, his participants used the Internet 100 minutes per day, and roughly 6% of the participants were considered as high-users (above 400 minutes per day). The participants in the high-users category reported more negative consequences compared to the low-users participants.

The concern for this particular population was further brought into public attention in May 2000 when William Woods University announced a program whereby undergraduates could earn up to $5000 against tuition fees if they scored enough points by attending various cultural events on campus. It was reported that the aim of the program was to reduce students' Internet use, although the formal description did not emphasise this (Kubey, Lavin, & Barrows, 2001). They then conducted their own study in which a paper and pencil survey was administered to 576 students in Rutgers University. Their survey included 43-multiple-choice items on Internet usage, study habits, academic performance, and personality. Internet dependency was measured with a five-point Likert-scale item, asking participants how much they agreed or disagreed with the following statement: "I think I might have become a little psychologically dependent on the Internet." To test the validity of the measure, they checked if the participant's self-report reflected other behavioural characteristic consistent with dependency and heavier usage (e.g. guilt, lack of control, using the Internet less if they had more friends, academic impairments, etc.). Participants were categorised as Internet dependent if they chose 'Agree' or 'Strongly Agree' to the statement.

Of the 572 valid responses, 381 (66%) were females and the age ranged between 18 and 45 years old with a mean age of 20.25 years. Fifty-three participants (9.3%) were classified as Internet dependent, and males were more prevalent in this group. Age was not found to be a factor, but first year students (mean age not reported) were found to make up 37.7% of the dependent group. Dependents were four times more likely than non-dependents to report academic impairment due to their Internet use, and they were significantly 'more lonely' than other students. In terms of their Internet usage, dependents that were also academically impaired were found to be nine times as likely to use synchronous functions of the Internet (MUDs and IRC/chat programs). The authors proposed that these types of application are important outlets for lonely people (especially students who just moved away to college) as they can keep in touch with family and friend, and find someone to chat to at anytime and no other me-

dium can offer such an opportunity. More recently, Nalwa and Anand (2003) found that students who were dependent on the Internet had higher scores on the loneliness scale, and their online use had affected their performance and work in school.

Niemz, Griffiths and Banyard (2005) surveyed 371 British students. In a questionnaire which included the pathological Internet use (PIU) scale (Morahan-Martin & Schumacher, 2000), the General Health Questionnaire (GHQ-12), a self-esteem scale, and two measures of disinhibition, results showed that 18.3% of the sample were considered to be pathological Internet users, whose excessive use of the Internet was causing academic, social and interpersonal problems. Other results showed that pathological Internet users had lower self-esteem and were more socially disinhibited. However, there was no significant difference in GHQ scores. However, there are methodological concerns as the study used the PIU Scale and relied on a self-selected sample.

Other studies such as those by Kennedy-Souza (1998), Chou (2001), Tsai and Lin (2003), Chin-Chung and Sunny (2003), Nalwa and Anand (2003). Kaltiala-Heino, Lintonen and Rimpela (2004), and Wan and Chiou (2006) that surveyed very small numbers of students and adolescents are simply too small and/or methodologically limited to make any real conclusions. From the studies so far discussed (in this section and the preceding one on comparison studies), it is clear that most of these "prevalence type" studies share common weaknesses. Most use convenient, self-selected participants who volunteer to respond to the survey. It is therefore difficult to plan any kind of comparable groups. Most studies did not use any type of validated addiction criteria (such as withdrawal symptoms, salience, tolerance, relapse etc.), and those that did assumed that excessive Internet use was akin to other behavioural addictions like gambling and/or used very low cut-off scores which would increase the percentage of those defined as addicted. As Griffiths (2000a) observed, the instruments used have no measure of severity, no temporal dimension, they have a tendency to over-estimate the incidence of the problems, and they do not consider the context of Internet use, (i.e., it is possible for some people to be engaged in very excessive use because it is part of their job or they are in an online relationship with someone geographically distant).

Griffiths (2000a; 2000b) noted the importance of case studies in the study of Internet addiction. Griffiths' own research on Internet addiction has attempted to address three main questions: (1) What is addiction? (2) Does Internet addiction exist? (3) If Internet addiction does exist, what are people addicted to? He adopted an operational definition of addictive behaviour as any behaviour (including Internet use) that included six core components of addiction, namely salience, mood modification, tolerance, withdrawal symptoms, conflict and relapse. Using these criteria, Griffiths asserts that Internet addiction exists in only a very small percentage of users, and most of the individuals who use the Internet excessively just use the Internet as a medium through which they can engage in a chosen behaviour.

Griffiths also claims that Young's (1999) classifications of Internet addiction are not really types of Internet addiction as the majority of the behaviours involve use of the medium of the Internet to fuel other non-Internet addictions. In conclusion, Griffiths stated that most studies to date have failed to show that Internet addiction exists outside a small minority of users. He therefore suggested that case studies might help in indicating whether or not Internet addiction exists, even if these are unrepresentative.

Griffiths (2000b) outlined five case studies of excessive users that were gathered over the space of six months. The first case was that of 'Gary', a 15-year old British student. He was an only child who spent up to six hours online on weekends. His mother reported that his academic performance had been affected by his Internet use. He suffered from neurofibromatosis, a condition that could result in varying degrees of behavioural

problems, and he always had problems socially. He had difficulties making friends and he suffered from teasing and bullying, and inferiority complex, which in turn caused him to get depressed. His parents stated that he viewed his computer as a 'friend', which led him to spend a lot of time using it at the cost of spending less time with family and friends. Griffiths commented that this case would fit into the stereotype of a computer 'addict'; a teenage male with little social life and low self-esteem, who used the computer as an escape from his problems and depression.

The second case was that of 'Jamie', a 16-year old British college student. He had few familial and physical problems, although he was very overweight. He reported spending about 70 hours per week on his computer, including 40 hours per week online. He described himself as 'sci-fi mad', participated on a *Star Trek* forum, which resulted in expensive phone bills. He reported to using the Internet, which he claimed was the most important thing in his life, to change his moods. He appeared to be displaying the core components of addiction in that he experienced loss of control when using the Internet, he thought about the Internet when he was offline, he had irregular sleeping patterns, and he displayed withdrawal symptoms such as irritability and shaking. He did not consider himself as an addict, and he had no desire to make friends offline. Griffiths noted that Jamie seemed to use the Internet mainly for social reasons, and it could be because of his obesity that he preferred online to face-to-face interactions.

The third case study was of 'Panos', a 20-year old Greek male university student. He was used to playing computer games since he was a child, and he claimed that he had been 'addicted' to the games he used to play, neglecting anything else. He believed that the feelings he had as a young child could then be recreated by playing online games. He stated that being online helped him adjust to university life. He spent up to 50 hours per week online, and his academic work had suffered as a consequence of his Internet use. Griffiths noted that Panos only seemed to display some of the core components of addiction, and in contrast to Gary and Jamie, did not deny that he had a problem with his computer use. His use could be viewed as a way to cope with living in a foreign country, and unsurprisingly, he used the Internet mostly for game playing given that he had been 'addicted' to game playing when he was a child.

The fourth case was that of 'Jodie', a 35-year old unemployed Canadian female who used the Internet for a minimum of 40 hours per week solely for Internet Relay Chat. She described herself as 'disabled, overweight and not at all attractive'. She viewed her Internet use as a way of life instead of an addiction, as all her relationships were based online. She was married to someone she met online, but lived in separate places although she did not see this as a problem as they chatted online for up to 4 hours each night. She claimed that she became moody and depressed if she did not go online, as she felt lonely without the IRC. Griffiths observed that she used the Internet purely for socializing and she did not view her excessive use as being a problem as it was justified by her situation.

The final case study was that of 'Dave', a 32-year old British male, who had a happy married life before he discovered the Internet. He changed when he had to stay home because of a change of job, and he became depressed and reserved. His wife claimed that he had changed his sleeping patterns in order to use the Internet within two months of staying home, becoming angry and anxious when he was not online. Within three months of being at home, Dave left his wife to go to America to be with a woman he met on the IRC, whom he had been calling up to six times a day. He had proposed marriage to the woman before even seeing her, and his wife stated that the Internet was the cause of their marriage break-up. Although he came back for a short time, admitting that he had begun to realise the damage of losing his family and job, he had gone back to the US. His wife claimed that he was not using the Internet anymore. Griffiths remarked that although Dave seemed to display some of the addiction components, his Internet use was symptomatic, motivated by his need to chat with his new partner. His use seemed to diminish once he was together with the woman he had been having an online affair with.

Griffiths concluded that out of the five case studies discussed, only two were 'addicted' according to the components criteria. In short, these two case studies ('Gary' and 'Jamie' – both adolescent males) demonstrated that the Internet was the most important thing in their lives, that they neglected everything else in their lives to engage in the behaviour and that it compromised most areas of their lives. They also built up tolerance over time, suffered withdrawal symptoms if they were unable to engage in using the Internet, and showed signs of relapse after giving up the behaviour for short periods.

In the other cases of very excessive Internet use, Griffiths claimed that the participants had used the Internet as a way to cope with, and counteract other inadequacies (e.g., lack of social support in real life, low self-esteem, physical disability, etc.). Griffiths also observed that it was interesting to note that all of the participants seemed to be using the Internet mainly for social contact and he postulated that it was because the Internet could be an alternative, text-based reality where users are able to immerse themselves by taking on another social persona and identity to make them feel better about themselves, which in itself would be highly rewarding psychologically (Griffiths, 2000b). In the next section, we focus more specifically on the attraction of the Internet to people including adolescents as a sub-group.

THE ATTRACTION OF THE ONLINE WORLD TO ADOLESCENTS

One of the main attractions of the Internet irrespective of age is the ability to form relationships with other online users. Prolonged contact and communication with each other can form the basis of social support. For example, regular visits to a certain group (e.g., a specific chat room, playing a particular MUD, or posting to the same Forum), will raise familiarity and closeness amongst other group members, and thus a sense of community is established. Like other communities, online culture also has its own set of ethics, values, norms, language and signs, which all group members adapt to over time. Kiesler, Siegal, and McGuire (1984) pointed out that this creates the opportunity to disregard normal conventions in interaction through the removal of time and space, work and play, and boundaries of privacy.

Intimacy develops more quickly among online users. In cyberspace, social conventions and rules of politeness are gone, allowing a person (such as an adolescent) to reveal and ask about personal details on an initial virtual meeting. The immediacy and openness in sharing personal details about one's life fosters intimacy. As a user becomes more involved in a specific group online, they are able to take more risks of voicing controversial opinions that they might not be able to make in real life. For adolescents and adults alike, the Internet provides anonymity, which removes the threat of confrontation, rejection and other consequences of the behaviour. The formation of such close bonds in such a short time may attract those with low self-esteem and low social skills to turn to the Internet for new relationships. Such rewarding online behaviour may be particularly attractive for adolescents. Indeed, a study by Joinson (2004) showed that low self-esteem users showed a significant preference toward e-mail communication compared to high self-esteem users. This pattern was reversed for face-to-face preferences.

Results from another (non-adolescent) study has suggested that self-esteem could account for both positive and negative differences between online and offline attitudes (Widyanto, Griffiths, Brunsden & McMurran, 2008). In other words, it would seem that the lower the individual's self-esteem, the bigger discrepancy there would be between their online and offline attitudes. This difference between the online and offline attitudes has raised the question of whether or not an inconsistency also exists between participants' self-esteem when they are online and offline. It is possible that this discrepancy exists, especially in those participants with higher scores on the Internet problems questionnaire. If being online enhances their confidence, they are more likely to spend more time online, which could in turn cause them problems in terms of their Internet use.

Research has shown that changes in self-esteem are associated with significant changes in an individual's social environment, such as moving to a new city, changing jobs, and (for adolescents) going to university (Harter, 1993; Ruble 1994). McKenna and Bargh (2000) noted that when individuals join an online group (e.g., chat rooms, MUD Games, forums, etc.), they are obtaining a group of new acquaintances who do not have any connection with their offline group. Thus, initiating online interactions would give them an opportunity to alter some elements of self that they present, and this would result in increased feelings of self-worth (McKenna & Bargh, 1998).

It was reported that the ability to (re)create one's persona online could be one major reason that the Internet is so attractive. This may also be particularly attractive for adolescents. As Suler (2002) stated, *"one of the interesting things about the Internet is the opportunity it offers people to present themselves in a variety of different ways. You can alter your style of being just slightly or indulge in wild experiments with your identity by changing your age, history, personality, physical appearance, even your gender"* (p. 455). The Internet provides individuals with anonymity, the freedom to be whoever they want to be. Users are in control of how much personal information they choose to reveal or conceal. In some cases, this might lead to dininhibition, whereby individuals feel more confident as they are protected by their anonymity that they become more honest and open about their opinions and feelings. The Internet can facilitate new relationship formations, which gives individuals a chance to express aspects of themselves they are not normally able to express in their offline relationships. Therefore, it can be expected that interactions via the Internet would encourage individuals to take on more aspects of their true self (McKenna & Bargh, 2000). In the next section, we examine more closely how excessive Internet use occurs.

WHY DOES EXCESSIVE INTERNET USE OCCUR?

Most of the research that has been discussed appears to lack theoretical basis as surprisingly few researchers have attempted to propose a theory of the cause of Internet addiction despite the number of studies conducted on the field. Furthermore, most of the research (to date) does not distinguish between adults and adolescents, nor does it examine any developmental pathology. Davis (2001) proposed a model of the etiology of pathological Internet use (PIU) using the cognitive-behavioural approach. The main assumption of the model was that PIU resulted from problematic cognitions coupled with behaviours that intensify or maintain maladaptive response. It emphasized the individual's thoughts/cognitions as the main source of abnormal behaviour. Davis stipulated that the cognitive symptoms of PIU might often precede and cause the emotional and behavioural symptoms rather than vice versa. Similar to the basic assumptions of cognitive theories of depression, it focused on maladaptive cognitions associated with PIU.

Davis described Abramson, Metalsky, and Alloy's (1989) concepts of *necessary, sufficient,* and *contributory* causes. A *necessary* cause is an etiological factor that must be present or must have occurred in order for symptoms to appear. A *sufficient* cause is an etiological factor whose presence/occurrence guarantees the occurrence of symptoms, and a *contributory* cause is an etiological factor that increases the likelihood of the occurrence of symptoms, but that is neither necessary nor sufficient. Abramson also distinguished between *proximal* and *distal* causes. In an etiology chain that results in a set of symptoms, some causes lie toward the end of the chain (proximal), while others in the beginning (distal). In the case of PIU, Davis claimed that distal cause was underlying psychopathology (e.g., depression, social anxiety, other dependence, etc.), while the proximal cause was maladaptive cognitions (i.e., negative evaluation of oneself and the world in general). The main goal of the paper was to introduce maladaptive cognitions as proximal sufficient cause of the set of symptoms for PIU.

Distal contributory causes of PIU were discussed. It was explained in a diathesis-stress framework, whereby an abnormal behaviour was caused by a predisposition/vulnerability (diathesis) and a life event (stress). In the cognitive-behavioural model of PIU, existing underlying psychopathology was viewed as the diathesis, as many studies had shown the relationship between psychological disorders such as depression, social anxiety and substance dependence (Kraut et al, 1998). The model suggested that psychopathology was a distal necessary cause of PIU, i.e. psychopathology must be present, or must have occurred in order for PIU symptoms to occur. However, in itself, the underlying psychopathology would not result in PIU symptoms, but was a necessary element in its etiology.

The model assumed that although a basic psychopathology might predispose an individual to PIU, the set of associated symptoms was specific to PIU and therefore should be investigated and treated independently. The stressor in this model was the introduction of the Internet, or the discovery of a specific function of the Internet. Although it might be difficult to trace back an individual's encounter with the Internet, a more testable event would be the experience of a function found online, e.g., the first time the person used an online auction, found pornographic material online, etc.

Exposure to such functions was viewed as a distal necessary cause of PIU symptoms. In itself, this encounter did not result in the occurrence of symptoms of PIU. However, as a contributory factor, the event could be a catalyst for the developmental process of PIU. A key factor here was the reinforcement received from an event (i.e., operant conditioning, whereby positive response reinforced continuity of activity). The model proposed that stimuli such as the sound of a modem connecting or the sensation of typing could result in a conditioned response. Thus, these types of secondary reinforcers could act as situational cues that contribute to the development of PIU and the maintenance of symptoms.

Central to the cognitive-behavioural model was the presence of maladaptive cognitions that were viewed to be proximal sufficient cause of PIU. Maladaptive cognitions were broken down into two subtypes; perceptions about one's self, and about the world. Thoughts about self are guided by ruminative cognitive style. Individuals who tend to ruminate would experience a higher degree in severity and duration of PIU, as studies have supported that rumination is likely to intensify or maintain problems, partly by interfering with instrumental behaviour (i.e., taking action) and problem solving. Other cognitive distortions include self-doubt, low self-efficacy and negative self-appraisal. These cognitions dictate the way in which individuals behave, and some cognitions would cause specific or generalized PIU. Specific PIU referred to the over-use and abuse of a specific Internet function. It was assumed to be the result of a pre-existing psychopathology that became associated with an online activity (e.g., compulsive gamblers might realize that they could gamble online and ultimately showed symptoms of specific PIU as the association between need and immediate reinforcement became stronger). However, it should be noted that not every compulsive gambler showed symptoms of PIU.

On the other hand, generalized PIU involved spending excessive amounts of time online with no direct purpose, or just wasting time. The social context of the individual, especially the lack of social support they received and/or social isolation, was one key factor that played a role in the causality of general PIU. Individuals with general PIU were viewed as being more problematic, as their behaviour would not even exist in the absence of the Internet.

Based on Davis' model, Caplan (2003) further proposed that problematic psychosocial predispositions causes excessive and compulsive Computer-Mediated (CM) social interaction in individuals, which in turn increases their problems. The theory proposed by Caplan, examined empirically, had three main propositions:

- Individuals with psychosocial problems (e.g., depression and loneliness) hold more negative perceptions of their social competence compared to others.
- They prefer CM interactions rather than face-to-face ones as the former is perceived to be less threatening and they perceive themselves to be more efficient in an online setting.
- This preference in turn leads to excessive and compulsive use of CM interactions that then worsens their problems and creates new ones at school, work and home.

In Caplan's (2003) study, the participants consisted of 386 undergraduates (279 females and 116 males), with the age ranging from 18 to 57 years old (mean age=20 years). This study used Caplan's (2002) Generalized Problematic Internet Use Scale (GPIUS), a self-report assessing the prevalence of cognitive and behavioural symptoms of pathological Internet use along with the degree to which negative consequences affected the individual. The GPIUS had seven subscales – mood alteration, perceived social benefits, perceived social control, withdrawal, compulsivity, excessive Internet use, and negative outcomes. Also included in this study were validated depression and loneliness scales.

It was found that depression and loneliness were significant predictors of preference for online social interaction, accounting for 19% of the variance. In turn, participants' preference for online social interaction was found to be a significant predictor of their scores on pathological Internet use and negative outcomes. The data also suggested that excessive use was one of the weakest predictors of negative outcomes whereas preference for online interaction, compulsive use, and withdrawal were among the strongest. Overall, loneliness and depression were not found to have large, independent effects on negative outcomes. The result of this study appeared to support the proposition that preference for online socialization was a key contributor to the development of problematic Internet use.

Caplan noted two unexpected results in the data. Firstly, loneliness played a more significant role in the development of problematic Internet use compared to depression. He attempted to explain this finding by stating that loneliness was theoretically the more salient predictor, as negative perception of social competence and communication skills is more pronounced in lonely individuals. On the other hand, a wide variety of circumstances that might not be related to a person's social life could result in depression (e.g., traumatic experiences). Secondly, using the Internet to alter mood was found to be lacking in influence on negative outcomes. For instance, it was proposed by Caplan was that there are various different circumstance in which individuals use the Internet to alter their mood, and different usages of the Internet would case different mood alterations. For example, online game playing would be exciting and fun, while reading the news could be relaxing. Therefore, in itself, using the Internet to alter mood might not necessarily lead to the negative consequences associated with preference for online social interaction, excessive and compulsive use, and experiencing psychological withdrawal.

The limitations to this study included the need for future empirical evidence pertaining to the causality of specific CM communication characteristics that could lead to the preference for online social interaction. Also, the data were collected from a primarily sample that did not display very high degrees of problematic Internet use (median for preference was 1.28 on a scale ranging from 1 to 5 (i.e, most participants did not prefer online over face-to-face social interactions). Finally, the study did not take into account the role that an individual's actual social skill and communication preference played in the development of problematic Internet use, despite the theory's emphasis on perceived social competence. In the next section, we take a more qualitative approach and look at what those who use the Internet say in their own words.

INTERNET USERS IN THEIR OWN WORDS

Widyanto (2007) attempted to explore if individuals feel differently when they are online and when they are offline. Adult participants were asked to complete a short questionnaire, and the short answers that the participants gave in response to the two open-ended questions were analysed one by one, and some common themes were identified. The first question was, *"Please describe the person you are when you are online"*, and the second was *"Bearing in mind your previous answer, do you feel any differently when you are offline? If so, can you please describe the difference(s)?"* It should be noted that not all the participants gave answers that could be analysed. For example, many participants just stated *"I feel exactly the same"* or *"Normal, like when offline"* to the first question, and *"Same"* or *"No different"* to the second. However, others—mostly adolescents and young adults—gave more descriptive and informative answers to the questions. From these longer answers, some themes emerged repeatedly. Some of the most common themes (i.e., disinhibition, anonymity, isolation, control, escape from reality, information access) are presented below:

Disinhibition: One of the most common themes that had emerged through the analysis of how differently participants feel online and offline related to their increased confidence online, due to the disinhibition effect. This effect is often associated with increased confidence, honesty, and openness when online. Below are some examples of the participants' responses.

"[When I'm online, I feel like] *someone worth talking to, with some interesting to say given the right topic. In chat rooms with lots of people (10 or more), I am quite happy to interrupt a conversation with my own thoughts on the subject in question. [When offline], I feel more reluctant to start a conversation about something I want to talk about, and find it more difficult to contribute to conversations in large groups*" (Female, 20-years old).

"*I am more sociable online! I have no inhibitions, so I feel more confident, maybe more blunt/ honest. I don't have to see this person's face if I upset them. When I am offline, I am more introverted; I will keep more thoughts to myself. Partly because I don't want to offend others/be rude, but mostly because I don't enjoy conversing as much in person*" (Male, 20-years old).

"*When I am online I become a more confident person, I pluck up the confidence to confront situations that I would not normally face. Some of the issues I confront people with I would not be able to do face-to-face.*" (Female, 19-years old)

"[When online I am] *not myself at all…I am far more confident and as a result my personality changes. When I'm offline I'm not as confident, you can talk to the opposite sex with more ease on the net as you are not face-to-face*" (Female, 19-years old).

"*When I am online, usually participating on a message board, I express my opinion openly and feel as if my thoughts should be shared with others online. When I am offline, I may be more hesitant to express my thoughts, depending on my surroundings and the topic at hand. When online, I am aware that my peer group is of the same interest that I am*" (Female, 21-years old)

"*Usually, I feel better* [online] *because I use forums or chat to people who can relate to situations taking place in my life. I feel that I am socially inept, but on the Internet, I have absolutely no problem speaking with others. I have more time to consider my words, and I have anonymity so I don't have to limit my thoughts. I know that I have thought-provoking ideas, and on the Internet I can express them. Through the Internet, I am able to be someone I want to be. I feel more confident than in person and I feel good that others are able to respect my opinions. I know that I do well in almost anything I do, but I often feel that my accomplishments aren't good enough. I also feel unable to communicate with other and I become anxious when I think about what other people think about me. When I am offline, I keep myself and my ideas more reserved. Because of this, I feel incapable of carrying on a good conversation/debate, and I feel less respected and/or understood*" (Female, 17-years old).

Anonymity: This relates to the fact that some participants feel like they can be anyone online due to the absence of physical presence and any other kind of identity, which is inevitable in face to face interactions.

"*Being online is freeing, you can be anything or anybody you want. Nobody can see or judge you. On the net, I can be the person I always wanted to be.* [Offline I feel] *very different. People judge you on a physical level, and I find that difficult to live with at times*" (Female, 29-years old).

"[Online] *I feel I can be who I want to be. I'm an admin in a large and popular website, so I get, I guess what you would call, a feeling of power.* [Offline] *I feel limited to being other people's perception of who I am. I don't really feel as important offline as I am online*" (Female, 19-years old).

Within this theme, some participants mentioned how the anonymity may lead to a feeling of equality. Those with physical disabilities in real life, for example, thought that the Internet provided a place where they were the same as everyone else.

"When I am online I feel as though I am fine, and any problem I have I let drift away while I work on other things like homework assignments, researching graduate schools and programs, etc. [I] only [feel] *a little* [different offline] *in that I have a knee injury that prevents me from doing some things that most people take for granted, and when I am online I don't have to worry about all the things I can't do because I'm focused on whatever I am doing online"* (Female, 20=years old)

"[When online I feel] *much the same as I am when offline just a little more sure of myself as using a PC puts me on a level with fully-sighted people"* (Male, 19-years old).

"[When online I feel like] *someone who has no mobility problems! [Offline, my] physical limitations* [are] *overly apparent to the eye"* (Female, 34-years old).

Others also mentioned this feeling of equality due to the lack of physical presence online.

"[Online] *I feel like there are no prejudgements made about appearance/accent etc., so everyone is treated exactly the same. [Offline] sometimes I feel self-conscious about what other people think of me as a first impression before they get to know me"* (Female, 20-years old).

"[Online I feel] *literate, in control, mature, respectful, and able to command respect. (That's true for any written medium though, not just the Net). The only difference is that when I'm offline, people judge me by my appearance and consequently treat me with contempt or disdain. From what I gather, I must have the appearance of a slacker – because this is how people treat me – they are invariably surprised when they found out I can string more than two words together…For some people, the spoken word is not always the easiest means of communication…"* (Male, 25-years old).

"[Online I am] *confident, slightly arrogant, friendly. [Offline] I'm not very confident, shy and self-loathing, the way I look affects the way I act which is obviously not an issue on the Interne."* (Male, 19-years old).

Isolation: Some participants stated that they sometimes feel isolated. However, this varies in terms of the situation. Some claimed that the Internet makes them feel isolated from the rest of the world.

"[Online I feel] *isolated, [I] need to get out and do something physical, i.e. sport. [Offline] I feel better as [I'm] not staring at a computer screen"* (Male, 22-years old).

"[Online I feel] *unmotivated and lazy. Offline there's much more activity to keep me active. On the net I become connected to the screen and block out everything else around me"* (Male, 22-years old).

"[Online I feel] *harassed, not enough time to sift through crap to pull out what I need from* [the] *net. [I also feel like a] bad parent as my daughter nags me when I'm browsing. [Offline] I don't feel like a bad parent as [I] am able to deal with constant questioning by 7 year old when I'm not reading from the screen"* (Female, 36-years old).

"[Online] *I am like a zombie and am unable to concentrate on what people say to me due to concentrating on the computer"* (Male, 18-years old).

On the other hand, others claimed the opposite – that they feel isolated in real life and turn to the Internet to feel more in touch.

"I'm still myself just as offline. The difference is when I'm offline, I feel isolated from the world" (Male, 33-years old).

"When I am online, I feel that I am more connected with the outside world…When I am offline, I don't feel as connected to the outside world, I don't pay attention to what is going on around me, I am much more sheltered from the realities of the real world" (Female, 21-years old).

"When online, I feel that I am 'included' especially when on a chat program as things are

being discussed between friends and you tend to feel part of what is happening, you get to hear things first hand" (Female, 19-years old).

"*When I'm not logged in to messenger and IRC I feel like I am out of contact with the world. It would be like taking a phone away from kids that have grown up with [it]*" (Male, 20-years old).

Control: Another common theme that emerged from the analysis was related to control. Some participants stated that they felt more in control when they are online with regards to the information available to them.

"*It is good to know that I have the information of the WWW at my fingertips, so [I] feel in control of my learning. [Offline I feel] at a loose end as to start and find the info I need*" (Female, 41-years old).

"*[Online] I feel that I am in control of what I am doing. I sometimes prefer to use the Internet for long periods of time as the amount of information and data is valuable to me and my studies*" (Female, 21-years old).

"*[Online] I feel a bit useless, as I'm not that good with computers, but I still feel in control of what I'm doing and confident I can manage certain tasks. [Offline] I feel less in control of the situation but I do feel more able to cope as I understand the world around me while I haven't a clue about computers.*" (Female, 18-years old).

Other participants had also mentioned the issue of control, but regarding to the information they could choose to divulge or reveal about themselves online. Some participants talked about how the Internet allows them to hide their more negative qualities.

"*[Online] I'm pretty similar to when I'm not, but I can often hide any bad qualities. [Offline I feel] maybe less adequate*" (Female, 18-years old).

"*[Online] I am able to present my better qualities to others and omit the worse ones. I am also held in high regards as someone who can offer advice and assistance*" (Male, 27-years old).

"*[Online] I feel slightly more ideal, like my small faults can be glossed over*" (Female, 24-years old).

Escape from reality: A few of the participants mentioned that the Internet allows them to escape from reality.

"*[Online] I feel like I'm in a different world and it's great 'cos I can do what I want and everybody wants to talk to me. I hate it offline. It's like a bad comedown from taking drugs or something. It's like withdrawal symptoms. I use the Internet to get away from all the crap and stress that's going on in my life*" (Female, 24-years old).

"*Online I can be anyone I want to be. No one will know unless I tell them! Offline I have to be me, because everyone around me knows me. So obviously there is a difference. Its very boring though being just me! Having an alter-ego…in a chat room can be very exciting*" (Male, 19-years old).

"*[Online] you can be anyone. I have been an 18 year-old blonde girl for a laugh on chat [rooms]. [Offline] people could see that I am a 38 year-old bloke*" (Male, 38-years old).

"*[Online I am] much more goal-getting. Much more 'excitable'. I am an eccentric either way, but when I am in a chat room, I BECOME a God… My online personality doesn't care about things as much as the real me does. In the past, I have strived to become my online personality…I was successful for a while, then in shambles, I became myself again and discovered a whole heck of a lot of difference in who I wanted to be and who I really am*" (Female, 26-years old).

"*I feel like [the Internet is] an escape from reality but it doesn't last forever*" (Female, age undisclosed).

"*[Online] I feel as though I am invincible. [Offline] I feel as though I am just an ordinary person with an ordinary life*" (Female, 26-years old).

"*[Online I feel] untouchable. Your identity is known [offline] therefore [I] feel less untouchable*" (Male, 21-years old).

Information access: Several participants also talked about how the Internet provided them with easy access to information.

"*[Online] I just feel normal. Perhaps a bit*

empowered by the information at my fingertips" (Female, 19-years old).

"[I] *feel competent online and enjoy getting information quickly and gaining knowledge on things I would not otherwise be able to find out*" (Female, 22-years old).

"[Offline I feel] *restricted to books – always aware of the nearest Internet access point as books are often a 2nd choice for information*" (Male, 27-years old).

However, for some participants the wealth of information provided by the Internet could cause some frustration.

"[Online I feel] *a bit overwhelmed with the information to be sifted through. Sometimes I feel so out of place and floating in unreality because it all seems just too much. The truth is that, because it is mostly research information which I truly need that I am looking at, I feel as if I am not doing well because I am being overwhelmed. I think that the people who used lots of books before our time were better off because books have boundaries and the net does not have any. The info highway gets too much most times*" (Female, age undisclosed).

"*When I'm online looking for information about assignments I can become frustrated with not being able to find the right information or I feel annoyed that the net can be difficult to search. I can quite happily live without the Internet or being online*" (Female, 31-years old).

Having examined individual accounts, in the final section we examine issues surrounding online and offline identities and some of the psychological implications.

ONLINE VS. OFFLINE IDENTITY

The Internet is fast becoming one of the most utilised methods of communication. It has also turned into a place where users such as adolescents can meet and talk with each other using functions such as forums, chat rooms, and online.

As a result, online communities (and adolescent subcultures) have been established. The online community is evidently different from a real life one. Since the individuals involved exist only in cyberspace, their presence is only a representation of their real selves. This can be in the form of an avatar or a username. In essence, users do not have a physical presence in cyberspace. Because of this, the online community has its own culture and set of etiquette, called 'netiquette'. According to Shea (1994), the one thing that users forget about when communicating with other people online is that there is a person behind the computer screen. She maintained that in an ironic way, despite its global reach, the Internet is an impersonal medium precisely because of this lack of physical presence.

One related topic that is also often discussed regarding online communities is what is termed the fluidity of the online self (Reid, 1998). This refers to the fact that being online permits users to explore different facets of their personalities (since they are not restricted by their physical selves). Being online allows users to mask almost every aspect of their identity such as gender, age, race, and class (McCrae, 1996; Stone, 1991). To a certain extent, online communities offer users the opportunity to escape from the constraints of society. Some participants in the study stated that one of the main draws of being online is the possibility to escape from reality. This theme was closely related to the anonymity of being online. For some participants, being online meant that they could be anyone they wished to be. In other words, they have control over the information they want other users to know about themselves. For some participants, this could bring about a feeling of equality, as they thought that they were perceived on the basis of their personalities instead of physical appearance.

This is especially true for those who have disabilities in real life. The Internet serves as a place where their disabilities made no difference to other's perception of them. For others, the

Internet provided them with a place where they could experiment with their identities (something that adolescents may engage in more than their adult counterparts). In some extreme cases, the identity exploration can go as far as changing gender and age online (Hussain & Griffiths, 2008). Some participants mentioned the fact that they could conceal their more negative qualities and enhance their more positive ones. McKenna and Bargh (2000) stated that in online interactions, users present idealised versions of themselves. In an earlier study, they compared participants who communicated face-to-face, to those who communicated online. It was found that those who interacted online were more able to present their ideal qualities. Therefore, it seems that people are seen the way they want to be seen online.

The lack of physical presence and anonymity could be some of the main causes of a phenomenon that seems to be unique to online communication, namely the disinhibition effect. Among users, this effect has been used to describe behaviour ranging from being impolite (Kiesler, Zubrow, Moses, & Geller, 1985) to the use of capitals, which is considered as the equivalent of shouting, and exclamation marks (Sproull & Kiesler, 1986). According to Zimbardo (1977), inhibition can be defined as behaviour that is constrained as it is governed by self-consciousness, awareness of social implications, and worries about public perception. By this definition, disinhibition can be described as the absence of, or the opposite of these factors. Disinhibition can be viewed as the result of reduced public-awareness, which would lead to decreased concern about others' opinions (Prentice-Dunn & Rogers, 1982).

With reference to online behaviour, disinhibition can be summarised as behaviour that is comparatively less inhibited than behaviour in real life. Thus, online disinhibition is not defined as hostile or rude behaviour, but behaviour that is the result of less self-awareness and regard for the judgement of others. Internet users are more honest, open and expressive online. They can be more free to express their thoughts as they are protected by their anonymity.

Anonymity has been known to have positive effects, as illustrated by a study conducted by Gergen, Gergen, and Barton (1973). They found that individuals who met and interacted in a darkened room where they could not see one another tend to disclose more details of their lives compared to those who met in a lighted room. Those who interacted in a darkened room also left with a better impression of the other person. Therefore, in terms of online research, this disinhibition effect might be advantageous, in that the participants would be more likely to give honest answers compared to other methods.

It is important to note that many of our online interactions are not anonymous. In many networking sites such as *MySpace* and *Friendster,* it is difficult, if not impossible, to remain anonymous. The purpose of sites like these is to expand one's network of friends through existing ones. Therefore, relationships that started here, although they were started online, would mostly originate from offline friends. Similarly, anonymity is limited in email communications, as most of those we interact with through this method are people we know already. However, users still have a degree of control over their anonymity, especially in functions that remove them completely from any real life contacts. In other words, individuals can still remain anonymous in places such as chat rooms, forums, and online games.

CONCLUSION

This chapter has demonstrated that research into adolescent Internet addiction is a relatively little studied phenomenon although most effects found among adult users are thought to occur among adolescents too. Clearly, more research is needed before the debate on whether Internet addictions are distinct clinical entities is decided. From the sparse research, it is evident that Internet use appears to be at least potentially addictive. There is also the question of developmental effects, i.e., does Internet addiction have the same effect regardless of age? It could well be the case that the Internet has a more pronounced addictive effect in young people but less of an effect once they have reached their adult years.

The labels "Internet Addiction", "Internet Addiction Disorder", "Pathological Internet Use", "Problematic Internet Use", "Excessive Internet Use" and "Compulsive Internet Use" have all been used to describe more or less the same concept, (i.e., that an individual could be so involved in their online use as to neglect other areas of their life). However, it would seem premature at this stage to use one label for the concept, as most of the studies conducted in the field so far have presented varying degrees of differences and conflicting results.

Most of the studies conducted in the field so far had presented varying degrees of differences in their results, and even some conflicting ones. Furthermore, it seems like the Internet has been used to refer to one general thing in all the above labels. In fact, the Internet consists of many different types of functions, each with different characteristics from the others. Certain functions on the Internet, such as archives and search engines, were designed to gather information. Other functions, such as email, chat rooms, and forums are use to communicate with other users. Even within these interactive functions, there was still a difference synchronous and asynchronous functions. Synchronous functions are those that allow users to communicate with each other on real time. An example is an online chat room, where one user could type a message, and the other(s) would be able to see this message straight away and reply. On the other hand, asynchronous functions are those that involve a delay in replies, such as emails. The Internet also enable users to do various things online such as shopping, gambling, playing games, blogging, banking, making travel arrangements, and many more.

Taking into account the diversity of the functions offered by the Internet, it seems highly unlikely that 'Internet Addiction' exists to any great extent. 'Internet Addiction' implies that an individual is addicted to the experience of being online, despite whatever function they are using. What seems to be more probable is for an individual's addiction to be associated to a function that happens to be online. Making the distinction between viewing the Internet as one general application and breaking it down into the specific functions available on it might have important implications on future research. The Internet consist of so many diverse functions, with different uses and therefore, different types of user who has different reasons for using a particular function. As Morahan-Martin (2005) pointed out *"rather than focus on a unified concept of Internet abuse, it may be more helpful to conceptualise and study disturbed patterns separately according to specific Internet activities"* (p. 45).

As mentioned earlier in the chapter, there is clearly a need to distinguish between addictions *to* the Internet and addictions *on* the Internet. Gambling addicts who chooses to engage in online gambling, as well as a computer game addicts who play online are not Internet addicts – the Internet is just the place where they conduct their chosen (addictive) behaviour. These people display addictions *on* the Internet. However, there is also the observation that some behaviours engaged on the Internet (e.g., cybersex, cyberstalking, etc.) may be behaviours that the person would only carry out on the Internet because the medium is anonymous, non-face-to-face, and disinhibiting (Griffiths, 2000c, 2001).

In contrast, it is also acknowledged that there are some case studies that seem to report an addiction to the Internet itself (e.g., Young, 1996b; Griffiths, 2000b). Most of these individuals use functions of the Internet that are not available in any other medium, such as chat rooms or various role playing games. These are people addicted *to* the Internet. However, despite these differences, there seem to be some common findings, most notably reports of the negative consequences of excessive Internet use (neglect of work and social life, relationship breakdowns, loss of control, etc.), which are comparable to those experienced with other, more established addictions. In conclusion it would appear that if Internet addiction does indeed exist, it affects only a relatively small percentage of the online population and there is very little evidence that it is problematic among adolescents. However, exactly what it is on the Internet that they are addicted to still remains unclear.

REFERENCES

Abramson, L. Y., Metalsky, G. I., & Alloy, L. B. (1989). Hopelessness depression: A theory-based subtype of depression. *Psychological Review, 96,* 358–372. doi:10.1037/0033-295X.96.2.358

Anderson, K. J. (1999, August). *Internet use among college students: Should we be concerned?* Paper presented at the annual meeting of the American Psychological Association, Boston.

Brenner, V. (1997). Psychology of computer use: XLVII. Parameters of Internet use, abuse, and addiction: The first 90 days of the Internet Usage Survey. *Psychological Reports, 80,* 879–882.

Caplan, S. E. (2002). Problematic Internet use and psychosocial well-being: Development of a theory-based cognitive-behavioral measurement instrument. *Computers in Human Behavior, 18,* 553–575. doi:10.1016/S0747-5632(02)00004-3

Caplan, S. E. (2003). Preference for online social interaction: A theory of problematic Internet use and psychosocial well-being. *Communication Research, 30,* 625–648. doi:10.1177/0093650203257842

Chin-Chung, T., & Sunny, L. (2003). Internet addiction of adolescents in Taiwan: An interview study. *Cyberpsychology & Behavior, 6,* 649–652. doi:10.1089/109493103322725432

Chou, C. (2001). Internet heavy use and addiction among Taiwanese college students: An online interactive study. *Cyberpsychology & Behavior, 4,* 573–585. doi:10.1089/109493101753235160

Davis, R. (2001). A cognitive-behavioral model of pathological Internet use. *Computers in Human Behavior, 17,* 187–195. doi:10.1016/S0747-5632(00)00041-8

Gergen, K. J., Gergen, M. M., & Barton, W. H. (1973). Deviance in the dark. *Psychology Today, 7,* 129–130.

Gold, S. (1993). *Court acquits teenage hacker.* Retrieved March 27, 2002, from http://www.eff.org/pub/Net_culture/Hackers/uk_court_acquits_teenage_hacker.article

Griffiths, M. (1998). Internet addiction: Does it really exist? In J. Gackenbach (Ed.), *Psychology and the Internet: Intrapersonal, interpersonal and transpersonal applications* (pp. 61-75). New York: Academic Press.

Griffiths, M. D. (1995). Technological addictions. *Clinical Psychology Forum, 76,* 14–19.

Griffiths, M. D. (1996a). Internet addiction: An issue for clinical psychology? *Clinical Psychology Forum, 97,* 32–36.

Griffiths, M. D. (1999). Internet addiction: Internet fuels other addictions. *Student British Medical Journal, 7,* 428–429.

Griffiths, M. D. (2000a). Internet addiction – time to be taken seriously? *Addiction Research, 8*(5), 413–418. doi:10.3109/16066350009005587

Griffiths, M. D. (2000b). Does Internet and computer "addiction" exist? Some case study evidence. *Cyberpsychology & Behavior, 3,* 211–218. doi:10.1089/109493100316067

Griffiths, M. D. (2001). Sex on the Internet: Observations and implications for sex addiction. *Journal of Sex Research, 38,* 333–342.

Griffiths, M. D. (2005). A "components" model of addiction within a biopsychosocial framework. *Journal of Substance Use, 10*, 191–197. doi:10.1080/14659890500114359

Griffiths, M. D. (2008). Internet and video-game addiction. In C. Essau (Ed.), *Adolescent addiction: Epidemiology, assessment and treatment* (pp. 231-267). San Diego, CA: Elselvier.

Hamilton, K., & Kalb, C. (1995, December 18). They log on, but they can't log off. *Newsweek.*

Harter, S. (1993). Causes and consequences of low self-esteem in children and adolescents. In R. Baumeister (Ed.), *Self-esteem: The puzzle of low self-regard* (pp. 87-116). New York: Plenum.

Hussain, Z., & Griffiths, M. D. (2008). Gender swapping and socialising in cyberspace: An exploratory study. *Cyberpsychology & Behavior, 11*, 47–53. doi:10.1089/cpb.2007.0020

Joinson, A. (2004). Self-esteem, interpersonal risk, and preference for e-mail to face-to-face communication. *Cyberpsychology & Behavior, 7*(4), 472–478. doi:10.1089/cpb.2004.7.472

Kaltiala-Heino, R., Lintonen, T., & Rimpela, A. (2004). Internet addiction? Potentially problematic use of the Internet in a population of 12-18 year-old adolescents. *Addiction Research and Theory, 12*, 89–96. doi:10.1080/1606635031000098796

Kennedy-Souza, B. (1998). Internet addiction disorder. *Interpersonal Computing and Technology: An Electronic Journal for the 21st Century, 6*(1-2). Retrieved December 10, 2003, from http://www.emoderators.com/ipct-j/1998/n1-2/kennedy-souza.html

Kiesler, S., Siegal, J., & McGuire, T. (1984). Social psychological aspects of computer-mediated communication. *The American Psychologist, 39*(10), 1123–1134. doi:10.1037/0003-066X.39.10.1123

Kiesler, S., Zubrow, D., Moses, A., & Geller, V. (1985). Affect in computer-mediated communication: An experiment in synchronous terminal-to-terminal discussion. *Human-Computer Interaction, 1*, 77–104. doi:10.1207/s15327051hci0101_3

Kraut, R., Patterson, M., Lundmark, V., Kiesler, S., Mukophadhyay, T., & Scherlis, W. (1998). Internet paradox: A social technology that reduces social involvement and psychological well being? *The American Psychologist, 53*, 1017–1031. doi:10.1037/0003-066X.53.9.1017

Kubey, R. W., Lavin, M. J., & Barrows, J. R. (2001). Internet use and collegiate academic performance decrements: Early findings. *The Journal of Communication, 51*, 366–382. doi:10.1111/j.1460-2466.2001.tb02885.x

Marks, I. (1990). Non-chemical (behaviourial) addictions. *British Journal of Addiction, 85*, 1389–1394. doi:10.1111/j.1360-0443.1990.tb01618.x

McCrae, S. (1996). Coming apart at the seams: Sex, text and the virtual body. In L. Cherry & E. Reba Weise (Eds.), *Wired women: Gender and new realities in cyberspace*. Seattle, WA: Seal Press.

McKenna, K. Y., & Bargh, J. A. (1998). Coming out in the age of the Internet: Identity "de-marginalization" through virtual group participation. *Journal of Personality and Social Psychology, 75*, 681–694. doi:10.1037/0022-3514.75.3.681

McKenna, K. Y., & Bargh, J. A. (2000). Plan 9 from cyberspace: The implications of the Internet for personality and social psychology. *Personality and Social Psychology Review, 4*(1), 57–75. doi:10.1207/S15327957PSPR0401_6

Moore, D. (1995). *The emperor's virtual clothes: The naked truth about the Internet culture*. Chapel Hill, NC: Alogonquin.

Morahan-Martin, J. (2005). Internet abuse: Addiction? Disorder? Symptom? Alternative explanations? *Social Science Computer Review, 23*(1), 39–48. doi:10.1177/0894439304271533

Morahan-Martin, J., & Schumaker, P. (1997). *Incidence and correlates of pathological Internet use.* Paper presented at the 105th Annual Convention of the American Psychological Association, Chicago, IL.

Nalwa, K., & Anand, A. P. (2003). Internet addiction in students: A cause of concern. *Cyberpsychology & Behavior, 6*(6), 653–656. doi:10.1089/109493103322725441

Niemz, K., Griffiths, M. D., & Banyard, P. (2005). Prevalence of pathological Internet use among university students and correlations with self-esteem, GHQ and disinhibition. *Cyberpsychology & Behavior, 8*, 562–570. doi:10.1089/cpb.2005.8.562

O'Neill, M. (1995, March 8). The lure and addiction of life on-line. *The New York Times.*

Prentice-Dunn, S., & Rogers, R. (1982). Effects of public and private self-awareness on deindividuation and aggression. *Journal of Personality and Social Psychology, 43*, 503–513. doi:10.1037/0022-3514.43.3.503

Reid, E. (1998). The self and the Internet: Variations on the illusion of one self. In J. Gackenbach (Ed.), *Psychology and the Internet: Intrapersonal, interpersonal and transpersonal applications.* New York: Academic Press.

Ruble, D. N. (1994). A phase model of transitions: Cognitive and motivational consequences. In M.P. Zanna (Ed.), *Advances in experimental social psychology* (Vol. 26, pp. 163-214). New York: Academic.

Scherer, K. (1997). College life on-line: Healthy and unhealthy Internet use. *Journal of College Student Development, 38*, 655–665.

Shea, V. (1994). *Netiquette.* San Francisco, CA: Albion

Sproull, L., & Kiesler, S. (1986). Reducing social context cues: Electronic mail in organizational communication. *Management Science, 32*, 1492–1512. doi:10.1287/mnsc.32.11.1492

Stone, S. (1991). Will the real body please stand up? Boundary stories about virtual culture. In M. Benedikt (Ed.), *Cyberspace: First steps.* Cambridge, MA: MIT Press.

Suler, J. R. (2002). Identity management in cyberspace. *Journal of Applied Psychoanalytic Studies, 4*, 455–460. doi:10.1023/A:1020392231924

Surratt, C. G. (1999). *Netaholics: The creation of a pathology.* New York: Nova Science Publishers.

Tsai, C.-C., & Lin, S. S. J. (2003). Internet addiction of adolescents in Taiwan: An interview study. *Cyberpsychology & Behavior, 6*, 649–652. doi:10.1089/109493103322725432

Wan, C., & Chiou, B. (2006). Why are adolescents addicted to online gaming? An interview study in Taiwan. *Cyberpsychology & Behavior, 9*, 762–766. doi:10.1089/cpb.2006.9.762

Widyanto, L. (2007). *Internet addiction: Assessment and the online and offline selves.* Unpublished doctoral dissertation, Nottingham Trent University, UK.

Widyanto, L., Griffiths, M. D., Brunsden, V., & McMurran, M. (2008). The psychometric properties of the Internet related problem scale: A pilot study. *International Journal of Mental Health and Addiction, 6*, 205–213. doi:10.1007/s11469-007-9120-6

Yellowlees, P. M., & Marks, S. (2007). Problematic Internet use or Internet addiction? *Computers in Human Behavior, 23*(3), 1447–1453. doi:10.1016/j.chb.2005.05.004

Young, K. (1996). Internet addiction: The emergence of a new clinical disorder. *Cyberpsychology & Behavior, 3*(1), 237–244.

Young, K. (1998). *Caught in the Net.* New York: John Wiley & Sons.

Young, K. (1999). Internet addiction: Evaluation and treatment. *Student British Medical Journal, 7,* 351–352.

Young, K., & Rodgers, R. (1998). *Internet addiction: Personality traits associated with its development.* Paper presented at the 69th annual meeting of the Eastern Psychological Association.

Zenhausen, B. (1995, February 26). *Preliminary draft of the DSM-V committee in cyberdisorders.*

Zimbardo, P. (1977). *Shyness: What is it and what to do about it.* London: Pan Books.

Chapter 4
Connected at any Cost:
Adolescent Developmental Needs and Online Relationship Formation

Susan M. Miller
Kent State University, USA

Kenneth L. Miller
Youngstown State University, USA

Christine Allison
Kent State University, USA

ABSTRACT

The goal of this chapter is to explore the formation of online relationships in the dual contexts of adolescent cognitive and psychosocial development and characteristics of Internet communication technologies. Research revealed that teens use the Internet to support existing, offline relationships and that such use is associated with closer relationships. For those who form online relationships, these are viewed as close or even romantic in nature. However, when compared along various dimensions, online relationships demonstrate weaker ties than do offline relationships. In general, extroverted teens are more likely to form online relationships, although, if that is their purpose, so do introverted teens. Forming online relationships may rest with the teen's awareness of how to present him or herself given the anonymity of the cue-free Internet environment.

INTRODUCTION

The purpose of this chapter (and indeed this book) is to explore relationships among adolescent development and the use of Internet technologies that influence the formation of online relationships. The focus on adolescence is designed to illuminate unique developmental characteristics and needs of that group which influence use of the Internet environment for forming relationships.

Developmental characteristics of the adolescent include unfolding abilities to think abstractly, to consider multiple points of views, to engage in counterfactual reasoning, and to reason deductively. These characteristics describe the stage of cognitive development identified by Jean Piaget (1967) as formal operational reasoning. For each stage of cognitive development Piaget described a

DOI: 10.4018/978-1-60566-926-7.ch004

form of egocentricism or limitation in thinking. A fundamental limitation for the adolescent is that these new-found abilities mean that they can envision utopian conditions while criticizing the state of the real world. The developing capacity for metacognition (i.e., being able to think about their thinking) translates to a high degree of self-consciousness. This characteristic is mirrored by new-found self-centeredness – the teen's belief that s/he is special, invulnerable, and omnipotent.

These egocentric characteristics are often discussed in terms of psychosocial and affective behaviors typical of adolescents. Erikson's (1950/1993) psychosocial theory provides a heuristic description of the opposing forces felt by most adolescents – the press to find their identity in society while overcoming their sense of confusion about who they will become. As adolescents experience new ways of seeing the world, they are afforded expanded interpersonal and social opportunities. Adolescent development takes place in a sphere of otherness, where the important social referents are other adolescents.

The importance of peer relationships is reflected by the frequency with which teenagers use the Internet for social communication. Data from a National Center for Education Statistics 2003 survey (N = 56,000 families) revealed that about 70% of students in grades 6 to 8, and 79% of high school students used the Internet (DeBell & Chapman, 2006). Older adolescents were more likely to use the Internet for social communication: 64% of high school students and 45% of 6 through 8 graders used the Internet for emailing/instant messaging.

One difficulty in constructing a sufficient, if not comprehensive, understanding of online adolescent relationship formation is the rapidly evolving nature of Internet communication technologies. Teens who participated in early research studies (just over a decade ago) were limited in their communication goals by the types of applications available to them (i.e., public arenas such as listservs and chat rooms or private spaces using email). After 1997/1998, instant messaging emerged as a communication tool. Around this time social network sites began to support communication among individuals already connected, but teens had little access until MySpace began to attract teenagers in 2004. Facebook, originally designed for college students, was opened to high school students in 2005 (Boyd & Ellison, 2007). An early study of novice online users found that adolescents used multi-user domains (MUDs) to meet new people (Subrahmanyam, Greenfield, Kraut, & Gross, 2001). Referring to current massive multiplayer online role-playing games (i.e., MMOs or MMORPGs), Yee (2006) reported that 20% of male users and 4.4% of female users were between 12 and 17 years old. As communication technologies become even more ubiquitous (e.g., multimedia phones, or integrated clothing and personal accessories) it is likely that the ways in which teens use and integrate them will dramatically evolve.

Chapter Objectives

The goal of this chapter is to explicate relationships among adolescent development, characteristics of Internet communication tools, and online relationship formation. After reading this chapter, the intended readers (i.e., researchers, teachers, students, and parents) should understand:

1. The major cognitive and psychosocial developmental characteristics that emerge occur during adolescence
2. The affordances offered by the Internet for formation and support of online relationships in the context of anonymous and cue-free Internet communications
3. Associations among types of online relationships, Internet affordances, and relationship quality

4. Psychosocial, motivational, and environmental variables that may influence the co-construction of adolescent online relationships
5. Teen vulnerability in online relationships based on development needs for friendships and a search for identity
6. Resources for adolescent safety and well-being in online environments

BACKGROUND ON THE DEVELOPING ADOLESCENT

Adolescence is the transition period from childhood to adulthood. During this period individuals at about 11 or 12 years of age begin a new stage of cognitive and psychosocial development. Jean Piaget's theory of cognitive development provides a useful framework for understanding the thinking of adolescents (Elkind, 1967, 1984; Rosser, 1994). At about six or seven years of age children begin to reason logically about the physical world: they understand the concept of numbers and one-to-one relationships necessary for mathematical logic, they can group objects into classes and sub-classes, and can demonstrate reversibility in thinking. Piaget called this stage concrete operational thinking: children develop reasoning skills about the concrete real world, but are not able to think logically about abstract or counterfactual ideas (Rosser, 1994).

Around the age of 11 or 12 years, given appropriate situational presses such as those that occur in formal educational settings as well as informal learning environments, cognitive structures emerge that allow reasoning at the abstract level. This is Piaget's stage of formal operational thinking. Whereas younger children can only think about events that actually happen or define concepts in terms of visible features and actions, adolescents are freed from confines of fact-based thinking and can now think and reason about abstract propositions or concepts. Abstract thinking means that adolescents begin to

understand and use simile, metaphor, and parody (Elkind, 1984) and these new ways of thinking fascinate the teenager.

Each stage of cognitive development is associated with limitations that are a function of that particular way of seeing the world - an idea Piaget called *egocentrism*. The same reasoning skills involved in abstract and hypothetical-deductive reasoning enables adolescents to think about their own thinking (i.e., metacognition) as well as think about what others might be thinking. Initially, this new perspective can result in an uncomfortable degree of self-consciousness. The teenager really does believe he or she is at center-stage - a form of adolescent egocentricism that David Elkind (1984; Elkind & Bowen, 1979) called the *imaginary audience*. Because of their limited experience thinking in the abstract realm, many teenagers, especially those in the early formal operational years, believe that all eyes (adoring or critical) are on them. As any parent or educator knows, they are not to be dissuaded from a belief that how they look or behave is of ultimate concern to others.

Adolescent self-consciousness is mirrored by a multi-faceted sense of self-centeredness that Elkind called *personal fable*: the teen's belief that they are unique and special, invulnerable to harm or injury, and omnipotent (Alberts, Elkind, & Ginsberg, 2007; Eklind, 1967). In the minds of many teenagers, their sense of personal fable protects them from negative repercussions of their behaviors; they enjoy the belief that nothing bad ever happens to the hero/heroine of a story. Invulnerability and the sense of uniqueness have been associated with mental health problems for some teens (Aalsma, Lapsley, & Flannery, 2006).

Although the idea of personal fable as a type of adolescent egocentricism is based on Piaget's cognitive developmental theory, personal fable connects underlying cognitive structures to the commonly-recognized affective and behavioral characteristics of most adolescents. Because they believe they are unique and special, most teenagers are sure "no one else has experienced what I am feeling" or "no one can understand me." (Elkind, 1967). These beliefs can lead a teenager to feel different and isolated from others. The adolescent's sense of invulnerability ("it can't happen to me") has been linked to adolescent risk-taking and their sense of omnipotence leads them to believe that they can handle any situation.

As adolescents experience new ways of seeing the world they are concurrently afforded expanded interpersonal and social opportunities. Rapid physical and sexual growth fuels the adolescent to reconsider what s/he has learned and who s/he is in light of the demands and opportunities of the adult world (Erikson, 1950/1993). Adolescence is the period when identity formation is the major concern. The adolescent is not just focused on understanding who s/he is now ("Who am I"?); abstract reasoning skills permit consideration of future possibilities. Thus, the adolescent considers questions such as "Who will I become?" "What type of occupation will I have?" "Will I be successful?" Foundational questions of identity include future occupation, ideology, world view, sexual orientation, as well as religion, politics, relationships, culture, personality, and body image (Santrock, 2009). As Erikson noted, the myriad possibilities envisioned by the adolescent can lead to a sense of role confusion at this stage. This confusion may involve uncertainty about the future: "What will be my place in society?"

One strategy used by adolescents to avoid a sense of confusion is to "fall in love" which certainly influences the teen's drive to form new relationships. Another strategy to stave off this sense of confusion is the formation of cliques and social groups. Being a member of an ingroup provides a temporary sense of security in being different (and generally better) than the outgroup. These ingroup-outgroup associations are often based on transient and trivial artificial social identifiers which change from year to year (Erikson, 1950/1993). Adherence to ingroup mores highlights a second characteristic of the

adolescent at this stage of development: the importance of ideology to the adolescent who is struggling to develop adult ethics and values (Erikson, 1950/1993). With newfound cognitive abilities teens are able to construct elaborate abstract theories to change the world based on altruistic values (Piaget, 1967). Concurrently, the adolescent's sense of specialness, in the words of Piaget a "disquieting megalomania and conscious egocentricity" (p. 66), provides the certainty that s/he can create this vision.

Adolescent growth involves the unfolding of new cognitive skills and personal awareness, which at any given point in time are likely to be tenuously held and tenuously executed. Adolescents are risk-takers (Lightfoot, 1997). They are particularly vulnerable, straining against a system of policies and conventions that protected them as children, but they are not yet ready to assume the roles and responsibilities of adults. One reason that we as a society are interested in, and concerned about, the affordances offered by cyber-communication tools are potential threats that the use of these technologies hold for vulnerable adolescents.

GROWING UP CONNECTED

Adolescent Use of the Internet for Relationship Formation

The Need for Connection

The cognitive and psychosocial needs of adolescents create the impetus for relationship formation, but place many at considerable risk for developing less than desirable connections. Successful relationship development requires partners who are able to self-disclose and establish intimacy, skills associated with self-awareness and self-confidence. The wide availability of public and private Internet environments may promote development of healthy and meaningful relationships for many adolescents. However, for those experiencing problems traversing the landscape of adolescence, the same communication options may create opportunities to experiment with relationship-building in unhealthy ways, communicate without the responsibilities imposed by real world interactions, and develop meaningless, pathological, and even dangerous relationships.

Most teenagers want to communicate with each as often as possible. It is as though they are compelled to share their new ways of thinking with others who are in the same stage of cognitive awakening. It is not surprising, then, that teenagers make use of the latest technologies to establish or extend these relationships. Compared to adult users, adolescents more frequently use Internet communication technologies such as instant messaging, chat rooms (Kraut, et al., 1998; Lenhart, Rainie, & Lewis, 2001) and MUDs (Subrahmanyam, Greenfield, Kraut, & Gross, 2001). In most cases the content of online conversations among existing friends are consistent with the developmental level of adolescents: (a) "friends and gossip" (Gross, 2004, p. 642); (b) "mundane as well as the most emotionally fraught and important conversations of their daily lives" (Lenhart, et al., 2001, p. 10) and (c) "small talk – gossip and news of the day, with a here-and-now flavor (Subrahmanyam, et al., 2001, p. 14).

For these types of communication it appears that instant messaging, followed by email, is the communication tool of choice. Gross's survey in 2000/2001 of 261 teenagers (7th and 10th graders) found that instant messaging was the most frequently cited Internet communication tool (used about 40 minutes daily) followed by email (used about 22 minutes daily); considerably less time was spent using chats or message boards (roughly 7 minutes each). Eighty-two percent of instant messaging occurred with existing friends. During the same time frame, the Pew Internet & American Life survey of 754 adolescents ages 12 to 17 revealed similar results (Lenhart, et al., 2001). As part of an early Internet study from

Carnegie Mellon University HomeNet Project, data from 110 teenage participants (ages 10 to 19) also revealed that, except for homework, the greatest use of the Internet was to communicate with local and distant friends (Subrahmanyam, et al., 2001).

It would be a mistake to suggest that teens use the Internet only to communicate with existing friends. In the studies previously cited, a small percentage of adolescent participants reported using the Internet to meet strangers, sometimes for the purpose of making new friends. In these instances the content of communication was consistent with typical adolescent issues. Analysis of chat room discourse found an emphasis on sexuality and identity (Subrahmanyam, Greenfield, & Tynes, 2004) and an analysis of social networking sites revealed a similar emphasis on sexuality and various risk-taking behaviors (Williams & Merten, 2008).

A substantial number of teenagers purposefully use the Internet to connect with strangers. Without providing precise data, Gross (2004) reported that a few teens spent online time to meet new people using communication tools such as bulletin boards and chat rooms. In the PEW study, 32% of the teen participants reported using the Internet in order to make new friends (Lenhart, et al., 2001). Although a larger number of teen participants reported using MUDs and chat rooms to meet new people in the HomeNet project, the study took place prior to the availability of instant messaging or social network sites (Subrahmanyam, et al., 2001). A recent study of 156 teens (ages 15 to 18) revealed that over a quarter communicated in chat rooms with individuals that they had not previously known, although over half typically communicated online with existing friends (Subrahmanyam & Lin, 2007).

Social networking and relationship formation also occurs in online gaming environments. Parks and Roberts (1998) surveyed 235 users of MOOs (MUDs, object oriented). Participants in this study ranged in age from 13 to 74 years; half were between the ages of 17 and 26. In contrast to the previous studies, almost all respondents (93.6%) reported that they formed a personal relationship online and 86.6% of the relationships were with opposite sex: 40.6% were close friendships (communicated 3 to 4 times weekly), 26.3% were friendships (communicated 1 to 2 times weekly), and 26.3% were romantic relationships (communicated daily).

One advantage of online communication for teens appears to be that they can simultaneously engage in other activities such as completing homework, downloading music, playing games, and telephoning (Gross, 2004; Lenhart, et al., 2001). Authors of the PEW *TeenageLife Online* noted "multitasking is a way of life" for teens (Lenhart, et al., p. 10). Online communication is becoming a group social activity: over 80% of teens reported being together in a group to send an instant message to another friend or friends also grouped together. Most teens use the Internet as another communication affordance to stay in touch with their close and not-so-close circle of friends. Instant messaging has not replaced the telephone but has become ubiquitous for social networking (Gross, 2004; Lenhart, et al.)

The Quality of Online Relationships

The degree to which a relationship is meaningful can be defined in terms of *strong ties* versus *weak ties* (Granovetter, 1973; Kraut, et al., 1998; Mesch & Talmud, 2006). Several qualities define this strong to weak continuum: closeness, emotional intimacy, reciprocal trust, self-disclosure, a shared history of experiences, and the ability to communicate about a large range of topics are thought to be associated with stronger ties. Researchers have advanced two hypotheses about the impact of the increased opportunities for online communication as they relate to the quality of relationships: the *reduction hypothesis* assumes that friendships initiated online are of lesser quality and hinders the building of intimate offline/real world friends;

the *stimulation hypothesis* postulates that online communication increases the depth and breadth of online and/or offline relationships. It is difficult to establish conclusive support for either hypothesis given the changing nature of Internet communication affordances and contradictory research results, although mounting evidence favors the Internet as extending and supporting relationships (Blais, et al., 2008).

The perceived value of online communication to enhance existing relationships is illustrated by findings from the PEW study (Lenhart, et al., 2001) which revealed that most teens used instant messaging to communicate with friends and classmates. Almost half reported that such communications improved their relationships with existing friends. More frequent communications were associated with perceived improvement. For a large number of adolescents (61%), time spent online with close relationships did not reduce time spent with friends in face-to-face situations. Cross-cultural support for the stimulation hypothesis was found in a study of 665 Dutch adolescents ages 10 to 16 years (Valkenburg & Peter, 2007). Almost all (88%) used the Internet to communicate and more frequent online communications were associated with perceptions of closer relationships to such friends.

Two frequently cited studies in support of the reduction hypothesis (Kraut, et al., 1998; Nie & Ebring, 2000 in Bargh & McKenna, 2004) have been frequently criticized for flaws in methodology and interpretation (e.g., McKenna & Bargh, 2000). Kraut and colleagues followed 93 families (110 children ages 10 to 19) which were provided with computers and Internet access as part of Carnegie Mellon's HomeNet Project. The first sample drawn in 1995 was from families who had teenagers enrolled in one of four Pittsburgh, Pennsylvania, high schools; the second sample drawn in 1996 also was not random. Initial findings (from year one or two depending on the family's start date) revealed that the frequency of online communication negatively influenced participants' social networks and communication among family members. Online communication was also associated with increased loneliness (Kraut, et al., 1998). In comments critical of this study, McKenna and Bargh (2000) noted that although reported findings were statistically significant, the actual impact was slight. In fact, as participants in the study used the Internet for a longer period of time the opposite effect was found (Kraut, et al., 2002). Commenting on data from the 110 adolescents in the HomeNet project, Subrahmanyam, et al., (2001) nonetheless concluded that online relationships were weaker than offline relationships. Respondents reported they felt less close to the individual with whom they communicated most frequently online compared to the person with whom they communicated most frequently offline. Relationships that started online rarely progressed to face-to-face meetings. The same pattern was reported by Subrahmanyam & Lin (2007). For most of the 156 teenagers in their study who started online relationships, the relationships did not progress to face-to-face meetings.

Contradictory results were found in two studies with older participants. In a sample of 568 newsgroup users, McKenna, Green, & Gleason (2003) found that a large percentage of online relationships migrated to other communication modes: telephone (63%), cards/letters (54%), and photographs (56%). Eventually a substantial percent (54%) met face-to-face. Almost all respondents reported that online relationships were "as real, as important, and as close" (p. 22) as offline relationships and a large percentage of these relationships continued after 2 years. The average age for participants in this study was 32 years (range 13 to 70 years) which reflects different cognitive and psychosocial abilities to form and maintain relationships than those of adolescents.

In an older sample of users of MOOs, in which half of the 235 users were ages 17 to 26 years (Parks & Roberts, 1998), most participants reported making 4 to 15 new online relationships and almost all relationships migrated to other communication modes: email (80%), telephone (66.8%), cards/letters (54.5%), and photographs (40.5%). Eventually a substantial percent (40%) met face-to-face. These individuals rated their online close relationships moderate to high on all but one measure of relationship quality. For the 155 participants who also provided information regarding their offline relationships, no differences between online and offline relationships were reported in terms of perceived breadth, depth, and use of language unique to the relationship. Yet, other measures favored offline relationships: (a) they were of longer duration and consisted of more frequent interactions and (b) they were statistically significantly rated as more interdependent, predictable/understandable, committed, and convergent than online relationships.

Similar findings in favor of offline relationships were reported from a one-year longitudinal study of 884 adolescents with average age of 15 years (Blais, et al., 2008). Best friendships and romantic relationships developed through instant messaging (presumably with existing friends) were statistically significantly associated with increases in three beneficial relationship qualities: (a) commitment, (b) intimacy/companionship, and (c) trust/communication. Best friendships and romantic relationships in chat rooms (presumably with previously unknown individuals) were statistically significantly associated with decreased intimacy and companionship as well as more alienation and conflict in romantic relationships. Adding to the equivocal nature of research findings on this topic is the fact that although findings were statistically significant in both studies, the small differences in quality between offline and online relationships makes it difficult to ignore the potential value of online relationships.

More compelling evidence for stronger offline than online relationships comes from a study of 987 Israeli adolescents with an average age of 15.5 years (Mesch & Talmud, 2006). Friendships made online were rated lower on the dimensions of intimacy, strength, and duration compared to offline friendships. Online relationships exhibited less *multiplexity* of content and activities. This is the idea that the closeness of a relationship is a function of (a) a shared history with multiple experiences and (b) a wide range of content topics that can be discussed. Multiplexity in a relationship is particularly relevant for teen relationships in light of their identity explorations. Teens reported they were more likely to talk with offline friends about personal problems and romance issues (although no differences were found for more neutral topics such as school, parents, friends, and hobbies). They also reported sharing a greater number of activities with offline friends. Some activities such as telephone conversations and meetings at school or friends' homes were also shared with friends made online but these occurrences were fewer in number.

In summary, teens perceive that online communication improves relationships with existing friends. Although some teenagers report close online relationships with individuals they met online, evidence suggests that these relationships do not migrate to offline involvement. Even when teens report feeling close to their online partners, when asked to compare offline and online relationships along various measures of relationship quality, they reported that relationships started online were weaker than those made offline. If Mesch & Talmud's (2006) multiplexity distinguishes meaningful relationships from those less meaningful, it appears unlikely that truly meaningful relationships can be made online. One defining feature of multiplexity is that the individuals create a shared history consisting of multiple experiences. Communicating only online does not provide opportunities for adolescents to develop shared experiences across a range of activities and time. On the other hand, communicating online with offline friends about offline shared experiences may serve to strengthen the sense of shared history.

Troubled Teens Online

As adolescents engage in the process of identity exploration, self-awareness and other relationship-building skills are characteristically under-developed. While most teens are successful in navigating the search for identify, for others a host of innate and environmental factors may interact with developmental needs to create significant problems in identity formation and relationship development. Alienation from parents and authority figures, a burgeoning sex drive, loneliness, social anxiety, egocentric thinking, poor judgment, and a limited sense of self in the context of overwhelming needs for making connections to others leads many adolescents to create less than ideal relationships. Bound by the egocentricism of adolescence, teenagers are often unable to evaluate the qualities of another person's intentions independent of the role that person plays in the teen's own imaginary audience. The issue is one of under-differentiation by the teen between his/her thoughts and feelings and the thoughts and feelings of others (Elkind, 1984).

Of concern to parents and others is that the most vulnerable teens are least likely to make good judgments when engaging in online communications with strangers. This concern is supported by in-depth analyses of teens who made close or romantic relationships with individuals they met online. A study of 1501 adolescents (10 to 17 years old) revealed that 25% reported making casual relationships and 14% reported making close or romantic relationships with individuals they met online (Wolak, Mitchell, & Finkelhor, 2002). Further analyses of data from the subset of teens (N = 210) who reported close or romantic online relationships yielded two red-flag variables (Wolak, Mitchell, & Finkelhor, 2003). For both male and female adolescents, teens who demonstrated high levels of depression, victimization (typically by peers), or other problematic life events were more likely than other teens to make close online relationships. So too were teens who reported some type of difficulty with their parents. For girls, this difficulty was child-parent conflict which consisted of behaviors such as yelling, nagging, and reduction of privileges; for boys, this difficulty was a low level of communication with parents. Girls who were classified as highly troubled or who reported high child-parent conflict were twice as likely as other girls to develop intimate online relationships. For both girls and boys, access to the Internet at home and high Internet use were also statistically significant predictors of forming close online relationships. Other predictor variables for making close online relationships were being White, non-Hispanic for boys and being slightly older (ages 14-17 compared to 10 to 13) for girls.

The concern for troubled teens making online relationships arises from substantial evidence that troubled or victimized teens are more likely to be at risk for re-victimization or abuse (Finkelhor, Omrod, & Turner, 2007; Finkelhor, Omrod, Turner, & Hamby, 2005). There is evidence that this phenomenon extends online (Mitchell, Finkelhor, & Wolak, 2007). Wolak, Finkelhor, and Mitchell (2008) reported that individuals who were classified as high-risk, unrestricted interactors in online interactions were more likely to be adolescents, to engage in high levels of Internet use, and to use a wide variety of online communication tools. Such high-risk individuals were reported to be substantially more likely to produce clinically significant scores for rule-breaking behavior, depression, and social problems and to report victimization by others in the real world. In the Wolak, et al. 2003 study, troubled teens who formed close online relationships (compared to untroubled teens) were more likely to form online romantic relationships (19% versus 6%), to have been approached for an face-to-face meeting (22% versus 11%), and to have met their close or romantic partner face-to-face (30% vs. 18%). Of the 48 adolescents who eventually met face-to-face, troubled teens put themselves at greater risk as they were less likely to have told

their parents prior to the meeting (44% vs. 26%). The researchers noted that having not informed parents or friends about their online relationships, these troubled teens lacked protective guidance from parents or peers. As an indicator that these teens may have formed unrealistic expectations, they were more likely to say that the person they met face-to-face did not look as they expected (28% vs. 11%).

Online Presentations of Self

One frequently cited hypothesis regarding teen use of the Internet for relationship formation is that teenagers who have difficulty forming friendships offline use the Internet to *compensate* for lack of requisite social skills. The anonymity of online communication is thought to provide a shield that protects the teen from negative consequences or repercussions (e.g., rejection) that can occur in face-to-face attempts to form relationships. In this cue-free environment, teens may be more likely to self-disclose personal information. Given that the primary goal of adolescence is to develop a personal identity, do adolescents use the anonymous comfort of the Internet to express their *true selves,* or, perhaps, as we think is more accurate, an idealized version of themselves?

Results from an innovative lab experiment with pairs of previously unacquainted male and female undergraduate college students suggest that self-disclosure is related to perceived online intimacy and closeness. In this study (McKenna, Green, & Gleason, 2003, study 3) unacquainted student pairs met in an Internet chat room and also face-to-face. Unknown to the participants, the stranger they met online and the stranger they met face-to-face was the same individual. The students reported liking the person they met online more than the person they met face-to-face. This liking was associated with ratings of intimacy and closeness of the online conversation but not of the face-to-face conversation. Why was the online stranger better liked? The answer may be revealed from a parallel series of studies with college undergraduates. Bargh, McKenna and Fitzsimons (2002) found that undergraduate students were better able to present their (presumably) true selves during online conversations with strangers than in face-to-face encounters. This conclusion was based on a match between students' description of their true selves and the descriptions of students made by online strangers (and not by the strangers after the face-to-face meeting). The researchers made an important point about this conclusion – the study's methodology could only determine that the teens were successful in communicating a *self* online to an unknown individual. Whether this was the teen's true self that emerged as a result of the anonymity of the Internet or an idealized self that was presented online cannot be determined from this study. Researchers also found that students projected characteristics they associated with an ideal close friend onto the online, but not face-to-face stranger. It is uncertain whether it is the teen's true self or an idealized version that is being presented in online communications.

A long history of research in the field of computer-mediated communication suggests that the lack of salient personal cues in online environments may act to level the playing field among individuals as they communicate (e.g., Sproull & Kiesler, 1991). The absence of cues regarding age, sex, attractiveness, disabilities, status, and other characteristics are thought to create an environment that enables individuals to freely self-disclose or to selectively present an idealized self (see review by Walther, 1996). The lure of a seemingly risk-free environment could be attractive to socially anxious or introverted teenagers. This was found to be true in the study of an older sample (average age 32 years) of newsgroup users (McKenna, Green, & Gleason, 2003, studies 1 and 2). Socially anxious and lonely participants were more likely to disclose their real selves in online relationships. Might the same be true for adolescents? Are socially anxious or introverted teens more comfortable expressing themselves

online and are they more likely to seek new relationships online? The alternative to this idea, referred to as the *rich get richer hypothesis*, is that extroverted individuals who are more comfortable making friends offline will also be more comfortable making friends online. A survey of 493 Dutch adolescents (average age 13.4 years) revealed that extroversion indirectly predicted online relationship formation (Peter, Valkenburg, & Schouten, 2005). In this study, formation of an online relationship was directly related to the frequency of online communication and the degree of self-disclosure in the communication (a finding consistent with the lab studies reported previously). Despite the frequently-posed hypothesis that introverted adolescents take advantage of the anonymous and cue-free online environment to make friends, introverted teens in this study used the Internet less frequently and self-disclosed less than did extroverted teens. Although it was extroverted teenagers who were more likely to make friends online, a subset of introverted teens did form online relationships. These teens professed a motivation to use the Internet deliberately for making online friends. A subsequent survey of 412 Dutch adolescents (average age 14.1 years) revealed similar findings (Peter, Valkenburg, & Schouten, 2006). Introversion was not associated with meeting strangers online. The 11% of teens who talked only or predominately with strangers online said they did so for entertainment value or to meet new friends. The researchers concluded that motivation to make online friends may supersede the influence of personality characteristics in the formation of online relationships. They followed-up on this conclusion with a larger survey of 1,340 adolescents (Schouten, Valkenburg, & Peter, 2007). Findings from this study lead the researchers to suggest that it was not the anonymity of the Internet or the reduced cues in the virtual environment *per se* that led teenagers to self-disclosure, but rather the teenagers' awareness that they could take advantage of these Internet features to control the presentation of an online self. These teens felt less inhibited and, in turn, increased self-disclosures. This behavior held true for both socially anxious and normal teenagers.

Experimenting with Alternative Selves

The primary goal of adolescence is to develop a personal identity. The teen years provide manifold opportunities to explore and try out tentative identities in order to determine a goodness of fit with the evolving adolescent's psyche, beliefs, values, and goals. Although experimentation is crucial for a successful integration of personal identity, the process is typically fraught with detours, blind alleys, and poor fits that are dynamically abandoned or revised as an emergent self becomes increasingly crystallized with time and experience. With a more comprehensible sense of identity, adolescents are able to communicate this understanding to others in their search create meaning through relationships. In the absence of such understanding, the process of forming meaningful relationships is significantly impaired.

Internet-based communication and social gaming tools provide myriad opportunities for adolescents to test evolving identities and relationships. In the developmental press of adolescence, many will use these online communication opportunities to clandestinely present tentative approximations of the *real self* to both meet immediate needs and determine reactions to an unsure and untried sense of self. Based on feedback from online friends or gamers, adolescents may continuously edit their cyber presentations of self until responses affirm a meaningful fit with an emergent identity. Others with more developed identities may use these tools to test the uncertain waters of creating and maintaining meaningful relationships.

In the previously mentioned study by Gross (2004), half of the 261 adolescents reported they pretended to be someone else while communicating online and this typically occurred while they were in the company of friends or family (rather than alone). Almost all pretended to be older and about 20% pretended to be of the opposite sex or sexual orientation. Only a few (11%) indicated that they were deliberately testing other persona or identities; half pretended "as a joke" (p. 643) or to protect their identity (16%).

A long history of online game-playing, from early text-based domains (MUDs) through current massive multiplayer online role-playing games (MMOs or MMORPGs), has provided abundant opportunities for teenagers to practice forming and testing hypotheses, use combinatorial analysis skills, and engage in counter-factual reasoning. The popularity of these environments may result from the corresponding emergence of adolescent cognitive and psychological capabilities and the logical but fantasy worlds of online games. The suspended reality of online games may enable adolescents to experience aspects of the personal fable (i.e., specialness, invulnerability, omnipotence) or explore different aspects of themselves in relative safety (Calvert, Mahler, Zehnder, Jenkins, & Lee, 2003). In most MMORPG environments, players select a role or avatar and engage in a quest or compete for rewards by communicating with virtual, non-player characters who parlay quests, direct players to other virtual non-player characters, or provide advice on how to continue play. It is through the suggested quests that the adolescent's sense of specialness, invulnerability, and omnipotence may be perpetuated through rich fantasy-like descriptions. For example, in currently popular "World of Warcraft" one virtual non-player character states "you have already proven your bravery to me, but if you truly wish to face the necromancer, then you must now prove your skill against his minions." Such interactions often communicate moral and ethical worldviews that allow a teen player to test behaviors based on those values while extending the myth of personal fable (Wolf, 2007).

Avatars can act in the virtual environment and engage in real-time interplay with other players and non-player characters. Through standard or player-created macros, the avatar can be made to engage in a variety of behaviors including an offer of verbal thanks or welcome to other players or demonstrate emotions such as throwing a kiss or jumping for joy. This sense of real-time communication encourages a real-world sense of personal fable. This gaming environment also engenders the ability to create and manipulate multiple identities within that personal fable (Gee, 2007). Turkle (2001) proposed that the game itself engenders a player to take multiple perspectives or adopt different identities in reaction to actions or statements made by non-player characters. For example, in a scenario where a player has completed a quest to discover the nest and kill a monster bird and is then told that the bird has fledglings who will be left alone, the avatar's identity is transformed from brave conqueror to compassionate caretaker.

A developmental value of these online game worlds may be that the fantasy-stories permit adolescents to use their emotions in order to direct their new cognitive abilities. According to Egan (2001), an important value of stories is that, unlike real life, they have a beginning, middle, and end. This closure brings children "a rare security and satisfaction" regarding how to feel about what is being learned (Egan, 2001, para. 23). Given the turmoil that most adolescents feel, they too may experience "a rare security and satisfaction" at a game's endpoint. Egan's' comments about children's fantasy stories may also apply to adolescent fantasy: "Fantasy creates the sense that there is something beyond or behind the surface of the everyday world. The sense of that mysterious something beyond or behind everyday reality can stimulate wonder and inquiry" (para. 55) which, in turn may be an "essential prerequisite for flexible scientific understanding" (para.54). Fantasy environments are not without pitfalls, however, for adolescents who are unable to appreciate the "transcendent quality" (Egan & Gajdamaschko, p. 13) that a character embodies rather than

over-identifying with more salient trappings of a particular character.

Another hazard of engaging in fantasy gaming environments is the impact on offline relationships. Results of a nearly two-year study revealed that time spent online gaming during high school years improved the quality of offline friendships but decreased relationship quality with parents (Willoughby, 2008). A one-year longitudinal study found that teens who played online games and engaged primarily in other entertainment activities showed decreases in commitment, trust, and communication in romantic relationships (Blais, et al., 2008). However, these authors' did not specify the types of games and assumed that playing games was a solo activity. Contrary to this solo-play belief, the multiplayer format is similar to MySpace and Facebook in that individuals can connect with their friends rather than be solo players in a world of strangers. Even within the context of game playing with strangers, 94% of online text-based gamers had formed close or romantic relationship with other players (Parks & Roberts, 1998).

Strategies for Promoting Adolescent Safety Online

Research findings presented in this chapter suggest that many, if not most, adolescents communicate online with friends and strangers without adverse consequences. However, these findings also reveal that for troubled adolescents the use of such tools is associated with far-reaching negative outcomes. In an effort to create safer online communication environments for children and adolescents, a wide-ranging number of organizations have taken action by providing guidelines for teen safety online (e.g., Federal Bureau of Investigation, 2008; Literacy Matters, n.d.). A typical list of parental guidelines for Internet safety is posted on the website of the St. Louis Children's Hospital. These include: "establish clear rules for Internet use and develop an Internet safety contract with their teen," "keep the computer in a public place in the house," "use an Internet filtering device to limit access to inappropriate sites," "instruct teens to never arrange face-to-face meeting with a person they have met on-line," "establish an open line of communication with teens to discuss the activities they enjoy on-line and about the people they talk to or meet while on-line" (Hallman, 2008, p. 2). However, for at-risk, troubled teens open lines of communication with parents are frequently non-existent.

More investigations of the kind associated with the Crimes against Children Research Center (e.g., Mitchell, Wolak, Finkelhor, 2008) are needed to identify the sub-groups of teens who are most vulnerable and the conditions that increase their vulnerabilities. The importance of this research lies in an opportunity to identify and isolate variables that are most problematic. For example, of great concern to parents and others is the amount and type of personal information that teens often present on their social profile webpages (e.g., Williams & Merten, 2008). Should the focus be on educating teens about what and how they self-disclose? A recent research study suggested that it is not the content *per se* that led to inappropriate online contacts, but rather the act of responding to unknown persons online (Mitchell, Wolak, & Finkelhor, 2008). If this finding is replicated in future studies, then the corrective message to teens (i.e., not to respond) may provide greater protection for vulnerable adolescents.

The purposes of this chapter preclude an in-depth discussion of the nature and types of content presented on teen profiles sites or other online venues. However, these data have been reported (e.g., Greenfield, 2004; Tynes, Reynolds, & Greenfield, 2004; Subrahmanyam, Greenfield, & Tynes, 2004). Online, teenagers talk about sex (often crudely), display verbal aggression and overt prejudice, and risk making contact with strangers. These developmentally-related behaviors are not confined to the Internet (see Greenfield, 2004).

Some evidence (Tynes, Reynolds, & Greenfield, 2004) suggests that teenagers who use monitored chat rooms display fewer overt inappropriate communications. But this is much like saying teens act more appropriately in front of their parents. In monitored chat rooms teens use other communication strategies such as coded language to get their points across. The best design for safe online use of the Internet may be adult guidance, wisdom, and interventions that aid teens through the minefield of adolescent development (e.g. Greenfield, 2004; Tynes, 2007).

IDEAS FOR FUTURE RESEARCH

Given the breadth of topics addressed in this chapter, a host of unanswered questions emerge for future investigation. We present a few ideas (in order of our personal interest). First, it is not without significance that adolescence is commonly discussed in terms of a search for identity. Despite slightly different starting points, the research avenue pursued by Schouten, Valkenberg, and Peter and the research developed by Bargh, McKenna, and colleagues converge on the importance of the self that is presented online. Communicating online with someone unknown may be the adolescent's opportunity to present (a) his/her hidden, but *true self,* (b) an unconscious projection of his/her *idealized self,* or (c) through a calculated and controlled use of the anonymous and cue-free Internet environment, a *select version of his/her self.* The research methodology required to examine these questions will be challenging especially considering the argument by Greenfield and Yan (2006) to address the co-constructed nature of the Internet environment.

Second, a corollary of the search for identity is the reduction in confusion and anxiety provided by being a member of a group. Being a group member provides security for social affiliation but also requires the member to adopt and adhere to the mores of the group (Erikson, 1950/1993). This becomes problematic when the group is based on racial/ethnic stereotypes, criminal behaviors, or other negative characteristics. It may be possible to use the Internet and gaming environments to help adolescents see beyond group boundaries (e.g., Amichai-Hamburger & McKenna, 2006). For example, many MMOPRGs include factions which create a sense of identity for a player; however, as the player progresses through the game, s/he can join another faction with players outside his/her initial group.

Third, do the multiple perspectives provided by the structure of most online games or by contact with more mature players facilitate an adolescent's emergence from egocentric limitations? Online gaming can provide opportunities to communicate with older adolescents or adults. Do adolescent perspectives change as the game scenarios bridge the gap between their understanding of the world and that of another player who may present with greater maturity, self-confidence, or cognitive complexity? With successive playing of the same games and associated constructs, do players begin to perceive that others experience the same feelings and similar beliefs? Might this same phenomenon occur in other online venues as well?

CONCLUSION

Research findings on relationships among adolescent developmental needs, use of online communication tools, and relationship development provide intriguing, yet incomplete, results. In this section we draw conclusions designed to provide possible explanations for these findings by focusing on the irregularly expanding cognitive and psychosocial abilities demonstrated by adolescents.

Adolescent cognitive developmental characteristics include unfolding abilities to think abstractly, to consider multiple points of view, to engage in counterfactual reasoning, and to reason deductively. These abilities are characteristic of,

and related to, a capacity for metacognition (i.e., executive processing or an ability to think about thinking). Metacognitive abilities create opportunities for self-awareness and the frequently observed adolescent trait of self-centeredness, which characteristically present as beliefs in specialness, invulnerability, and omnipotence. A belief in specialness may lead some adolescents to a related, but irrational, belief that no one is capable of understanding their uniqueness. This belief may spawn feelings of disconnection with others and psychological isolation. Similarly, a belief in personal invulnerability may lead some adolescents to the perhaps understandable, yet irrational, belief that no harm will come to them when they engage in risk-taking behaviors. In these ways, emergent cognitive abilities have a significant impact on emotional and psychosocial development during adolescence.

Consistent with the path of cognitive development, adolescent psychosocial growth is unique and irregular. Rapid physical and sexual maturation provide opportunities to experiment with newfound abilities in a world of ever-increasing demands. Requisite for understanding one's place in this new world order is an emergent and consistent search for identity that places demands on newly acquired cognitive abilities to imagine oneself in a host of future possible worlds. Combined with expanding cognitive and psychosocial abilities, emergent self-awareness produces an understanding that life is, by nature, a social experience. A burgeoning libido and budding options for social connectedness create unprecedented opportunities for success in making meaningful relationships as well as for failure in navigating the turbulent waters of relationship formation. Depending on these and other factors such as personal maturity, psychological health, and family/peer support, some adolescents will create and maintain healthy relationships while others will seek to make connections at any cost.

Internet technologies provide adolescents with an enormous array of communication tools for making social connections. Email, listserves, chat rooms, instant messaging tools, social network sites, multi-user domains (MUDs), and massive multiplayer online role-playing games (MMOs or MMORPGs) are but a sample of such tools used by adolescents. To the extent that they are tools, they have no valence in determining the extent to which adolescents communicate effectively or form meaningful relationships. However, these tools offer anonymity and ubiquity for making connections. These are broad technological characteristics that draw the attention of researchers, teachers, and parents who are concerned for the nature and types of connections that adolescents make online. A host of questions remain unanswered (i.e., does the anonymity offered by the Internet permit an individual to disclose his/her true self or present an idealized self?) Additional research is required to identify correlations among specific technological characteristics and relationship quality.

Evidence is overwhelming that adolescents use Internet communication tools to support existing, offline relationships. Online communication serves to promote stronger ties by providing opportunities for frequent contact among friends without diminishing the frequency of offline contacts. Online communication extends the breadth of contact among existing friends and is perceived to increase relationship intimacy and closeness. The frequency with which teenage friends communicate with each other is consistent with the egocentric adolescent's sense of self-centeredness. More importantly, such connections may mitigate the negative aspects of being special, replacing a sense of psychological isolation and feeling misunderstood with the company of like companions.

Adolescents who form online relationships perceive them as being close, even romantic, in nature, although rarely do these relationships migrate to offline interactions. These findings should also be interpreted in the context of comparison to offline relationships. When asked to compare the quality of online relationships with face-to-face relationships, adolescents report that online relationships are characterized by weaker bonds. However, the value of these less intimate online connections may be that they provide substance to an otherwise imaginary audience of the adolescent's world.

Research findings fail to support the popular idea that introverted adolescents use the anonymity provided by the Internet to make friends online. In fact, except for a small subset who deliberately set-out to make friends online, introverted teenagers use the Internet less frequently and self-disclose less online than do their extroverted counterparts. Extroverted teenagers, who are better able to make friends face-to-face are also better at making online connections.

A concern for teenagers who form online relationships, without a balance of intimate offline friendships, is strengthened by findings that teenagers who formed close online relationships were more likely to report high levels of depression, victimization (typically by peers), or other problematic life events. These teenagers were also more likely to report relationship problems with parents. Such adolescents exhibit difficulty in negotiating the challenges of cognitive and psychosocial demands and it is unlikely that making online friends alone will provide enough positive support to overcome these challenges. Continued vigilance is required to determine the conditions that yield more positive than negative outcomes.

It is reasonable to say that the degree to which adolescents are successful in developing meaningful relationships is a function of the extent to which cognitive and psychosocial stages of development have been successfully negotiated. This function incorporates some degree of reciprocity as meaningful relationships can mediate the effects of cognitive egocentricism and psychosocial experimentation. Connecting online strengthens relationships among existing friends; less clear is the degree to which online-only relationships serve as a psychological safeguard for developing adolescents.

REFERENCES

Aalsma, M. C., Lapsley, D. K., & Flannery, D. L. (2006). Personal fables, narcissism, and adolescent adjustment. *Psychology in the Schools*, *43*, 481–491. doi:10.1002/pits.20162

Alberts, A., Elkind, D., & Ginsberg, S. (2007). The personal fable and risk-taking in early adolescence. *Journal of Youth and Adolescence*, *36*, 71–76. doi:10.1007/s10964-006-9144-4

Amichai-Hamburger, Y., & McKenna, K. Y. A. (2006). The contact hypothesis revisited: Interacting via the Internet. *Journal of Computer-Mediated Communication*, *11*, 825–843. doi:10.1111/j.1083-6101.2006.00037.x

Bargh, J. A., & McKenna, K. Y. A. (2004). The Internet and social life. *Annual Review of Psychology*, *55*, 573–590. doi:10.1146/annurev.psych.55.090902.141922

Bargh, J. A., McKenna, K. Y. A., & Fitzsimons, G. M. (2002). Can you see the real me? Activation and expression of the "true self" on the Internet. *The Journal of Social Issues*, *58*, 33–48. doi:10.1111/1540-4560.00247

Blais, J. J., Craig, W. M., Pepler, D., & Connolly, J. (2008). Adolescents online: The importance of Internet activity choices to salient relationships. *Journal of Youth and Adolescence*, *37*, 522–536. doi:. doi:10.1007/s10964-007-9262-7

Boyd, D. M., & Ellison, N. B. (2007). Social network sites: Definition, history, and scholarship. *Journal of Computer-Mediated Communication*, *13*, article 11. Retrieved from http://jcmc.indiana.edu/vol13/issue1/boyd.ellison.html

Calvert, S. L., Mahler, B. A., Zehnder, S. M., Jenkins, A., & Lee, M. S. (2003). Gender differences in preadolescent children's online interactions: Symbolic modes of self-presentation and self-expressions. *Applied Developmental Psychology*, *24*, 627–644. doi:10.1016/j.appdev.2003.09.001

DeBell, M., & Chapman, C. (2006). *Computer and Internet use by students in 2003* (NCES 2006-065). U. S. Department of Education. Washington, DC: National Center for Educational Statistics.

Egan, K. (2001). *The cognitive tools of children's imagination*. Paper presented at EECREA. Retrieved March 3, 2009, from http://www.educ.sfu.ca/kegan/Cognitive_tools_and_imagin.html

Egan, K. (n.d.). *Fantasy and reality in children's stories*. Retrieved March 3, 2009, from http://www.educ.sfu.ca/kegan/FantasyReality.html

Egan, K., & Gajdamaschko, N. (n.d.). *Some cognitive tools of literacy*. Retrieved March 3, 2009, from http://www.educ.sfu.ca/kegan/Vygotskycogandlit.pdf

Elkind, D. (1967). Egocentrism in adolescence. *Child Development*, *38*, 1025–1034. doi:10.2307/1127100

Elkind, D. (1984). *All grown up & no place to go: Teenagers in crisis*. Reading, MA: Addison-Wesley.

Elkind, D., & Bowen, R. (1979). Imaginary audience behavior in children and adolescents. *Developmental Psychology*, *15*, 38–44. doi:10.1037/0012-1649.15.1.38

Erikson, E. (1950/1993). *Childhood and society*. New York: W. W. Norton.

Federal Bureau of Investigation. (n.d.). *A parent's guide to Internet safety*. U. S. Department of Justice, FBI, Cyber Division. Retrieved January 4, 2008, from http://www.fbi.gov/publications/pguide/pguidee.htm

Finkelhor, D., Omrod, R. K., & Turner, H. A. (2007). Re-victimization patterns in a national longitudinal sample of children and youth. *Child Abuse & Neglect, 31*, 479–502. doi:10.1016/j. chiabu.2006.03.012

Finkelhor, D., Omrod, R. K., Turner, H. A., & Hamby, S. L. (2005). The victimization of children and youth: A comprehensive, national survey. *Child Maltreatment, 10*, 5–25. doi:. doi:10.1177/1077559504271287

Gee, J. P. (2007). Learning by design. In P. Messaris & L. Humphreys (Eds.), *Digital media: Transformation in human communication* (pp. 173-186). New York: Peter Lang.

Granovetter, M. (1973). The strength of weak ties. *American Journal of Sociology, 73*, 1361–1380.

Greenfield, P. M. (2004). Developmental considerations for determining appropriate Internet use guidelines for children and adolescents. *Applied Developmental Psychology, 25*, 751–762. doi:10.1016/j.appdev.2004.09.008

Greenfield, P. M., & Yan, Z. (2006). Children, adolescents, and the Internet: A new field of inquiry in developmental psychology. *Developmental Psychology, 42*, 391–394. doi:10.1037/0012-1649.42.3.391

Gross, E. F. (2004). Adolescent Internet use: What we expect, what teens report. *Applied Developmental Psychology, 25*, 633–649. doi:10.1016/j. appdev.2004.09.005

Hallman, J. (2008). *Adolescent update: Keeping adolescents safe online.* St. Louis Children's Hospital. Retrieved December 30, 2008, from http:// www.stlouischildrens.org/content/AdolescentUp-dateKeepingAdolescentsSafeOnline.htm.

Kraut, R., Kiesler, S., Boneva, B., Cummings, J., Helgeson, V., & Crawford, A. (2002). Internet paradox revisited. *The Journal of Social Issues, 58*, 49–74. doi:10.1111/1540-4560.00248

Kraut, R., Patterson, M., Lunmark, V., Kiesler, S., Mukopadyay, T., & Scherlis, W. (1998). A social technology that reduces social involvement and psychological well-being. *The American Psychologist, 53*, 1017–1031. doi:10.1037/0003-066X.53.9.1017

Lenhart, A., Rainie, L., & Lewis, O. (2001). *Teenage life online. The rise of the instant-message generation and the Internet's impact on friendship and family relationships.* PEW Internet and American Life Project, Washington, DC. Retrieved September 9, 2008, from http://www. pewinternet.org/pdfs/PIP_Teens_Report.pdf

Lightfoot, C. (1997). *The culture of adolescent risk-taking.* New York: Guilford Press.

Matters, L. (n. d.). *Ensuring safety.* Retrieved January 4, 2008, from http://www.literacymatters. org/content/research/ensure.htm

McKenna, K. Y. A., & Bargh, J. A. (2000). Plan 9 from cyberspace: The implications of the Internet for personality and social psychology. *Personality and Social Psychology Review, 4*, 57–75. doi:10.1207/S15327957PSPR0401_6

McKenna, K. Y. A., Green, A. S., & Gleason, M. E. J. (2002). Relationship formation on the Internet: What's the big attraction? *The Journal of Social Issues, 58*, 9–31. doi:10.1111/1540-4560.00246

Mesch, G., & Talmud, I. (2006). The quality of online and offline relationships: The role of multiplexity and duration of social relationships. *The Information Society, 22*, 137–148. doi:10.1080/01972240600677805

Mitchell, K. J., Finkelhor, D., & Wolak, J. (2007). Youth Internet users at risk for the most serious online sexual solicitations. *American Journal of Preventive Medicine, 32*, 532–537. doi:. doi:10.1016/j.amepre.2007.02.001

Parks, M. R., & Roberts, L. D. (1998). "Making MOOsic": The development of personal relationships on line and a comparison to their off-line counterparts. *Journal of Social and Personal Relationships*, *15*, 517–537. doi:10.1177/0265407598154005

Peter, J., Valkenburg, P. M., & Schouten, A. P. (2005). Development a model of adolescent friendship formation on the Internet. *Cyberpsychology & Behavior*, *8*, 423–430. doi:10.1089/cpb.2005.8.423

Peter, J., Valkenburg, P. M., & Schouten, A. P. (2006). Characteristics and motives of adolescents talking with strangers on the Internet. *Cyberpsychology & Behavior*, *9*, 526–530. doi:10.1089/cpb.2006.9.526

Piaget, J. (1967). *Six psychological studies*. New York: Random House.

Rosser, R. (1994). *Cognitive development: Psychological and biological perspectives*. Boston: Allyn and Bacon.

Santrock, J. W. (2009). *Child development* (12th ed.). Boston: McGraw-Hill.

Schouten, A. P., Valenburg, P. M., & Peter, J. (2007). Precursors and underlying processes of adolescents' online self-disclosure: Developing and testing an "Internet-attribute-perception" model. *Media Psychology*, *10*, 292–315. doi:. doi:10.1080/15213260701375686

Sproull, L., & Kiesler, S. (1991). *Connections: New ways of working in the networked organization*. Cambridge, MA: MIT Press.

Subrahmanyam, K., Greenfield, P., Kraut, R., & Gross, E. (2001). The impact of computer use on children's and adolescents' development. *Applied Developmental Psychology*, *22*, 7–30. doi:10.1016/S0193-3973(00)00063-0

Subrahmanyam, K., Greenfield, P., & Tynes, B. (2007). Constructing sexuality and identity in an online teen chat room. *Applied Developmental Psychology*, *25*, 651–666. doi:10.1016/j.appdev.2004.09.007

Subrahmanyam, K., & Lin, G. (2007). Adolescents on the Net: Internet use and well-being. *Adolescence*, *42*, 659–677.

Turkle, S. (2001). Who am we? In D. Trend (Ed.), *Reading digital culture* (pp. 236-250). Malden, MA: Blackwell Publishers.

Tynes, B., Reynolds, L., & Greenfield, P. M. (2004). Adolescence, race, and ethnicity on the Internet: A comparison of discourse in monitored vs. unmonitored chat rooms. *Applied Developmental Psychology*, *25*, 667–684. doi:10.1016/j.appdev.2004.09.003

Tynes, B. M. (2007). Internet safety gone wild? Sacrificing the educational and psychosocial benefits of online social environments. *Journal of Adolescent Research*, *22*, 575–584. doi:10.1177/0743558407303979

Valkenburg, P. M., & Peter, J. (2007). Preadolescents' and adolescents' online communication and their closeness to friends. *Developmental Psychology*, *43*, 267–277. doi:10.1037/0012-1649.43.2.267

Walther, J. B. (1996). Computer-mediated communication: Impersonal, interpersonal, and hyperpersonal interactions, *Communication Research*, *23*(1), 3-43. Retrieved from http://crx.sagepub.com/cgi/content/abstract/23/1/3

Williams, A. L., & Merten, M. J. (2008). A review of online social networking profiles by adolescents: Implications for future research and intervention. *Adolescence*, *43*, 253–273.

Willoughby, T. (2008). A short-term longitudinal study of Internet and computer games use by boys and girls: Prevalence, frequency of use and psychosocial predictors. *Developmental Psychology, 44*, 195–204. doi:10.1037/0012-1649.44.1.195

Wolak, J., Finkelhor, D., & Mitchell, K. (2008). Is talking online to unknown people always risky? Distinguishing online interaction styles in a national sample of youth Internet users. *Cyberpsychology & Behavior, 11*, 340–343. doi:. doi:10.1089/cpb.2007.0044

Wolak, J., Mitchell, K. J., & Finkelhor, D. (2002). Close online relationships in a national sample of adolescence. *Adolescence, 37*, 441–455.

Wolak, J., Mitchell, K. J., & Finkelhor, D. (2003). Escaping or connecting? Characteristics of youth who form close online relationships. *Journal of Adolescence, 26*, 105–119. doi:10.1016/S0140-1971(02)00114-8

Wolf, M. J. P. (2007). On the future of video games. In P. Messaris & L. Humphreys (Eds.), *Digital media: Transformation in human communication* (pp. 187-195). New York: Peter Lang.

Yee, N. (2006). The demographics, motivations and derived experiences of users of massively-multiuser online graphical environments. *Presence (Cambridge, Mass.), 15*, 309–329. doi:10.1162/pres.15.3.309

Chapter 5
The Internet and Adolescent Sexual Identity

Bryant Paul
Indiana University, USA

Lelia Samson
Indiana University, USA

ABSTRACT

This chapter considers the potential role of the Internet in the process of adolescent sexual identity construction. It starts by providing evidence of the ever-increasing role the Internet is playing in the lives of adolescents and by considering the potential impact such a technology is likely to have given the transitional nature of the adolescent brain. A consideration of theoretical approaches for understanding the role the Internet is likely to play in individuals' sexual self-identity development is then undertaken. A review of the specific role Internet communication technologies have come to play in the process of adolescent sexual socialization is then carried out. In doing so the authors argue that future research addressing the role of the Internet in the process of adolescent sexual socialization and identity development must consider both the specific structure of the adolescent brain and the unique nature of the Internet as a source of information and an opportunity for social networking.

INTRODUCTION

Adolescence is a period of great psychological and social transformation. Puberty is a major developmental milestone of adolescence. The changes occurring during puberty signal the transition into adolescence from childhood. These changes are initiated by the synthesis and release of various steroid hormones. This in turn results in the

onset of secondary sexual characteristics as well as often striking changes in individuals' mood, positive affect, sensation seeking and behavior (Petersen, Silbereisen, & Sorenson, 1996, p. 5). It is with this sometimes tumultuously transitioning brain that adolescents are often forced to develop a new sense of self identity; one befit for a world suddenly marked by so much physical, social, and psychological change. Given all of the chemical, biological, and (related) psychological changes occurring during adolescence it should come as little

DOI: 10.4018/978-1-60566-926-7.ch005

surprise that the development of one's sexual self-identity is one of the most complex experiences marking the period of transition from childhood to adulthood.

Researchers have long accepted that one of the primary tasks of adolescence is the development of a sense of self or identity (Erikson, 1968). This includes development on the part of individuals of a sense of how they fit into their social and physical worlds, as well as a perception of how they are perceived in those worlds by others. A fundamental part of the construction of every young person's self-definition is the development of a sexual identity (Buzwell & Rosenthal, 1996; Chilman, 1983; Gagnon & Simon, 1987). According to Buzwell and Rosenthal (1996), sexual identity, in addition to an individual's sexual preferences, perceptions of masculinity and femininity, or what they perceive to be appropriate or inappropriate sexual behaviors, also includes "...an individual's perception of his or her 'qualities' in the sexual domain" or "...their perceptions of the *sexual self*" (p. 490). These preferences and perceptions, it is argued, are largely a function of, among other things, the interplay between an individuals' psychological constitution and their social experiences (DeLamater & Friedrich, 2002; Sisk, 2006). Key to understanding the development of adolescent sexual identity is therefore a consideration of both the structure of the adolescent mind and the nature and types of information and experiences upon which individuals rely in constructing this dimension of their self concept.

Although media have long been assumed to have a primary role in the process of sexual socialization (for reviews, see Escobar-Chaves et al., 2005; Ward, 2003; see also, Brown, 2000), recent research has demonstrated that the Internet is a particularly powerful source of information for young people regarding issues of sexual identity (Bremer & Rauch, 1998; Kraus & Russell, 2008; Peter & Valkenburg, 2008; Suzuki & Calzo, 2004). Adolescents have been found to frequently use the Internet to communicate about and explore their sexualities. This includes everything from the discussion of a broad range of sexual topics, to virtual dating, to participating in episodes of "virtual sex" (Subrahmanyam, Greenfield & Tynes, 2004; Subrahmanyam, Smahel, & Greenfield, 2006).

The current chapter argues that adolescents' growing reliance on the Internet as a source of information exchange, entertainment, and potential social networking (both of a sexual and nonsexual nature) means that it is playing an increasingly important role in the development of young peoples' sexual identities. Any understanding of contemporary sexual identity development must therefore include a consideration of the role of the Internet in this process. Further, we argue that specific attention must be given to understanding how various characteristics associated with the unique technological nature of the Internet are likely to be processed by, and influential on the distinctive adolescent mind. An understanding of this interaction will allow researchers, clinicians, and educators to better aid adolescents in effectively preparing for, and dealing with the process of sexual identity construction in today's world.

BACKGROUND

Adolescents' Use of the Internet

Data from the United States and the United Kingdom indicate that the amount of time adolescents spend online has continued to increase since the Internet first became publicly available in the early 1990's (Jackson, 2008; Livingstone et al., 2005). The number of teenagers using the Internet grew 24% between the years 2000 and 2004 (PEW, 2005). Recent research by the Pew Internet and American Life Project (2007) indicates that overall, 93% of adolescents use the Internet, particularly as a venue for social interaction. Sixty-one percent of the teens interviewed in the Pew study reported going online as part of their daily routine in 2006, with 34% of those claiming multiple daily use. Addditional research has found older adolescents (those ages 15-17) more likely to go online than younger adolescents (Jackson, 2008).

Though they often have different reasons for doing so, male and female adolescents have been found to be equally as likely to go online in general (PEW, 2007). Females, for example, are significantly more likely than males to access and contribute to blogs, whereas males were twice as likely as females to post content to video-sharing sites such as YouTube. A majority of all teens however, reported watching videos on video sharing sites.

Adolescents report high levels of use of a wide range of pursuits on the Internet. Certain online activities are more popular with this age group than others. Activities in which a majority of adolescent Internet users claim to participate include E-mailing, viewing entertainment news websites, playing games, instant messaging, creating or accessing user-created content, getting information about education, visiting chat rooms, visiting social networking sites, gathering information on politics, and downloading music (PEW, 2005). Research suggests the majority of adolescent online pursuits fall into one of five general categories (Gross, 2004; Roberts et al., 2005; Seiter, 2005). These include communication, information, entertainment, self-expression, and escape. Importantly however, adolescents consistently report their most common reason for using the Internet as communicating with their peers (Bargh & McKenna, 2004; Boneva et al., 2006; Gross, 2004; Jackson, 2008; PEW, 2007; Roberts et al., 2005).

Data from a national study of U.S. adolescents in the indicate that nearly 55% of teens maintain a profile on a social networking site, such as MySpace or Facebook (PEW, 2007). Further, adolescents appear to take an 'in for a dime, in for a dollar' approach to social networking sites;

with a wide majority of those reporting use of social networking sites also reporting that they read the blogs of others (70%) and have posted comments to a friend's blog (76%) on those sites. Regardless of whether or not they participate in social networking websites specifically, research has consistently shown that maintaining and expanding ones social network is a primary objective and activity among adolescents (For a review see Jackson, 2008).

Clearly the role of the Internet in adolescents' lives continues to expand. Although adolescent Internet use has been found to supplement—rather than replace—the use of more traditional forms of communication (Subrahmanyam et al., 2000), the characteristics of the adolescent mind such that the unique features of the Internet make it a particularly important tool in the potentially difficult process of adolescent sexual identity construction. In the next section we consider how the adolescent mind is theoretically likely to process and be influenced by online information in constructing a sexual self-identity.

Approaching Adolescent Sexual Identity Development Theoretically

Research focusing on the development of sexuality has focused on two primary categories of theoretical perspectives: essentialist theories and social constructionist theories (DeLamater & Hyde, 1998; Moore & Rosenthal, 2006). Put perhaps overly simplistically, essentialism focuses more on biological processes in sexuality, whereas social constructionist perspectives place more attention on the role of culture. More specifically, essentialists work from the perspective that certain phenomena are largely a function of natural or biological processes. Essentialist theoretical perspectives, including evolutionary psychology and Erickson's (1968) eight stages of human development, focus primarily on the important functions of genetics and biological factors in shaping sexual identity and behavior (for a review see Moore & Rosenthal,

2006). Social constructionists, on the other hand, emphasize the role of individual interpretations of their own experiences in predicting sexual attitudes and behaviors. Perspectives falling into this category, such as sexual scripts theory (Gagnon & Simon, 1973; Simon & Gagnon, 1986) and various discourse analytic approaches, tend to argue that sexuality is a fluid, complex, and largely learned social construct; and that it is strongly influenced by the interpretation of both sexual and nonsexual cultural experiences. Although most scholars working from either perspective typically acknowledge the basic existence, and potential influence of both the social and biological in the process of sexual identity development, they differ significantly on the emphasis they place on these dimensions (Moore & Rosenthal, 2006).

It has been argued that the differences in ontological and epistemological assumptions underlying the essentialist and social constructionist perspectives make their fusion difficult (DeLameter & Hyde, 1998; Moore & Rosenthal, 2006). Both have their critics and supporters. As Moore and Rosenthal (2006) point out however, the purpose of good theory in the current context is to provide

"...*new insights and new ways of viewing and understanding [sexual] behavior. They help us forge conceptual links between the plethora of data available on teenagers' sexual behavior, attitudes, knowledge and beliefs...What is important is that we view these theoretical approaches not as static, but as developing frameworks that can eventually lead to better integration of research data, case material, common sense and personal experience*" (p. 65).

It is with this in mind that we take what has been called a biosocial approach in attempting to best understand the development of adolescent sexuality generally and the role of the Internet and social networking technology in the process of adolescent sexual socialization and identity construction specifically.

The Adolescent Mind and Sexual Self-Identity

Developmental psychologists have postulated that human psychosocial development occurs in a series of ordered stages. Erickson (1968), for instance, argued that there are eight distinct developmental stages of human development, which collectively span from birth to death. According to Erickson, individuals can only effectively move from an earlier stage to a later one by successfully fulfilling the developmental works or *tasks* that are required as part of the earlier stage. The perspective holds that a failure to complete the relevant developmental tasks in an earlier stage will likely result in difficulties fulfilling other tasks in later stages. So for instance, a toddler (stage 2) that fails to develop self-esteem, perhaps due to being consistently stifled by adults or an older sibling when attempting to master certain simple, yet important physical skills, may fail to develop the healthy sense of autonomy needed to successfully initiate play with others when they are a preschooler (stage 3).

Significant changes in brain structure occur during puberty and continue into early adulthood. These structural changes have been shown to impact various cognitive abilities in adolescents. For instance, increased frontal lobe development, pruning of the white matter, increased axon myelination, changes in the dopamine inputs and the limbic system have all been documented to occur during puberty.

Sisk (2006) emphasizes the importance of the "organizational role of gonadal steroid hormones, which become elevated during puberty, in sculpting the adolescent brain and programming adult sexual behavior" (p. 10). The initial synthesis and release of the gonadotropin-releasing hormone (GNRH) and Luteinizing-hormone releasing hormone (LHRH) within the hypothalamic neurons (Sisk et al., 2006) activates the secretion of pituitary gonadotropins, luteinizing hormones (LH), and follicle-stimulating hormones (FSH).

Together, these regulate the development, growth, pubertal maturation, and reproductive processes of the human body. They do so by triggering the release of the gonadal hormones testosterone, progesterone, and estrogen. Importantly, these steroid hormones are responsible for the organizational remodeling of neural circuits underlying sexuality during puberty (Sisk et al., 2006). In addition to "sculpting" the adolescent brain, pubertal hormones are also responsible for activating sexually differentiated nervous system responses that facilitate the expression of sexual behavior in specific social contexts. Based on this perspective, Sisk (2006) argues against a simplistic causational model of individual differences in sexual behaviors in adulthood, and instead supports a model focusing on the complex three-way interaction between pubertal hormones, the adolescent brain, and social experience (p. 11).

Intricately related to sexuality, emotional reactions undergo tumultuous changes during adolescence. There are striking changes in mood, positive affect, sensation seeking, and behavior, (Petersen et al., 1996) all of which are possibly explained by the neurophysiological transformations within the mesolimbic system (the brain region associated with emotional reactions). Parts of the 'mammalian' or emotional brain, the amygdala, the hippocampus, and the caudate nucleus significantly increase in volume, connectivity, and activation during adolescence (Benes, 1989; 1998; Giedd et al., 1997). These structural changes may explain adolescents' tendency toward intuitive appraisals of emotional stimuli based on 'gut feelings' rather than complex cognitive consideration, as well as their increased difficulty with impulse control.

These critical changes are accompanied by dramatic neurocognitive transformations in the higher cortical areas. The adolescent brain undergoes significant structural and functional changes, particularly in areas associated with higher cognition (Casey et al., 2005). A number of researchers have documented a significant decrease in gray-matter density in the prefrontal cortex during this developmental period (Gogtay et al., 2004; Sowell et al., 2004; Toga et al., 2006). It has been suggested that a rapid expansion in gray-matter volume results in a subsequently lower density. A possible interpretation is that during this period the juvenile neural systems are being pruned to allow for a cognitive metamorphosis into a leaner, more elastic brain (Toga et al., 2006). It results in more functionally efficient associations between abstract cognitive concepts during adolescence and adulthood. According to Toga and colleagues (2006), the exuberant increase in brain connections occurring during childhood "...is followed by an enigmatic process of dendritic 'pruning' and synapse elimination, which leads to a more efficient set of connections that are continuously remodeled throughout life" (p. 148). The dramatic losses in white-matter indicate a culling of the juvenile synapses, resulting in a metamorphosis into a more plastic brain.

It can be argued that this loss of fixed juvenile associations allows for more open associations, necessary for abstract thinking and for the development of postconventional reasoning. The processes described above offer a possible neural foundation for the characteristic theorized by Erikson to manifest during the 5th stage of psychosocial development: challenges to conventional authority, pre-existent morals, and social structures (Erikson, 1968). It links with other characteristics identified by Erikson (1968) as typical of this stage of psychosocial development: autonomy and rebellion against authority figures or ready-made adult models (Erikson, 1968).

It has also been found that cortical activity in ventral PFC changes from diffuse in childhood to more focal activation during late adolescence (Casey et al., 2005; Durston et al., 2002). That is, task-related activations become more finely-tuned and efficient, while task-unrelated associations are eliminated. Findings have shown this process to be positively correlated with both age and performance on learning tasks (Casey et al., 2005; Durston et al., 2002). Strengthening the relevant connections and culling the excessive and redundant ones also contributes to the plasticity of the adolescent brain, resulting in an efficient ability to 'think freely.'

Childhood is distinguished from young adolescence by the extreme biological, psychological, and social changes occurring rapidly within and around the individual (Brooks-Gunn, 1988; Brooks-Gunn & Paikoff, 1997). Adolescence therefore becomes a period during which young people are forced to develop a sense of who they are in the face of significant competing external and internal influences. They do this by turning to what must seem like a rapidly changing world and attempting to make sense of it with a mind, which, as discussed above, is going through a serious and fundamental transition of its own.

Erickson (1968) argues that the primary tasks associated with the adolescent stage of development (stage 5) have to do with defining ones identity as an individual in a greater society. Given this confluence of factors, it is not surprising that adolescence is the period during which individuals often experience what Erickson refers to as their first significant crisis of identity. This crisis, often results in a seemingly paradoxical response on the part of adolescents, wherein the individual will seek individuality by identifying strongly with specific groups or cliques. The tendency is for members of this age group to develop a mistrust of what they perceive as traditional adult models and authority figures. They come instead to rely on their peers more than ever before for information about how the world works and what role they are expected to play in it.

Not surprisingly, great development in individuals' sexual self-identities tends to occur during adolescence. Bodily changes during puberty "… include physical growth, growth in genitals and girls' breasts, and development of facial and pubic hair. These changes signal to the youth and to others that he or she is becoming sexually mature" (DeLamater & Friedrich, 2002, p. 11). Rapidly changing bodies and a related sudden increase in sexual interest combine to increase the relevance of adolescents' sense of their sexual selves. As a result adolescence is a key period of psychosocial development, during which the potential psychological and social impact of information of a sexual nature can be expected to increase significantly. Research suggests this information has a significant impact on the construction of adolescents' sexual self-identity (Buzwell & Rosenthal, 1996; Farrar, 2006). It should probably also be noted that although many adolescents may already have a stored set of information of a sexual nature based on pre-adolescent experiences with sexual information and behaviors, newly experienced sexual information is likely to take on a previously unobserved relevance in the quickly changing adolescent mind.

The development of a sexual identity is a central component of the construction of the adolescent self concept. Biological changes resulting from the onset of puberty initiate, and interact with changes in the social forces with which adolescents are forced to cope. The sudden changes occurring during adolescence in terms of cognition, anatomy and social pressures make it a period during which information about sexually normative behavior is fundamentally influential. The information and experiences of adolescents serve then, of necessity, as the primary foundation upon which their sexual schemas will be based (Gagnon & Simon, 1973). Normative beliefs about what it means to be sexual, how one is supposed to express gender identity, proper sexual relationship management, and what are appropriate and inappropriate sexual attitudes and behaviors are all influenced by the nature of this information and these experiences. With greater information, number of experiences, and subsequent considerations of both, so too are expected to develop more complex sexual schemas. The consistency of these schemas, along with individual differences, in terms of motivations for seeking information and for going through various sexual episodes, will influence how one processes this information and these experiences.

Thus a cyclical process of constant sexual identity development is expected to occur, by which newly encountered information is processed and reacted to by minds which are constantly being shaped and reshaped by those experiential phenomena. As an individual's sexual schemas become more complex, we can expect specific information and incidents to have a declining impact on their overall sexual identity. As a result, the period of adolescence, particularly early adolescence, during which sexual schemas are relatively undeveloped and malleable, must be viewed as a key period of sexual identity development.

THE INTERNET AND DEVELOPMENT OF ADOLESCENT SEXUAL SELF-IDENTITY

As has been demonstrated above, the Internet has become a central source of social information and a primary means of social interaction for adolescents. Its role in the sexual socialization of young person's can therefore only be increasing. Only through continuing to study the manner by which adolescents interact in, and consume and process information provided by the Internet and other social networking technologies can researchers and clinicians hope to continue to better understand and potentially positively influence the development of their sexual identities.

As an opportunity for social exploration and networking the Internet holds the potential to play an enormous role in the development of adolescent sexual identities. Research has consistently shown that both peers and media play a significant role in the formation of adolescents' sexual attitudes, beliefs and behaviors (Berndt & Savin-Williams, 1993; Brown, 2000; Brown et al., 2006; Connolly, Furman, & Konarski, 2000; Kallen, Stephenson & Doughty, 1983; Kraus & Russell, 2008; Lefkowitz, Boone, & Shearer, 2004; L'Engle, et al., 2006; Martino et al., 2005; Taylor, 2005). The multimedia, networked nature of the Internet means that it

offers greater connectivity between peers, as well as access to content from more traditional media sources than any pre-existing medium. Further, the perceived anonymity and ease of access afforded by the Internet makes it an ideal place for seeking and/or sharing sensitive information about sex and sexuality (Huffaker & Calvert, 2005). In other words, it offers a heretofore unseen gateway to sexual socialization.

Development of Sexually Normative Attitudes and Behaviors

Perhaps it is the ubiquity of the Internet in the lives of today's adolescents that represents its greatest power. According to Livingtone (2008), "…for teenagers, the online realm may be adopted enthusiastically because it represents 'their' space, visible to the peer group more than to adult surveillance, an exciting yet relatively safe opportunity to conduct the social psychological task of adolescence…" (p. 397). For adolescents, the online world is a small, but very significant part of the real world. Information about social or behavioral norms obtained through online interactions with others they think are the same age, and who they believe are experiencing the same fears, questions, and insecurities as they are themselves are highly influential on their worldview and likely behaviors. Although the average adolescent no doubt discounts some of the information they receive from online sources as a result of perceptions of source credibility, such information possesses many of the characteristics (i.e., a source perceived as similar to the self; the apparent lack of adult monitoring and supervision by which it is distributed) likely to make it highly impactful.

Although scant empirical research has considered the effects of exposure to online sexually explicit materials on adolescent sexual beliefs, attitudes, and predicted behaviors, recent findings suggest such exposure is becoming a growing concern. Data suggest that an increasing number of adolescents are consuming sexually explicit online material (Brown & L'Engle, 2009; Flood, 2007; Kraus & Russell, 2008; Lo & Wei, 2005; Peter & Valkenburg, 2006; 2008; Wolak, Mitchell & Finkelhor, 2007). Recent survey research by Peter and Valkenburg (2008) and Kraus and Russell (2008) suggests that this exposure is positively correlated with levels of sexual uncertainty and positive attitudes toward early and uncommitted sexual behaviors. These findings seem to be in line with previous research demonstrating a relationship between higher levels of exposure to sexually explicit content online and more sexually permissive attitudes (Lo & Wei, 2005; Peter & Valkenburg, 2006). Research by Brown and L'Engle (2009) found that early exposure to sexually explicit content in adolescents predicted less progressive gender role attitudes and even an increased likelihood of sexual activity for both male and female respondents.

Moreover, consumption of sexual media has been shown to increase erroneous beliefs on the part of adolescents regarding peers' sex-related norms, attitudes and permissiveness (Brown & L'Engle, 2009; Chia & Lee, 2008). Further, these misperceptions have been found to indirectly influence adolescents' own personal levels of reported sexual permissiveness. Although the nature of this research precludes the establishment of the causal nature of this relationship, such findings seem to fit well into a perspective stressing the potential for adolescents to be learning sexual scripts from their exposure to sexually explicit online content.

Information Seeking

The high levels of accessibility, interactivity, and perceived anonymity of the Internet make it a particularly valuable resource for adolescents dealing with the potentially sensitive issue of sexual identity. Huffaker and Calvert (2005) argue that "the internet has provided a new context for identity exploration, as the virtual world provides a venue to explore a complex set of relationships that is flexible and potentially anonymous." In line with this idea, Turkle (1995) notes that the online world is likely a useful source for both the exploration/development of sexual and gender identities, as well as a place for learning specific romantic and sexual scripts. Research has found that 59% of teens that go online on a daily basis read blogs (PEW, 2007). Suzuki and Calzo (2004) note that many teens rely on websites that offer the opportunity to question and respond to their peers regarding sensitive personal topics as invaluable sources of information, opinion, and even emotional support. Subrahmanyam et al. (2004) found that sex and sexuality were popular topics discussed by adolescents in online chat rooms. These researchers point out that the anonymous nature of the virtual world may be better suited for exploring issues of identity, sexuality, and sexual health than the real world.

The same characteristics that make the Internet an unprecedented source of information relevant to adolescent social and psychological well-being also make it a potentially dangerous one. The lack of expert supervision in many of these information environments means that misinformation has the potential to flow as easily as truth. Those interested in predatory behaviors, taking advantage of others, and/or in misrepresenting themselves to the detriment of message consumers can do so online with little fear of repercussion. Although research has shown the potential for expert monitoring of message boards and blogs to reduce the amount of misinformation distributed by online sources (Subrahmanyam, Smahel, & Greenfield, 2006), there is still plenty of information to be found online that is based wholly on rumor, conjecture, and misinformed opinion. In addition, knowing that a particular source might be monitored by an adult is also likely to negatively impact adolescents' willingness to communicate candidly regarding sensitive issues. If a large proportion of adolescents are aware of this tendency, they may very well turn to forums that they know are unmonitored for more candid discussion of these issues. As a result adolescents may very well be drawn to less reliable sources for important information on sex and sexuality because they perceive them as more free-flowing, less likely to be censored, and therefore more likely to contain the true beliefs of their peers.

Trying a Sexual Identity on for Size

The Internet also allows individuals unprecedented opportunities for experimentation with their sexual identity. The anonymous nature of much online communication allows individuals of any age to present themselves as anyone or anything they desire. Findings from the Pew Internet and American Life Project (2007) for instance, suggest that 56% of teens with online profiles admitted to posting false information. This has the potential for at least two distinct repercussions. First, it means that adolescents who base their beliefs about the attitudes, behaviors, and even physical characteristics of others in their peer group on such information are likely at least somewhat misinformed. Second, and from a far more pro-social perspective, adolescents and others might be able to use the opportunity to post such (mis)information to anonymously find out how their peers are likely to react to it.

Teens experiencing issues of gender confusion, or other crises related to sexual identity could be well served by online social networking opportunities. Beyond offering such individuals the prospect of confidentially interacting with others who might be experiencing similar crises, the Internet offers an opportunity to interact with others in the actual guise of an alternative sexual identity (Huffaker & Calvert, 2005). This can be as basic as a member of one gender operating or posting to blogs as a member of the opposite gender, to participating in sexual acts as a member of one's own or opposite sex in synthetic worlds, such as Second Life or Red Light Center.

By offering actual depictions of sexual encounters using avatars, synthetic worlds further offer the opportunity for individuals to learn specific sexual behaviors with which they are unfamiliar in the real world. Gender is really nothing more than a key stroke in virtual environments, while sexual preference is but a willingness to allow one's avatar to run one particular digital script over another when presented an opportunity to do so with someone else's avatar. In this sense, synthetic worlds offer a potentially far safer means to experience the sexual experimentation that often to marks the lives of adolescents.

Of course these virtual experiences also have the potential to incite deeper sexual identity crises in some. In exploring new sexual experiences, individuals may find themselves suddenly aroused by, or attracted to behaviors they think or know are dangerous or socially, legally, and/or morally unacceptable. Among these are virtual sexual interactions including depictions of rape, pedophilia, or even something as simple as unprotected sexual contact between strangers. Depending on the individual, such virtual experiences could have serious consequences in the real world. Though likely uncommon, it is not beyond the realm of possibilities that certain individuals could learn that certain problematic sexual behaviors are arousing in the synthetic world and develop a desire to try such behaviors out in the real world.

The opportunity for online sexual interactions may also influence adolescents by impacting their normative beliefs and attitudes about appropriate sexual and romantic behaviors. The virtual sex practiced in online environments could be internalized as normative behaviors by adolescents. The sexual scripts of those partaking in such behaviors could be seriously impacted. This could include anything from the development a sense of appropriate sexual positions during coitus to the proper ways of approaching a potential romantic partner.

Online communication also offers the potential for creating and extending real life relationships. One small study found that 33% percent of a sample of experienced Internet users between the ages of 12 and 22 reported their first sexual experience occurred online (Smahel, 2003). The Internet offers adolescents the opportunity to establish new relationships with people with whom they may have limited or no contact in the real world. Considering the social and physical awkwardness that often marks this stage in the human developmental process, it is possible some adolescents might find interacting in a more confidential environment easier than doing so in a face-to-face context. Most (though not all) research suggests however, that adolescents who have more well-established social contacts in the real world tend to also have more and better social connections in the online world (for a review see Jackson, 2008; Subrahmanyam & Lin, 2007; van den Eijnden et al., 2008).

FUTURE TRENDS

There is little doubt that the Internet and social networking technology will continue to play an increasingly seminal role in the lives of adolescents and members of all age groups. As noted, data suggest that adolescents continue to access and rely upon the Internet in increasing numbers, and with rising intensity every year (PEW, 2007). The unique nature of the Internet as a means of information dissemination makes it likely to be increasingly utilized by young persons in their sexual identity development, particularly those in the early and most uncertain stages of the process. The combined increasing ubiquity, general anonymity, and interactivity that are hallmarks of Internet communication make it a particularly well suited tool for use in exploring sexual and other dimensions of identity development among members of this age group. It should therefore not be surprising that, as has been discussed, an increasing proportion of adolescents already report turning to various Internet sources for information related to issues of sex and sexuality. In response,

researchers should continue to increase their attention towards the role of the Internet in the process of sexual socialization.

Special consideration should be given to those adolescents who might be considered most at risk for developing crises related to their sexual identity. Here we are not simply referring to those individuals who are struggling in coming to terms with their sexual orientation. As discussed, the concept of sexual identity refers to far more than sexual orientation. Specific attention should be given to adolescents who appear to be having a particularly difficult time with any part of the sexual identity development process. The role of the Internet as both a contributor to, and/or a potential solution for such problems must be considered. For example, researchers should continue to compare and contrast the positive and negative repercussions of relying on Internet sources for sexual information and socialization (e.g., unmonitored websites, blogs, and social networking sites) with those of more traditional, non-media sources (e.g., school, parents, real world peer relationships). Particular attention should also focus on how Internet use might interact with certain individual differences in adolescent psychology and personality. Such interactions could potentially result in various levels and types of sexual dysfunction.

It may quickly become apparent that media literacy programs, such as those aimed at improving adolescents' online information processing skills are needed to help adolescents better utilize the Internet in the process of general socialization in addition to sexual socialization. Considering the amount of information and, perhaps more importantly, misinformation that is available through the Internet from peers, those claiming to be experts, and those specifically interested in doing harm to members of this age group, aiding adolescents in becoming more efficient and efficacious processors of online communication seems likely to help in all aspects of identity development. Programs should be developed that help adolescents better seek out, process, and put into perspective the onslaught of sexually-related information they will continue to encounter on the Internet in coming years. Such programs could take the form of a unit in curricula related to either general sex education or media literacy. Perhaps both would be best.

CONCLUSION

This chapter considered the potential role of the Internet in adolescent sexual identity construction. It began by underscoring the importance of understanding the complex interrelationships within this process between the rapidly transitioning adolescent body and brain, and the types of social stimuli generally experienced by young persons as they develop a sexual self-identity. It then noted the increasing ubiquity of various Internet communication activities (a particular social stimulus) in the lives of young people. Theoretical perspectives best suited to help researchers understand the processes by which adolescents go about constructing their individual sexual self-identities were then considered. We next examined the specific role Internet communication technologies already do, and are likely to continue to play in the process of sexual socialization. Finally, we considered what the future is likely to hold in terms of adolescents' use of the Internet as a tool in this process. Researchers and clinicians interested in the issue of the development of sexual identity among adolescents would do well to give greater attention to the increasingly central role the Internet and other social networking technologies can be expected to play in sexual identity development. In doing so they should focus substantial attention on the complex interrelationship between the structure of the biologically transitioning adolescent mind and the nature and impact of the Internet as a source of information and social networking.

REFERENCES

Bargh, J. A., & McKenna, K. Y. A. (2004). The Internet and social life. *Annual Review of Psychology*, *55*, 573–590. doi:10.1146/annurev.psych.55.090902.141922

Benes, F. M. (1989). Myelination of cortical-hippocampal relays during late adoescence. *Schizophrenia Bulletin*, *15*(4), 585–593.

Benes, F. M. (1998). Brain development, VII. Human brain growth spans decades. *The American Journal of Psychiatry*, *155*(11), 1480.

Berndt, T. J., & Savin-Williams, R. C. (1993). *Peer relations and friendships*. Oxford, UK: John Wiley & Sons.

Boneva, B. A., Quinn, A., Kraut, R., Kiesler, S., & Shklovski, I. (2006). Examining the effect of Internet use on television viewing: Details make a difference. In R. Kraut, M. Brynin, & S. Kiesler (Eds.), *Computers, phones, and the Internet: Domesticating information technology: Oxford series in human-technology interaction* (pp. 70-83). New York: Oxford University Press.

Bremer, J., & Rauch, P. K. (1998). Children and computers: Risks and benefits. *Journal of the American Academy of Child and Adolescent Psychiatry*, *37*(5), 559–560. doi:10.1097/00004583-199805000-00019

Brooks-Gunn, J. (1988). Antecedents and consequences of variations in girls' maturational timing. *Journal of Adolescent Health Care*, *9*, 365–373. doi:10.1016/0197-0070(88)90030-7

Brooks-Gunn, J., & Paikoff, R. (1997). Sexuality and developmental transitions during adolescence. In J. Schulenberg, J. L. Maggs, & K. Hurrelmann (Eds.), *Health risks and developmental transitions during adolescence* (pp. 190-219). New York: Cambridge University Press.

Brown, J. D. (2000). Adolescents' sexual media diets. *The Journal of Adolescent Health, 27*(2Supplement), 35–40. doi:10.1016/S1054-139X(00)00141-5

Brown, J. D., & L'Engle, K. L. (2009). X-rated sexual attitudes and behaviors associated with US early adolescents' exposure to sexually explicit media. *Communication Research, 36*(1), 129–151. doi:10.1177/0093650208326465

Brown, J. D., L'Engle, K. L., Pardun, C. J., Guo, G., Kenneavy, K., & Jackson, C. (2006). Sexy media matter: Exposure to sexual content in music, movies, television, and magazines predicts black and white adolescents' sexual behavior. *Pediatrics, 117*(4), 1018–1027. doi:10.1542/peds.2005-1406

Buzwell, S., & Rosenthal, D. (1996). Constructing a sexual self: Adolescents' sexual self-perceptions and sexual risk-taking. *Journal of Research on Adolescence, 6*, 489–513.

Casey, B. J., Tottenham, N., Liston, C., & Durston, S. (2005). Imaging the developing brain: What have we learned about cognitive development? *Trends in Cognitive Sciences, 9*(3), 104–110. doi:10.1016/j.tics.2005.01.011

Chia, S. C., & Lee, W. P. (2008). Pluralistic ignorance about sex: The direct and the indirect effects of media consumption on college students misperception of sex-related peer norms. *International Journal of Public Opinion Research, 20*(1), 52–73. doi:10.1093/ijpor/edn005

Chilman, C. (1983). The development of adolescent sexuality. *Journal of Research and Development in Education, 16*, 16–25.

Connolly, J., Furman, W., & Konarski, R. (2000). The role of peers in the emergence of heterosexual romantic relationships in adolescence. *Child Development, 71*(5), 1395–1408. doi:10.1111/1467-8624.00235

DeLamater, J., & Friedrich, W. N. (2002). Human sexual development. *Journal of Sex Research, 39*, 10–14.

DeLamater, J. D., & Hyde, J. S. (1998). Essentialism vs. social constructionism in the study of human sexuality. *Journal of Sex Research, 35*, 10–18.

Durston, S., Thomas, K. M., Yang, Y. H., Ulug, A. M., Zimmerman, R. D., & Casey, B. J. (2002). A neural basis for the development of inhibitory control. *Developmental Science, 5*(4), F9–F16. doi:10.1111/1467-7687.00235

Erikson, E. H. (1968). *Identity: Youth and crisis.* New York: Norton.

Escobar-Chaves, S. L., Tortolero, S. R., Markham, C. M., Low, B. J., Eitel, P., & Thickstun, P. (2005). Impact of the media on adolescent sexual attitudes and behaviors. *Pediatrics, 116*, 303–326. doi:10.1542/peds.2004-2541

Farrar, K. M. (2006). Sexual intercourse on television: Do safe sex messages matter? m*Journal of Broadcasting & Electronic Media, 50*(4), 635–650. doi:10.1207/s15506878jobem5004_4

Flood, M. (2007). Exposure to pornography among youth in Australia. *Journal of Sociology (Melbourne, Vic.), 43*(1), 45–60. doi:10.1177/1440783307073934

Gagnon, J. H., & Simon, W. (1973). *Sexual conduct: The social sources of human sexuality.* Chicago: Aldine.

Gagnon, J. H., & Simon, W. (1987). Sexual scripts: Permanence and change. *Archives of Sexual Behavior, 15*, 97–120.

Giedd, J. N., Castellanos, F. X., Rajapakse, J. C., Vaituzis, A. C., & Rapoport, J. L. (1997). Sexual dimorphism of the developing human brain. *Progress in Neuro-Psychopharmacology & Biological Psychiatry, 21*(8), 1185–1201. doi:10.1016/S0278-5846(97)00158-9

Gogtay, N., Giedd, J. N., Lusk, L., Hayashi, K. M., Greenstein, D., & Vaituzis, A. C. (2004). Dynamic mapping of human cortical development during childhood through early adulthood. *Proceedings of the National Academy of Sciences of the United States of America, 101*(21), 8174–8179. doi:10.1073/pnas.0402680101

Gross, E. F. (2004). Adolescent Internet use: What we expect, what teens report. *Journal of Applied Developmental Psychology, 25*, 633–649. doi:10.1016/j.appdev.2004.09.005

Huffaker, D. A., & Calvert, S. L. (2005). Gender, identity, and language use in teenage blogs. *Journal of Computer-Mediated Communication, 10*(2), 26.

Jackson, L. A. (2008). Adolescents and the Internet. In P. E. Jamieson & D. Romer (Eds.), *The changing portrayal of adolescents in the media since 1950* (pp. 377-411). New York: Oxford University Press.

Kallen, D. J., Stephenson, J. J., & Doughty, A. (1983). The need to know – recalled adolescent sources of sexual and contraceptive information and sexual behavior. *Journal of Sex Research, 19*, 137–159.

Kraus, S. W., & Russell, B. (2008). Early sexual experiences: The role of Internet access and sexually explicit material. *Cyberpsychology & Behavior, 11*(2), 162–168. doi:10.1089/cpb.2007.0054

L'Engle, K. L., Brown, J. D., & Kenneavy, K. (2006). The mass media are an important context for adolescents' sexual behavior. *The Journal of Adolescent Health, 38*(3), 186–192. doi:10.1016/j.jadohealth.2005.03.020

Lefkowitz, E. S., Boone, T. L., & Shearer, C. L. (2004). Communication with best friends about sex-related topics during emerging adulthood. *Journal of Youth and Adolescence, 33*, 339–351. doi:10.1023/B:JOYO.0000032642.27242.c1

Livingstone, S. (2008). Taking risky opportunities in youthful content creation: Teenagers' use of social networking sites for intimacy, privacy and self-expression. *New Media & Society, 10*(3), 393–411. doi:10.1177/1461444808089415

Livingstone, S., Bober, M., & Helsper, E. J. (2005). Active participation or just more information? Young people's take-up of opportunities to act and interact on the Internet. *Information Communication and Society, 8*(3), 287–314. doi:10.1080/13691180500259103

Lo, V. H., & Wei, R. (2005). Exposure to Internet pornography and Taiwanese adolescents' sexual attitudes and behavior. *Journal of Broadcasting & Electronic Media, 49*(2), 221–237. doi:10.1207/s15506878jobem4902_5

Martino, S. C., Collins, R. L., Kanouse, D. E., Elliott, M., & Berry, S. H. (2005). Social cognitive processes mediating the relationship between exposure to television's sexual content and adolescents' sexual behavior. *Journal of Personality and Social Psychology, 89*(6), 914–924. doi:10.1037/0022-3514.89.6.914

Moore, S., & Rosenthal, D. (2006). *Sexuality in adolescence: Current trends*. New York: Routledge/Taylor & Francis Group.

Peter, J., & Valkenburg, P. M. (2006). Adolescents' exposure to sexually explicit material on the Internet. *Communication Research, 33*(2), 178–204. doi:10.1177/0093650205285369

Peter, J., & Valkenburg, P. M. (2008). Adolescents' identity experiments on the Internet - consequences for social competence and self-concept unity. *Communication Research, 35*(2), 208–231. doi:10.1177/0093650207313164

Petersen, A., Silbereisen, R. K., & Sorenson, S. (1996). Adolescent development: A global perspective. In K. Hurrelmann & S. F. Hamiliton (Eds.), *Social problems and social contexts in adolescence* (pp. 3-38). Edison, NJ: Aldine Transaction.

Pew Internet & American Life Project. (2005). *Teens and technology: Youth are leading the transition to a fully wired and mobile nation.* Retrieved June 30, 2008, from http://www.pewinternet.org/pdfs/PIP_Teens_Tech_July2005web.pdf

Pew Internet & American Life Project. (2007). *Social networking websites and teens: An overview.* Retrieved June 30, 2008, from http://www.pewinternet.org/pdfs/PIP_Teens_Social_Media_Final.pdf

Roberts, D. F., Foehr, U., & Rideout, V. (2005). *Kids and media in America.* New York: Cambridge University Press.

Seiter, E. (2005). *The Internet playground: Children's access, entertainment and mis-education.* New York: Peter Lang.

Simon, W., & Gagnon, J. H. (1986). Sexual scripts: Permanence and change. *Archives of Sexual Behavior, 15,* 97–120. doi:10.1007/BF01542219

Sisk, C. (2006). New insights into the neurobiology of sexual maturation. *Sexual and Relationship Therapy, 21,* 5–14. doi:10.1080/14681990500470009

Smahel, D. (2003). Communication of adolescents in the Internet environment. *Československá Psychologie, 47,* 144–156.

Sowell, E. R., Thompson, P. M., Leonard, C. M., Welcome, S. E., Kan, E., & Toga, A. W. (2004). Longitudinal mapping of cortical thickness and brain growth in normal children. *The Journal of Neuroscience, 24*(38), 8223–8231. doi:10.1523/JNEUROSCI.1798-04.2004

Subrahmanyam, K., Greenfield, P. M., & Tynes, B. (2004). Constructing sexuality and identity in an online teen chat room. *Journal of Applied Developmental Psychology, 25,* 651–666. doi:10.1016/j.appdev.2004.09.007

Subrahmanyam, K., & Lin, G. (2007). Adolescents on the Net: Internet use and well-being. *Adolescence, 42*(168), 659–677.

Subrahmanyam, K., Smahel, D., & Greenfield, P. (2006). Connecting developmental constructions to the Internet: Identity presentation and sexual exploration in online teen chat rooms. *Developmental Psychology, 42,* 395–406. doi:10.1037/0012-1649.42.3.395

Subrahmanyam, S., Kraut, R. E., Greenfield, P. M., & Gross, E. F. (2000). The impact of home computer use on children's activities and development. *The Future of Children, 10,* 123–144. doi:10.2307/1602692

Suzuki, L. K., & Calzo, J. P. (2004). The search for peer advice in cyberspace: An examination of online teen bulletin boards about health and sexuality. *Journal of Applied Developmental Psychology, 25*(6), 685–698. doi:10.1016/j.appdev.2004.09.002

Taylor, L. D. (2005). Effects of visual and verbal sexual television content and perceived realism on attitudes and beliefs. *Journal of Sex Research, 42*(2), 130–137.

Toga, A. W., Thompson, P. M., & Sowell, E. R. (2006). Mapping brain maturation. *Trends in Neurosciences, 29*(3), 148–159. doi:10.1016/j.tins.2006.01.007

Turkle, S. (1995). *Life on the screen: Identity in the age of the Internet.* New York: Simon & Schuster.

van den Eijnden, R., Meerkerk, G. J., Vermulst, A. A., Spijkerman, R., & Engels, R. (2008). Online communication, compulsive Internet use, and psychosocial well-being among adolescents: A longitudinal study. *Developmental Psychology, 44*(3), 655–665. doi:10.1037/0012-1649.44.3.655

Ward, L. M. (2003). Understanding the role of entertainment media in the sexual socialization of American youth: A review of empirical research. *Developmental Review, 23,* 347–388. doi:10.1016/S0273-2297(03)00013-3

Wolak, J., Mitchell, K., & Finkelhor, D. (2007). Unwanted and wanted exposure to online pornography in a national sample of youth Internet users. *Pediatrics*, *119*(2), 247–257. doi:10.1542/peds.2006-1891

Section 2
Current Legal Perspectives and Future Legal Needs

Chapter 6
The Role of Law in Adolescent Online Social Communication and Behavior

Larry L. Burriss
Middle Tennessee State University, USA

ABSTRACT

What in the world is a chapter on law doing in a book on psychology, behavior and affect (that's af'ekt, not ə fekt')? Well, the analogy of a game comes to mind. The psychologist may ask such questions as, why do the players do what they do? How do they feel about the activity? How do they interact with other players? Certainly these questions are important. But at the same time the players have to play by the rules. And that's where the law comes in.

INTRODUCTION

Some 2,300 years ago the philosopher Aristotle said, "The law is reason free from passion." At the philosophical level Aristotle's statement is certainly true: attorneys, and teachers, must deal with the law as it exists, not as they would like it to be.

But the law is not an abstraction found only in case law, statutes and administrative rules. At its most fundamental level the law deals with people, and that means the law must be responsive to both reason and passion. Although Aristotle's statement

about the law quoted above is well known, less well known, but certainly as relevant, is what he said earlier: "Whereas the law is passionless, passion must ever sway the heart of man." That is why, for example, a person who commits a crime in the "heat of passion" is less culpable than one who carefully and meticulously plans and executes a crime.

Thus both the lawyer and the teacher or school administrator must ask such questions as: How should a particular law be applied? What are the trends in the law? How has the law changed? For our purposes the question becomes, What is the triple connection between the law, the adolescent and electronic social networking?

DOI: 10.4018/978-1-60566-926-7.ch006

A Mythology of Freedom

The First Amendment to the United States Constitution states, "Congress shall make no law…abridging the freedom of speech, or of the press…." On the surface those words are clear and unambiguous. However, in actual application the U.S. Supreme Court has never taken those words literally. There are hundreds of laws and regulations that infringe on free speech and free press. Whether those laws *should* be in place is a question for ethicists. How to deal with those restrictions and limitations is a question for both attorneys and those who are directly affected by the law.

This then leads to the question, should a given law be applied differently to different groups? Again, we turn to the U.S. Supreme Court for an answer, and that answer is an ambiguous, "maybe yes, maybe no." In general we can say that the application of a given law based on race, religion, gender and national origin is unconstitutional. But what about age? Here the law is just as clear, but the application is more difficult: of course we apply the law differently depending on the age of the person involved. In both criminal and tort law, courts generally follow what is known as the "Rule of Sevens" (*Cardwell v. Bechtol*, 1987): under the age of 7, a child is generally considered to have "no capacity"; between 7 and 14 there is a rebuttable presumption of no capacity; between 14 and 21, a rebuttable presumption of capacity; over 21, capacity. Thus an adolescent is considered to understand the consequences of what he or she is doing, although this capacity may be challenged by the opposing side.

Location is Everything

Although it is sometimes said the Internet (and by extension, a social network) is simultaneously both everywhere and nowhere, the fact is the Internet is accessed from a real (as opposed to a virtual) somewhere. There is an intersection of the virtual and real worlds. And it is at that intersection that the law is in a state of flux.

Ever since the invention of the telegraph (and perhaps, even before), the law has had difficulty keeping up with technology. In the late 1800s, movies sprang upon the public before states and cities imposed regulations and censorship boards (Vivian, 2008, p. 139). The development of broadcasting was impeded because there was no regulation (Vivian, 2008, pp. 151-152). Indeed, it was the broadcasters themselves who asked the federal government to impose regulations. And the Internet? Well, some people have compared the Internet to the wild, wild West where lawlessness and individualism run rampant (Dempsey, 2007, p. 75; Schwartz, 2008, p. 29).

Nevertheless there is a body of law dealing with adolescents and media. Here the central question is often, "Where did the child's action take place?" In a curriculum-related activity? In an open school laboratory? At a school-related off-campus activity? At an off-campus location unrelated to any school activity?

All of these moving parts make for some interesting Boolean logic constructions and Venn diagrams. There is the "Law and the Adolescent" circle. The "First Amendment" circle. The "Internet" circle. The "social networking" circle. But isn't social networking part of the Internet? Isn't the First Amendment part of the law? Does Internet regulation include regulation of social networks? Does the First Amendment trump any attempts to regulate Internet behavior?

So Where are We?

Because of these questions, and a myriad of others, this chapter will proceed along three fronts: (1) Schools, adolescents and messages, (2) Schools, adolescents and the Internet, and (3) Case law involving adolescent social networking sites including FaceBook, YouTube and Second Life.

That is why it is important to have a chapter on law in a book dealing primarily with emotions, feelings and sentiments. What goes on inside the heads of adolescents is certainly important and worthy of exploration, but this exploration must be tempered by what happens in the external world as well. This is not to discount the psychological components of social network activities, but rather to stress the importance the "rules of the game" play in these virtual worlds.

ISSUES, CONTROVERSIES, PROBLEMS

High school kids sure cause a lot of trouble! It would be a lot easier if they just did what they were told and let adults do their thinking for them. "Ah," but the high schoolers say, "We're adults and we want to be treated like adults. It's our newspaper or yearbook or web page, and we should be able to run it the way we want." And here's what the school administration says: "The newspaper or web page is a function of the curriculum; it uses school money and personnel, and therefore should be controlled by the administration." So then how do we bring these two divergent points of view together? Well, the guiding principles are what the courts say someone can and cannot do. Ours is a nation of laws, and if students violate the law, then they must pay the consequences. If they willfully violate the law in order to make a point, then they must be willing to suffer the consequences.

What have the courts said in recent years about what students can and cannot do in terms of free speech in the high school? What the courts have tried to do is balance the right of free speech against the requirement of the state to provide an education. Any speech, or other activity that is disruptive to the educational process is not allowed. At this point we need to recognize that in dealing with the law and court cases we can't get involved in ethics and morality; statements such as "should" and "should not" are often irrelevant. The law is the law. We may disagree with the law;

we may want the law changed; we may think the law is wrong. But the law is the law. And that is a fundamental principle of the American legal system. We have to start with what the law actually says, not with what we want the law to say; not with what the law ought to say; not with what the law should say. Unfortunately (at least for school administrators), the law is just not that clear-cut with respect to children:

The law of children has developed in a patchwork and inconsistent fashion. Decisionmakers including Congress, state legislatures, the Supreme Court, and state courts have created laws and decided cases without a comprehensive vision of what it means to be a child or how children think and behave. Particularly troublesome is the varying manner in which the question of psychological capacity has been addressed by decisionmakers, if at all.

Some areas of the law view children as "infants" who do not have the capacity to act. . . .

Other areas of the law presume capacity in all instances or disregard the question of capacity altogether. (Cunningham, 2006)

In that light we need to examine, in general terms, what students can, or cannot express in the school setting. Notice I did not say "what students can 'say' in the school setting." As we will see, the courts have said that there are varieties of speech, and oral speech is only one kind of expressive activity.

We also must consider what the courts have said about the relationships between the Internet, schools and students. This is an evolving area in the law, and the reader is cautioned that what is permissible today may not be permissible tomorrow. Numerous court cases are inexorably making their way through the court system, and it may still be several years before we can say with any assurance what the rules are.

We can say, with some assurance, that in terms of legal theory and practice, adolescents fall into something of a legal netherworld: as noted above, some of them are children and some are adults. Or rather, sometimes some of them are children and sometimes some of them are adults. In some cases, legal rulings are made on the basis of the "appropriateness" of various kinds of material and expressive activity. There are also question of the age of the sender and the age of the receiver.

So let's begin by looking at how the law differentiates between ages. As discussed elsewhere in this book, the age at which a child becomes an adolescent varies from culture to culture, from child to child, and even within the child himself. The law, however, likes to deal in absolutes as much as possible, and judges like to lay down bright lines in determining the applicability of the law. In this regard a seminal court case involving age comes from Tennessee, (*Cardwell v. Bechtol*, 1987) and addressed the issue of whether or not a minor could consent to medical treatment. Here the court, as noted earlier in this chapter, has explicated the "Rule of Sevens": If the child is under the age of seven, there is a presumption of "no capacity." If the child is between the ages of seven and fourteen there is a rebuttable presumption of no capacity (the court will begin by assuming the child has no "capacity," and it is then up to the opposing attorney to convince the court otherwise). Between the ages of fourteen and twenty-one there is a rebuttable presumption of capacity. At age twenty-one the child is presumed to have know and understand the results of their actions (i.e., have capacity) (Cardwell v. Bechtol, 1987, p. 745).

But notice the problem: most students enter high school at age 15, and therefore have a "rebuttable presumption of capacity." Most laws addressing student rights deal with high school students, but more and more laws and court cases address adolescents, who can be 13 or younger, and thus

in junior high or middle school. At this age there is a "rebuttable presumption of no capacity."

In preparing this chapter the author ran a series of simple searches on the legal database WestLaw® to see how many cases include education and freedom of expression terms. The results, while admittedly not quantitatively rigorous, nevertheless show where most of the controversy lies: of 214 cases in which the court has used the phrase "freedom of expression," nearly one-quarter (23.4 percent) also include one of the school-related terms. Further, of the 50 cases using the phrase "freedom of expression" and one of the school terms, 66.0 percent used the term "high school," 26.0 percent used the term "secondary school," and 8 percent used the term "junior high school." (Table 1)

Again, while this brief review may not stand up to rigorous quantitative analysis, it does show a substantial interest on the part of the court in educational and free speech issues, and that high school free speech issues predominate.

At this point we will move into the first prong of our two-tiered paradigm (the intersection of free speech and social networking sites): issues of schools and free speech. Although some 50 cases have approached this issue, four have most clearly laid out the boundaries of this discussion.

Expanding the boundaries. *Tinker v. Des Moines Independent Community School District*, 393 U.S. 503 (1969). As far back as 1943, in *West Virginia State Board of Education v. Barnett*, the Supreme Court addressed the issue of expression in public schools. *Tinker*, however, was the first time the Court faced the issue of "pure speech" (p. 508).

In 1965 public support for the war in Vietnam was wavering. As a sign of protest towards the war John F. Tinker, age 15, his sister Mary Beth Tinker, age 13, sister Hope Tinker, age 11, brother Paul Tinker, age 8, and a family friend, Christopher Eckhardt, age 16, wore black armbands to school. The action was in contravention to a hastily passed school policy prohibiting the

Table 1. Cases containing education and freedom of expression terms

Expression	Hits
Freedom of Expression	214
High School	418
Secondary School	119
Junior High School	35
Middle School	23
"Freedom of Expression" and "High School"	33
"Freedom of Expression" and "Secondary School"	13
"Freedom of Expression" and "Junior High School"	4
"Freedom of Expression" and "Middle School"	0

wearing of armbands. The students were asked to remove the armbands, and when they refused, they were suspended.

The case reached the Supreme Court in November 1968, and the Court issued its opinion in February 1969. The Court noted that in wearing the armbands the students had not interfered with normal school operations, and that other students had worn buttons and symbols representing a variety of social and political activities and causes, including "the Iron Cross, traditionally a symbol of Nazism" (p. 510).

Because there was no disruption of the school day, nor was there any evidence there would be disruption, the Court ruled the students should not have been suspended. Then, using a phrase that has almost taken on a life of its own, Justice Abe Fortas wrote, "It can hardly be argued that either students or teachers shed their constitutional rights to freedom of speech or expression at the schoolhouse gate. This has been the unmistakable holding of this Court for almost 50 years" (p. 506).

In summary, the Court held that unless the school could show either an imminent likelihood of serious disruption, or actual serious disruption, symbolic speech by students was protected under the First and Fourteenth Amendments to the U.S. Constitution.

Limits on Indecent Expression. *Bethel School District No. 403 v. Fraser*, 478 U.S. 675 (1986). Matthew Fraser, a high school senior, was apparently on the short list for high school graduation speakers when he delivered an election campaign speech consisting almost entirely of extended sexual metaphors and innuendos, and ran afoul of his school's "disruptive conduct" rule." His speech may have been clever, but it led to the beginning of an erosion of the freedoms outlined in *Tinker*.

In April 1983, Fraser delivered a speech in support of the candidacy of friend and student council nominee Jeff Kuhlman. The speech was part of a civic engagement project attended by some 600 students from Bethel High School, Pierce County, Washington.

The short speech, in its entirety, reads:

I know a man who is firm -- he's firm in his pants, he's firm in his shirt, his character is firm -- but most . . . of all, his belief in you, the students of Bethel, is firm."

Jeff Kuhlman is a man who takes his point and pounds it in. If necessary, he'll take an issue and nail it to the wall. He doesn't attack things in spurts—he drives hard, pushing and pushing until finally—he succeeds."

Jeff is a man who will go to the very end -- even the climax, for each and every one of you."

So vote for Jeff for A.S.B. vice-president -- he'll never come [long pause] between you and the best our high school can be. (p. 687)

Fraser had shown the speech to several teachers, and at least two said it was "inappropriate." During the speech itself, "Some students hooted and yelled; some by gestures graphically simulated the sexual activities pointedly alluded to in respondent's speech. Other students appeared to be bewildered and embarrassed by the speech." (p. 678)

Fraser was told the speech had violated a school disciplinary rule which stated, "Conduct which materially and substantially interferes with the educational process is prohibited, including the use of obscene, profane language or gestures." As a result he was given a three day suspension and he was removed from consideration as a graduation speaker. He served two days of the suspension and was later allowed to give a speech at the school's graduation exercises.

Fraser brought suit, claiming among other things, that his punishment violated his First Amendment rights. Both the district court and appellate court ruled in favor of the student. The U.S. Supreme Court, on the other hand, disagreed.

In distinguishing this case from *Tinker*, the court said that students' speech rights are not coextensive with adult political speech, and that [I]t is a highly appropriate function of public school education to prohibit the use of vulgar and offensive terms in public discourse. . . . Nothing in the Constitution prohibits the states from insisting that certain modes of expression are inappropriate and subject to sanctions. . . . The determination of what manner of speech in the classroom or in school assembly is inappropriate properly rests with the school board. (p. 683)

Here the Court applied what is known as the "time, place, manner" test for school speech. Outside the school, the speech would have been protected, particularly if it could be shown it was, in fact a political speech. However, because the language used (not the political intent, but the words actually used) violated school policy, it could be enjoined.

There was no doubt Fraser's speech was was offensive and indecent. But what about speech that is merely inappropriate? What are the rules? Again, we turn to the Supreme Court.

Limits on Inappropriate Expression. *Hazelwood School District v. Kuhlmeier*, 484 U.S. 260 (1988). If we combine *Tinker* and *Fraser* we could conclude that so long as student speech is not "too" offensive and is not "too" indecent, it is protected. Speech that is obviously offensive and indecent is seen as incompatible with the basic mission of high schools: education in an environment free from distractions. But what if the expression is neither offensive nor indecent, but rather "inappropriate" in the mind of school officials? That was the issue in *Hazelwood*.

In May 1983, students in a journalism class at Hazelwood East High School in St. Louis County, Missouri, prepared the school year's final edition of *Spectrum*. The paper had a circulation of 4,500, and was distributed in both the school and the local community. There was no question that the paper was under the ultimate control of school officials, although *which* official was open to question: the classroom teacher or school administration. The paper was part of a class, and a sizeable portion of the paper's funding was provided by the local school board. The usual policy was for the newspaper advisor, the classroom teacher, to submit the paper to the school principal for review before publication.

This particular six-page issue contained two stories the principal found objectionable. One dealt with the impact of divorce on students in the school. The other described three students' experiences with pregnancy. Because there was no time to remove the two stories and rearrange the remaining material the principal chose to remove the two pages containing the offending material.

The students then made photocopies of the excised pages and distributed them throughout the school. They also sought injunctive relief in federal district court.

At trial in federal district court, the judge said the school principal was justified in removing the material. The court of appeals disagreed and said:

Because Spectrum is a member of the press and especially because Spectrum is the sole press of the student body, Spectrum has a responsibility to that student body to be fair and unbiased in reporting, to point out injustice and, thereby, guard student freedoms, and to uphold a high level of journalistic excellence. This may, at times, cause Spectrum to be unpopular with some. Spectrum is not printed to be popular. Spectrum is printed to inform, entertain, guide and serve the student body-no more, and hopefully, no less[.] (Kuhlmeier v. Hazelwood School District, 1986, p. 1373)

The United States Supreme Court, however, reversed the court of appeals, and said that student press rights are not coextensive with those of adults, and since the school paper was controlled by the school administration, the administration had final authority over what could or could not be published.

Limits on Out-of-School Expression. *Morse v. Frederic,* 127 S.Ct. 2618 (2007). So far court decisions had placed limits on what students may do or say inside the school building, a fairly constrained area. But what happens when the student moves outside the building itself, yet is still involved in a school-sponsored activity?

In January 2002, the Olympic Torch was making its way through Juneau, Alaska, on its way to the Winter Olympics in Salt Lake City, Utah.

Persons carrying the torch were scheduled to run along the street in front of Juneau-Douglas High School, and the school principal, Deborah Morse, decided to allow students and staff to leave the school building proper and watch the event from either side of the street.

As the torch passed by, student Joseph Frederick and his friends unfurled a large banner with the words "BONG HiTS [sic] 4 JESUS" clearly visible. Morse told the students to take the banner down, and all of the students except Frederick complied. He was subsequently suspended for 10 days for violating Juneau School Board Policy 5520, which states, "The Board specifically prohibits any assembly or public expression that ... advocates the use of substances that are illegal to minors.... Disorderly students will be disciplined in accordance with law and Board policy." (1998) Frederick was also accused of violating a board policy regarding conduct at school-sponsored activities: "Pupils who participate in approved social events and class trips are subject to district rules for student conduct; infractions of those rules will be subject to discipline in the same manner as are infractions of rules during the regular school program." Juneau School District, 1985).

Frederick sued in Federal District Court, which ruled in favor of the school. The Ninth Circuit Court of Appeals reversed and the school subsequently appealed to the United States Supreme Court, which reversed the appellate court, thus ruling against Frederick and in favor of the school.

In his narrow 5-4 decision, Chief Justice John Roberts conceded the conflict between *Tinker* on the one hand, and *Fraser* and *Hazelwood* on the other: students do indeed have rights, but these rights are limited because of the special relationship schools have with their students. This responsibility is even more pronounced when the message being delivered seems to promote drug use:

Our cases make clear that students do not "shed their constitutional rights to freedom of speech or expression at the schoolhouse gate." Tinker v. Des Moines Independent Community School Dist., 393 U.S. 503, 506, 89 S.Ct. 733, 21 L.Ed.2d 731 (1969). At the same time, we have held that "the constitutional rights of students in public school are not automatically coextensive with the rights of adults in other settings," Bethel School Dist. No. 403 v. Fraser, 478 U.S. 675, 682, 106 S.Ct. 3159, 92 L.Ed.2d 549 (1986), and that the rights of students "must be 'applied in light of the special characteristics of the school environment.'" Hazelwood School Dist. v. Kuhlmeier, 484 U.S. 260, 266, 108 S.Ct. 562, 98 L.Ed.2d 592 (1988) (quoting Tinker, supra, at 506, 89 S.Ct. 733). Consistent with these principles, we hold that schools may take steps to safeguard those entrusted to their care from speech that can reasonably be regarded as encouraging illegal drug use. We conclude that the school officials in this case did not violate the First Amendment by confiscating the pro-drug banner and suspending the student responsible for it. (p. 2622).

So what can we conclude: student speech and expression is protected on school property, unless that speech and expression is disruptive to normal school operations or is incompatible with the normal school "message."

If only it were that easy.

ENTER THE INTERNET

I was giving a university tour to a small family group that included a mother, father, teenager (a prospective student) and a six-year-old. I took them through classroom buildings, the library, labs and the student union. At the end of the tour everyone seemed satisfied. Everyone except the youngest member of the group who ask, "But where is the university?"

One could just as well ask, "But where is the Internet?" We can find the hardware fairly easily. We can see the content, at least when it is displayed on the hardware. But the actual Internet? As Gertrude Stein is reported to have said, "There's no there there."

Current Internet law, as it relates directly to school operations, is currently in a state of flux. Numerous portions of numerous federal laws dealing with children, schools and the Internet have been struck down, usually on vagueness or overbreadth grounds.

Although this book deals primarily with adolescent use of the Internet, it is instructive to quickly review how the courts have dealt with laws that have attempted to protect children who are using the Internet and that have attempted to regulate Internet conduct in schools and libraries.

Communications Decency Act (CDA), 47 USC § 223. Overturned in *Reno v. American Civil Liberties Union*, 521 U.S. 844 (1997).

The CDA was designed to protect minors from harmful material on the Internet. The Court, however, found the restrictions were "content-based," and would deny access by adults to material that would be inappropriate for children, thus violating the First Amendment.

Child Pornography Prevention Act (CPPA), 18 USC §§ 2256(8)(B) and 2256(8)(D) (1996). Overturned in *Ashcroft v. Free Speech Coalition*, 535 U.S. 234 (2002)

The CPPA sought to expand existing child pornography laws by prohibiting sexually-related material that "appear[ed] to be of a minor," but were, in fact, not minors. The law also dealt with the advertising and distribution of such material. The Court ruled that the law, as enacted, would also prohibit access by adults to material that would be considered inappropriate for children. In addition, because the law used the phrases "appears to be" and "conveys the impression" the Court said the law was vague and overbroad, and could be used to ban such plays such as *Romeo and Juliet*, in which the main characters are young teenagers.

Child On-Line Protection Act (COPA), 47 USC § 231 (1998). Overturned in *Ashcroft v. American Civil Liberties Union*, 542 U.S. 656 (2004).

In response to the Court's ruling in *Reno*, Congress passed the Child Online Protection Act, designed to prevent minors from accessing pornographic material online. The Act specifically required that a credit card or "any other reasonable measures that are feasible under available technology." be used to access such material (§ 231(c)(1)). The American Civil Liberties Union and several on-line publishers immediately sued to prevent enforcement of the act. The Court ruled that Congress had not shown that credit card use would not prevent access by minors to pornographic material, and that blocking and filtering software was a less restrictive means of control.

Children's Internet Protection Act (CIPA), 17 USC § 1701 et seq (2000). Upheld in *United States v. American Library Association*, 539 U.S. 194 (2003).

In 2000, Congress passed the Children's Internet Protection Act, which required libraries that receive federal funds to install blocking software in order to prevent access by minors to certain kinds of Internet material. The American Library Association challenged the law, which was upheld by the Supreme Court.

The Court said that libraries have always been able to decide what materials to provide, and that deciding which Internet access to provide was analogous to deciding which books to purchase. Because filtering software can be turned on and off, the Court said, material that is inappropriate for children would still be accessible by adults.

Children's On-Line Privacy Protection Act (COPPA), 15 USC § 6501-6506 (1998). Not to be confused with COPA, this act applies to websites that collect information from children under 13 years old. The Act itself has not be challenged, and it has been used by the Federal Trade Commission against numerous companies that appeal to children, and has successfully levied fines up to $1-million for repeated violations of the Act's provisions.

As with so much of First Amendment law, the Court has attempted to balance freedom to expression with the compelling state interest in protecting children from harm. Into this mix we must also put material that is inappropriate for children, but not for adults. If, somehow, Congress could craft a law that allowed access for adults, but blocked access by children, such a law might stand up to judicial scrutiny. The Children's Internet Protection Act (supra) comes close, but introduces yet another variable: blocking and filtering software.

ENTER THE COURTS

Among the almost mythic stories about school behavior are the ones where the student gets caught passing a note in class. Even worse are the intercepted notes that make comments about the teacher. Students have also carved comments on desktops and surreptitiously written notes on the chalkboard (now, the marker board). And they have almost always gotten caught, and almost assuredly, the punishment was swift and certain.

Today, however, the Internet has made worldwide distribution of offensive messages easier than ever. It is also apparent many youth think the anonymity of the Internet means they won't get caught. But quite the contrary is true: it is easier than ever to catch the perpetrators. "In fact, the long arm of a school official all-too-often reaches far off campus into private homes to punish students who create--on their own time and with their own computers--Web sites that assail administrators and tweak teachers." (Calvert, 2001)

What happens, then, if we link concerns about student expressive conduct (supra) and student Internet use? Courts have conceded that the Internet has made the issue more difficult. Said the Pennsylvania Supreme Court, "the advent of the Internet has complicated analysis of restrictions on speech." (*J.S. v. Bethlehem School District*, 2002, p. 863) Although the United States Supreme Court has not yet addressed this issue of student speech vis-à-vis the Internet, lower courts have been more amenable to free speech and the dissemination of ideas.

Beussink ex rel. Beussink v. Woodland R-IV School District, 30 F.Supp. 2d 1175 (E.D. Mo. 1998).

Using his home computer, on his own time, Brandon Beussink created a web page containing vulgar statements about Woodland High School, teachers, the principal and the school's own homepage. There was no indication the page caused any disruption at the school, beyond upset feelings on the part of the principal and some teachers.

Nevertheless Beussink was suspended for 10 days, which caused him to fail all of his second semester junior year classes.

Beussink sought an injunction prohibiting enforcement of the suspension, which the district judge in the case granted. In granting the injunction the judge wrote that "Beussink's homepage did not materially and substantially interfere with school discipline." (at 1182) The judge noted that speech that interferes with normal school operations may be prohibited, but that unpopular speech, that did not interfere, was protected.

Once again, the Court applied a disruption test, rather than an offensiveness test to determine whether the First Amendment or school rules would trump.

Boucher v. School Board of the School District of Greenfield, 134 F.3d 821 (7th Cir. 1998)

But what about the *potential* for disruption? Other First Amendment cases, most notably *Brandenburg v. Ohio* (1969), have distinguished between "mere advocacy" and "imminent lawless action." There is still a kind of calculus, however, which balances the "gravity of the evil," (p. 453) the nature of the advocacy and the likelihood of the action taking place. It was at this confluence that high school student Justin J. Boucher got into trouble.

Writing under the pseudonym "Sacco and Vanzetti," Boucher penned an article for *The Last*, an underground (non-school sponsored) newspaper, in which he provided profanity-laced instructions detailing how to hack into the school's computers. School officials quickly determined Boucher was the author of the article, and in July 1997 he was expelled from school.

Boucher claimed his First Amendment rights were being violated, and a federal district court agreed, ordering the school not to enforce the expulsion. The school board appealed, and the Seventh Circuit Court of Appeals upheld the expulsion.

The court gave a passing nod to *Tinker*, noting students do not "shed their constitutional rights to freedom of speech or expression at the schoolhouse gate," but then quickly returned to the *Hazelwood* standard of substantial interference with the school. The court ruled that (1) allowing the injunction to stand would undermine general school authority, and (2) there was the potential for serious disruption of the school's computer system and thus school operations.

Interestingly, the circuit court judge suggested to Boucher a way that might have salvaged the article: "Boucher does not contend that the article was intended merely as some sort of *parody* of anarchist high school hackers a defense that might have been more promising than the ones offered" (p. 828. Italics in original. Footnotes omitted).

Emmett v. Kent School District No. 415, 92 F.Supp 2d 1088 (W.D. Wash 2000).

So how serious must the perceived threat be before it triggers a response from school officials? The judge in *Boucher* mentioned "parody," and the Supreme Court has ruled that parody is a protected form of speech in both privacy (*Hustler Magazine v. Falwell*, 1988) and copyright (*Campbell v. Acuff-Rose*, 1994) cases. But what about parody that *appears* to pose a threat?

That was the gist of Emmett, and the background was so simple it can easily be repeated from the district court decision:

Plaintiff, Nick Emmett, is an eighteen-year-old senior at Kentlake High School. He has a grade point average of 3.95, is co-captain of the basketball team, and has no disciplinary history. On February 13, 2000, he posted a web page on the Internet that was created from his home without using school resources or time. The web page was entitled [sic] the "Unofficial Kentlake High Home Page," and included disclaimers warning a visitor that the site was not sponsored by the school, and for entertainment purposes only. It contained some commentary on the school administration and faculty. Two aspects of the site are at issue. The page posted mock "obituaries" of at least two of the Plaintiff's friends. The obituaries were written tongue-in-cheek, inspired, apparently, by a creative writing class last year in which students were assigned to write their own obituary. The mock obituaries became a topic of discussion at the high school among students, faculty, and administrators. In addition, the Plaintiff allowed visitors to the web site to vote on who would "die" next—that is, who would be the subject of the next mock obituary.

On Wednesday, February 16, an evening television news story characterized Plaintiff's web site as featuring a "hit list" of people to be killed, although the words "hit list" appear nowhere on the web site. That night, Plaintiff removed his site from the Internet. The next day, he was summoned to the school principal's office, and eventually told that he was placed on emergency expulsion for intimidation, harassment, disruption to the educational process, and violation of Kent School District copyright (p. 1089).

Were there overt threats on the web page, and if so, how serious should they have been taken? The court, while perhaps not seeing the humor in the pages, nevertheless saw a minimal threat:

Web sites can be an early indication of a student's violent inclinations, and can spread those beliefs quickly to like-minded or susceptible people. The defendant, however, has presented no evidence that the mock obituaries and voting on this web site were intended to threaten anyone, did actually threaten anyone, or manifested any violent tendencies whatsoever. (p. 1090)

Thus the *Emmett* court said that if there is no indication the student intends to cause harm, and the school cannot reasonably show any potential for harm, then the First Amendment trumps school fears.

Killion v. Franklin Regional School District, 136 F. Supp. 2d 446 (W.D. Pa. 2001).

So far all of the cases have dealt with Internet messages that are somehow connected with the school. But what about electronic speech that refers to a teacher, yet is not delivered to the school?

In March 1999 high school student Zachariah Paul created an e-mail, at home, making comments that teachers considered "rude, abusive and demeaning" (p. 455) and "lewd and obscene" (p. 456). Although Paul sent the e-mail, he did not distribute it to his school; other students did.

The school suspended Paul, and his parent Joanne Killion (hence the name on the case) sued, claiming a First Amendment violation.

After an extensive review of the history of school disruption and free speech cases, the Court said (1) the e-mail had not caused disruption at the school and (2) even if it had, Paul was not the proper person to sue, because he had not sent or delivered the missive to the school itself.

J.S. v. Bethlehem School District, 807 A.2d 847 (Pa. 2002).

At what point, we can ask, does the "potential" for harm and disruption move into action? That was the issue addressed by the Pennsylvania Supreme Court in 2002. The court's opinion provides a graphic description of the web page in question:

The site was entitled [sic] "Teacher Sux." It consisted of a number of web pages that made derogatory, profane, offensive and threatening comments, primarily about the student's algebra teacher, Mrs. Kathleen Fulmer and Nitschmann Middle School principal, Mr. A. Thomas Kartsotis. The comments took the form of written words, pictures, animation, and sound clips.

Within the web site were a number of web pages. As noted above, certain of the web pages made reference to Principal Kartsotis. Among other pages was a web page with the greeting "Welcome to Kartsotis Sux." Another web page indicated, in profane terms, that Mr. Kartsotis engaged in sexual relations with a Mrs. Derrico, a principal from another school, Asa Packer School.

The web site also contained web pages dedicated to Mrs. Fulmer. One page was entitled [sic] "Why Fulmer Should be Fired." This page set forth, again in degrading terms, that because of her physique and her disposition, Mrs. Fulmer should be terminated from her employment. Another animated web page contained a picture of Mrs. Fulmer with images from the cartoon "South Park" with the statement "That's right Kyle [a South Park character]. She's a bigger b____ than your mom." [Footnote 3. For purposes of this opinion, blanks will be used rather than the actual profane words that were spelled out in the web site.]

Yet another web page morphed a picture of Mrs. Fulmer's face into that of Adolph Hitler and stated "The new Fulmer Hitler movie. The similarities astound me." Furthermore, there was a hand-drawn picture of Mrs. Fulmer in a witch's costume. There was also a page, with sound, that stated "Mrs. Fulmer Is a B____, In D Minor." Finally, along with the criticism of Mrs. Fulmer, a web page provided answers for certain math lessons.

The most striking web page regarding Mrs. Fulmer, however, was captioned, "Why Should She Die?" Immediately below this heading, the page requested the reader to "Take a look at the diagram and the reasons I gave, then give me $20 to help pay for the hitman." The diagram consisted of a photograph of Mrs. Fulmer with various physical attributes highlighted to attract the viewers' attention. [Footnote 4. Lines from the photograph of Mrs. Fulmer connected to four statements regarding the author's reasons why Mrs. Fulmer should "die." The statements were: (1) "Is it a rug, or God's Mistake?" (2) "Puke Green Eyes" (3) "Zit!" and (4) "Hideous smile."] Below the statement questioning why Mrs. Fulmer should die, the page offered "Some Words from the writer" and listed 136 times "F ___ You Mrs. Fulmer. You Are A B ____. You Are A Stupid B ____." Another page set forth a diminutive drawing of Mrs. Fulmer with her head cut off and blood dripping from her neck. (p. 851)

The web page provoked considerable discussion in the school, and, perhaps more importantly, resulted in serious mental and emotional harm to Mrs. Fulmer, necessitating psychotropic medicine and a medical leave of absence, which in turn resulted in substitute teachers being used in her classes.

School officials claimed the web site constituted a threat against Mrs. Fulmer, and in general disrupted normal school operations; as a result J.S. was issued a three-day suspension.

The case made its way to the Pennsylvania Supreme Court, which ruled that although the site was not a "true threat" (p. 860) it did cause substantial disruption:

- Mrs. Fulmer suffered severe emotional injuries and had to take a medical leave of absence.
- Because of Mrs. Fulmer's absence, substitute teachers had to cover her classes, impacting students.

- Some students became anxious for their personal safety.
- Parents expressed concern about the safety of the school and about the use of substitute teachers.

In sum, the web site created disorder and significantly and adversely impacted the delivery of instruction. Indeed, it was specifically aimed at this particular school district and seemed designed to create precisely this sort of upheaval. Based upon these facts, we are satisfied that the School District has demonstrated that J.S.'s web site created an actual and substantial interference with the work of the school to a magnitude that satisfies the requirements of *Tinker*. Thus, for the reasons stated above, we find that the School District's disciplinary action taken against J.S. did not violate his First Amendment right to freedom of speech. (p. 675)

So where does that leave us? Quite frankly, on rather boggy ground, with only treacherous pathways through the mire. In general, the First Amendment protects student expression, but the nature of the expression, its impact and where the message originates also must be considered.

WHITHER SOCIAL NETWORKING?

Given what we know about the law, students and free expression, including expression over the Internet, how do social networking sites such as Second Life fit into the equation? What are the rules regarding the kind of expressions the court has already dealt with when the expression occurs on MySpace, FaceBook, Second Life, or any of the myriad of other social networking sites?

The easy answer appears to be, "there is no connection." The courts have not dealt with this kind of issue. That may be facially true, but what the courts often do with a new issue is rule by analogy: the court will look at the similarities and differences between old and new issues, will next

look at past rulings, and will then determine how best to apply the old rules (called *precedents* in legal parlance) to the new situation.

Layshock v. Hermitage School District, 496 F.Supp.2d 587 (W.D. Pa. 2007).

In terms of the application of old rules to news technologies, *Layshock* simply went back to basics, and applied the *Tinker* rule concerning disruption to material posted on the social networking site MySpace.

In late December 2005, Justin Layshock created what he called a "parody" MySpace profile of his high school principal. He created the parody after school hours, using his grandmother's computer. The site contained vulgar comments, generally related to the word "big." After the profile was posted, several other students also posted parody sites about the principal.

As early as October 2005 the school had attempted to block access to MySpace on school computers. This effort, however, was unsuccessful, and several students and teachers apparently accessed the parody.

Layshock was subsequently given a 10-day suspension and was told he would not be allowed to participate in any school activities, or be allowed to attend his graduation the following June. The reason for the disciplinary action, according to the school, was that Layshock had caused substantial disruption to school operations, and had been disrespectful to school officials.

In terms of disruption, there was some effort made by the school to block access to MySpace, and student computer use at the school was restricted for approximately four days. Nevertheless, the court ruled the disruption was not substantial enough to warrant punishment.

Requa v. Kent School Dist. No. 415, 492 F.Supp.2d 1272, (W.D.Wash., 2007).

A different social network posting, however, using different reasoning, elicited a different response from the court.

In June 2006, Gregory Requa posted on YouTube a video of his English teacher. The video included scenes surreptitiously shot in her class, as well as various production elements including music, text and slow motion scenes. The video included text comments on the teacher's personal hygiene, as well as video of cluttered work areas, another student making "rabbit ears" and "pelvic thrusts" behind the teacher, and scenes of the teacher's buttocks as she walked away from the camera and bent over.

School officials were never able to conclusively determine who actually shot, edited and posted the video, but despite Requa's denials, several students identified him as being involved in the production process, and perhaps in the actual shooting. Requa admitted posting a link on his home page to the video, but he also averred he removed the link after a local television station aired the production as part of a story about similar videos on the social network. As of September 2008, however, the video was still available on YouTube at http://www.youtube.com/watch?v=aHIJMWr1Zy0

Requa was given a 40 day suspension, with 20 days being remitted upon completion of a research paper. Other students also received similar suspensions. After exhausting his administrative remedies, Requa took his case to Federal District Court, claiming his First Amendment and due process rights were being violated.

Given a choice, Federal courts would rather not deal with First Amendment issues, if there are other grounds for upholding a lower judicial or administrative ruling. In this instance the court said the video was "lewd and offensive and devoid of political or critical content" (at 1279) and thus did not reach First Amendment protection.

Instead, the court denied the plaintiff's request for a temporary restraining order on the ground that the video constituted sexual harassment (and thus caused significant disruption) and that the secret filming violated explicit school regulations concerning the use of audio and video recorders.

Spanierman v. Hughes, --- F.Supp.2d ----, 2008 WL 4224483 (D. Conn., 2008).

Up to this point all of the cases cited have involved student activities on web pages or in social networking sites, and generally have involved student activities that make teachers and administrators uncomfortable. But what happens when a teacher's on-line activities violate school policy or lead to distress on the part of students? Those were the issues in our last case.

Jeffrey Spanierman was a newly-hired English teacher at Emmett O'Brien High School in Ansonia, Connecticut. In the course of his employment he created a MySpace profile, and encouraged his students to use the site to communicate with him. The site contained a picture of Spanierman, pictures of students and "pictures of naked men with what [a school guidance counselor] considered 'inappropriate comments' underneath them." (p. 2) In addition, the site contained conversations with students which the counselor considered "very peer-to-peer like." (p. 2)

In addition, several students who had accessed the page said it made them uncomfortable. Spanierman was asked to remove the page, which he did. He almost immediately, however, launched a new page under a different name, but with almost exactly the same content. Following an administrative hearing, Spanierman was placed on administrative leave, and later his contract for the next school year was not renewed. He then filed suit in Federal District Court, claiming his due process and First Amendment rights had been violated. The defendants responded by filing a motion for summary judgment, which the court granted.

The court spent most of its decision discussing Spanierman's due process claim. The court found that all administrative procedures had been followed, and that he was not "terminated," but rather his contract simply not renewed. The court also determined that his speech was generally not protected as dealing with public policy, but rather was private speech that was, in fact, inappropriate in a teacher-student relationship.

In light of the potential for abuse, and in an effort to maintain appropriate student-teacher relationships, several states, are now considering legislation that will place an outright ban on teacher-student relationships via social networking sites. Other school districts allow such contacts, but only through district-sponsored sites. (Simon, 2008)

Sites such as Second Life, of course, have the potential for adding another layer of virtual reality to these problems. A student can create an almost limitless collection of avatars; enough to populate an entire classroom or school. These avatars can represent the student, teachers, administrators or other students. They can be made to do and say whatever the "creator" wants. They can have an almost limitless array of body types, parts and physical attributes.

Given that adolescents can, as we have seen, be extremely cruel in their verbal descriptions of faculty and staff, sites such as Second Life present new issues of false light invasion of privacy, the traditional elements of which are:

Publication…

…with malice…

…that creates a false impression…

…that is highly offensive to a reasonable person.

It does not take much imagination to see how students in the previously cited court decisions could turn their verbal descriptions into visual depictions. And as other decisions showed, the responsible party will be the student, not the publisher/owner of the virtual world.

ACCEPTABLE USE POLICIES

So what can school administrators do to protect themselves from lawsuits filed by aggrieved parents and students? The quick answer is: not much. However, there are some precautions that can show good-faith on the part of the schools in protecting students' free speech rights, as well as letting students know what kinds of behaviors are acceptable and which are not. These precautions are found in Acceptable Use Policies (AUP).

An AUP has three purposes: First, it allows parents to grant (or not grant) their children Internet access. Second, it provides guidelines for what is, or is not, appropriate when students do access school-provided Internet resources. Third, it tells students what sanctions will be imposed for violating these rules. But note, the AUP may not impose a blanket prohibition on student expression. The rules concerning disruption, appropriateness, control and free speech still apply.

Perhaps the best way to craft an AUP is to provide a list of "dos and don't." While there may be a tendency to writer an all-inclusive list, administrators should resist this temptation. In today's rapidly-changing electronic environment such a list may quickly become outdated. In addition, it is impossible to include all possible behaviors, so in a questionable situation will boil down to asking, "If it isn't in the policy is it allowed or prohibited?" And those are the kinds of questions that lead to lawsuits.

Thus the AUP should be general enough to cover a majority of situations that may arise. Of course, if there are "dos and don'ts," then there must be sanctions imposed for violations of the policy. Remember, most students will abide by the rules, and most of the time students who violate the rules do not do so deliberately. Thus it is a small number of students who will be the targets of sanctions.

And what should the sanctions be? The general rule is to make the punishment fit the crime. The most prevalent sanction is to deny the student Internet privileges at the school. More flagrant violations could lead to suspension. But whatever reward/punishment scheme is adopted, it must be applied fairly and consistently.

The written policy must also include provisions for due process and should be signed by the student, the student's parents, and a representative of the school (or district). The Virginia Department of Education has an excellent electronic publication detailing how to create an acceptable use policy, and includes examples from other states, as well as templates for creating an Acceptable Use Policy.

Fortunately a number of other schools have already created Acceptable Use Policies. A simple Internet search will yield hundreds, if not thousands of such policies. Here are a few sites to get you started:

http://www.gnn.com/gnn/meta/edu/features/archive/aup.htm

lhttp://www.wentworth.com/classroom/aup.htm

http://www.bham.wednet.edu/policies.htm

http://www.erehwon.com/k12aup/

MOVING INTO THE FUTURE?

At this point you may be saying to yourself, "Can any good come out of this?" Yes, there are some positive benefits to social networking sites, but rather than throw their hands up in despair, teachers and administrators should remember that it was only a few years ago that computers were introduced into the classroom, and even fewer years when the Internet arrived. And we all survived, and in many case thrived and found new and exciting ways to use this new technology. Now it may be time for the next step, and integrate social networking sites into the curriculum.

Some schools have gone so far as to build virtual campuses where students and faculty can gather for classes and casual interactions. Of course, as noted previously, faculty must be extremely careful not to overstep the bounds of propriety and appropriate student-teacher relationships.

A safer option is for the school to merely establish a presence in one of the virtual worlds, and simply provide information about the school and school activities. But is it also possible to teach in a virtual world? Some colleges and universities are indeed experimenting with virtual classrooms, as an extension of synchronous interactions. Indeed it is not much of a leap from synchronous communication via a keyboard, to establishing a more elaborate virtual classroom complete with demonstrations and avatars asking and answering questions. Most of these experiences, however, provide supplemental materials rather then replacing the brick-and-mortar school. Second Life in particular allows "citizens" to upload content that can be used as classroom material.

For those interested in pursuing the application of virtual worlds to the classroom, here are some web sites that may be useful:

http://bellevuecollege.edu/informatics/VWTAFinal.pdf

http://dokimos.org/secondlife/education/

http://www.simteach.com/

http://slgames.wordpress.com/2007/04/12/alternatives-to-second-life-uber-edition/

CONCLUSION

The United States Supreme Court has yet to deal with adolescents and social networking sites such as Second Life. However, using the concept of "reasoning from analogy" we can surmise what the new rules for the ever-expanding CyberVillage might look like.

- Speech that occurs in school and deals with public policy and does not cause substantial disruption is almost certainly protected.
- Expression that occur in the school building itself, or as part of an officially-sanctioned off-school-property function, whether part of the curriculum or not, and is disruptive or runs counter to the school's basic educational mission, is not protected.
- Speech that is "merely" offensive, and is created off-campus, is probably protected, even if the message is later distributed in the school.

• Expression that causes or has the potential to cause serious disruption, or that can be considered a "true threat," is not protected.

Given the current legal climate, it is critical that schools develop written policies regarding the role of the school in education for civility, free speech, disruption, threats and proper computer use, and how computer use relates to these areas.

REFERENCES

Aristotle, A. (2008). *Politics. Book III, part XV.* (B. Jowett, Trans.). Retrieved September 28, 2008, from http://classics.mit.edu/Aristotle/politics.3.three.html

Aristotle, A. (2008). *Politics. Book III, Part XVI.* (B. Jowett, Trans.). Retrieved September 28, 2008, from http://classics.mit.edu/Aristotle/politics.3.three.html

Ashcroft v. American Civil Liberties Union, 542 U.S. 656 (2004).

Ashcroft v. Free Speech Coalition, 535 U.S. 234 (2002).

Bethel School District No. 403 v. Fraser, 478 U.S. 675 (1986).

Beussink ex rel. Beussink v. Woodland R-IV School District, 30 F.Supp. 2d 1175 (E.D. Mo. 1998).

Boucher v. School Board of the School District of Greenfield, 134 F.3d 821 (7th Cir. 1998).

Brandenburg v. Ohio, 395 U.S. 444 (1969).

Calvert, C. (2001). Off-campus speech, on-campus punishment: Censorship of the emerging Internet underground. *Boston University Journal of Science and Technology Law, 7*, 244–245.

Campbell v. Acuff-Rose, 510 U.S. 569 (1994).

Cardwell v. Bechtol, 724 S.W. 2d 739 (Tenn. 1987).

Child On-Line Protection Act (COPA), 47 USC § 231 (1998).

Child Pornography Prevention Act (CPPA), 18 USC §§ 2256(8)(B) and 2256(8)(D) (1996).

Children's Internet Protection Act (CIPA), 17 USC 1701 et seq (2000).

Children's On-Line Privacy Protection Act (COPPA), 15 USC § 6501-6506 (1998).

Communications Decency Act (CDA), 47 USC § 223 (1996).

Cunningham, L. (2006). A question of capacity: Towards a comprehensive and consistent vision of children and their status under law. *University of California at Davis Journal of Juvenile Law and Policy, 10*, 277.

Dempsey, J. X. (2007, November/December). The Internet at risk. *EDUCAUSE Review*, 72–82.

Emmett v. Kent School District No. 415, 92 F.Supp 2d 1088 (W.D. Wash 2000).

Hazelwood School District v. Kuhlmeier, 484 U.S. 260 (1988).

Hustler Magazine v. Falwell, 485 U.S. 46 (1988).

J.S. v. Bethlehem School District, 807 A.2d 847 (Pa. 2002).

Juneau School District. (1985, January 8). *Policy manual: Policy 5850, social events and class trips.*

Juneau School District. (1998, February 17). *Policy manual: Policy 5520, disruption and demonstration.*

Killion v. Franklin Regional School District, 136 F. Supp. 2d 446 (W.D. Pa. 2001).

Kuhlmeier v. Hazelwood School District, 795 F.2d 1368, 1372 (8th Cir. 1986), *rev'd*, 484 U.S. 260 (1988).

Layshock v. Hermitage School District, 496 F.Supp.2d 587 (W.D. Pa. 2007).

Morse v. Frederic, 127 S.Ct. 2618 (2007).

Reno v. American Civil Liberties Union, 521 U.S. 844 (1997).

Requa v. Kent School Dist. No. 415, 492 F.Supp.2d 1272, (W.D.Wash. 2007).

Schwartz, M. (2008, August 3). The trolls among us. *New York Times Magazine,* 27-30.

Simon, M. (2008). *Online student-teacher friendships can be tricky.* Retrieved August 13, 2008, from http://www.cnn.com/2008/TECH/08/12/studentsteachers.online/index.html20080813

Spanierman v. Hughes, --- F.Supp.2d ----, 2008 WL 4224483 (D. Conn. 2008).

Stein, G. quoted in Shapiro, F.S. (2006). *The Yale book of quotations.* New Haven, CT: Yale University Press.

Tinker v. Des Moines Independent Community School District, 393 U.S. 503 (1969).

United States v. American Library Association, 539 U.S. 194 (2003). Virginia Department of Education. (n.d.). *Acceptable use policies: A handbook.* Retrieved September 29, 2008, from http://www.doe.virginia.gov/VDOE/Technology/AUP/home.shtml

Vivian, J. (2008). *The media of mass communication.* New York: Pearson.

West Virginia State Board of Education v. Barnett, 319 U.S. 624 (1943).

Chapter 7
Do High School Students Benefit from the Children's Internet Protection Act?

Zheng Yan
State University of New York at Albany, USA

ABSTRACT

The Children's Internet Protection Act (CIPA; 2000) requires an Internet filtering and public awareness strategy to protect children under 17 from harmful visual Internet depictions and has been implemented nationwide since 2001. However, little literature is available documenting its impacts on children's Internet safety. This chapter first reviews CIPA as well as other existing regulations in protecting children on the Internet. It then presents empirical evidence that CIPA is associated with a decrease in high school students' Internet use at school but does not appear to have a beneficial effect on their knowledge of Internet safety or opportunities for Internet safety education.

INTRODUCTION

The Children's Internet Protection Act (CIPA) was signed into federal law on December 21, 2000 and became effective on April 20, 2001. Under CIPA, public schools and public libraries receiving E-rate funds are required both to use filtering and blocking programs to protect children under 17 from harmful visual depictions on the Internet and to provide public notices and public hearings to increase public awareness of Internet safety. In the United States, almost 100% of public schools

have implemented CIPA (Wells & Lewis, 2006), while approximately 60% of public libraries have done so (Jaeger, McClure, Bertot, & Langa, 2005). Thus, it is important to assess the impacts of CIPA on young Internet users and to determine whether they benefit from CIPA. However, few empirical studies have been conducted to assess the impacts of CIPA on young Internet users. The objectives of this chapter are twofold: (a) To provide a broad conceptual context of the issue of children's Internet safety by reviewing federal regulations on Internet safety of children and (b) to demonstrate the complexity of children's Internet safety in the real-life world by presenting a specific case in assessing the

DOI: 10.4018/978-1-60566-926-7.ch007

impacts of CIPA on children and adolescents in public schools.

INTERNET SAFETY PROTECTION STRATEGIES IN THE UNITED STATES

Among a wide variety of mass media (e.g., telephone, radio, movies, television, and Internet), only television and the Internet have caused widespread concerns specifically related to children, resulting in regulation at the federal level.

For television, there is one federal regulation entitled the Children Television Act of 1990 (CTA). The primary goals of CTA are to restrict advertising during children's television and to increase educational and informational television programs for children. Specifically, based on rules made by the Federal Communications Commission (FCC), television stations must (a) air the core programs that is specifically designed to serve the educational and informational needs of children ages 16 for at least 30 minutes in length between the hours of 7:00 a.m. and 10:00 p.m. with a regularly scheduled weekly program; b) identify the core programs by displaying the "E/I" icon denoting that the program is "educational and/or informational." and (c) limit the amount of commercial matter that may be aired in certain children's television programming to 10.5 minutes per hour on weekends and 12 minutes per hour on weekdays. Starting in 2007, FCC further required that at least three hours per week of the core programs must be provided on the main programming stream. CTA as well as FCC's rules have been implemented nationwide for nearly two decades to help children to learn important knowledge and values from television and to protect children from overcommercialization on television.

In contrast to television, there are six federal regulations concerning children and the Internet: (a) the Child Online Protection Act of 1998, (b) the Neighborhood Children's Internet Protection Act of 1999, (c) the Children's Online Privacy Protection Act of 2000, (d) the Children's Internet Protection Act of 2000, (e) the Deleting Online Predators Act of 2006, and (f) Internet Safety Education Act of 2007. These Internet-related regulations are unprecedented in the human history, signifying the serious societal concerns about the negative consequences of the Internet on children. These concerns about children's safety on the Internet (e.g., exposing to pornography and being online victimization) are much more worrisome than those about impacts of commercialization and lack of learning on the television. As a result, these concerns lead to a series of federal regulation efforts to protect children on the Internet.

Among the six regulations concerning children and the Internet, CIPA is particularly important for several reasons: (a) It has been considered constitutional and implemented the most widely in the United States (despite that the American Library Association and other free speech advocates have been challenging it for violating the first amendment), compared to the Child Online Protection Act of 1998 that the Supreme Court ruled unconstitutional. (b) It is the typical strategy using by all the five Internet-children regulations in restricting Internet access for children, compared to the Children's Television Act that primarily requires offering educational programs for children. (c) It represents the latest federal strategy to be adopted, given that the Deleting Online Predators Act of 2006 and the Internet Safety Education Act of 2007 are both still in the debating stage. (d) It has drawn the largest amount of public attention and has become the focal point of legal issues related to the Internet and children among parents, policy makers, researchers, and other concerned parties. Thus, CIPA can be considered as the most representative and best known federal policy among the Internet-related regulations and is the primary focus of the present chapter.

CIPA consists of nine sections, including five major sections specifying two major strategies for protecting children online (mainly in Sections 1711, 1712, 1721, and 1732) as well as four minor sections describing various definitions and procedural issues for implementing the strategies (mainly in Sections 1701, 1703, 1731, 1732, 1733, and 1741).

Section 1711 of CIPA specifies the primary Internet protection strategy—the filtering strategy—in public schools. Specifically, it amends the Elementary and Secondary Education Act of 1965 by limiting funding availability for schools under Section 254 of the Communication Act of 1934. Through a compliance certification process within a school under supervision by the local educational agency, it requires schools to include the operation of a technology protection measure that protects students against access to visual depictions that are obscene, child pornography, and harmful to minors under 17.

Section 1712 specifies the same filtering strategy in public libraries. Specifically, it amends Section 224 of the Museum and Library Service Act of 1996/2003 by limiting funding availability for libraries under Section 254 of the Communication Act of 1934. Through a compliance certification process within a library under supervision by the Institute of Museum and Library Services (IMLS), it requires libraries to include the operation of a technology protection measure that protects students against access to visual depictions that are obscene, child pornography, and harmful to minors under 17.

Section 1721 is a requirement for both libraries and schools to enforce Internet safety policy with the Internet safety policy strategy and the filtering technology strategy as condition of universal service discounts. Specifically, it amends Section 254 of the Communication Act of 1934 and requests both schools and libraries to: (1) monitor the online activities of minors and operate a technical protection measure; and (2) provide reasonable public notice and hold at least one public hearing or meeting to address the Internet safety policy. This is through the certification process regulated by FCC.

Section 1732, the fourth major section, with another title of Neighborhood Children's Internet Protection Act (NCIPA), amends the amends Section 254 of the Communication Act of 1934 and requires schools and libraries to adopt and implement an Internet safety policy. It specifies five types of Internet safety issues: (a) access by minors to inappropriate matter on the Internet, (b) safety and security of minors when using email, chat rooms, and other online communications, (c) unauthorized access, (d) unauthorized disclosure, use, and dissemination of personal information, and (e) measures to restrict access to harmful online materials.

In summary, the key features of CIPA are: (a) The target impact of CIPA is to protect children from harmful visual depictions on the Internet. (b) The target strategies to generate the target impact are the primary strategy of filtering and the secondary strategy of public awareness. (c) The target population for implementing the two strategies is young Internet users under 17. (d) The target organizations for implementing the two strategies are both public schools and pubic libraries that receive the E-rate funding.

ASSESSING IMPACTS OF THE INTERNET SAFETY PROTECTION STRATEGIES

Assessment of the impact of a media regulation such as CIPA or CTA concerns two important questions: What impacts are assessed (e.g., assessing impacts of CIPA on children's online behavior or assessing impacts of CTA on educational television programs for children)? How are the impacts assessed (e.g., using a laboratory experiment design or a quasi-experiment design)? The first question concerns assessing the content of impacts, and the second concerns selecting the methodology for assessing impacts. These two questions will be discussed in detail in this section.

It is important to differentiate six different kinds of impacts, including media effects vs. regulation impacts, regulation impacts on media vs. regulation impacts on children, regulation impacts on children's behaviors vs. regulation impacts on children's non-behavioral aspects, since different kinds of impacts lead to a different kind of research questions.

First, it is important to differentiate media effects from regulation impacts. Many researchers in various fields such as media psychology and media communications extensively examine media effects (e.g., Zillmann & Bryant, 2002), while researchers in other fields such as developmental psychology and information science focus on regulation impacts (e.g., Calvert & Kotler, 2003). Media effects are generally defined as psychological effects of form, content, and technology of the mass media that affect how media consumers think and behave (Zillmann & Bryant, 2002). There is extensive literature examining media effects (e.g., Gunter, 2002; Harris, 2004; Perse, 2001; Zillmann & Bryant, 2002). For instance, researchers have examined effects of pornography on the Internet on sexual attitudes (Gunter, 2002; Huston, Wartella, Donnerstein, Scantlin, & Kotler, 1998; Thornburgh & Lin, 2002). In contrast, regulation impacts in this study are defined as impacts of specific local, state, and federal regulations on media, society, and individuals (Calvert & Kotler, 2003; Jaeger, McClure, Bertot, & Langa, 2005; Jordan, Schmitt, & Woodard, 2001; Kunkel & Goette, 1997; Kunkel & Wilcox, 2001; Parsad & Jones, 2005; Wells & Lewis, 2006). For instance, Jordan, Schmitt, and Woodard (2001) examined impacts of the Children's Television Act on educational content of major television channels. Here the emphasis of these studies is on a specific regulation (e.g., CTA or CIPA) rather than on a specific medium (e.g., television or Internet).

Second, it is important to differentiate regulation impacts on media from regulation impacts on children. Among the regulation impacts studies, some researchers assess regulation impacts on media (e.g., examining whether filtering programs reduce students' exposure to harmful online materials at school after CIPA?), while others examine regulation impacts on children (e.g., examining whether children benefit from CIPA cognitively and socially?). There is relatively extensive literature on regulation impacts on media (e.g., Greenfield, Pickwood, & Tran, 2001; Jaeger, McClure, Bertot, & Langa, 2005; Jordan, Schmitt, & Woodard, 2001; Kunkel & Goette, 1997; Wells & Lewis, 2006). For instance, some researchers have examined how many public schools have implemented CIPA (Wells & Lewis, 2006) and others have examined how effective various filtering and blocking programs currently on the market can filter the harmful visual depictions (Greenfield, Pickwood, & Tran, 2001; Rideout, Richardson, & Resnick, 2002). In contrast, there is very limited literature that has directly examined regulation impacts on children rather than on media. For instance, Calvert and Kotler (2003) examined the impacts of CTA on children's preferences and comprehension of educational and informational content. This study is considered to be the first and best direct examination of the impact of CTA on elementary-school-age children's learning since it provides the direct evidence that CTA is having the intended effects.

Third, it is important to differentiate impacts on children's behaviors from impacts on children's non-behavioral aspects. A regulation might have a wide variety of impacts on child development, which can be further divided into two major categories: impacts on children's behaviors (e.g., Does CIPA reduce students' online risk behaviors such as visiting pornography sites or chatting with online strangers?) and impacts on children's non-behavioral aspects (e.g., Does CIPA improve students' knowledge of Internet safety and increase their awareness of Internet safety?). Moreover, behavioral aspects and non-behavioral aspects generally interact with each other related. For instance, extensive literature on indicates that children's good knowledge is not only important source/outcome of certain positive behaviors but also a protective factor of certain risk behaviors (e.g., Hofer & Pintrich, 1997 & 2002; Schmmer, 1993). Thus, for protecting children from harmful online materials and assessing impacts for the filtering and awareness strategies, basic knowledge about the Internet safety and appropriate education experience of Internet safety are relevant and fundamental.

Among the six different but related types of impacts discussed above, there exists extensive literature examining effects of pornography exposure on children, but limited literature focuses on impacts of CIPA in protecting children from harmful materials on the Internet. Furthermore, there are studies focusing on the impacts of CIPA on media (e.g., scope of implementation and efficiency of filtering), but no single empirical study directly assesses impacts of CIPA on child development, neither on behavioral nor on non-behavioral aspects, which might partly result from methodological challenges in conducting such a study.

In addition to the conceptual challenges of assessing different types of impacts, there are five existing methodological challenges for assessing the impact of the two protection strategies of CIPA on children.

The first is an ethical/legal challenge. Under CIPA, it is not only unethical but also illegal to intentionally allow school students to expose harmful pornography on the Internet. This make it unlawful to conduct a true experiment (Shadish, Cook, & Campbell, 2002) by randomly assigning children to access to either an unfiltered or a filtered Internet environment in order to examine the impacts of CIPA on students' unsafe behaviors and pornography attitudes.

The second is a sampling challenge. Given that nearly 100% of American public schools have implemented CIPA in 2005, it is practically impossible to either have random samples with and without filtering experience after 2001 when

CIPA went into effect or have a random sample to longitudinally examine students' differences before and after CIPA was implemented in 2001.

The third is a data collection challenge. While CIPA requires installing filtering and blocking programs to protect students from harmful depictions, it does not explicitly permit tracking students' Internet use in order to protect their privacy, according to Section 1702 of CIPA. This makes it technically infeasible to directly collect observational data of students' online behavior by installing Internet tracking programs in the school computer system and tracking individual students' online activities at school.

The fourth is a participant challenge. CIPA covers a broad age span of young Internet users, from about 1 year old to 17 years old. Different ages are associated not only with children's cognitive, language, social, and physical development, but also with their online experiences and online behaviors. Given that age is a particularly important factor in children's understanding of and interaction with the Internet (e.g., Yan, 2005, 2006, in press), it is a challenge to decide how participants should be chosen (i.e., elementary school students, middle school students, high school students, or all school students under 17).

The last is an organizational challenge. CIPA concerns both public schools and public libraries. While 100% of public schools have implemented CIPA, only about 60% of public libraries have done so. This makes it challenging to compare the impacts of CIPA on schools and libraries.

In summary, while it is urgent and important to assess whether students really benefit from CIPA, there are various conceptual challenges and unique methodological challenges for such an assessment effort. Researchers need to design and conduct a thoughtful and innovative study to address these challenges and to assess the impact of CIPA on young Internet users empirically and effectively.

AN EMPIRICAL STUDY OF ASSESSING IMPACTS OF CIPA'S TWO INTERNET SAFETY PROTECTION STRATEGIES

To assess the impacts of the two internet safety protection strategies used in CIPA, recently I conducted an empirical study. It assessed high-school students' basic knowledge about, and perceived education of, Internet safety in order to investigate the effects of regulation on non-behavioral aspects of adolescent development, given the existing conceptual and methodological challenges. Specifically, he study examined four research questions:

1. Are there significant differences in the basic knowledge of Internet safety between high school and undergraduate students? It could be reasoned that if the filtering strategy of CIPA works well and has a significant impact on high school students, given the relatively similar ages between these two groups, high school students should only have been exposed to fully filtered well-protected Internet environments in school and consequently should show limited knowledge of Internet safety. In contrast, college students should have been exposed to completely unfiltered Internet environments in school and thus should show sophisticated knowledge of Internet safety issues.

2. Are there significant differences in the perceived education of Internet safety between high school and undergraduate students? If the awareness strategy of CIPA works well and has a significant impact on high school students, then high school students should receive observable efforts toward promoting public awareness such as informal Internet safety classes, and thus should report a higher level of attendance at informal Internet classes at school than that of college students.

3. Are there significant differences in frequency and duration of Internet use at school between the high school and undergraduate students? If CIPA works well and has a significant impact on high school students, then high school students should use the Internet much less than college students (high school students might be less interested in using school computers installed with filtering programs whereas college students can access to the Internet freely).

4. Are there significant differences in frequency and duration of Internet use at home between the high school and undergraduate students? It could be reasoned that no differences of Internet use at home should be observed between high school students and college students, simply because CIPA only applies to public schools and public libraries but not to students' private homes.

METHOD

The study used the quasi-experimental design (Shadish, Cook, & Campbell, 2002), in which high-school students served as the experimental group and went online with the CIPA restriction. Undergraduate college students served as the control group, going online without the CIPA restriction. This research design allowed experimental manipulation of two dependent variables (i.e., the filtering strategy and the awareness strategy) and at the same time met the ethical and legal challenges of assessing the impacts of CIPA on minors. Furthermore, since high school students represented the oldest age group under CIPA and undergraduate students represented the youngest possible age group without the restriction of CIPA, these two groups had the smallest age gap but very different online environments. In some ways, this partially reduced the major confounding factor of a chorological age difference between high school students and undergraduate

Figure 1. Demographic characteristics of the sample (N = 407)

Student	Mean Age (*SD*)	*n*	Female	Male
High School				
Sophomore	15.40 (0.518)	78	37	41
Junior	16.48 (0.503)	76	36	41
Senior	17.54 (0.535)	61	23	38
Total	16.39 (1.000)	216	96	120
Undergraduate				
Sophomore	18.87 (0.991)	45	40	5
Junior	20.50 (0.864)	66	44	22
Senior	21.71 (0.986)	80	60	20
Total	20.62 (1.460)	191	144	47

students, while recognizing that some potential confounding factors (e.g., dissimilarities in their cognitive development or in social environment) might exist between high school students and undergraduate students.

To enhance the quasi-experimental design with two nonequivalent rather than random samples, the study cross-examined the difference between Internet use at school where CIPA was implemented and Internet use at home where CIPA was not. The comparison of school and home use for the two groups provided a control for another important potential confounding factors, that is, different Internet use at school and at home by these two groups (Shadish et al., 2002). As a result, the study included two independent variables, namely the filtering strategy and awareness strategy, and four dependent variables, namely basic knowledge of Internet safety, perceived education of Internet safety, Internet use at school, and Internet use at home.

In addition, the study was designed to focus only on students' basic knowledge and perceived education of Internet safety, as two non-sensitive variables to assess impacts of CIPA's two protection strategies, rather than on their unsafe online behaviors or knowledge toward child pornography. This decision, together with purposefully choosing only high-school adolescents rather than younger

age groups and purposefully collecting students' self-report data rather than computerized data based on Internet tracking programs for protecting individual student's privacy, should help minimize potential harm to participants during the present empirical study of assessing impacts of CIPA on minors.

A total of 407 students participated in the study (see Figure 1 for demographic details). Among them, 216 were high school students from grades 10 - 12, with a mean age of 16.39 (SD = 1.00), and 191 were undergraduate students ranging from sophomores to seniors, with a mean age of 20.62 (SD =1.46). There were relatively more female high school students than male (96 vs. 120) and more male undergraduate students than male ones (144 vs. 47). The high school students were from a public high school in New York State. The high school had over 1,600 students, with 2.4% of students eligible for free or reduced price lunch. Among them, 88.5% were Caucasian, 3.7% African American, 2.8% Hispanic, and 5.0% Asian. Comparably, the undergraduate students were from a public university in New York State. The university had a student population of more than 12,000, with 79% of them being Caucasian, 8% African American, 7% Hispanic, and 6% Asian.

To keep the high school group and undergraduate group close in age, no first year high school students were included. To keep the high school and undergraduate groups distinguished from each other in age, no undergraduate first year students were included in the study. This also allowed undergraduate students participating in the study to have at least two years of online experience without filtering programs.

The study was conducted during the 2006 spring semester. CIPA was enacted in December of 2000, took effect in April of 2001, and it was implemented in the high school in 2001. Thus, all the high school students in the present sample had at least 5 years of online experience with the restriction of CIPA but no online experience without the restriction of CIPA. In contrast, all undergraduate students were in high school when CIPA was enacted. They had approximately one year or more of online experience with the CIPA restriction, and approximately two years or more of online experience without the CIPA restriction. High school students reported that they used the Internet more than 4-5 years at both school and home; similarly, undergraduate students reported that they used the Internet more than 4-5 years at both school and home. As a result, their online experience had been influenced by CIPA.

A 22-item survey was developed and used to collect the data. Twelve survey items were multiple-choice questions that collected data about demographic information and students' use and learning of the Internet, while 10 were open-ended questions for assessing students' basic knowledge about the Internet safety.

The items assessing students' use and learning of the Internet included questions about frequency of internet use at school, which solicited students' responses (1 = never used, 2 = every month, 3 = every week, and 4 = every day) to the survey question, "How often do you use the Internet at school?"; duration of internet use at school, which assessed students' responses (1 = 0-1 year, 2 = 2-3 years, 3 = 4-5 years, and 4 = over 5 years) to the question, "How long have you been using the Internet at school?"; frequency of internet use at

home, based on students' responses (1 = never used, 2 = every month, 3 = every week, and 4 = every day) to the survey question, "How often do you use the Internet at home?"; duration of internet use at home, which elicited students' responses (1 = 0-1 year, 2 = 2-3 years, 3 = 4-5 years, and 4 = over 5 years) to the question, "How long have you been using the Internet at home?"; perceived education of internet safety, which asked students to report how many informal Internet education they have received at school (1 = never, 2 = once, 3 = twice, and 4 = three or more) in response to the question, "Have you taken a class or a workshop about the Internet at school?"

The 10 open response questions assessing basic knowledge of internet safety focused on the impact of the Internet filtering strategy of CIPA on students' knowledge of Internet safety. Example items are "What kinds of BAD things could the Internet do for us" (Please give 3-5 examples)? "What kinds of BAD things could happen to us when we use email?" "Do you need to be careful when you go to WWW?" Responses were scored as representing one of four levels of knowledge if the Internet: (1) Minimal knowledge indicates that an individual knows very little about the positive or negative social consequence of the Internet and expresses little precaution of Internet safety; (2) Limited knowledge indicates that an individual has a general but limited sense of the positive or negative social consequence and a vague precaution of Internet safety; (3) Substantial knowledge indicates a clear understanding of the positive and negative social consequences of the Internet and a proper attitude towards Internet safety; (4) Sophisticated knowledge indicates a balanced and comprehensive knowledge of the profound positive and negative social consequences of the Internet and a thoughtful attitude towards Internet safety. The present study adopted the coding method used in previous studies (see Yan, 2005 & 2006 for more details),

The author and two trained graduate assistants independently coded 10% of the data on students' basic knowledge of Internet safety. The standard procedure was taken to develop the coding system, to train coders, to code the data, and to estimate the kappa coefficient indicating interrater agreement. The estimated interrater agreement using the Kappa coefficient was .82. Coding discrepancies between coders were resolved through discussion prior to data analysis.

RESULTS

Both qualitative and quantitative results are presented to address the four research questions of the study. Eight cases selected based on both representativeness of the four levels of Internet safety knowledge and diversity in demographics are presented first to qualitatively illustrate differences in basic knowledge of Internet safety, perceived education of Internet safety, as well as Internet use at school and at home between four high school students and four undergraduate students. Statistical results are then summarized to quantitatively estimate the differences between 216 high school students and 191 undergraduate students.

Qualitative Comparisons between High School Students and Undergraduate Students

Two Cases with Minimal Knowledge of Internet Safety

Case 1 was a 17 year old female studying in Grade 11. She used the Internet at home every day but used the Internet at school only weekly. She had used the Internet at home and school for more than five years. She reported that she had never attended any workshop about the Internet at school and had learned about the Internet most from her siblings. Based on her responses to the survey regarding her basic knowledge of Internet safety, the good things the Internet could do for people are helping us with school, having easy access to shopping services, learning, and using email to help us to talk to others and using websites to find out good information. The bad things that could happen to people are influencing us, getting us into bad experiences, viruses may be emailed to us, but nothing really bad could happen by using websites. She stated that people do not need to be careful when going to either WWW or using email since "nothing has happened yet" and "she has no clue".

Case 2 was a 20 year old male undergraduate sophomore majoring in history. He used the Internet at home and at school every day and had used the Internet at home and at school for more than 5 years. He had never attended any Internet workshops and learned about the Internet most by himself. Based on his responses to the survey regarding his basic knowledge of Internet safety, the good things that could happen to people are research, pleasure, and communication, specifically, keeping in touch with friends and family via email and learning from websites. He specified that, in general, there is nothing bad on the Internet, except that viruses can be spread. He stated that people do not need to be careful when going to WWW since it is not harmful, but people do need to be careful when using email since viruses are spread through email.

These two cases suggest that (a) these two students had sufficient online experience both at school and at home, (b) neither reported any Internet safety education experiences, and (c) their basic knowledge of Internet safety is minimal and their attitude toward Internet safety is naïve. In the present study there were 12 out of 216 high school students (10.0%) and 22 out of 191 undergraduate students (11.5%) showing such minimal knowledge.

Two Cases with Limited Knowledge of Internet Safety

Case 3 was an 18 year old male in Grade 12. He used the Internet at home every day and at school every week. He had used the Internet for more than five years both at home and at school. He had never attended an Internet workshop at school and had learned about the Internet most by himself. His responses to the survey regarding his basic knowledge of Internet safety indicated that he saw the good things that could happen to people as talking to Grandma in China, learning to grow trees, and diagnosing herpes; and the bad things that could happen to people included viruses, worms, pictures of Chelsea Clinton, talking to strangers when using email, and becoming obsessed. He stated that people should be careful when going to WWW or using email since strangers can get information.

Case 4 was a 20 year old female undergraduate junior majoring in political science. She used the Internet at home every day and at school every week. She had used the Internet for more than five years at home and at school. She had taken one workshop about how to use the Internet but learned about the Internet most from her parents. Regarding her knowledge of Internet safety, she believed that good things about the Internet include helping us with research, and connecting us with family and friends who we normally do not see. She listed two bad things about the Internet, including stolen identification information and getting viruses that ruin our computers. She stated that people need to be careful when using WWW, since it might not be what you thought and that people need to be careful when using email since there are viruses.

These two students had sufficient online experience at home, while they used the Internet less at school. Neither reported any Internet safety education experience, and their basic knowledge of Internet safety was notable but very limited. There were 121 out of 216 high school students (57.3%) and 86 out of 191 undergraduate students (45.0%) showing such limited knowledge.

Two cases with Substantial Knowledge of Internet Safety

Case 5 was a 16 year old girl in Grade 11. She used the Internet at home every day and at school every week. She had used the Internet at home and at school for 4-5 years. She had never had an Internet workshop and had learned about the Internet most from her relatives. She reported that she like the Internet because one can find facts and AIM; she did not like pop-ups, viruses, porn sites, hackers. The good things on the Internet include finding facts, contact with people with email and AIM, learning about things. The bad things on the Internet include: bad websites, porn pop-ups, viruses, and that strangers can get information about you. On the Internet there are porn stars and pedophiles. Many porn sites want to use children for sex. She stated that we need to be careful when we go to WWW since there is porn and viruses and we also need to be careful when we use email since there are viruses and bad images.

Case 6 was a 21 year old female senior majoring in psychology. She used the Internet every day both at home and at school. She had used the Internet for 4-5 years both at home and at school. She had attended an Internet workshop about how to build a personal website and learned about the Internet most from her classmates. She listed the good things the Internet can do for people as research, email, and AIM; and the bad things included porn, child porn, pedophiles, and terrorists. Specifically, email might be sent out to the wrong person and seeing things we do not want to look at. She stated that people need to be careful when going to WWW since you never know what happens when using email since the government could be screening it.

These two students had sufficient online experience at home and used the Internet less at school.

Neither reported any Internet safety education experience, their basic knowledge of Internet safety was substantial and their attitude toward Internet safety was cautious. There were 60 out of 216 high school students (28.4%) and 72 out of 191 undergraduate students (37.7%) showing such limited knowledge.

Two Cases with Sophisticated Knowledge of Internet Safety

Case 7 was a grade 12 male student aged 18 years. He had used email every day at home for 6 years and at school every month for 4-5 years. He had never attended any Internet workshops and learned about the Internet most by himself. Regarding his knowledge of Internet safety, he reported that the good things on the Internet include greater access to information, facilitation of college applications, supplanting the use of paper so environmental consequences are diminished, ease of communicating through email, and finding information without driving to a library. The bad things on the Internet included facilitating play of action games, exposure to ads, the ease for people to buy things they do not need, and spyware that can attack computers. He stated that "We need to be careful when we go to WWW since one should avoid obscene sites, sites intended to harm one's computer, and sites that involve giving away personal information that is not over a secure server since there are identity thieves. It is essential not to open attachments from unfamiliar email senders. On the Internet there are many learners and researchers but there are identity thieves and hackers."

Case 8 was a 21 year old female senior English major. She had used the Internet at home and at school every day for more than five years. She attended one workshop learning about how to search the web for information but had learned about the Internet most by herself. As for her knowledge of Internet safety, she listed the good things that the Internet could do for people as providing more information, better knowledge, creating a small global environment, using email to keep in touch with long lost friends, and using the web to have more information access. She listed the bad things the Internet could do to people as child molesters gaining access to children better, pornography, a lot of wrong information, hacking and stolen identity, email use can lead to no personal contact, and using websites we can lose the ability to learn from books. She stated that people should be careful when going to WWW since there is porn, stalkers, etc. and we should be careful when using email since people need to be aware of the information you use.

Comparing these latter two cases, these two students had sufficient online experience at home and at school. Neither reported any Internet safety education experience, their basic knowledge of Internet safety is sophisticated and their attitude toward Internet safety is careful. There were nine out of 216 high school students (4.3%) and 11 out of 191 undergraduate students (5.8%) showing such limited knowledge.

Quantitative Comparisons of High School Students and Undergraduate Students[1]

Students' Internet safety knowledge was assessed based on four levels (1 = minimal knowledge, 2 = limited knowledge, 3 = substantial knowledge, and 4 = sophisticated knowledge). Contrary to expectations, the average level of knowledge of Internet safety of high school students (M = 2.56, SD = .730) was between Levels 2 and 3 and higher than that of undergraduate students (M = 2.45, SD = .772), $F(1, 400) = 2.11$, p = .147, η^2 = .005.

Contrary to expectations, the number of the perceived education experiences of Internet safety of high school students was lower for high school students (M = 1.57, SD = .912) than for undergraduate students M = 1.67, SD = .872), $F(1, 404) = 1.36$, p = .363, η^2 = .005).

As shown in Figure 2, the frequency of Internet use at school among high school students was substantially lower than that of undergraduate students. Compared to frequency of Internet use at school, duration of Internet use at school by high school students was somewhat lower than that of undergraduate students, but this difference was not significant.

Compared to the Internet use at school, the high school students' frequency of Internet use at home was slightly lower than that of undergraduate students, but this difference only approached the level of significance. Compared to frequency of Internet use at home, duration of high school students' reported Internet use at home was significantly lower than that of undergraduate students.

Why do High School Students not Benefit their Understanding of the Internet Safety from the Filtering Strategy? Why do High School Students not Report Sufficient Internet Safety Education Efforts at School?

One of the findings of this study was that high school students show slightly more sophisticated knowledge of Internet safety than undergraduate students, but this difference is not statistically significant. The minimal difference in basic knowledge of Internet safety between the two groups suggests that the primary filtering strategy of CIPA does not have a significant positive impact on high school students' Internet safety knowledge, given that (a) the high school students and undergraduate students are the closest adjacent age groups and share much developmental similarity and (b) there are marked differences in the online environments at school, the filtered one in the high school and unfiltered one at the university. If the filtering strategy works well, and school is the sole or primary resource for students' online experiences, then high students should almost always be exposed to filtered content and should

show naive understanding compared to undergraduate students.

Why might the CIPA filtering strategy fail to benefit adolescents' understanding of the Internet safety? One possibility is that high school students are in middle- to- late adolescence and may be curious about sexuality due to the physical and psychological developmental changes they are experiencing. Filtering and blocking online sexual materials in schools might increase their sexual curiosity so that they might use various strategies and seek different sources to satisfy their curiosity. If this is the case, it would also explain why they used the Internet at school less than they did at home (and much less than undergraduate students did at school), as was found in the study. Perhaps good sex education and online safety education should be offered to better protect high school students' Internet safety.

Second, the filtering strategy enforced only in public schools and public libraries simply might not work. Schools are not the only channel, or even not the primary channel, for students to access to the Internet. Students are exposed to pornography and other harmful materials through diverse mass media (e.g., TV, movies, cell phones, and magazines) in diverse locations (e.g., their own homes, neighborhoods, friends' homes, grandma's house, cyber café, and community centers) rather than merely in public schools or public libraries. CIPA's filtering strategy might substantially reduce students' sexual exposure online in public schools and libraries, but is offers limited control given the wide variety of harmful visual materials existing online and offline. The implication is that, to best protect students' Internet safety, diverse and comprehensive strategies focusing on various social institutions such as home and community should be used.

The second major finding of the study was that high school students did not report more perceived efforts of Internet safety education than undergraduate students. The minimal difference in the perceived education of Internet safety sug-

Figure 2. Results of ANOVAs examining differences in frequency of high school and undergraduate students' Internet use at school and duration of Internet use both at school and at home (N = 407)

	M	SD	F	p	η^2
I. At School					
Frequency of Internet use			211.183	.000	.343
High School	2.74	.652			
Undergraduate	3.66	.626			
Duration of Internet use			1.597	.207	.004
High School	3.04	.797			
Undergraduate	3.15	.899			
II. At Home					
Frequency of Internet use			3.048	.082	.007
High School	3.81	.516			
Undergraduate	3.89	.389			
Duration of Internet use			23.230	.000	.055
High School	3.36	.759			
Undergraduate	3.70	.658			

gests that the awareness strategy of CIPA does not have a significant positive impact on high school students' Internet safety education experience, given that the high school students and undergraduate students are the closest adjacent age groups developmentally and there are mandated Internet safety awareness strategies used at high schools but not at universities. If the awareness strategy worked well and high school students receive sufficient exposure to the Internet safety issues, then high students should report more perceived Internet safety education efforts than the undergraduate students.

Why do high school students not report sufficient Internet safety education efforts? There are several potential explanations. First, it is possible that they might not report the existing efforts or might not pay attention to these efforts. Thus, efforts should be made to design age-appropriate awareness programs to increase their proactive awareness of Internet safety. Second, although universities are not required to provide the safety programs, strong Internet safety awareness programs might be available for undergraduates. This might increase undergraduates' awareness and thus no differences were found between high school students and undergraduate students. However,

both groups have only received less than one informal Internet safety workshop, and thus this speculation should be ruled out.

Another finding of the study was that differences between high school students and undergraduate students were observed only in frequency of Internet use at school but not in duration of Internet use at school, frequency of Internet use at home, and duration of Internet use at home. First, differences in frequency of Internet use at school and at home, may be a side effect of the filtering strategies that occur at school. In the filter-free environment, high students and undergraduate students show similar Internet use patterns, using the Internet almost every day. In contrast, high school students use the Internet much less than undergraduate students, with reported Internet use dropping from almost once a day to less than once a week. Second, students started to use the Internet at home at an earlier time point than at school. Thus, Internet use at home can be considered one of the primary sources of students' Internet experience. Perhaps CIPA should emphasize awareness and offer or even emphasize filtering and blocking not only on public schools and libraries but in the home and community to best protect children and young adolescents. In addition, the duration and frequency of Internet use at home reflects the "natural" course of Internet use, without the restriction of CIPA. And indeed, our examination of internet use shows that the impact of CIPA on internet use occurs only at school.

CONCLUSION

What future studies need to be done in order to more thoroughly understand if CIPA or other Internet safety regulations are working or not? The study presented above suggests at least four specific lines of research.

First, the study mainly focused on only one aspect of the possible impact, students' basic knowledge of Internet safety, and other aspects such as online attitudes, online behaviors, as well as physical, cognitive, social, and emotional development are likely to play important roles. Further research is needed to assess the impact on younger groups in order to obtain a more comprehensive assessment of the utility of the Internet filtering strategy.

Second, the study mainly focused on the impact of the filtering strategy only on one age group, the high school students, rather than on all younger groups under 17 (e.g., Gross, 2004; Yan, 2005, 2006). Further research is needed to assess the impact on various aspects of potential impacts, such as online behavior and social development.

Third, the study was limited to students' perceived efforts of Internet safety rather than directly assessing student awareness, online attitudes and online behaviors. Little is known about effects of the quality and quantity of various awareness strategies, such as school Internet safety policies, honor codes, informal Internet safety classes, public meetings, pop-up safety messages when logging on, and/or parental education. Thus, research is needed to assess the role of various awareness strategies to increase understanding of the impact of CIPA's public awareness strategy.

Last, the study used the single survey question on perceived safety education, which might

not capture students' real experiences. Multiple items should be developed to examine the true implementation of the awareness strategy. Thus, research is needed to improve the awareness strategy assessment section of the survey instrument to better understand the impact of CIPA's public awareness strategy.

In conclusion, it is urgent and important to assess the real impact of CIPA as well other Internet safety regulations on young Internet users. Furthermore, it is complex and challenging to conduct a valid and solid assessment in the real-life world. The study presented in this chapter offers the empirical evidence of a lack of some anticipated positive impacts of CIPA on young Internet users. Unquestionably, the intended beneficial impact of CIPA was to establish protections for youth from inappropriate content that can be found readily on the Internet. The findings of the study suggest that high school students at least have reduced their use of the internet in school, as compared to outside of school. However, this does not mean that the CIPA goals were realized. To improve knowledge and awareness of Internet safety among young Internet users and ultimately to best protect their Internet safety, it is important to develop effective Internet safety education programs and to enhance home-based and community-based Internet safety activities rather than focusing solely on the filtering strategy at schools. Follow-up studies that assess the regulation impact on elementary school students and/or on students' attitudes and behaviors of Internet safety would help develop a comprehensive assessment of the impacts of CIPA on children's Internet safety.

REFERENCES

Calvert, S. L., & Kotler, J. A. (2003). Lessons from children's television: The impact of the Children's Television Act on children's learning. *Journal of Applied Developmental Psychology, 24*(3), 275–335. doi:10.1016/S0193-3973(03)00060-1

Greenfield, P., Pickwood, P., & Tran, H. H. (2001). *Effectiveness of Internet filtering software products*. Retrieved October 26, 2004, from http://www.aba.gov.au/internet/research/filtering/filtereffectiveness.pdf

Greenfield, P. M. (2004). Inadvertent exposure to pornography on the Internet: Implications of peer-to-peer file-sharing networks for child development and families. *Journal of Applied Developmental Psychology, 25*, 741–750. doi:10.1016/j.appdev.2004.09.009

Gross, E. F. (2004). Adolescent Internet use: What we expect, what teens report. *Journal of Applied Developmental Psychology, 25*, 633–649. doi:10.1016/j.appdev.2004.09.005

Hofer, B. K., & Pintrich, P. R. (1997). The development of epistemological theories: Beliefs about knowledge and knowing and their relation to learning. *Review of Educational Research, 67*, 88–140.

Hofer, B. K., & Pintrich, P. R. (2002). *Personal epistemology: The psychology of beliefs about knowledge and knowing*. Mahwah, NJ: Erlbaum.

Huston, A. C., Wartella, E., Donnerstein, E., Scantlin, R., & Kotler, J. (1998). *Measuring the effects of sexual content in the media: A report to the Kaiser Family Foundation*. Oakland, CA: The Kaiser Family Foundation.

Jordan, A., Schmitt, K., & Woodard, E. (2001). The developmental implications of commercial broadcasters' educational offerings. *Journal of Applied Developmental Psychology, 22*(1), 87–102. doi:10.1016/S0193-3973(00)00068-X

Kunkel, D., & Goette, U. (1997). Broadcasters' response to the Children's Television Act. *Communication Law and Policy, 2*, 289–308.

Kunkel, D., & Wilcox, B. L. (2001). Children and media policy. In D. G. Singer & J. L. Singer (Eds.), *Handbook of children and the media* (pp. 589-604). Thousand Oaks, CA: Sage.

Parsad, B., & Jones, J. (2005). *Internet access in U.S. public schools and classrooms: 1994–2003* (NCES 2005–015). U.S. Department of Education. Washington, DC: National Center for Education Statistics.

Rideout, V., Richardson, C., & Resnick, P. (2002). *See no evil: How Internet filters affect the search for online health information*. Retrieved October 26, 2004, from http://www.kff.org/entmedia/20021210a-index.cfm

Schmmer, M. (1993). Epistemological development and academic performance among secondary students. *Journal of Educational Psychology, 85*, 1–6.

Shadish, W., Cook, T., & Campbell, D. T. (2002). *Experimental and quasi-experimental designs for generalized causal inference*. Boston: Houghton Mifflin.

Thornburgh, D., & Lin, H. S. (Eds.). (2002). *Youth, pornography, and the Internet*. Washington, DC: National Academic Press.

Wells, J., & Lewis, L. (2006). *Internet access in U.S. public schools and classrooms: 1994–2005* (NCES 2007-020). U.S. Department of Education. Washington, DC: National Center for Education Statistics.

Yan, Z. (2005). Age differences in children's understanding of complexity of the Internet. *Journal of Applied Developmental Psychology, 26*, 385–396. doi:10.1016/j.appdev.2005.04.001

Yan, Z. (2006). What influences children's and adolescents' understanding of the complexity of the Internet? *Developmental Psychology, 42*, 418–428. doi:10.1037/0012-1649.42.3.418

Yan, Z. (in press). Useful resources, important messages: The explosion of parenting books on adolescents and social networking sites. *Journal of Applied Developmental Psychology*.

Zillmann, D., & Bryant, J. (Eds.). (2002). *Media effects: Advances in theory and research* (2ⁿᵈ ed.). Mahwah, NJ: Erlbaum.

ENDNOTE

[1]   All the results of ANOVA reported in this section were completely consistent with those of the Mann-Whitney U test.

Section 3
Recent Research Findings, Educational Perspectives and Practical Applications

Chapter 8
Effects of Motives for Internet Use, Aloneness, and Age Identity Gratifications on Online Social Behaviors and Social Support among Adolescents

Louis Leung
The Chinese University of Hong Kong, Hong Kong

ABSTRACT

The advent of new media technologies, such as e-mail, blogs, MSN, online games, mobile phones, iPods, MP3, PS3, NDS, video on demand (VOD), and DVDs, to name a few, has dramatically changed both the nature and number of social compensation and mood management devices available to most youngsters. Although previous research has examined how the Internet has become an important resource for information and entertainment, little research has focused on the ways in which individuals use the Internet for social communication and support. In particular, how personality traits, such as perception of aloneness and age identity gratifications, together with motives for Internet use impact Internet habits and perceived social support are much-neglected areas of research. This chapter investigates how differences in these constructs among adolescents and children influence their online social behavior (such as use of instant messaging, online games, and participating in forums).

INTRODUCTION

The advent of new media technologies, such as e-mail, blogs, MSN, online games, mobile phones, iPods, MP3, PS3, NDS, Wii, video on demand (VOD), and DVDs, to name a few, has dramatically changed both the nature and number of *social compensation* and *mood management* devices available to most youngsters. Although previous research has examined how the Internet has become an important resource for information and entertainment, little research has focused on the ways in which

DOI: 10.4018/978-1-60566-926-7.ch008

individuals use the Internet for social communication and support. Online social network sites such as Facebook, Friendster, and MySpace allow individuals to present themselves, and establish and maintain relationships with others (Raacke & Bonds-Raacke, 2008). How personality traits, such as perception of *aloneness* and *age identity gratifications,* together with *motives for Internet use* impact Internet habits and social support are, however, much-neglected areas of research. In this chapter we will examine how the Internet plays a role in influencing mediated social support and how these psychological variables motivate online social communication and behavior.

BACKGROUND

Motives for Internet Use

With the introduction of e-mail, instant texting technologies (such as ICQ, MSN, Messenger, Google Talk, and Net Meeting), the Internet and other computer-mediated communication (CMC) technologies seem to ideally fulfill social deficiency needs. Increasingly, the Internet serves interpersonal utility functions (such as relationship building, social maintenance, and social recognition) as much as entertainment and information utility functions. Motivations for Internet use (such as for interpersonal utility, social bonding, social identity, and showing affection)—as found in studies into the motives for Internet use (e.g., Papacharissi & Rubin, 2000; Leung, 2003; Stafford & Gonier, 2004)—can also be collectively identified as motives for *social compensation* – similar to the motivations for television viewing.

As the Internet is becoming more and more like television, a second dimension of Internet motives can be conceptualized from the theoretical discussion on the role of arousal in television viewing behavior (Donohew, Finn, & Christ, 1988; Zillmann, 1985; Zillmann, 1988a, 1988b). These authors propose that the traditional motives of

relaxation, entertainment, arousal, and information seeking in television viewing compose a cluster of viewing motives on the basis of *human stimulation* needs. Grounded in Blumler's (1979; 1985) uses and gratifications framework, recent research into motivations for Internet use has found similar motives, (e.g., entertainment, surveillance, to pass time, and escape). In fact, the psychological basis for human stimulation needs is well documented and provides the grounding for high level elaboration in theorizing stimulus, arousal, human needs, and well-being (Berlyne, 1971; LaRose, Mastro, & Eastin, 2001). Because today's Internet has been transformed and possesses many functions that are similar to television, we could also use Zillmann's term, *mood management,* to describe the concept of arousal-oriented motivations for Internet use, including entertainment, information seeking, diversion, and relaxation.

To understand the relationship between the motives for Internet use and online social communication behavior, mood management theory can be applied to describe how individuals with different personality traits might use the Internet in a similar manner to television, to block anxious thoughts and replace dysphoric moods. Knobloch (2003) argued that the aim of mood management is to alter disagreeable moods, enhance mediocre feelings and to maintain pleasant moods. With the ubiquitous nature and a wide assortment of entertainment available on the Internet, its mood-regulating content is becoming more and more accessible and convenient. Such content affects human behavior such as thinking and memory (Ellis & Moore, 1999), perceptions of others and of the self (Forgas & Bower, 1987), and feelings about one's environment; therefore, the use of the Internet (such as online games, ICQ, chartrooms, or web searches) and its influence on mood and how mood affects Internet use is an important area of study. Past research has established current mood state to be a key factor for selective exposure to media, especially for entertainment choices (Knobloch & Zillmann, 2002; Zillmann,

Schweitzer, & Mundorf, 1994). However, few of the available published studies have examined the perceptions of *need for aloneness* and *age identity gratifications* in relation to media consumption habits. This chapter investigates the generality of social compensation and mood management concepts by examining the relationship between these motives for Internet use and personality differences.

Aloneness

Many people use aloneness and loneliness interchangeably (Pierce, Wilkinson & Anderson, 2003); however, individuals can feel alone, but not in the sense of being lonely (Parsons, 1997). According to the American Heritage Dictionary of the English Language (1992), aloneness does not necessarily imply feelings of unhappiness. Instead, aloneness can be viewed as being self-reliant, hopeful, and resourceful and as having self-determination and being able to engage in self-reflection (Pierce, Wilkinson & Anderson, 2003).

People are born with the need both to be alone and to be connected with others (Buchholz & Chinlund, 1994). Aloneness, like attachment, is regarded as necessary for human growth, with loneliness being aloneness' negative extreme (Buchholz & Catton, 1999). By examining the perceptions of adolescents, they found that adolescents are able to distinguish between the state of loneliness and the need to be alone (Galanaki, 2004). They recommend that future research explore more positive dimensions of aloneness, including when adolescents choose to be alone, what they do while alone, and how they feel after being alone (Buchholz & Catton, 1999). For adolescents who concentrate on identity formation (Blos, 1962; Erikson, 1968), aloneness needs and abilities may be especially important. 'Leave me alone' is probably among adolescents' most used phrases. Larson (1990) has conducted extensive research on the time adolescents spend alone, and

sees aloneness as a time of reflection, rest, and self-renewal. Along with Larson's work, there is a growing body of literature on aloneness that focuses on the positive effects of solitude (Griffin, 2001; Griffin & Kent, 1998; Moustakas, 1989; Storr, 1988). Buchholz and colleagues have explored aloneness as a developmental need, essential for all phases of personal growth (Buchholz & Chinlund, 1994; Buchholz & Tomasi, 1994; Galanaki, 2005; Memling & Buchholz, 1994). Winnicott (1965) shares the belief with Buchholz and his associates that the capacity to be alone is part of a healthy maturation process and is learned, similar to attachment, wherein individuals have to learn how to relate.

The Internet has some unique qualities: it is mediated, it is not face-to-face, it is interactive, and can be anonymous (e.g., blogs, forums, chat rooms, and instant messaging). Adolescents and children who want to be alone may, therefore, choose the Internet as their preferred means to explore the social world. They may have different social compensation and mood management needs that motivate their Internet use. Based on these literatures, this research hypothesizes in H_1 that the more adolescents and children express their desire to be alone, the more their motivations for using the Internet will be allied to (a) social compensation and (b) mood management.

Age Identity Gratifications

Age identity plays a significant role in young adults' mass, interpersonal, intergenerational, and intercultural communication (McCann, Kellermann, Giles, Gallois & Viladot, 2004). Age identity seems to act as a 'pre-interactional' tendency whereby a strong sense of identification with a particular group (e.g., young adults) influences communication with outgroup members (e.g., older people). Social age identity involves the importance of a person's age group to his/her self-concept, that is, the valuing, liking, and being proud of one's age group; one's age group membership being important and central to who a person is; and the sense of attachment, inclusion, and belonging with one's age group (Gartska et al., 1997; Harwood, 1999; Westerhof & Barrett, 2005). Social age identity is the importance of a person's age group to his/her sense of self. Beginning with Hall (1905), psychologists have described adolescence as a time of change, involving interpersonal relationships, more time spent with peers, and less with family members.

Harwood (1999) contends that age identity is associated with television viewing choices, especially for mood regulating contents. Lin, Hummert, and Harwood (2004) examine how age identities are presented in an online discussion forum. Online messages were examined using discourse and content analyses. Evidence of a tension between positive and negative age identities emerged in the analysis. Despite this, little social scientific work has examined the ways in which age identities may be related to Internet use. Previous researches have demonstrated that the Internet is the preferred medium for the Net-generation to socialize or to compensate social deficiency, to get information, and to manage their moods or be entertained (Leung, 2003). Thus, this chapter tries to shed light on the following hypothesis in H_2: the more adolescents and children show strong age identification, the more their motivations for using the Internet will be allied to (a) social compensation and (b) mood management.

Social Support

In a review of social indicators research, Cobb (1976) defined social support primarily as information leading the subject to believe that he or she is cared for and loved, that he/she is esteemed and valued, and he/she belongs to a network of communication and mutual obligation. Other scholars have defined social support as interpersonal transactions involving affect, affirmation, aid, encouragement, and validation of feelings (Abbey, 1993; Hlebec, Manfreda, Vehovar, 2006;

Kahn & Antonucci, 1980). House (1986) gave a third definition in which social support involves the flow between people of emotional concern, instrumental aid, information, or appraisal.

Existing measures of social support are rather varied because of the different definitions of social support and the lack of a clear conceptualization of the construct (Cohen & Syme, 1985; Donald & Ware, 1984). Recent research, however, has generally attempted to measure the *functional components* of social support because functional support is most important and can be of various types providing: (1) *emotional* support which involves caring, love, and sympathy, (2) *instrumental* support which provides material aid or behavioral assistance and is referred to by many as tangible support, (3) *information* support which offers guidance, advice, information, or feedback that can provide a solution to a problem, (4) *affectionate* support which involves expressions of love and affection, and (5) *social companionship* (also called *positive social interaction*) which involves spending time with others in leisure and recreational activities (Sherbourne & Stewart, 1991).

Past research found that Internet-based support groups – including newsgroups, message boards, and listservs for specific medical conditions, have been successful in improving some intermediate patient outcomes in clinical trials involving caregivers to Alzheimer patients and for patients with AIDS (Brennan, Moore, & Smyth, 1995; Brennan, Ripich, & Moore, 1991; Gallienne, Moore, & Brennan, 1993). Heavy users of Internet-based peer support groups for people suffering from depression that offered information and support were more likely to have resolution of depression during follow-up than less frequent users (Houston, Cooper, & Ford, 2002). Similarly, past research has demonstrated that frequent and increasing use of the community computer network and the Internet significantly influences social capital formation (Kavanagh & Patterson, 2001).

Taking particular care in considering the

theoretical constructs of motivations for Internet use (such as mood management and social compensation), need for aloneness, age identity gratifications, and social support into this research, this chapter investigates how differences in these constructs among adolescents and children influence their online social behavior (such as use of instant messaging, online games, and participating in forums). We expect that the use of the Internet for social compensation and mood management motives and the effect of aloneness and age identity are potent variables that can influence online social communication behavior and the perception of social support. Therefore, this research posed in H_3 that the more adolescents and children exhibit a high level of perceived social support (from online and offline sources), the more their motivations for using the Internet will be allied to social maintenance and mood management.

Offline Social Activities

In this chapter, we seek to add more understanding of the dynamics involved by analyzing a number of indicators, in addition to demographics, motives for Internet use, and personality variables, in their relationships as to how online social behaviors as well as offline social activities (such as communicating face-to-face with family/relative, friends, and schoolmates and frequency of going to movies, going on picnics or to BBQs, window shopping, and going to parties or karaoke in their leisure time) can influence perception of social support. As a result, we posed two research questions:

1. To what extent can demographics, motives for Internet use, personality traits (i.e., aloneness and age identity), online social behaviors, and offline social activities predict perceived social support?
2. In what ways can demographics, motives for Internet use, personality traits (i.e., aloneness and age identity), and offline social activities predict online social behaviors?

DESCRIPTION OF DATA AND RESEARCH METHOD

Data were gathered from a probability sample of 717 adolescents and children ranging in age from 8 to 18 who responded to a telephone survey in February 2005. Telephone numbers were drawn from the most recent edition of the territory telephone directory in Hong Kong by first randomly selecting a page, then randomly selecting a column within the page, and finally randomly selecting a name with a phone number in the column. Non-eligible respondents (i.e., younger than 8 and older than 18), numbers that were unobtainable, and numbers that were not answered after five attempts were excluded. In addition, eligible respondents had to be PC users with access to the Internet at home. The survey instrument was pilot tested before the actual fieldwork was conducted. The response rate was 57.8 percent.

Measurements

Motivations for Internet Use. Initially, motivation items used in previous Internet research were included in the survey questionnaire. Additional items were gathered by a focus group of 26 students to refine the unique motives associated with Internet use for this age group. A pilot study on motives for Internet use with 23 items was carried out for 51 respondents to eliminate bad items and to solicit new ones. The final questionnaire consisted of 17 motivation statements. Respondents were asked: How satisfied are you with the Internet in helping you do the following things? A 5-point Likert scale where 1 = not at all satisfied and 5 = very satisfied was used. A principal components factor analysis (with Varimax rotation) grouped these items into four motivation dimensions with an eigenvalue greater than 1.0, explaining 50.78 percent of the variance. The four-factor solutions were labeled "entertainment," "relationship maintenance," "recognition gaining," and "information seeking." Cronbach's alpha

Table 1. Motives for Internet use

How satisfied are you with the <u>Internet</u> in helping you to do the following things?	Mean	SD	Factors			
			1	2	3	4
Entertainment/Escape						
1. To make me feel less tense	3.39	1.04	.79			
2. To relax	3.50	1.09	.73			
3. To have fun or a good time	3.52	1.04	.68			
4. To forget about my problems	2.91	1.17	.67			
5. To feel less lonely	3.38	1.17	.58			
Relationship Maintenance						
6. To let others know I care about their feelings	2.79	1.10		.68		
7. To stay in touch with people I don't see very often	3.65	1.18		.63		
8. To show others encouragement	3.00	1.11		.62		
9. To feel involved with what's going on with other people	3.12	1.14		.61		
10. To meet new people	3.12	1.24		.50		
Social Recognition						
11. To feel important	2.34	1.04			.80	
12. To impress people	2.00	.97			.73	
13. To gain status	2.44	1.10			.68	
14. To improve my identity in the world	2.81	1.14			.54	
Information Seeking						
15. Found things I need to know about daily life	3.94	1.03				.82
16. Helped me keep up with news that isn't available elsewhere	3.79	1.05				.73
17. Gave me immediate knowledge of big news events	3.74	1.09				.64
Eigenvalues			5.08	1.96	1.32	.91
Variance explained (%)			29.86	11.52	7.78	5.35
Cronbach's Alpha			.79	.70	.71	.65

Scale used: 1 = Very dissatisfied and 5 = Very satisfied

values were .79 for entertainment (five items); .70 for relationship maintenance (five items); .71 for recognition gaining (four items); and .65 for information seeking (three items). Similar to Blumler's (1985) and Zillmann's (1988a, 1988b) characterization, entertainment and information seeking were regarded as mood management, and relationship maintenance and social recognition were treated as motives for Internet use for social compensation.

Aloneness. To assess aloneness, the 9-item need for aloneness measure was used. The scale items (e.g., "Being able to use the Internet in solitude helps me explore my private self; chatting on the Internet can be a coping strategy for dealing with stress; and aloneness is an opportunity for me to self-regulate my emotions") were used on a 5-point scale ranging from "strongly disagree" (1) to "strongly agree" (5), with high scores indicating higher need for aloneness. The factor structure of aloneness was examined and the results indicated the existence of a single factor with a high internal consistency reliability of .74. Evidence of the construct validity of the scale was provided by a significant positive relationship with social compensation (r = .36, p<.001) and mood management motives (r = .28, p<.001).

Age Identity Gratifications. Although single-item indicators of age identity gratification have been commonly used, this chapter used three items to assess the age identity gratifications construct. Three scale items including: "I am satisfied with the way I use the Internet to connect with people with whom I can identify; to share with people in similar situations to those I experience; to enjoy chatting with people who are like me," were used on a 5-point scale ranging from "strongly disagree" (1) to "strongly agree" (5). Cronbach's alpha was acceptable at .70.

Social Support. To assess social support, a battery of 19 items within four subscales developed by The Rand and Medical Outcome Study (MOS) teams was adopted with slight modifications. The

five original dimensions of social support were reduced to four as emotional support and informational support were merged because they were highly correlated and overlapped considerably. As a result, the four subscales were "tangible," "affectionate," "social companionship," and "emotional or informational" supports. It was recommended that the subscale scores rather than the total score be used. Moreover, items from the tangible support subscale were excluded because tangible support mainly refers to medical or health-related assistance from friends or close relatives rather than being affective or emotionally related. Respondents were asked how often each of the support items measured in the remaining three dimensions was available to them if needed either online or offline. A 5-point scale was used where; 1 = none of the time, 2 = a little of the time, 3 = some of the time, 4 = most of the time, and 5 = all

Table 2. Factor analysis of social support

How often is each of the following kinds of support available to you if you need it via either online or offline?	Mean	SD	Factors		
			1	2	3
Social companionship					
1. someone you can count on to listen to you when you need to talk	3.86	1.07	.73		
2. someone to do things with to help you get your mind off things	3.29	1.25	.66		
3. someone to share your most private worries and fears with	3.67	1.13	.62		
4. someone who understands your problems	3.55	1.11	.61		
5. someone to confide in or talk to about yourself or your problems	3.83	1.08	.59		
Affectionate					
6. someone to have a good time with	3.94	1.02		.75	
7. someone who comforts you sincerely	3.71	1.12		.71	
8. someone to love and make you feel wanted	3.79	1.07		.65	
9. someone who shows you love and affection	3.62	1.13	.43	.65	
Emotional/information					
10. someone to give you information to help you understand a situation	3.46	1.12			.85
11. someone whose advice you really want	3.69	1.10			.68
12. someone to turn to for suggestions about how to deal with a personal problem	3.67	1.06			.64
Eigenvalues			5.81	.84	.72
Variance explained (%)			48.44	7.01	5.96
Cronbach's Alpha			.80	.81	.75

Scale used: 1=none of the time, 2=a little of the time, 3=some of the time, 4=most of the time, and 5=all of the time; N = 717 of the time. A principal components factor analysis extracted three factors and explained 71.8% of the variance. The three factors were "social companionship" with alpha = .80, "affectionate" (alpha = .81), and "emotional and informational" support (alpha = .75).

Online Social Behavior. Online social behavior was measured by asking adolescents and children how often they used the three most popular Internet activities, namely use of instant messaging (e.g., MSN, ICQ, QQ, and chat rooms), online games, and forums. Specifically, they were asked how much time *last week* they spent online on these Internet activities using a 7-point scale where 1 = never, 2 = less than an hour, 3 = about an hour, 4 = more than one but less than two hours, 5 = two to less than three hours, 6 = three to less than four hours, and 7 = four or more hours.

Offline Social Activities. To assess offline social activities, respondents were asked to estimate (1) how many minutes the previous day they had spent face-to-face with (a) family/relative, (b) friends, and (c) schoolmates engaging in a conversation which lasted three minutes or more (casual 'hi and bye' interactions were not included) and (2) how

often they (a) went to movies, (b) went on picnics or to BBQs, (c) went window shopping, and (d) went to parties or karaoke at in their leisure time on a 5-point Likert scale with 1 = not often and 5 = very often. Responses to these items were first standardized and then combined to yield a composite score reflecting the level of social activities respondents engaged in offline.

Relationships between Aloneness, Age Identity, Social Support and Internet Motives

H_1 predicted that the more adolescents and children express the desire to be alone, the more their motivations for using the Internet will be allied to (a) social compensation and (b) mood management. Regression results in Table 3 show that both relationship maintenance (β=.14, p<.001) and social recognition (β=.27, p<.001) were significantly linked to aloneness. This indicates that the more adolescents and children have the need for aloneness, the more *social compensation* will motivate Internet use. In contrast, aloneness was predictive only for entertainment and escape

Table 3. Regression of demographics, and personality on motives for Internet use

Predictors	Social Compensation Motives		Mood Management Motives	
	Relationship Maintenance	Social Recognition	Entertainment and Escape	Information Seeking
	β	β	β	β
Demographics				
Gender (male=1)	.04	-.02	.05	.01
Age	-.05	-.10**	-.09**	-.08*
Family income	-.02	.01	.01	-.06
Personality				
Aloneness	.14***	.27***	.24***	.02
Age identification gratifications	.74***	.44***	.54***	.51***
R^2	.60	.32	.39	.27
Final adjusted R^2	.60	.32	.39	.26
N =	655	659	667	661

Notes: Figures are standardized beta coefficients.
*p<=.05; **p<=.01; ***p<=.001

(β=.24, p<.001). Such a result supports the notion that the more adolescents and children want to be alone, the more they will use the Internet to relax, have fun, forget about problems, feel less tense and lonely, meet new people, show encouragement, stay in touch, and care about others. No significant link was found between the aloneness and information seeking motive. As a result, H_1 was largely supported.

Likewise, H_2 proposed that the more adolescents and children exhibit strong age identity gratification, the more their motivations for using the Internet will be allied to (a) mood management and (b) social compensation. As shown in

Table 3, age identity gratification was a significant predictor of both social compensation motives (such as relationship maintenance (β=.74, p<.001) and social recognition (β=.4, p<.001)) and mood management motives (such as entertainment and escape (β=.54, p<.001) and information seeking (β=.51, p<.001)) when using the Internet. Therefore, H_2 was fully supported.

As a whole, aloneness and age identity significantly predicted social compensation and mood management motives in adolescents' and children's Internet use in four separate regression analyses with variance explained ranging from 26 to 60 percent. As indicated in Table 3, the younger

Table 4. Regression of demographics, Motives for Internet use, personality, online social behavior, and offline social activities on social support

Predictors	Social Support		
	Social Companionship	Affectionate	Emotional/Information
	β	β	β
Demographics			
Gender (male=1)	-.14**	-.24***	-.07
Age	-.12**	-.09*	-.01
Family Income	-.04	.03	.06
Motives for Internet Use			
Entertainment and Escape	-.05	-.01	-.03
Relationship Maintenance	.11	.12*	.19**
Social Recognition	-.01	-.06	-.03
Information Seeking	.15**	.20***	.20***
Personality			
Aloneness	-.02	-.04	-.11*
Age Identity Gratification	.00	.02	-.02
Online Social Behavior			
Instant Messaging	-.01	-.02	-.08
Online Game	-.11*	-.08*	-.02
Forum	.00	-.09	-.08
Offline Social Activities	.16***	.19***	.14**
R^2	.12	.21	.14
Final adjusted R^2	.10	.19	.12
N =	585	585	587

Notes: Figures are standardized beta coefficients.
*p<=.05; **p<=.01; ***p<=.001

the respondent, the more he/she was motivated by social recognition, entertainment/escape, and information seeking motives.

H_3 predicted that the more adolescents and children exhibit a high level of perceived social support (from both online and offline sources), the more their motivations for using the Internet will be allied to (a) social maintenance and (b) mood management. Regression results in Table 4 show that relationship maintenance was predictive of affectionate (β=.12, p<.05) and emotional/information (β=.19, p<.01). Similarly, the information-seeking motive was also significantly linked to social companionship (β=.15, p<.01), affectionate (β=.20, p<.001), and emotional/information (β=.20, p<.001) dimensions of social support. But entertainment/escape and social recognition motives were not significant. This suggests that adolescents and children with a high motivation to use the Internet for mood management or social compensation tend to perceive that they can obtain all three levels of social support when they need them. Thus, H_3 was partially supported.

Predicting Social Support

To determine what factors predict social support, multiple regressions were run (as shown in Table 4). Results show that offline social activities (β=.16, p<.001) were the strongest predictors of social companionship in social support, followed by information seeking motive (β=.15, p<.01), gender (β=-.14, p<.01), age (β=-.12, p<.01), and playing online games (β=-.11, p<.05). When affectionate was used as the dependent variable, being female (β=-.24, p<.001), information seeking (β=.20, p<.001), offline social activities (β=.19, p<.001), relationship maintenance (β=.12, p<.05), being young (β=-.09, p<.05), and online games (β=-.08, p<.05) were significant predictors. As for the emotional/information dimension of social support, information seeking (β=.20, p<.001) and relationship maintenance (β=.19, p<.001) were the strongest predictors, followed by offline social

activities (β=.14, p<.01) and aloneness (β=-.11, p<.05). Interestingly, age identity gratification, instant messaging, and forums were not significant in any of the regression analyses. Altogether, the predictors included in the regression equations explained 10 to 19 percent of the variance.

Predicting Online Social Behavior

To assess what predicted online social behavior, three parallel regression equations were analyzed using instant messaging, online games, and forums as dependent variables. Results in Table 5 show that being older (β=.35, p<.001), active in offline activities (β=.30, p<.001), and strongly motivated by relationship maintenance (β=.16, p<.01) were predictive of instant messaging use on the Internet. Playing online games as a social and entertainment online activity was significantly predicted by being male (β=.21, p<.001), motivated by entertainment/escape (β=.15, p<.01) and relationship maintenance (β=.15, p<.01) motives, but less for information seeking needs (β=-.12, p<.05), having a lower family income (β=-.12, p<.01), and wanting to be alone less (β=-.09, p<.05). These three equations explained 10 to 29 percent of the variance.

CONCLUSION

Effects of Personality Traits

The results of this study showed that personality traits (such as the need for aloneness and age identity gratifications) significantly predicted motives for Internet use for social compensation (i.e., recognition gaining and relationship building) and mood management (i.e., entertainment and information seeking). This indicates that it is much more desirable when adolescents and children experience bad moods and the desire to be alone is strong to be entertained, find companionship, and be socially recognized through a non-face-

Table 5. Regression of demographics, motives for Internet use, personality, offline social activities on online social behavior

Predictors	Online Social Behavior		
	Instant Messaging	Online Game	Forum
	β	β	β
Demographics			
Gender (male=1)	-.01	.21***	-.03
Age	.35***	-.01	.33***
Family Income	.02	-.12**	-.10*
Motives for Internet Use			
Entertainment and Escape	.05	.15**	.08
Relationship Maintenance	.16**	.15**	.04
Social Recognition	-.06	.08	.05
Information Seeking	-.05	-.12*	-.09*
Personality			
Aloneness	-.06	-.09*	.02
Age Identity Gratification	.02	-.11	.00
Offline Social Activities	.30***	.08	.15***
R^2	.30	.11	.20
Final adjusted R^2	.29	.10	.19
N =	612	598	595

Notes: Figures are standardized beta coefficients.
*$p<=.05$; **$p<=.01$; ***$p<=.001$

to-face channel in solitude and in isolation. This supports the notion that being alone provides the opportunity to self-reflect and get away from others (Pierce, Wilkinson & Anderson, 2003). In fact, being able to use the Internet in solitude may help adolescents and children explore the private self and find a partner with whom they can converse who helps them cope with stress. With the Internet being mediated, non-face-to-face, interactive, and sometimes anonymous, adolescents and children who want to be alone may prefer it as a means to explore the social world (Leung, 2001).

The current analysis also demonstrates that age identity gratification predicts Internet motives, especially for social compensation and mood management, which most adolescents and children of similar ages tend to seek frequently on the Internet. The predictive ability of age identity

gratification is exceptionally strong (with beta weight ranging from .44 to .74). This indicates a strong influence of age identity gratifications (i.e., youngsters in the same age groups who greatly desire to use the Internet to connect with people they can identify with, share with people in similar situations to those they experience, and enjoy chatting with people who are like them) on Internet motives. On one level it may seem self-evident that respondents will seek to connect with individuals online who have similar characteristics to themselves (Atkin, 1985; Hoffer & Cantor, 1991); however, it is interesting that increased age identity gratification did not seem to affect either perceived social support or translate into *action* in the choice of online social behavior. This could be because there is more than a single universal desire among adolescents and children to engage in certain online social behaviors despite the fact that the three online activities we chose were the most common. Similarly, the desire varies with individual variations in the endorsement of age identity gratification measure.

Internet Motives and Perceived Social Support

As hypothesized, the motivations for Internet use of individuals who are better able to access different types of social support are characteristically more allied to mood management and social maintenance. In particular, those who perceived that they had strong affectionate and emotional/information social support tended to be those who were strongly motivated by relationship maintenance needs (Wright, 2000). This makes sense as the more adolescents and children can obtain more relationship maintenance gratifications online, the more they will perceive that their affectionate and emotional/information social supports are always available to them. The same explains why information seeking gratifications can predict perceived social companionship, affectionate, and emotional/information social support because information seeking online may mean seeking information through personal blogs, e-mails, participating in chat rooms, and even socializing through Facebook. Through these activities, adolescents can get information to help understand a situation, receive advice, or get suggestions about how to deal with a personal problem.

Online Social Behavior and Social Support

When actual online social behaviors were used as predictors, perceived social support was linked only to online games: instant messaging and forums were not significant. This may be due to the fact that the online social behaviors chosen for the analyses (i.e., instant messaging, online game, and forums) were not the normal channels

through which adolescents and children receive social support (e.g., in getting advice, suggestions, and sharing private worries and problems). Instant messaging (e.g., MSN, ICQ, or chat rooms) is generally used to pass time and exchange gossip (Leung, 2001), while online games are for entertainment, diversion, and escape, and forums are for in-depth discussion on specific topics. Channels such as personal blogs and e-mail may be better online environments for showing love and affection, caring for others, giving encouragement, and comforting others when they are in need. Furthermore, online games were significantly related to social companionship and affectionate dimensions of social support but the relationship was negative. According to Kraut, Patterson, Lundmark, Kiesler, Mukopadhyay, and Scherlis (1998), this may be because online game, which is computer-mediated, is a less adequate medium for social communication than the telephone or face-to-face interactions it displaces. Online friends are superficial and bonds are easily broken, with many of the social relationships people maintain online through online games being less substantial and sustaining than relationships that people have in other areas of life (Leung & Lee, 2005). In fact, strong social ties are relationships that generally buffer people from life's stresses. More online time may take away from more valuable offline social contact. Heavy online game players, as a result, tend to perceive that they have difficulties getting social companionship and affectionate social support either online or offline, which may be why online social behaviors exhibit little or no effect on perceived social support for adolescents and children.

Offline Social Activities and Online Social Behavior

It is also worth noting that the more *offline* social activities adolescents and children participate in (such as face-to-face conversation with family and friends, going to movies, picnics, BBQs, and parties), the more *online* social behaviors they will have (especially instant messaging and participating in forums). This suggests that offline social activities, in some way, *activate* or *complement* online social behaviors or help enlarge social networks (Rosengren & Windahl, 1989). Similarly, offline social activities also had a strong effect on social support. This effect seems to be the dominant factor influencing perceived social support as compared to personality and online social behavior. The data, however, further reflects that social support has not been transferred from offline social activities to online social behaviors, despite the Internet increasingly becoming the preferred social medium for adolescents and children.

Although the conceptual relationships in this research are based on sound theoretical assumptions and are empirically supported, the present results should be interpreted in light of the methodological limitations of the study. It is important to note that some concepts in the questionnaire, such as aloneness, age identity gratifications, and social support (e.g., being alone gives solitary time to self-reflect, being able to use the Internet in solitude helps you explore your private self, and the Internet allows you to connect with people you can identify) may have been difficult for respondents, particularly 8- to 10-year olds, to understand, or they may not have been applicable to them. As a result the overall result may have been affected.

FUTURE TRENDS

Spending time with friends face-to-face may be considered a normal developmental step among adolescents and important for their identity development. The heavy use of online social communication technologies may also, in fact, be a natural developmental behavior for adolescents and children as demonstrated in this research. Future research should widen the scope of this study by comparing results for different age groups. Although the findings are consistent with the predictions of theories revealed, they do not demonstrate a cause and effect relationship. Use of quasi-experimental and longitudinal designs would improve the strength of the findings. The ability to acknowledge beneficial aloneness, or solitude, seems to be a developmental aim that had not yet been reached; the majority of 7- to 10-year-old children may have great difficulty in perceiving the positive functions of aloneness or recognizing the fact that aloneness can be beneficial, especially if restriction and isolation within one's room have been used as a punishment for bad behavior. Therefore, future research might examine the consequences of age identity gratification-driven online social behaviors. To what extent will we be able to identify specific positive or negative outcomes associated with socializing online that are associated with these age identity gratifications?

REFERENCES

Abbey, A. (1993). *The effect of social support on emotional well-being*. Paper presented at the First International Symposium on Behavioral Health, Nags Head, North Carolina.

American heritage dictionary of the English language. (1992). (CD-ROM). Redmond, WA: Microsoft Corporation.

Atkin, C. K. (1985). Informational utility and selective exposure to entertainment media. In D. Zillmann & J. Bryant (Eds.), *Selective exposure to communication* (pp. 63-92). Hillsdale, NJ: Lawrence Erlbaum.

Berlyne, D. E. (1971). *Aesthetics and psychology*. New York: Appleton-Century-Crofts.

Blos, P. (1962). *On adolescence*. New York: The Free Press.

Blumer, J. G. (1985). The social character of media gratifications. In K. E. Rosengren, L. A. Wenner, & P. Palmgreen (Eds.), *Media gratifications research* (pp. 41-60). Beverly Hills, CA: Sage.

Blumler, J. G. (1979). The role of theory in uses and gratifications studies. *Communication Research*, *6*, 9–36. doi:10.1177/009365027900600102

Brennan, P. F., Moore, S. M., & Smyth, K. (1995). The effects of a special computer network on caregivers of persons with Alzheimer's disease. *Nursing Research*, *44*, 166–172. doi:10.1097/00006199-199505000-00007

Brennan, P. F., Ripich, S., & Moore, S. M. (1991). The use of home-based computers to support persons living with AIDS/ARC. *Journal of Community Health Nursing*, *8*, 3–14. doi:10.1207/s15327655jchn0801_1

Buchholz, E. S., & Catton, R. (1999). Adolescents' perceptions of aloneness and loneliness. *Adolescence*, *34*(133), 203.

Buchholz, E. S., & Chinlund, C. (1994). En route to a harmony of being: Viewing aloneness as a need in development and child analytic work. *Psychoanalytic Psychology*, *4*, 354–374.

Buchholz, E. S., & Tomasi, S. (1994). *Differentiating aloneness from loneliness: The alone state in theory and research* (unpublished manuscript).

Cobb, S. (1976). Social support as a moderator of life stress. *Psychosomatic Medicine*, *38*, 301–314.

Cohen, S., & Syme, L. (1985). *Social support and health*. Orlando, FL: Academic Press.

Donald, C. A., & Ware, J. E. (1984). The measurement of social support. In R. Greenley (Ed.), *Research in community and mental health* (Vol. 4, pp. 325-370). Greenwich, CT: JAI Press.

Donohew, L., Finn, S., & Christ, W. G. (1988). The nature of news' revisited: The roles of affect, schemas, and cognition. In L. Donohew, H. E. Sypher, & E. T. Higgins (Eds.), *Communication, social cognition, and affect* (pp. 195-218). Hillsdale, NJ: Lawrence Erlbaum.

Ellis, H. C., & Moore, B. A. (1999). Mood and memory. In T. Dalgleish & M. J. Power (Eds.), *Handbook of cognition and emotion* (pp. 193-210). Chichester, UK: Wiley.

Erikson, E. (1968). *Identity: Youth and crisis*. New York: Norton.

Forgas, J. P., & Bower, G. H. (1987). Mood effects on person-perception judgments. *Journal of Personality and Social Psychology*, *53*, 53–60. doi:10.1037/0022-3514.53.1.53

Galanaki, E. (2004). Are children able to distinguish among the concepts of aloneness, loneliness, and solitude? *International Journal of Behavioral Development*, *28*(5), 435–443. doi:10.1080/01650250444000153

Galanaki, E. (2005). solitude in the school: a neglected facet of children's development and education. *Childhood Education*, *81*(3), 128–133.

Gallienne, R. L., Moore, S. M., & Brennan, P. F. (1993). Alzheimer's caregivers: Psychosocial support via computer networks. *Journal of Gerontological Nursing*, *19*, 15–22.

Garstka, T. A., Branscombe, N. R., & Hummert, M. L. (1997). *Age group identification across the life span* (unpublished manuscript).

Griffin, M. (2001). The phenomenology of the alone condition: More evidence for the role of aloneness in social facilitation. *The Journal of Psychology*, *135*(1), 125–128.

Griffin, M., & Kent, M. V. (1998). The role of aloneness in social facilitation. *The Journal of Social Psychology*, *138*(5), 667–669.

Hall, G. S. (1905). *Adolescence*. New York: Appleton and Co.

Harwood, J. (1999). Age identification, social identity gratifications, and television viewing. *Journal of Broadcasting & Electronic Media, 43*, 123–136.

Harwood, J. (1999). Age identity and television viewing preferences. *Communication Reports, 12*(2), 85.

Hlebec, V., Manfreda, K. L., & Vehovar, V. (2006). The social support networks of Internet users. *New Media & Society, 8*(1), 9–32. doi:10.1177/1461444806058166

Hoffer, C., & Cantor, J. (1991). Perceiving and responding to mass media characters. In J. Bryant & D. Zillmann (Eds.), *Responding to the screen: Reception and reaction processes* (pp. 63-102). Hillsdale, NJ: Erlbaum Associates.

House, J. S. (1986). Social support and the quality and quantity of life. In F. M. Andrew (Ed.), *Research on the quality of life*. Ann Arbor, MI: Survey Research Center, Institute for Social Research, University of Michigan.

Houston, T. K., Cooper, S., & Ford, D. E. (2002). Internet support groups for depression: A 1-year prospective cohort study. *The American Journal of Psychiatry, 159*(12), 2062–2068. doi:10.1176/appi.ajp.159.12.2062

Kahn, R. L., & Antonucci, T. C. (1980). Convoys over the life course: Attachment, roles and social support. In P. B. Baltes & O. Brim (Eds.), *Lifespan development and behavior* (Vol. 3). Boston: Lexington Press.

Kavanagh, A. L., & Patterson, S. J. (2001). The impact of community computer networks on social capital and community involvement. *The American Behavioral Scientist, 45*(3), 496–510. doi:10.1177/00027640121957312

Knobloch, S. (2003). Mood adjustment via mass communication. *The Journal of Communication, 53*(2), 233–150. doi:10.1111/j.1460-2466.2003.tb02588.x

Knobloch, S., & Zillmann, D. (2002). Mood management via the digital jukebox. *The Journal of Communication, 52*, 351–366. doi:10.1111/j.1460-2466.2002.tb02549.x

Kraut, R., Patterson, M., Lundmark, V., Kiesler, S., Mukopadhyay, T., & Scherlis, W. (1998). Internet paradox: A social technology that reduces social involvement and psychological well-being? *The American Psychologist, 53*, 1017–1031. doi:10.1037/0003-066X.53.9.1017

LaRose, R., Mastro, D., & Eastin, M. S. (2001). Understanding Internet usage: A social-cognitive approach to uses and gratifications. *Social Science Computer Review, 19*(4), 395–414. doi:10.1177/089443930101900401

Larson, R. W. (1990). The solitary side of life: An examination of the time people spend alone from childhood to old age. *Developmental Review, 10*, 155–183. doi:10.1016/0273-2297(90)90008-R

Larson, R. W. (1997). The mergence of solitude as a constructive domain of experience in early adolescence. *Child Development, 68*, 80–93. doi:10.2307/1131927

Leung, L. (2001). College student motives for chatting on "ICQ." . *New Media & Society, 3*(4), 483–500. doi:10.1177/14614440122226209

Leung, L. (2003). Impacts of Net-generation attributes, seductive properties of the Internet, and gratifications-obtained on Internet use. *Telematics and Informatics, 20*(2), 107–129. doi:10.1016/S0736-5853(02)00019-9

Leung, L., & Lee, P. S. N. (2005). Multiple determinants of life quality: The roles of Internet activities, use of new media, social support, and leisure activities. *Telematics and Informatics, 22*(3), 161–180. doi:10.1016/j.tele.2004.04.003

Lin, M., Hummert, M. L., & Harwood, J. (2004). Representation of age identities in on-line discourse. *Journal of Aging Studies, 18*(3), 261. doi:10.1016/j.jaging.2004.03.006

McCann, R. M., Kellermann, K., Giles, H., Gallois, C., & Viladot, M. A. (2004). Cultural and gender influences on age identification. *Communication Studies, 55*(1), 88.

Memling, M., & Buchholz, E. S. (1994). *Psychoanalytic reflections on the need for aloneness in children's literature* (unpublished manuscript).

Moustakas, C. E. (1989). *Loneliness.* New York: Prentice Hall.

Papacharissi, Z., & Rubin, A. M. (2000). Predictors of Internet use. *Journal of Broadcasting & Electronic Media, 44*(2), 175–196. doi:10.1207/s15506878jobem4402_2

Pierce, L. L., Wilkinson, L. K., & Anderson, J. (2003). Analysis of the concept of aloneness as applied to older women being treated for depression. *Journal of Gerontological Nursing, 29*(7), 20.

Raacke, J., & Bonds-Raacke, J. (2008). MySpace and facebook: Applying the uses and gratifications theory to exploring friend-networking sites. *Cyberpsychology & Behavior, 11*(2), 169–174. doi:10.1089/cpb.2007.0056

Rhodes, J. E., & Jason, L. A. (1990). A social stress of substance abuse. *Journal of Consulting and Clinical Psychology, 58*, 395–401. doi:10.1037/0022-006X.58.4.395

Rosengren, K. E., & Windahl, S. (1989). *Media matters: TV use in childhood and adolescence.* Norwood, NJ: Ablex.

Sherbourne, C. D., & Stewart, A. (1991). The MOS social support survey. *Social Science & Medicine, 32*, 705–714. doi:10.1016/0277-9536(91)90150-B

Stafford, T. F., & Gonier, D. (2004). What Americans like about being online. *Communications of the ACM, 47*(11), 107–112. doi:10.1145/1029496.1029502

Storr, A. (1988). *Solitude: A return to the self.* New York: The Free Press.

Westerhof, G. J., & Barrett, A. E. (2005). Age identity and subjective well-being: A comparison of the United States and Germany. *Journal of Gerontology, 60B*(3), S129.

Winnicott, D. W. (1965). *The maturational processes and the facilitating environment: Studies in the theory of emotional development.* New York: International University Process.

Wright, K. (2000). Computer-mediated social support, older adults, and coping. *The Journal of Communication, 50*(3), 100–118. doi:10.1111/j.1460-2466.2000.tb02855.x

Zillmann, D. (1982). Television viewing and arousal. In D. Pearl, L. Bouthilet, & J. Lazar (Eds.), *Television and behavior: Ten years of scientific progress and implications for the eighties (Vol. 2): Technical reviews* (pp. 53-67). Washington, DC: Government Printing Office.

Zillmann, D. (1985). The experimental exploration of gratifications from media entertainment. In K. E. Rosengren, et al. (Eds.), *Media gratifications research: Current perspectives.* Newbury Park, CA: Sage.

Zillmann, D. (1988a). Mood management through communication choices. *The American Behavioral Scientist, 31*, 327–340. doi:10.1177/000276488031003005

Zillmann, D. (1988b). Mood management: Using entertainment to full advantage. In L. Donohew, H. E. Sypher, & E. T. Higgins (Eds.), *Communication social cognition, and effect* (pp. 147-171). Hillsdale, NJ: Lawrence Erlbaum.

Zillmann, D., Schweitzer, J. J., & Mundorf, N. (1994). Menstrual cycle variation of women's interest in erotica. *Archives of Sexual Behavior, 23*, 579–597. doi:10.1007/BF01541499

Chapter 9
Fear for Online Adolescents:
Isolation, Contagion, and Sexual Solicitation

Myron Orleans
California State University at Fullerton, USA

ABSTRACT

The research literature regarding fears associated with online activities of adolescents was reviewed and assessed in relation to earlier research reported by the author. The original qualitative study focused on the interactions between the social networks of young adolescents and their computer usage. Particular attention was devoted to determining whether heavy computer use tended to isolate adolescent users. The findings challenged the common attributions of prevalent danger, that heavy youthful computer users would experience social isolation. That earlier research led to further questioning of the potential harm of computer use in relation to contagion effects and alarms raised regarding sexual solicitation via the Internet. Recent literature was examined to assess whether danger warnings have been magnified, distorted, or manipulated for ideological purposes. Contrary to popular considerations, the interpersonal lives and computer activities of early adolescents reciprocally reinforced patterns of behavior that lowered the likelihood of risk behaviors to a significantly greater degree than did direct parental involvement. Recommendations to responsible adults were offered to re-focus energies and efforts in directions that would support appropriate computer use and promote pro-social behaviors of online adolescents.

INTRODUCTION

Fear as a distinctive constructed social phenomenon has recently been the subject of not only of socio-psychological consideration but of public attention (Altheide, 2002; Glassner, 2000; Furedi, 2006; Stearns, 2006). As social structures and technologies have become more complex, offering more alternative sources of communication, fear has been directed toward the very avenues of access, particularly the Internet. Combined with persistent fears regarding youthful experimentation

DOI: 10.4018/978-1-60566-926-7.ch009

with all sorts of means of interaction, we have a substantial focal point of public concern. This paper addresses certain common perceptions and attributions regarding the presumed damaging effects of Internet communication on the lives of adolescents. Our focus here is on examining the consequences of perceived risk behaviors of adolescents engaged in online environments. The attributions of isolation, contagion and sexual solicitation as possible outcomes of online interaction will be explored.

The emergence of distinctive online cognitive environments for adolescents has posed significant challenges to many parents and adult guardians whose non-digital orientation opens up profound questions of intergenerational distancing, loss of trust, and, mainly, fear of youth's degradation. Adult anxiety regarding youth social isolation as a result of excessive online activity reflects a linear mode of thought along with a limited realist notion of the meaning of sociality. In previous research, this writer presented qualitative data suggesting that under certain conditions, actual socialization of youth was not negatively impacted by virtual computer activity (Orleans & Laney, 2000). A counter-intuitive finding indicated that lesser parental involvement with online activity was associated with higher levels of pro-social interaction in both online and face-to-face environments. Since this issue has remained a public concern (Gross, 2004; Mazalin & Moore, 2004; Sanders, Field, Diego, & Kaplan, 2000), further review of this issue is most certainly warranted and will presented here.

Further deepening the concerns of parents and professionals have been the features made possible through the advent of Web 2.0. This phenomenon refers to new ways of using the Internet to promote the formation of communities, collaborative environments, networks, file sharing sites, as well as wikis and blogs that have become commonplace in recent years. Myspace, Youtube, Facebook and Twitter are among the more popular social networking sites that are collectively and continually built with substantial involvement of adolescents. The participatory nature of such sites may exacerbate fears of some parents, however carefully these sites may be scrutinized.

Recent research on social networking sites has found, for example, that despite parental concern, teens generally responded "to negative online events" in ways that could be characterized as "healthy" (Rosen & Carrier, 2008). Additionally, authoritative parenting was found to predict the lowest frequency of negative behaviors. Other research suggests that personal disclosures are not as frequent as some parents may assume and that adolescent use of Myspace is most frequently responsible and reasonable (Hinduja & Patchin, 2008). Valkenburg, Jochen and Schouten (2006) found that peer interaction on friendship networking sites increased the range of social relationships with effects on self-esteem related to the quality of feedback received.

Fear of contagion through online interaction expresses the dread that young people will be exposed to and persuaded by negative, corruptive sorts of influences. Fear of exposure to and obsession with inappropriate sexual material and communication, to crude, violent imagery, to recipes for anti-social actions such as homicide or suicide, drug use, etc., to extreme cultic ideologies, to all sorts of commonly despised possibilities, foment in the minds of many parents. Thus, fear of adolescent isolation is contrasted with fears of the very wrong kinds of social influences experienced in online environments (Mitchell, Finkelhor, & Becker-Blease, 2007; Whitlock, 2006). Studies call for parental awareness of the dangers posed to address such issues without excessive hyperbole (Becker, El-Faddagh, Berson & Berson, 2005; Schmidt, 2004; Bross, 2005; Wolak, Finkelhor, Mitchell, & Ybarra, 2008).

While isolation and contagion fears reflect the duality of adult orientations toward online adolescent interpersonal experiences and subjective orientations, heightened concern regarding sexual solicitation and subsequent abductions of youth reflect fears of potentially devastating actions. Adult solicitation of youth through online communication is commonly presumed to be a reality, a lurking danger, and is viewed with the greatest concern (Wolak et al., 2008). Solicitation and then abduction is presumed to be a reality, with supposed documented cases indicating a potential to occur in the absence of responsible adult supervision. Youth runaways are frequently considered to have been influenced in their conduct by online solicitation, sometimes prepared through contagion. Solicitation may be thought of more as a direct person to person communication act, or more specifically, adult to adolescent process, while contagion is more of a collective process related to virtual assemblages in chatrooms and the like. Research reveals that reports of overall sexual solicitations is declining possibly due to law enforcement efforts as well as educational efforts aimed at white affluent youth while programs to improve awareness among minority youth has lagged (Mitchell et al., 2007).

While any imagined threat may have instances of enactment, the discussion of such possibilities rarely examine how this fear itself may affect attitudes, actions and interactions of youth, their parents, and others. Cautions, admonitions, preventions, and treatments, all play a role in the process of fear induction and propagation, and, in effect, magnify their consequences. This paper explores the role of fears in relation to adult involvement with online adolescents. Some proposals are offered regarding the management of fear through a balanced approach which takes into account actual dangers while reconsidering appropriate and productive adult responses to adolescent online activity.

FOUNDATIONS OF FEAR

The simple explanation for fear-mongering regarding youth Internet activity is that such concern sells. Sensationalism garners attention, sells space,

markets therapeutic services, promotes advocacy groups and associations, builds demand for reactive software, justifies organizations, and supports political, religious and ideological agendas. Such sites as www.loveourchildrenusa.org/, www.simpletoremember.com/vitals/dangers-of-the-internet.htm, www.protectkids.com/dangers/, www.gov.il/FirstGov/TopNavEng/EngSubjects/SafeSurfingEng/ParentsEng, www.webmd.com parenting/features/4-dangers-internet, www.iusb.edu/~sbit/pdf/dangerous-internet.pdf, and so forth have fueled the issue.

Perhaps at a somewhat deeper level, fear sustains the adult need to control the range and experiences of the young. This need to control may be rooted in a sense that youth will stray into some unknown sectors of meaning, invent alternative discourses, or engage with significances that are incomprehensible to adults. While the sources may be speculated upon, genuinely felt fear and anxiety seem to frame general adult, and specifically, parental perceptions of the online world-building actions of youth.

Popular and scholarly discussion of children and computers has generally lauded the educational benefits of home computers for children (Bross, 2005; Schall & Skeele, 1995; Williams, 1994). Large and growing proportions of youth in the United States have and will have regular access to a home computer or notebook, text messaging, Blackberry capabilities, and while usage varies, parents have long expected that their children need to use and will use a computer on a regular basis (Green, 1996).

At the same time, however, concern has been expressed regarding the possible isolating effects of computer communication on children (Gross, 2004; Mazalin & Moore, 2004, Sanders et al., 2000). Consideration of the presumed "nonsocial" nature of computers has led some to conclude that regardless of instrumental benefits, excessive preoccupation with computers may pose a danger to adults as well as to children (Kupfer, 1995; Stoeltje, 1996).

Serious concerns have also been raised about the contagion effects of high levels of Internet involvement. Young people may be exposed to all sorts of anti-social recipes for conduct including elaborated means of expressing violence toward others, but more pervasively, self-destructive acts such as purging, binging, mutilation, and ultimately suicide (Winkel, Groen, & Petermann, 2005). Additionally, fears regarding hate sites, sexual perversions, extreme behaviors, high-risk activities, drug use, and much more are thought to be purveyed via the Internet to corrupt youth. Particular types of young adults who exhibit self-harming traits, must be addressed distinctively in relation to online activities as they pose specific risks and vulnerabilities (Mitchell & Ybarra, 2007).

Much attention has been devoted to Internet-mediated sexual solicitation of youth by older predators (Berson & Berson, 2005; Padilla-Walker, 2006). Seduction into aberrant lifestyles and orientations are considered more feasible with the advent of the compelling technologies associated with the Internet. Deception and manipulation can be easily practiced via the Internet, where alternation of self and anonymity are the hallmarks of direct communication.

Responsible parental vigilance and negotiated regulation is promoted as the means through which youth can be regulated in online environments (Livingstone, 2005). Yet, it is inevitable that young people can hide their computer activities from their elders and excessive vigilance further divides generations diminishing trust and autonomy while implicitly emotionalizing leanings toward distanced, suspicion-generating relationships. Thus, excessive parental concern may prove counter-productive under some conditions.

Children's use of computers firmly affects their personal lives, family relationships and peer adjustment. Since computers constitute a significant and growing proportion of children's lives (Welch, 1995), it is not surprising that concerns have addressed the possibility that children will experience a diminution of social relationships, be exposed to malevolent interests, and place themselves in jeopardy. Fears have been frequently and even vociferously expressed that children's physical, personal and social development will be impaired by excessive computer usage (Dorman, 1997; Miller, 1993.)

Fear of the effects of digital technology is not new, nor has it escaped the attention of researchers (Suratt, 2006; Talbott, 1995; Turkle, 1995). Media critics have frequently proclaimed that television, music, video games, as well as computer games, damage children, diminish their social interaction, and place them at greater risk of subjection to anti-social influence (Freeman, 1997; Smith, 1995). Debates rage as to the reality of Internet "addition" (Collins, 2007; Suratt, 2006). Personal computers may have now taken over television's prominent position as the newest, most feared piece of technology in the home (Coffey & Horst, 1997). The anxiety felt by some adults has not apparently impacted the teenagers themselves who seem to continue to view the Internet favorably (Clemmitt, 2006).

Parental dread of children's computer misuse is further enhanced by exaggerated media depictions. For example, popular movies, such as far back as "Hackers" (Wickstrom, 1996), and as recently as "Live Free or Die Hard" (Neman, 2007) portrayed adolescents as cyberjunkies who compromise banking procedures, change television programming, twist government policies, foil the bad guys, save the world, but who do not participate in sports and barely associate with anyone outside their computer-related culture including their families. Magazines and newspapers have also contributed to the environment of anxiety with articles such as "Child molesters on the internet," (Trebilcock, 1997), "Snared by the net," (Rogers, Sandler, Duffy, Salcines, & Duignan-Cabrera, 1997), "Internet dangers (How to protect our children)," (Rubenstein, 1996), "Are we creating Internet introverts? Culture: Our children need to be in the real world," (Shulman, 1996), and more recently, "Babes in the Woods" (Flanagan, 2007). An assumption behind these critiques of young people's computer use is that a limited reservoir of time and energy is available to devote either to social or to non-social technological involvements. Zero sum thinking posits that technological activities necessarily reduce sociation, substitute ersatz experiences that are inherently frustrating because they waste time, energy, and sensibility, misdirect interests, focus on falsehoods instead of substance and substitute unrealities for social life and physical activity. This approach fears the loss of the self and the social to the technology (Kupfer, 1995; Stoeltje, 1996).

INTERNET BENEFITS

Alternative conceptualizations suggest that computers may actually promote certain kinds of sociations and advance pro-social and educational orientations (Aslanidou, and Menexes, 2008); Wellman, Salaff, & Dimitrova, 1996). Technology, in this view, may create occasions for social interaction and serve as topics of discourse. Rather than posit computer technology and social interaction as mutually exclusive options, this approach poses the possibility of reciprocal and reflexive interplay between the two phenomena (Leeds-Hurwitz, 1995; Pearce, 1994). Computer use may be thus thought of as a possible foundation for social interaction as well as its product. Explorations of virtual worlds convey lessons for life and promote learning of variable sorts. Youth gain sophistication, it is argued, by trial and error in the online environment. They experience autonomy and a form of self-responsibility through their navigations. Most significantly, it has been suggested that excessive fear of the Internet may cancel some of the substantial benefits offered (Tynes, 2007).

Earlier research reported a set of scenarios describing adolescent computer users under a variety of conditions that resulted in different kinds of youthful associations (Orleans & Laney, 2000). Young computer users were intensively observed in the naturalistic settings of their home environments to grasp the spontaneously expressed social meanings of their computing behavior. A phenomenological approach (Orleans, 1991) was used to describe and analyze the patterned computer-related actions and interactional world of the subjects. This kind of data did not permit empirical generalizations as to the proportion of children whose social life is enhanced vs. the proportion whose social life is diminished by computer use. Rather this qualitative data permitted the detailed description of the lived experience of the subjects under varying conditions. These conditions included parental involvement, orientations to computers, gender, degree of peer integration, computer sophistication as well as other variables.

Parents were likely to be important insofar as they configure their child's computer and establish parameters for use. Computational power and software capabilities were most frequently parental prerogatives related to their financial situation and to their purposes in providing the child with computer access. It was considered that a curvilinear relationship in which extremely low and high levels of parental involvement either precluded adolescent sociation or rendered it unlikely. Moderate amounts of parental consultation along with encouragement toward autonomy were predicted as the greatest likelihood of sociation connected with computer use.

A different orientation to computer use was hypothesized as likely to be associated with the quality and frequency of social interaction of early adolescents. Thus, some young adolescents were thought to see their computers as tools of personal expression and self-empowerment (Orleans & Walters, 1996). It was thought that they use the computer to expand interests, obtain information, improve academic performance, and to demonstrate mastery of a complex technology before family and peers. It was conjectured that the functional use of the child's personal computer in this scenario might impel him or her to try new computer activities, learn programming, resolve problems, and continuously upgrade capabilities. While ego enhancement might have driven some to do it all on their own, it was thought more likely that regular consultations with experienced peers would help early adolescent computer users become aware of new software, programming approaches, and trouble-shooting techniques. Thus, it was suggested that sociation might be promoted to the extent that the desire to perfect one's personal computer motivated the user to seek sophisticated peer assistance.

Children likely spend a great deal of time directly playing games against their computer and apparently isolating themselves (Chiou, 2008). But gamers, especially adolescents, often get together to play computer games (Barnett, Vitaglione, Harper, & Quackenbush, 1997; Buchman & Funk, 1996; Funk & Buchman, 1996: Olson, Kutner, & Warner, 2008). Increasingly, gamers were and are networked either in actual networks or via digital links. Online services are offering gamers opportunities to play via their proprietary services or at Internet sites. Game installations, including consultations providing technical support, sharing, shortcuts, codes, achievements and ways of improving scores, may promote sociation. Thus, to the extent that gaming implicates others, the surround of game playing poses a possibility of social interaction.

While the online world may appear to some as a substitute for interpersonal communication, a virtual sociality that provides only a false sense of connection, it affords many opportunities for children to genuinely interact. Young adolescents may discuss the benefits of e-mailing, blogging, networking, chatting, Web surfing, and the like. They can convince their own and peer's parents to allow online access, help each other to get online, share favorite sites, compare different plugins, discuss technical matters, and offer support for each other's online ventures. They may gather in groups to share online access and certainly do so through social networking sites. Additionally, some children may find it more fun to go online together rather than individually and do both alternatively. Thus, virtual social worlds and actual sociality can reciprocally co-exist even though time spent on the Internet may displace social activities (Nie, Hillygus & Erbring, 2002).

Researchers studying the impact of computer use on socialization initially found that online activity diminished the quantity of offline interaction (Kraut, Patterson, Lundmark, Kiesler, Mukopadhyay, & Scherlis, 1998). Subsequent research found that the negative effects on offline sociality declined with time but suggested that multiple if weaker online ties replaced stronger offline connections (Kraut, Kiesler, Boneva, Cummings, Helgeson & Crawford, 2002). The impact of computer usage on family boundaries was measured by Mesch (2006) who found that family cohesion was negatively associated when time on the Internet was spent for non-knowledge gathering social purposes but was enhanced in the use of the Internet for learning. Further, it was suggested that family-based Internet activities could enhance family cohesion when activities were focused on collective processes. Overall, it may reasonably be concluded that moderate, balanced use of the Internet by adolescents does not severely negatively affect offline social interaction.

The characteristics of early adolescent gender-based groups impact sociation experiences (Lever, 1978; Fine, 1988). Research on male groups suggests that activities and tasks constitute the prime focus of interactions. Communication regarding computers would seem to meet the standards exemplified in male groupings. There may well be an affinity between male sociation patterns and interaction concerning computers (D'Amico, Baron, & Sissons, 1995; Kinnear, 1995; Whitley, 1997). Since female play groups have been found to be less complex and more oriented toward socializing itself rather than toward activities or tasks (Lever, 1978), it may be somewhat less likely for female adolescents to use computer issues as a resource for sociation. However, the advent of Facebook, YouTube, blogging, etc., likely diminishes any gender differences. However, females report higher rates of online sexual solicitation (Mitchell, Wolak, & Finkelhor, 2008). Chatroom users were more likely to be persons categorized as "troubled" and were more vulnerable than others, but this was not associated with encountering problems online (Beebe, Asche, Harrison, & Quinlan, 2004). In any case, computer involvement might prove less likely to produce isolation among young females because of their direct orientation toward sociability. Thus, gender may impact computer-related sociation of early adolescents in four ways: 1) isolate males who are not involved in computer support social groupings; 2) integrate males who use computer-related communications as grounds for sociation; 3) somewhat reduce female sociation by promoting individual computer activities; 4) somewhat promote female sociation if they seek social support for their computer activities.

PARENTAL INVOLVEMENT

Although the previous study (Orleans & Laney, 2000) had hypothesized that adolescent computer users would require some parental assistance, the computer competence of all but the youngest users tended to obviate the need for intrusive involvement. Indeed, the activation of the subjects' social networks depended upon the gaps produced by their parents' relative disinclination to impose their frames upon the computer actions of their children. Specifically, it was determined that once adults had set up the computer basics and receded, even non-sophisticated children could move to a level of competence using their siblings and peers as primary resources.

In most instances observed, the parameters for computer use set by the parents encouraged family interaction, but also allowed for some degree of isolation. However, parental enmeshment in child-

hood and early adolescent computer use tended to preclude the computer serving as a resource in developing either a stronger family bond or friendship network. Thus, a fearful, authoritarian parent would be more likely to dissuade the child from engaging with the computer and peers productively.

Once children established themselves as being fully in charge of their computing, they were able to master the elements for their own purposes, principally online access, and conducted their activities with apparent self-responsibility. Groups of friends were observed together getting online to explore resources and gain the experiences they wanted in the absence of adults, self-regulating, collectively monitoring and alerting each other to possible problems.

In these limited instances of parental involvement in their children's computer use, it became apparent that the greater the autonomy the child was given, the more pro-social was his or her experience. Indeed, parental guidance rooted in their fear concerns seemed to dampen children's sociation with peers. Given leeway, the young computer users seemed to be stimulated to seek support from and involvement with their peers and avoided the feared pitfalls.

GROUP ORIENTATIONS

The previous research (Orleans & Laney, 2000) found that group solidarity and boundary definitions were established through the use of computer embedded language among peers in the absence of adults. Terms brought into the conversation from computer experience served to deepen the level of meaning and served to protect the subjects from predatory practice.

The research found that the reflexive, self-constituting process of sociation while computing allowed subjects to develop a protective sophistication. The subjects created a micro-social world which was itself a product of their computer activities and provided the context within which these computer activities occurred. Thus, the social dimension of computing was found to be inextricably bound to the computing acts themselves tying the youngsters into a defensive collectivity that could effectively ward off external threats. Interestingly, it was additionally found that successfully conducted adolescent computer activity led to increased self-confidence, character development, family discussion, and solidification of parent-child relationships in the absence of the fear orientation.

As for frequently dreaded computer games (Olson et al., 2008), the research found that gaming served not only as a focus of social activity, but as a topic of discourse and as a frame through which to experience ordinary communication. Gaming formed the backdrop for their talk while the subjective experience of it constituted the theme of the conversation. They engaged in heated and fruitful discourse, experiencing active communication that may have significant socialization benefit for all involved.

Young adolescents played computer games and experience social relationships under diverse social conditions. The research demonstrated a range of consequences of game playing including topical talk, framing, mediating, perspective interchange, role sharing, self-organization, reconstructed logics, strategic discourse, impression management and the like. When the subjects' mundane computer activities were viewed as sophisticated collective accomplishments, the socialization gain derived from these activities can be substantial and obviated feared consequences of isolation and compulsive participation. A rewards strategy using the notion that less rewards produces more attitude change has been proposed to address online compulsive gaming participation, i.e., gaming addiction, that holds great promise (Chiou, 2008). In experimental research, gamers were given lower levels of rewards under the condition of the perception of personal freedom of choice producing attitude change and disengagement from online

gaming. It is not unreasonable to suggest that focusing on the losses incurred in terms of social isolation effects experienced through gaming addiction might be used as an effective intervention tool to promote gaming disengagement.

A huge proportion of male computer activity was spent online. This time was by no means socially isolated time. Online communication was usually not a substitute for interpersonal communication, rather both often occurred simultaneously. Perhaps male gaming pursuits would not gain the endorsement of adults, but the proficiency with which boys create communities of interests suggests that collaborative online activities emerge readily among male adolescents (Kutner, Olson, Warner, & Hertzog, 2008).

Even when not using a computer for online activities, adolescents were observed in the earlier study (Orleans & Laney, 2000) to be using online access as a topic of conversation. They demonstrated the fluidity of youthful activities indicating the inseparability of online communication and face-to-face communication. Instead of isolating youth rendering them more vulnerable to predatory practice, it was found that virtual and real communications reflexively construct each other. Thus, adolescents bring their everyday real world experience to bear upon their online virtual communication providing a kind of protective shield. They reflexively integrate their online life into their ordinary talk spontaneously regulating online participation.

Gender

Until recently, far more of the research in this area has focused on male rather than on female adolescent computer use. Previous research (Orleans & Laney, 2000) showed that while females were comfortable with computers, it was comparatively rare to find them sharing computer interests and activities. Most of the female subjects performed their computer actions alone and computers did not discernibly enter into their conversations.

When communicating in relation to computers, females focused on the substance rather than on the technology which permitted broad exploration of different ways of relating.

Another gender differential in computer use that was observed was that girls rarely played music or had the television turned on while on the computer. The girls also used their computers more for homework than did the boys, who were more likely to play computer games. With exceptions, the girls were more likely to be serious about using the computer. They were more focused on using the computer for particular purposes and their demeanor while using was more somber than the boys. However comfortable the girls appeared with the computer, it occupied a marginal position in their world, rarely substituting for social contact but sometimes provoking sociation. The girls, however, did not seem to legitimate computer use as a social tool.

Research has shown that girls who have more conflicted relationships with parents and were more highly troubled were more likely to form closer online relationships than were other girls (Wolak, Mitchell & Finkhor, 2003). While all youth with poor parental communication and troubled relationships are more likely to be at-risk online than less troubled peers, it can be postulated that Internet usage might make some girls even more vulnerable than boys to contagion on such matters as suicide, eating disorders, sexual promiscuity, and crime since online relationship-formation may have greater personal significance in the absence of supportive familial environments.

For most of the girls who were observed in the previous study, substituting virtual for actual relationships would contradict their taken-for-granted way of doing their normal lives (Berger and Luckmann, 1966). That is, for them the ordinary social world was most salient. The computer may have been viewed as a useful tool, a transitional substitute for social bonding, but not as the paramount reality taking precedence over other aspects of one's social life (Furger, 1998).

Since girl culture emphasized direct interpersonal contact and conversation regarding purely human phenomena, engagement with the computer as a prime focus of communication was not performable (D'Amico et al, 1995; Kinnear, 1995; Whitley, 1997). Girls were more likely to do their computer work without compromising their sociality. The research did not show substantial diminution of social relations among active, apparently non-troubled computer-using females.

Popular and scholarly discussion of sexually-oriented material and seductive possibilities of Internet sites have spurred a great deal of concern, particularly focused on young females (Berson & Berson, 2005; Padilla-Walker, 2006). While some type of parental response is warranted, excessive parental focus following an authoritarian pattern could be counter-productive by unintentionally provoking curiosity and even exploration. The risk factor, although present, is of such a statistically insignificant likelihood, that in the absence of suspicious actions many perceived threats may be best left to general discussion rather than lead to intense concern. Supportive conversation and authoritative guidance by parents may be a more productive approach to effective parenting.

Rosen and Carrier (2008) suggest that parental fears of online threats were not matched either by the actual prevalence found in their research or by parental actions with regard to limit setting and monitoring practices. They suggest that open negotiation with adolescents to establish consensual parameters to online activity would have the most positive results. Eastin. Greenberg and Hofschire (2006) propose that evaluative and factual discussions of online communication are necessary to mediate Internet use. Further, Lee and Chae (2007) in their study of Korean families found that parental suggestions of Internet sites and co-use predicted higher levels of children's online education activity. On the other hand, they found that restrictive approaches did not affect children's Internet use.

Of relatively common interest among young females is celebrity idolization using the Internet and other means of inquiry (Engel & Kasser, 2005). Google searches for celebrities are a major Internet activity extending and deepening this preoccupation. While celebrity stalking is frequently discussed, it is rarely enacted and would appear to not be an issue of note for the vast majority of young females. Idolization is more of a para-social process without substantial negative consequence that most frequently plays a role in adolescent female socialization.

Systematic research has failed to support the publicity devoted to online predators who seduce naïve children using deceit and coercion (Wolak et al., 2008). However, Internet sex crime does occur more frequently as a matter of statutory rape where young adult offenders encounter and entice underage adolescents into relationships. It is indeed misleading to forewarn adolescents about the adult predator while ignoring this more typical pattern of seduction. The actual predators appear more acceptable to the young adolescent and engage with them in ways that are more apparently acceptable. Parents are urged to take into account these realities when addressing the romantic, sexual interests of their adolescents. The problems and hazards of engaging in relationships with adults who are only a few older should be explained while avoiding distorted stereotypes. Adolescents with higher risk factors, particularly victims of childhood sexual abuse are particularly vulnerable, likely requiring professional involvement. Factors predicting online victimization are explored more fully in Chapter 13 of this book.

Recommendations

Since this research did not find that computer use resulted in individual isolation and vulnerability, and in the absence of research that it does, it is recommended that the media abstain from emphasizing its dangers and threats to the common sensibility. Certainly, instilling fear and moral panic regarding young people's computer use is more likely to be profitable than would normal-izing discourse. However, to pathologize computer use without adequate justification does a serious disservice to our children and our future (Bross, 2005; Tynes, 2007). More directly, while parental anxieties cannot be fully alleviated by research and rational consideration, the focus of attention might be more effectively directed toward the particular areas of sensitivity to avoid diffusing the entire issue.

Adult anxiety regarding the damaging effects of online activity of adolescents suggested that the interactional networks that structure adolescent computer experience constrained rather than expanded risk-taking actions of adolescents. Since groups serve as a kind of protective shield for boys, actions to promote collectivized computer activities for girls may be warranted to provide some support.

A key recommendation derived from this study is to encourage the trend among female adolescents to further integrate actual and virtual interactions that support and expand interpersonal relations. While the girl-culture emphasis on the human dimension in social interaction is critically important, it might well include the use of computers and the cyber world as a topic of conversation and as a focus of activity. This would seem beneficial in terms of information development and educational activities, but also in terms of networking and collaborating. As adolescent females gain familiarity with the underlying technology they will be better prepared to anticipate and to innovate new designs and applications advancing their personal and, ultimately, their professional capabilities in the digital world.

How to engineer this is, of course, problematic, but games and computer activities that encourage social interaction will likely entice girls' participation (Corston and Colman 1996; Furger, 1998; Thomas, 1996; Vail, 1997). Social networking sites are definitely enticing greater female adolescent involvement than earlier forums for interaction. These sites such as Facebook and MySpace are expanding scope and options rapidly frequently drawing parents and other responsible adults into these activities on an online interactive basis. Further technological developments making greater graphic and creative participation available will enhance the quality of female integration of actual and virtual interactions.

Just as girls' athletic programs have developed substantially, perhaps in spite of culturally-rooted prejudices, and as girls are preparing to enter into many nonconventional occupations with many worthy adult female role models available, it is ever more apparent that adolescent females are increasingly motivated to approach computing as an ordinary, pleasant and productive feature of their social lives. As female online sociation has become commonplace, a major benefit of such female peer social networks and sites would possibly be to promote resistance to online contagions and solicitations while preparing for future technology-based endeavors.

Certainly, parents need to be aware of their children's computer activities. They need to be mindful, however, that their own excessive involvement may rob the children of their chance for discovery and peer socialization. Parents would be well advised to allow their children the opportunity to enjoy the computer without dread of its putative dangers while engaged in ongoing realistic discourses to mediate Internet experience. Children with adequate values socialization, normal peer relations and social support networks are unlikely to be vulnerable targets. Reasonable caveats and age appropriate limits established through open and reasonable discussion, along with wise selection of software, is likely to provide sufficient safeguards (Livingstone, 2007; Mitchell, Finklhor, & Wolak, 2005). While overall sexual solicitations seem to be declining, more serious and aggressive solicitations remain an issue requiring attention (Mitchell, Finkelhor, & Wolak, 2007). Programmatic approaches to improve regulatory capabilities of minority parents are needed. Parents ought to be reassured that the computer with Internet connection is essentially a benign,

productive device, which certainly can be misused, but is most likely to prove of significant benefit. Indeed, since computer and other informational technologies can promote family interaction, it is advised that families might focus more of their activities around computing and online activity (Kraut et al., 1996; Sun, 1995).

Similarly, the Internet should be best understood in terms of a virtual social world intersecting infinitely with actual social worlds. Our children are establishing their presence and communicating beyond their immediate social circles. They are discovering all sorts of representations of worlds within and beyond their familiarity, and hopefully, producing their own representations. Collective efforts of adolescents to participate on the Internet would seem to easily flow from their involvement. Adolescents are increasing self-aware of potential risks and take actions to protect themselves by limiting disclosures and other such deflecting strategies (Youn, 2005). Sharing and communicating interpersonally about the Internet, in general, is strongly advised, even if some pursuits may not be amenable to conventional tastes. In any case, the sparse verifiable examples of children lured away from home by online predators or atypical stories of children losing their souls to "cyberaddiction" should not dissuade parents and adults from supporting moderate and appropriate use of the Internet (Collins, 2007; Orleans, 1997; Suratt, 2006; Young, 1996).

Research has also shown that Internet use provides greater benefit for hearing-impaired adolescents (Barak & Sadovsky, 2008). Internet activity served to empower these youth and provided means for expanding range and intensity of social involvement. Such results suggest that the positive benefits far outweigh dangers for even the most potentially vulnerable young people. They used communication tools to overcome tendencies toward isolation achieving levels of well-being commensurate with non-impaired adolescents.

CONCLUSION

In sum, recommendations are offered which enhance awareness of the dimensions of online activity of youth that require attention. Computers and online access is deeply integrated into all aspects of contemporary life. Dystopic visions of a fragmented social world resulting from computerization have not materialized demonstrating the society's capacity to adapt. A more embracing research-based approach, starting with children, will facilitate the implementation of more effective resolutions of the social challenges posed by technological advances.

REFERENCES

Altheide, D. (2002). *Creating fear: News and the construction of crisis.* Chicago: Aldine.

Aslanidou, S., & Menexes, G. (2008). Youth and the Internet: Uses and practices in the home. *Computers & Education, 51*, 1375–1391. doi:10.1016/j.compedu.2007.12.003

Barak, A., & Sadovsky, Y. (2008). Internet use and personal empowerment of hearing-impaired adolescents. *Computers in Human Behavior, 24*, 1802–1815. doi:10.1016/j.chb.2008.02.007

Barnett, M. A., Vitaglione, G. D., Harper, K. K. G., & Quackenbush, S. W. (1997). Late adolescents' experiences with and attitudes toward videogames. *Journal of Applied Social Psychology, 27*(15), 1316–1334. doi:10.1111/j.1559-1816.1997.tb01808.x

Becker, K., EI-Faddagh, M., & Schmidt, M. H. (2004). Cybersuizid oder werther-effekt online: Suizidchatrooms und-foren im Internet. *Kindheit und Entwicklung, 13*(1), 14–25. doi:10.1026/0942-5403.13.1.14

Beebe, T. J., Asche, S. E., Harrison, P. A., & Quinlan, K. B. (2004). Heightened vulnerability and increased risk-taking among adolescent chat room users: Results from a statewide school survey. *The Journal of Adolescent Health, 35*, 116–123.

Berger, P., & Luckmann, T. (1966). *The social construction of reality: A treatise in the sociology of knowledge,* Garden City, NY: Doubleday.

Berson, I. R., & Berson, M. J. (2005). Challenging online behaviors of youth: Findings from a comparative analysis of young people in the United States and New Zealand. *Social Science Computer Review, 23*, 29–38. doi:10.1177/0894439304271532

Bross, D. C. (2005). Minimizing risks to children when they access the World Wide Web. *Child Abuse & Neglect, 29*, 749–752.

Buchman, D. D., & Funk, J. B. (1996). Video and computer games in the 90's: Children's time commitment and game preference. *Children Today, 24*(1), 12–15.

Chiou, W. B. (2008). Induced attitude change on online gaming among adolescents: An application of the less-leads-to-more effect. *Cyberpsychology & Behavior, 11*(2), 212–216. doi:10.1089/cpb.2007.0035

Clemmitt, M. (2006). Cyber socializing. *CQ Researcher, 16*(27), 625–648.

Coffey, S., & Stipp, H. (1997). The interactions between computer and television usage. *Journal of Advertising Research, 37*(2), 61–67.

Collins, L. H. (2007). A review of 'netaholism…' Another pseudodiagnosis. *PsycCRITIQUES, 52*(330), Article 3.

Corston, R., & Colman, A. M. (1996). Gender and social facilitation effects on computer competence and attitudes toward computers. *Journal of Educational Computing Research, 14*(2), 171–183.

D'Amico, M., Baron, L. J., & Sissons, M. E. (1995). Gender differences in attibutions about microcomputer learning in elementary school. *Sex Roles*, *33*(5-6), 353–385. doi:10.1007/BF01954574

Dorman, S. M. (1997). Video and computer games: Effect on children and implications for health education. *The Journal of School Health*, *67*(4), 133–138. doi:10.1111/j.1746-1561.1997.tb03432.x

Eastin, M. S., Greenberg, B. S., & Hofschire, L. (2006). Parenting the Internet. *The Journal of Communication*, *56*(3), 486–504. doi:10.1111/j.1460-2466.2006.00297.x

Engel, Y., & Kasser, T. (2005). Why do adolescent girls idolize male celebrities? *Journal of Adolescent Research*, *20*, 263–283. doi:10.1177/0743558404273117

Fine, G. A. (1988). Friends, impression management, and preadolescent behavior. In G. Handel (Ed.), *Childhood socialization*. New York: Aldine de Gruyter.

Freeman, M. (1997). Electronic media and how kids (don't) think. *Education Digest*, *63*(3), 22–27.

Funk, J. B., & Buchman, D. D. (1996). Playing violent video and computer games and adolescent self-concept. *The Journal of Communication*, *46*(2), 19–32. doi:10.1111/j.1460-2466.1996.tb01472.x

Furedi, F. (2006). *Culture of fear revisited: Risk-taking and the morality of low expectation*. New York: Continuum.

Furger, R. (1998). *Does Jane compute?: Preserving our daughters' place in the cyber revolution*. New York: Warner Books.

Glassner, B. (2000). *The culture of fear: Why Americans are afraid of the wrong things*. New York: Basic Books.

Green, K. C. (1996). The coming ubiquity of information technology. *Change*, *28*(2), 24–28.

Gross, E. F. (2004). Adolescent Internet use: What we expect, what teens report. *Journal of Applied Developmental Psychology*, *25*(6), 633–649. doi:10.1016/j.appdev.2004.09.005

Hinduja, S., & Patchin, J. W. (2008). Social networking and identity construction: Personal information of adolescents on the Internet: A quantitative content analysis of MySpace. *Journal of Adolescence*, *31*(1), 125–146. doi:10.1016/j.adolescence.2007.05.004

Kinnear, A. (1995). Introduction of micocomputers: A case study of patterns of use and children's perceptions. *Journal of Educational Computing Research*, *13*(1), 27–40. doi:10.2190/NA0H-1RV6-LFLU-23H0

Kraut, R., Kiesler, S., Boneva, B., Cummings, J., Helgeson, V., & Crawford, A. M. (2002). Internet paradox revisited. *The Journal of Social Issues*, *58*(1), 49–74. doi:10.1111/1540-4560.00248

Kraut, R., Patterson, M., Lundmark, V., Kiesler, S., Mukopadhyay, T., & Scherlis, W. (1998). Internet paradox: A social technology that reduces social involvement and psychological well-being? *The American Psychologist*, *53*, 1017–1031. doi:10.1037/0003-066X.53.9.1017

Kraut, R., Sherlis, W., Mukhopadhayay, T., Manning, J., & Kiesler, S. (1996). The HomeNet field trials of residential Internet services. *Communications of the Association for Computing Machinery. Inc.*, *39*(12), 55.

Kupfer, A. (1995). Alone together: Will being wired set us free?. *Fortune, 131*(Mar. 20), 94-96.

Kutner, L. A., Olson, C. K., Warner, D. E., & Hertzog, S. M. (2008). Parents' and sons' perspectives on video game play: A qualitative study. *Journal of Adolescent Research*, *23*, 76–96. doi:10.1177/0743558407310721

Lee, S. J., & Chae, Y. G. (2007). Children's Internet use in a family context: Influence on family relationships and parental mediation. *Cyberpsychology & Behavior*, *10*(5), 640–644. doi:10.1089/cpb.2007.9975

Leeds-Hurwitz, W. (1995). Introducing social approaches. In W. Leeds-Hurwitz (Ed.), *Social approaches to communication*. New York: The Guilford Press.

Lever, J. (1988). Sex differences in the complexity of children's play and games. In G. Handel (Ed.), *Childhood socialization*. New York: Aldine de Gruyter.

Livingstone, S. (2007). Strategies of parental regulation in the media-rich home. *Computers in Human Behavior*, *23*, 920–941. doi:10.1016/j.chb.2005.08.002

Mazalin, D., & Moore, S. (2004). Internet use, identity development and social anxiety among young adults. *Behaviour Change*, *21*(2), 90–102. doi:10.1375/bech.21.2.90.55425

Mesch, G. S. (2006). Family relations and the Internet: Exploring a family boundaries approach. *Journal of Family Communication*, *6*(2), 119–138. doi:10.1207/s15327698jfc0602_2

Miller, N. L. (1993). Are computers dangerous to children's health? *Education Digest*, *58*(5), 24.

Mitchell, K. J., Finkelhor, D., & Becker-Blease, K. A. (2007). Linking youth Internet and conventional problems: Findings from a clinical perspective. *Journal of Aggression, Maltreatment & Trauma*, *15*(2), 39–58. doi:10.1300/J146v15n02_03

Mitchell, K. J., Finkelhor, D., & Wolak, J. (2005). Protecting youth online: Family use of filtering and blocking software. *Child Abuse & Neglect*, *29*, 753–765.

Mitchell, K. J., Finkelhor, D., & Wolak, J. (2007). Youth Internet users at risk for the most serious online sexual solicitations. *American Journal of Preventive Medicine*, *32*(6), 532–537. doi:10.1016/j.amepre.2007.02.001

Mitchell, K. J., Wolak, J., & Finkelhor, D. (2007). Trends in youth reports of sexual solicitations, harassment and unwanted exposure to pornography on the Internet. *The Journal of Adolescent Health*, *40*, 116–126. doi:10.1016/j.jadohealth.2006.05.021

Mitchell, K. J., Wolak, J., & Finkelhor, D. (2008). Are blogs putting youth at risk for online sexual solicitation or harassment? *Child Abuse & Neglect*, *32*, 277–294. doi:10.1016/j.chiabu.2007.04.015

Mitchell, K. J., & Ybarra, M. L. (2007). Online behavior of youth who engage in self-harm provides clues for preventive intervention. *Preventive Medicine*, *45*, 392–396. doi:10.1016/j.ypmed.2007.05.008

Neman, D. (2007, June 18). Uneven 4th: 'Live Free or Die Hard' / Willis does a bang-up job, but film implodes at the end. *Richmond Times-Dispatch*, p. 15.

Nie, N. Hillygus. S. D., & Erbring, L. (2002). Internet use, interpersonal relations and sociability: A time diary study. In B. Wellman & C. Haythornthwaite (Eds.), *The Internet in everyday life*. Hoboken, NJ: Wiley-Blackwell.

Olson, C. K., Kutner, L. A., & Warner, D. E. (2008). The role of violent video game content in adolescent development: Boys' perspectives. *Journal of Adolescent Research*, *23*, 55–75. doi:10.1177/0743558407310713

Orleans, M. (1991). Phenomenological sociology. In H. Etzkowitz & R. M. Glassman (Eds.), *The renascence of sociological theory: Classical and contemporary*. Itasca, IL: F.E. Peacock Publishers.

Orleans, M. (1997). Caught in the Web: The phenomenon of cyberaddiction. In J. Behar (Ed.), *Sociological studies of telecommunications, computerization and cyberspace*. Oakdale, NY: Dowling College Press.

Orleans, M., & Laney, M. C. (2000). Children's use of computers in the home: Isolation or sociation? *Social Science Computer Review, 18*(1), 56–72. doi:10.1177/089443930001800104

Orleans, M., & Walters, G. (1996). Human-computer enmeshment: Identity diffusion through mastery. *Social Science Computer Review, 14*(2), 144–156. doi:10.1177/089443939601400202

Padilla-Walker, L. M. (2006). "Peers I can monitor, It's media that really worries me!": Parental cognitions as predictors of proactive parental strategy choice. *Journal of Adolescent Research, 21*, 56–82. doi:10.1177/0743558405282723

Pearce, W. B. (1994). *Interpersonal communication: Making social worlds*. New York: Harper-Collins.

Porter, P. B. (1993). Fostering collaborative word processing with writing disabled adolescents (Doctoral dissertation, University of Toronto, Canada). *Dissertation Abstracts International, 55-03A*, 0460.

Rogers, P., Sandler, B., Duffy, T., Salcines, M., & Duignan-Cabrera, A. (1997, August 11). Snared by the net: Lured to the Internet by fun and friends, some teens get caught in a web of trouble. *People*, 48.

Rosen, L. D., & Carrier, M. L. (2008). The association of parenting style and child age with parental limit setting and adolescent MySpace behavior. *Journal of Applied Developmental Psychology, 29*, 459–471. doi:10.1016/j.appdev.2008.07.005

Rossi, P. H. (1988). On sociological data. In N. J. Smelser (Ed.), *Handbook of sociology*. Newbury Park, CA: Sage Publications.

Rubenstein, C. M. (1996). Internet dangers. *Parents' Magazine (Bergenfield, N.J.), 71*(3), 145.

Sanders, C. E., Field, T. M., Diego, M., & Kaplan, M. (2000). The relationship of Internet use to depression and social isolation among adolescents. *Adolescence, 35*(138), 237–242.

Schall, P. L., & Skeele, R. (1995). Creating a home-school partnership for learning: Exploiting the home computer. *The Educational Forum, 59*(3), 244–249. doi:10.1080/00131729509336399

Shulman, M. (1996, May 9). Are we creating Internet introverts? Culture: Our children need to be in the real world. *Los Angeles Times*, p. 9.

Smith, J. (1955). *Understanding the media: A sociology of mass communication*. Creekskill, NJ: Hapmpton Press, Inc.

Stearns, P. N. (2006). *American fear: The causes and consequences of high anxiety*. New York: Routledge.

Stoeltje, M. (1996). Human costs in the computer age – commentary. *Journal of Systems Management, 47*(1), 57.

Sun, M. P. (1995). Effects of new media use on adolescents' family lives: Time use and relationships with family members in Taiwan (Doctoral dissertation, Ohio University). *Dissertation Abstracts International, 56-12A*, 4598.

Suratt, C. G. (2006). *The psychology of netaholics*. New York: Novinka Books.

Talbott, S. (1995). *The future does not compute*. Sebastopol, CA: O'Reilly and Associates.

Thomas, S. G. (1996). Great games for girls. *U.S. News and World Report, 121*(Nov. 25), 108.

Trebilock, B. (1997). Child molesters on the Internet: Are they in your home. *Redbook Magazine, 188*(April), 100–103.

Turkle, S. (1995). *Life on the screen: Identity in the age of the Internet*. New York: Simon and Schuster.

Tynes, B. M. (2007). Internet safety gone wild?: Sacrificing the educational and psychosocial benefits of online social environments. *Journal of Adolescent Research, 22*, 575–584. doi:10.1177/0743558407303979

Vail, K. (1997). Electronic school: Girlware. *The American School Board Journal, 184*(6), A18–A21.

Valkenburg, P. M., Jochen, P., & Schouten, A. P. (2006). Friend networking sites and their relationship to adolescents' well-being and social self-esteem. *Cyberpsychology & Behavior, 9*(5), 584–590. doi:10.1089/cpb.2006.9.584

Welch, A. (1995, May 25-29). *The role of book, television, computers and video games in children's day to day lives*. Paper presented at the Annual Meeting of the International Communication Association, Albuquerque, NM.

Wellman, B., Salaff, J., & Dimitrova, D. (1996). Computer networks as social networks: Collaborative work, telework, and virtual community. *Annual Review of Sociology, 22*, 213–238. doi:10.1146/annurev.soc.22.1.213

Whitely, B. E. (1997). Gender differences in computer-related attitudes and behavior: A meta-analysis. *Computers and Behavior, 13*(1), 1–22. doi:10.1016/S0747-5632(96)00026-X

Whitlock, J. L., Powers, J. L., & Eckenrode, J. E. (2006). The virtual cutting edge: The Internet and adolescent self-injury. *Developmental Psychology, 42*(3), 407–417. doi:10.1037/0012-1649.42.3.407

Wickstrom, A. (1996). Hackers (videotape review). *Video, 19*(April), 75.

Williams, G. III. (1994). Plugging kids into computers. *The American Legion, 136*(6), 23.

Winkel, S., Groen, G., & Petermann, F. (2005). Soziale unterstutzung in suizidforen. *Praxis der Kinderpsychologie und Kinderpsychiatrie, 54*(9), 714–727.

Wolak, J., Finkelhor, D., Mitchell, K. J., & Ybarra, M. L. (2008). Online 'predators' and their victims: Myths, realities, and implications for prevention and treatment. *The American Psychologist, 63*(2), 111–128. doi:10.1037/0003-066X.63.2.111

Wolak, K. J., Mitchell, K. J., & Finkelhor, D. (2003). Escaping or connecting? Characteristics of youth who form close online relationships. *Journal of Adolescence, 26*(1), 105–119. doi:10.1016/S0140-1971(02)00114-8

Youn, S. (2007). Teenagers' perceptions of online privacy and coping behaviors: A risk–benefit appraisal approach. *Journal of Broadcasting & Electronic Media, 49*(1), 86–110. doi:10.1207/s15506878jobem4901_6

Young, K. S. (1996). Psychology of computer use: XL. Addictive use of the Internet: A case that breaks the stereotype. *Psychological Reports, 79*(3), 251–270.

Chapter 10

Identifying Risk Factors and Enhancing Protective Factors to Prevent Adolescent Victimization on the Internet

Megan E. Call
University of Utah, USA

Jason J. Burrow-Sanchez
University of Utah, USA

ABSTRACT

The Internet is widely used among adolescents. Although the Internet is a beneficial tool for youth, some children and adolescents are at risk for being victimized online. Media reports portraying online predators and their victims have received increasing publicity. However, some information in these stories can be inaccurate or misleading. Therefore, it is important that mental health professionals and parents receive accurate information about online victimization in order to protect youth from harm. The purpose of this chapter is to provide research-based information on adolescent Internet use and the risk factors associated with online victimization. Further, recommendations for increasing protective factors are provided as a means to keep youth safe while using the Internet.

INTRODUCTION

A large number of adolescents in the United States use the Internet. In a recent survey of 935 youth, who were between 12-17 years old and lived in the United States, 93% of the sample reported using the Internet (Lenhart & Madden, 2007). More specifically, 89% of the sample stated that they used the Internet at least once a week and 61% used the Internet daily. Parent salary and education mediated Internet behavior among the youth in this study. Youth were more likely to use the Internet if

DOI: 10.4018/978-1-60566-926-7.ch010

their parents had a college education and a higher income in comparison to their counterparts whose parents had less education and earned a lower income. These youth reported using the Internet for a variety of reasons including educational, social, and entertainment purposes. Other research suggests that most parents view the Internet as a helpful tool for their children, believing that it is associated with academic success (Turow & Nir, 2000). However, despite the benefits the Internet provides for children and adolescents, there are negative aspects and risks associated with going online (Wolak, Fineklhor, Mitchell, & Ybarra, 2008).

The Internet has been described as a misleading medium because it provides a sense of privacy and anonymity to users but in reality, the Internet is a public entity where complete strangers can contact anyone via e-mail, SPAM messages, chat rooms and advertising (Gross, 2004; Jordan, 2002; Turow, 2001). Youth are not immune to this type of interaction. In their study, Lenhart and Madden (2007) found that 30% of their sample reported being contacted by or receiving messages from a complete stranger while using the Internet. Approximately 20% of these adolescents stated they were curious about these messages and replied to the sender for more information. Prior research has reported similar online behavior among teens and inferred that some online relationships are formed through these types of interactions. For instance, in a study of 1,511 youth and parents from the United Kingdom who were surveyed about their Internet use, 30% of participants reported that they had met a person online, 46% had given personal information to someone they met online, and 8% had face-to-face meetings with someone they met online (Livingstone & Bober, 2005). Similarly, the first Youth Internet Safety Survey (YISS) evaluated the online behavior of 1,501 youth from the United States who were between 10-17 years old and reported that 14% of their sample had formed close relationships with individuals met online (Finkelhor, Mitchell, & Wolak, 2000).

Some adolescents report finding solace in forming online relationships stating that it is more comfortable to share personal information via the Internet than in a face-to-face conversation (Gross, 2004). Unfortunately, a proportion of online relationships result in victimization where youth are solicited and groomed by sex offenders to participate in sexual and other harmful acts either on- or offline. Prior research indicates that certain factors place some youth more at risk for being victimized online in comparison to their peers (Mitchell, Finkelhor, & Wolak, 2001). Professionals in school or health settings are likely to encounter adolescents who have been victimized online; however, not all of these professionals routinely assess for risky online behaviors or previous victimizations when working with teens (Wells, Mitchell, Finkelhor, & Becker-Blease, 2006). In addition, these professionals may feel unprepared to address issues related to online victimization and Internet safety (Finn & Kerman, 2004) as there is limited information available in general on how to assist youth and their families with Internet safety issues (see Rosen, 2007; Wolak et al., 2008). The purpose of this chapter is to review the risk factors associated with online victimization as well as describe the protective factors that promote Internet safety and prevent online victimization from occurring.

BACKGROUND

There are three types of online victimization (Finkelhor, Mitchell, & Wolak, 2000). The first is sexual solicitation, where teens are requested to engage in wanted or unwanted sexual talk or sexual behavior with an adult. Unwanted exposure to sexual material is the second type of victimization. Sexual material includes images of naked individuals or people having sex that appear in conjunction with conducting online searches or opening e-mail messages.

The third type of victimization is Internet harassment, which is defined as aggressive or embarrassing comments made to or posed about a person online. Current research indicates that unwanted exposure to sexual material and sexual solicitation are the two most common types of online victimization. In the second Youth Internet Safety Survey (YISS-2), Wolak and colleagues (2006) found that among their sample of 1,500 adolescents, 34% were exposed to unwanted sexual material, 13% received a sexual solicitation and 9% were victims of Internet harassment during a one-year period. In contrast, Livingstone and Bober (2005) reported a greater occurrence of sexual solicitation in their survey findings where approximately 33% of youth received an unwanted sexual or nasty comment from strangers while online. Lastly, in their survey research on Internet harassment with 1,388 adolescents, Hinduja and Patchin (2007) determined that youth were more likely to be harassed online via instant messaging (males: 17%, females: 19.7%) in comparison to e-mail (males: 9.6%, females: 13%). Further, as these results suggest, female adolescents were deemed to be more susceptible to Internet harassment as opposed to male adolescents.

The majority of youth in these studies reported that they were not bothered by any form of online victimization; however, some did report experiencing emotional distress, mental health and social problems (Ybarra, Mitchell, Wolak & Finkelhor, 2006). For instance, approximately 25% of youth in the YISS-2 study reported feeling very upset or afraid after being sexually solicited or exposed to unwanted sexual material (Wolak et al., 2006). Youth also endorsed symptoms of stress after both types of incidents including feeling anxious or irritable, experiencing reoccurring thoughts about the incident, decreasing or stopping their online activity, and losing interest in other activities. Patchin and Hinduja (2006) reported similar ramifications for victims of Internet harassment. In their study, approximately half of the youth reported feeling frustrated (42.5%) or angry (40%) after being harassed, while almost one-third stated that the incident affected them at home (26.5%) or school (31.9%).

Even though some adolescents were upset when victimized online, some were unlikely to report these incidents to adults or other authority figures. In the YISS-2 study, approximately 50% of the youth did not report being solicited or exposed to unwanted sexual material. Further, 39% of youth who described feeling extremely distressed from seeing explicit sexual material online decided to remain silent (Wolak et al., 2006). Other research supports these findings where parents indicate that they are often unaware that their child has been victimized online (see Livingstone & Bober, 2005). Reasons why most youth do not report online victimization incidents to their parents, teachers or other authority figures include finding the solicitations or sexual material only minimally distressing, being too embarrassed or uncomfortable to discuss the incident, or believing that they might get in trouble for reporting it (Mitchell, Finkelhor, & Wolak, 2001).

Results from the research studies reviewed above indicate that not all adolescents who use the Internet are victimized online. In fact, prior findings suggest that youth are more likely to encounter intrafamilial sexual abuse, date rape, and gang violence than receive an online sexual solicitation from a stranger (Finkelhor & Dziuba-Leatherman, 1994). Also, less than half of youth who are victimized report feeling upset or disturbed by the incident. Although this information may be reassuring to caregivers and professionals, precautions still need to be taken to prevent online victimization. Especially since certain subgroups of youth are at higher risk of victimization than others (Mitchell, Finkelhor, & Wolak, 2001, 2003). Recent findings suggest that online victimization occurs within a confluence of risk factors, including psychosocial issues and general Internet use characteristics (Ybarra & Mitchell, 2008). It is important for parents and professionals who work with adolescents to be able to identify these risk factors in order to provide appropriate prevention and intervention. The next section addresses these risk factors in greater detail.

IDENTIFYING RISK FACTORS

Similar to other problem behavior such as substance abuse and violence, there are many factors that place youth at risk for being victimized online (Hawkins, Catalano, & Miller, 1992). Current research suggests that certain risk factors appear to be more harmful than others. Also, the likelihood of an adolescent being victimized online increases as the number of risk factors increase (Ybarra, Mitchell, Finkelhor, & Wolak, 2007). In order to discuss the influence of risk factors in greater detail, the following section has been organized into three categories including technology-based, interpersonal, and intrapersonal risk factors.

Technology-Based Risk Factors

Generally speaking, any involvement with the Internet can be considered a technology-based risk because information is shared and obtained in an environment that is typically unmonitored. Also, simple mistakes on the Internet can lead to negative consequences. For example, in qualitative interviews on viewing unwanted sexual material, adolescents reported that they were exposed to images of naked people and people having sex solely because they misspelled a word while conducting a online search (Wolak et al., 2006). A primary technology-based risk factor is disclosure of personal information online, which is defined as making information such as real name, telephone number, age or year born, or a picture of oneself available to others on the Internet (Ybarra et al., 2007). Adolescents share their personal information through many online mediums such as e-mail, social networking sites (e.g., Facebook or MySpace), blogs, chat rooms, or instant messaging. Contrary to popular belief and media reports, recent research suggests that teens tend to refrain from disclosing too much personal information online. Hinduja and Patchin (2008) analyzed 1,475 adolescent MySpace profiles and determined that only 8% of the sample included

their full name on their profile and 1% provided a telephone number. These findings indicate that only a small number of youth reveal personal information in their online profiles; however, the adolescents who do reveal personal information are at high risk for being victimized. For instance, convicted online sex offenders report that they devote time to reading online profiles of adolescents prior to initiating contact (Malesky, 2007). Therefore, the more information adolescents provide about themselves online, the greater the risk for being contacted by unknown individuals and becoming potential victims.

Other technology-based risk factors for adolescents include downloading pictures, videos or movies from file-sharing programs or intentionally visiting X-rated websites (Ybarra et al., 2007). These actions are problematic because they have the potential to place youth in contact with individuals unknown to them. Further, teens may be asked to submit their own sexual photos or be exposed to unwanted sexual material at these types of sites (Mitchell, Finkelhor, & Wolak, 2007a). Being able to access the Internet in a poorly monitored environment such as home or elsewhere also places adolescents at risk for victimization. Similar to the research conducted on television programming where adolescents who had television sets in their bedrooms were more likely to watch programs their parents would not approve (see Holz, 1998; Reyna & Farley, 2006), youth are more likely to view inappropriate websites or communicate with unknown individuals when given the freedom and privacy to do so (Ybarra et al., 2007). Whether a form of rebellion or need to individuate from family norms, teens who participate in risky online behavior often are unaware of the technological dangers of the Internet. Many adolescents do not understand the permanency or accessibility of placing personal information online, whether via an online profile page, chatroom or other Internet forum (Wells & Mitchell, 2008). Also, teens tend to be uninformed regarding the illegality of soliciting for or posting sexual material online. This lack of knowledge can be especially perilous for youth who meet and form close online interpersonal relationships with adults.

Interpersonal Risk Factors

Interpersonal risk factors involve an adolescent's capacity (e.g., maturity, decision-making skills) for interacting with others in both on- and offline environments. One major risk factor is when adolescents form relationships with unknown people on the Internet (Mitchell, Finkelhor, & Wolak, 2007). The risk for victimization increases when teens share personal information or talk about sex with an unknown individual while online. Interviews with convicted sex offenders reveal that the most common characteristic of a potential online victim was willingness to engage in sexual talk or discuss sexually related issues (Malesky, 2007). Therefore, disclosing personal information on the Internet (a technology-based risk factor) increases the adolescent's risk for victimization as the content becomes more personal and restrictions on accessibility are lowered. Instant messaging and chat rooms are often the mediums used for sexual solicitation and online harassment. However, social networking sites such as MySpace or Facebook, which are often deemed as safer modes of online interaction, can become dangerous if an adolescent places an unknown individual on their buddy or friend list depending on the program (Ybarra & Mitchell, 2007). It is important to note that the majority of online sex offenders do not disguise their identities or their intentions from their victims. Also, adolescents who meet online sex offenders in a face-to-face environment acknowledge that the purpose of the meeting is for engaging in sexual activity (Wolak et al., 2008). Previous research suggests that many teens report experiencing feelings of closeness or even love toward the online offender (Wolak, Mitchell, & Finkelhor, 2003a). These findings highlight some of the deceptive elements

of the relationship between a sex offender and a romantically-naïve adolescent.

In addition to online interactions with unknown individuals, adolescents are at risk for victimization if they participate in aggressive behavior while using the Internet (Ybarra et al., 2007). This includes making rude or nasty comments to someone online or using the Internet to harass or embarrass someone in a revengeful manner. Teens may participate in online aggressive behavior with their peers or in a solitary environment (Wolak et al., 2006). Current research indicates that adolescents who engage in online aggressive behavior are more than twice as likely to report having been victimized online in comparison to their peers (Ybarra et al., 2007). Youth who participate in this specific type of risky online behavior are also more likely to have social, academic and other problems (Ybarra & Mitchell, 2008). In particular, teens who have experienced offline victimization or have high levels of conflict in the home are more likely to engage in aggressive online behavior (Wells & Mitchell, 2008). It is unknown at this time whether these high-risk adolescents tend to engage in aggressive online behavior because of the issues they face offline, or if their actions online influence the likelihood of being harmed while offline. In any case, there appears to be a connection between negative on- and offline relationships for adolescents.

One of the most influential offline interactions for youth is the parent-child relationship where they receive information, rules and support while navigating their way to adulthood. Lack of parent-child communication about sex and other risky behaviors limit youth from being able to recognize the harm of an online or offline sexual solicitation (Fleming, Greentree, Cocotti-Muller, Elias, & Morrison, 2006) and possibly cause teens to seek information from peers and popular media sources which are not always accurate. More specific to Internet use, many parents do not talk to their children about their expectations for using the Internet at home nor do they adequately monitor the online behavior of their children (Livingstone, 2007; Livingstone & Bober, 2005). Research indicates that adolescents are more at risk to be victimized online if their parents do not establish and reinforce rules for Internet use in the home (Livingstone & Bober, 2006; Mitchell, Finkelhor, & Wolak, 2003). Online victimization is also more likely to occur if there is a high level of parent-child conflict in the home, which may include poor communication, lack of supervision and low emotional attachment. For instance, teens who engage in aggressive online behavior are more likely to report low emotional bonding toward their parents in comparison to adolescents who are not aggressive online (Ybarra & Mitchell, 2004). Similarly, in their study on youth online behavior, Ybarra and Mitchell (2005) found a significant relationship between viewing pornography via the Internet, a technology-based risk factor, and poor attachment with parents.

Lastly, adolescents with histories of offline sexual or physical abuse are considerably more likely to receive online sexual solicitations, especially aggressive solicitations (Mitchell, Finkelhor, & Wolak, 2007b, 2001). Research suggests that teens who were physically or sexually abused as children are more likely to exhibit symptoms of depression or anxiety, conduct and antisocial behaviors, and suicidal ideation (Fergusson, Boden, & Horwood, 2008). Further, adolescents who were abused as children tend to experience greater difficulty recognizing or responding to inappropriate sexual advances because they are unable to separate acts of violence or sex from expressions of love (Berliner & Elliott, 2002; Rogosch, Cicchetti, & Aber, 1995).

Intrapersonal Risk Factors

In addition to the risk factors associated with interpersonal relationships there are also intrapersonal factors that clearly place some adolescents at more risk for online victimization.

For instance, demographics such as gender, race and ethnicity moderate online victimization. Regarding gender, girls are more at risk than boys for online victimization (Wolak, Mitchell, & Finkelhor, 2004). Girls who become sexually active during early adolescence are especially susceptible to online victimization (Wolak et al., 2008) because they are more likely to participate in unsafe sexual practices (Ponton & Judice, 2004) and be intimately involved with older adults (Leitenberg & Saltzman, 2000, 2003; Manlove, Moore, Liechty, Ikramullah, & Cottingman, 2005). In terms of race and ethnicity, girls of African and African-American decent are more at risk to receive online requests for sexual pictures than their adolescent peers (Mitchell, Finkelhor, & Wolak, 2007a).

Research also indicates that teens who form close online relationships are at higher risk for being victimized in comparison to youth who solely converse online with known friends (Wells & Mitchell, 2008; Wolak, Mitchell, & Finkelhor, 2003b). Adolescents may form close online relationships for a variety of reasons. For example, teens experiencing depression and related mental health disorders are more likely to form online relationships to cope with or ameliorate their feelings of loneliness in comparison to their mentally healthy counterparts (Wolak, Mitchell, & Finkelhor, 2004). Adolescents who have difficulty forming supportive interpersonal relationships with others may also find solace in online relationships where self-disclosure can occur without the pressure of conversing in a face-to-face manner (Gross, 2004). Another vulnerable group is questioning or homosexual youth who use the Internet to seek contacts or information about their sexual orientation. In fact, one-fourth of online sex offender arrests involve relationships between adolescent males and adult men suggesting that some online offenders target homosexual youth in the guise of assisting with issues regarding sexual orientation (Wolak, Mitchell, & Finkelhor, 2004).

One of the primary problems with teens forming close relationships online is that they often to do not have the emotional maturity or decision-making capacity to discern if a relationship with an unknown individual could be beneficial or harmful. For instance, evidence from brain research indicates that the frontal lobe, which controls executive functions such as decision-making, is not fully mature during adolescence (Blakemore & Choudhury, 2006). This biological observation is likely related to the finding that adolescents tend to underestimate the harmful consequences and long-term effects associated with risk-taking behavior (Reyna & Farley, 2006). Also, many teens make decisions based on the perceived benefits of their intended behavior as opposed to the perceived risks. This finding is evidenced in Internet research where adolescents are more likely to trust information obtained on the Internet (National Public Radio, 2000) and are more willing to disclose personal information online in comparison to adults (Livingstone & Bober, 2006; Turow & Nir, 2000). Similar to decision-making, emotional regulation is also not fully developed until late-adolescence or early adulthood (Mash & Wolfe, 2005). This finding suggests that youth in early to mid-adolescence may struggle with emotional control when involved in romantic relationships whether on- or offline (Cauffman & Steinberg, 2000; Weinstein & Rosenhaft, 1991). Online relationships may be particularly difficult for adolescents to cope with emotionally because connections can be formed quickly and involve a high level of personal self-disclosure in comparison to the slower development of offline relationships (McKenna, Green, & Gleason, 2002). Online relationships also can be isolating because family members and peers are often unaware that such an intense and secretive relationship exists (McKenna et al., 2002). Thus, adolescents are more susceptible to being victimized and exploited online in comparison to adults because teens do not have the developmental capacity to handle the dangers associated with online relationships. In sum, there are a variety of intrapersonal factors that make youth vulnerable to online sex offenders. As discussed above, such factors are complex in nature and interact with other risk factors (e.g., technology, interpersonal), which combines to make the identification of adolescents at risk for online victimization a less than straight-forward process. However, the good news is that certain protective factors can buffer the negative effects of risk factors and this topic is discussed next.

ENHANCING PROTECTIVE FACTORS

In general, protective factors are anything that decreases the probability of a problem behavior from being expressed (Hawkins, Catalano, & Miller, 1992). Some examples of protective factors for adolescents include having good coping skills, associating with pro-social peers, and obtaining good grades in school. The majority of adolescent preventive interventions for problem behavior are designed with the intent to decrease risk factors and enhance protective factors.

Preventive interventions for promoting Internet safety have been slow to develop and primarily ineffective due to the quickly evolving nature of the Internet. Currently, the two most common prevention approaches used are to (1) tell teens to avoid disclosing any personal information online and (2) inform parents to mediate their children's Internet use at home (Wolak et al., 2008). These preventive interventions do little for Internet safety efforts because they do not address the primary risk factors associated with sexual solicitation and harassment, nor do they assist adolescents who are most vulnerable to online victimization. These approaches also do not incorporate evidence-based recommendations for promoting Internet safety. For instance, previous research suggests that parental involvement with the Internet should be more discussion and education-based as opposed to restrictive (Mitchell et al., 2001). Adolescents also should be better informed as to why they should not disclose personal information via the Internet. Preventive interventions need to be developed and evaluated to properly address the risk factors specific to online victimization and enhance the protective factors associated with healthy and safe Internet use. These approaches should be adapted to both school and home settings in order for teens to receive consistent prevention messages from all aspects of their lives. The remainder of this chapter discusses four components that should be included in future prevention programming to promote Internet safety: (1) educating adolescents about the dangers of the Internet and ways to promote positive online communication, (2) involving peers as agents of positive change, (3) involving family members to promote Internet safety and (4) addressing the needs of teens who are most vulnerable to online victimization.

Internet Safety Education

Internet safety strategies are taught to adolescents primarily in school-based settings and tend to focus on the dangers of posting personal information on the Internet (Wolak et al., 2008). Some schools even utilize scare tactics through films depicting naïve teenagers disclosing personal information via the Internet only to have their actions come back to haunt them in the form of online sexual predators or Internet scams. Previous research on other problem behavior indicates that the use of scare tactics is ineffective because most adolescents do not identify with the teens or scenarios portrayed, believing that they are immune from these types of situations (Lambie & Rokutani, 2002). It is therefore important for Internet safety education to be realistic and informative, applicable to actual adolescent online behavior, and specifically address the interactive aspects of the Internet. This form of prevention can occur in a variety of settings with older peers, parents, educators, religious leaders, mental health professionals,

mentors and physicians. Further, the information provided should be both developmentally and culturally appropriate for the adolescent audience (Greenfield, 2004).

A natural starting point for Internet safety interventions would be to discuss the elements of a healthy romantic relationship. It was mentioned previously that many adolescents in their early- to mid-teens struggle with decision-making and regulating emotions (Cauffman & Steinberg, 2000; Reyna & Farley, 2006). Thus, it seems logical to discuss with teens how it is natural to experience sexual and romantic feelings toward another person and though exciting, there are risks involved with committing to a romantic relationship whether on- or offline. Adolescents should be informed that romance and love does not involve manipulation, sexual solicitation or the exchange of sexual images (Wolak et al., 2008). Adolescents need to be educated about the existence of autonomy within a relationship and how it is acceptable to say "no" to situations or requests that seem uncomfortable, inappropriate, or violate their values (Wolak, Mitchell, & Finkelhor, 2003b). Specific to online relationships, teens should learn who online sex offenders are and the tactics they employ to seduce potential victims (Wolak et al., 2008). Adolescents should be taught that disclosing personal information via the Internet, whether in writing or images, is an action that could potentially be discovered by anyone including future employers, university selection committees and online offenders. Teens should also understand that it is potentially dangerous to talk with unknown individuals in chat rooms or place them on their buddy or friends list. Further, youth should be informed to never talk about sex with anyone while online, no matter the situation, as this action is strongly associated with online harassment and victimization (Malesky, 2007).

Prevention efforts involving education should also address aggressive online behavior or cyberbullying. Similar to discussing healthy romantic relationships, all adolescents should learn skills that would prevent them from being aggressive toward others whether on- or offline. These basic life skills could include problem-solving, decision-making, effective communication, stress management and anger management (Greenberg, 2003). Preventive interventions use a variety of settings to teach these skills including individual, group, and family interventions as well as in classrooms. Schools in particular are in a unique position to develop adolescent social skills and also deliver anti-cyberbullying messages and training. Feinberg (2003) recommends that cyberbulling prevention programs remain consistent across schools within the same district in order for students to receive the same training and information as they change grades or move to a different school. Cyberbullying education can be provided as a classroom curriculum or through school assemblies, media presentations and even peer mentoring (Diamanduros, Downs, & Jenkins, 2008). School personnel have also been encouraged to form specific committees to address cyberbullying in the schools and ensure that effective preventive interventions are implemented (Storm & Storm, 2005).

Lastly, it is important that prevention efforts address what adolescents should do if they are solicited or harassed online. Teens should be encouraged to report these incidences and receive information regarding whom to talk to (e.g., parent, teacher, school counselor, law enforcement). Adolescents should also be taught how to respond to an online sex offender. Appropriate actions would include blocking the offender from being able to read their online profile page, staying away from chat rooms, and removing the offender's name from their friend or buddy list. In the instance of cyberbullying, teens should be informed to not retaliate against the offender as this action will only perpetuate the cyberbullying problem and could also cause the victim further harm (Diamanduros, Downs, & Jenkins, 2008). Overall, adolescents should feel empowered to report these types of online incidences and un-

derstand that they will not be punished for doing so. Adolescents should also know that they play a valuable role in educating their peers about Internet safety and preventing online victimization and harassment from occurring.

Peer Involvement

Adolescents have been utilized as peer educators or peer leaders in interventions designed to prevent substance abuse, violence, teen pregnancy, diabetes, cancer and even oral health problems. Findings from prevention research suggest that peer-led preventive interventions are just as, if not more, effective than adult-led interventions (Cuijpers, 2002). More specifically, adolescents are more likely to endorse a preventative behavior if they receive the information from a peer as opposed to an adult (Erhard, 1999). Teens are knowledgeable resources for Internet safety education efforts due to their unique understanding of teenage online behavior and therefore, they should be included at all levels of online preventive interventions. For instance, adolescents should be consulted when designing a program curriculum in order to guarantee that the information being provided is developmentally appropriate and relevant to teen Internet use. Youth could also be involved in delivering the intervention such as teaching part of the curriculum, sharing personal and relevant stories, designing media campaigns, or even composing an informative newsletter or blog for their classmates. In addition, all adolescents should be trained to be agents of change in promoting positive online communication. Teens should be informed that online harassment occurs not only between an adolescent and adult online predator, but also among peers in the form of cyberbullying (Ybarra et al., 2008). Youth should be taught how to recognize and report inappropriate online behavior as well as how to enforce responsible and positive standards while using the Internet (Wolak et al., 2008). It is well known that peers become more influential during the period of adolescence;

however, an adolescent's family still continues to exert considerable influence during this period of development.

Family Involvement

Although it has been recommended for the majority of online prevention efforts to be focused on adolescents, parents can also serve as an important protective factor. For instance, Greenfield (2004) reports that having a warm and communicative parent-child relationship can serve as a protective factor for many problem behaviors. Parents can promote Internet safety in the home by openly talking to their children about the benefits and dangers of the Internet (Wolak et al., 2008). As mentioned in the education section above, parents can discuss with their children who online molesters are, how they manipulate and deceive youth, and what to do if they are solicited or harassed while online. These conversations should also inform adolescents why relationships with online predators are inappropriate and how they can cause harm. Fortunately, some resources are available for parents to talk to their children about online predators and cyberbulling (Willard, 2007). For example, Hinduja, Patchin and Burgess-Proctor (2006) created conversation starters for parents to engage their children in discussions about cyberbullying. Parents can also use Internet contracts that list parent expectations for safe and appropriate online behavior, which are signed by both the parent and adolescent (Hinduja & Patchin, 2007). There are many other ways to encourage and promote Internet safety in the home. For instance, parents can participate in their children's Internet activity or place the computer in a public space (e.g., kitchen) for easier monitoring. Parents should also establish and reinforce developmentally appropriate rules for using the Internet (Livingstone, 2007) such as what types of websites are appropriate to visit, time limitations with using the Internet for academic and entertainment purposes, Internet use when youth are home

alone, asking permission to use the Internet, what type of personal and family information youth are allowed to provide to others on the Internet, and who youth are allowed to converse with online (Greenfield, 2004).

Some parents try to use restrictive mediation, or filtering and blocking software, as a way to control Internet use in the home. These programs can create many unintended problems. For instance, some blocking software prevents access to educational or other appropriate types of websites (Fleming, Greentree, Cocotti-Muller, Elias, & Morrison, 2006). Filtering and blocking software has also been found to only modestly reduce exposure to negative online images and material (Mitchell et al., 2005). Unnecessary parent-child tension may be created through the use of restrictive mediation (Turow & Nir, 2000). In their research on adolescent online behavior, Livingstone and Bober (2006) reported that teens in their study expressed more concern about maintaining privacy from people they do know in comparison to unknown individuals. Further, they determined that youth do not like their parents to monitor or restrict their Internet use and therefore, find methods to avoid this invasion of privacy such as deleting their website history, hiding or mislabeling files, and minimizing a window when someone else came into the room. Based on these findings, parents should use interpersonal communication as opposed to restrictive mediation to protect their children from online solicitations and harassment (Mitchell et al., 2001).

Addressing Intrapersonal Risk Factors

Providing Internet safety education, using peers as agents of change, and involving parents are all important protective factors that can help prevent teens from being harmed online. However, more intensive preventive approaches should be utilized to assist those who are most vulnerable to online victimization and harassment. Assessment is the first step in identifying youth who are at risk for being harmed online. Although no questionnaire or assessment instrument is currently available, educators and other health professionals can informally determine an adolescent's risk level by asking him or her about such things as formation of online relationships, what he or she talks about while online and what types of websites are visited (Ybarra et al., 2007). During the assessment, it should be kept in mind that high-risk adolescents usually communicate online with unknown individuals and participate in at least four other previously mentioned risky online behaviors (Ybarra et al., 2007).

Once an adolescent is identified as being high-risk, he or she would likely benefit from counseling or other mental health services to address the inter- and intrapersonal factors associated with risky online behavior such as depression or self-esteem, previous sexual or physical abuse, sexual identity development, and other mental health issues (Wolak et al., 2008). Counseling services should also focus on decreasing risky online behavior such as forming close relationships online, talking about sex with unknown individuals or aggressively acting out on the Internet (Wolak et al., 2008). Counselors may want to use an educational approach to inform the adolescent about the illegality of online sexual solicitations and provide strategies for how to respond if solicited in the future (Wells & Mitchell, 2008). This could be accomplished by teaching the previously mentioned problem-solving and decision-making skills, as well as the social skills necessary to form positive relationships both on- and offline. Since preventive interventions with high-risk teens are more intensive in nature, they would be most effective delivered in a small group or one-on-one setting rather than in a classroom. It is important to note that not all preventive interventions are effective with high-risk teens. Therefore, it is crucial that assessment results be utilized to determine which preventive approach will work best for a specific adolescent (Wells & Mitchell, 2008).

FUTURE RESEARCH

Teen Internet use has become a recent phenomenon in the last decade and more research needs to be done to understand online behavior among adolescents and prevent online victimization from occurring. Specifically, more effort needs to be devoted toward learning about the risk factors associated with online victimization and harassment (Wolak et al., 2008). For instance, no research studies have measured if risky online behavior is associated with other problem behavior such as substance abuse, violence, or teen pregnancy. It would be important to know if the risk factors for these behaviors are related in order to develop effective prevention programming to target related problem behavior. Wolak and colleagues (2008) recommend that both quantitative and qualitative methods be used to further assess the risk factors associated with online victimization. They further suggest that this type of research be longitudinal in nature in order to comprehend the long-term effects of online victimization. In addition, from a more practical standpoint, a measurement instrument needs to be developed to assist educators and health professionals in identifying adolescents who are most vulnerable to online victimization in order for them to receive the appropriate services. Lastly, there is a great need to develop prevention programming for all youth but specifically those who are most vulnerable for online victimization (Wolak et al., 2008). This curriculum should be developed with the assistance of adolescents in order to ensure that teens are receptive to the program. This type of preventive intervention should be adaptable to both individual and group-based programming. Once developed, the curriculum needs to be evaluated for effectiveness before being disseminated across schools and health settings.

CONCLUSION

The Internet is a common source of information, entertainment and communication for youth. Although the rate of online sexual victimization and harassment is lower than portrayed in the media, some adolescents are more at risk than others for being harmed while using the Internet. Professionals who work with teens and parents can provide assistance by understanding the technological-based, interpersonal and intrapersonal risk factors that are associated with online victimization. Further, they can implement programming that enhances individual, peer, school, and family-based protective factors to prevent future online and offline victimization from occurring.

REFERENCES

Berliner, L., & Elliott, D. M. (2002). Sexual abuse of children. In *The APSAC handbook on child maltreatment* (2nd ed., pp. 55-78). Thousand Oaks, CA: Sage.

Blakemore, S. J., & Choudhury, S. (2006). Development of the adolescent brain: Implications for executive function and social cognition. *Journal of Child Psychology and Psychiatry, and Allied Disciplines*, *47*(3-4), 296–312. doi:10.1111/j.1469-7610.2006.01611.x

Cauffman, E., & Steinberg, L. (2000). (Im)maturity of judgment in adolescence: Why adolescents may be less culpable than adults. *Behavioral Sciences & the Law*, *18*, 741–760. doi:10.1002/bsl.416

CSRIU. (2008). *Center for Safe and Responsible Internet Use*. Retrieved from http://www.csriu.org

Cuijpers, P. M. (2002). Effective ingredients of school-based drug prevention programs: A systematic review. *Addictive Behaviors*, *27*(6), 1009–1023. doi:10.1016/S0306-4603(02)00295-2

Diamanduros, T., Downs, E., & Jenkins, S. J. (2008). The role of school psychologists in the assessment, prevention and intervention of cyberbullying. *Psychology in the Schools*, *45*(8), 693–704. doi:10.1002/pits.20335

Erhard, R. (1999). Peer-led and adult-led programs – student perceptions. *Journal of Drug Education*, *29*(4), 295–308. doi:10.2190/DK18-4305-W7AB-PLPE

Feinberg, T. (2003). *Bullying prevention and intervention*. Retrieved from http://www.nasponline.org/resources/principals/nassp bullying.aspx

Fergusson, D. M., Boden, J. M., & Horwood, J. L. (2008). Exposure to childhood sexual and physical abuse and adjustment in early adulthood. *Child Abuse & Neglect*, *32*(6), 607–619. doi:10.1016/j.chiabu.2006.12.018

Finkelhor, D., & Dziuba-Leatherman, J. (1994). Children as victims of violence: A national survey. *Pediatrics*, *94*(4), 413–420.

Finkelhor, D., Mitchell, K. J., & Wolak, J. (2000). *Online victimization: A report on the nation's youth*. Arlington, VA: National Center for Missing & Exploited Children.

Finn, J., & Kerman, B. (2004). Internet risks for foster families online. *Journal of Technology in Human Services*, *22*(4), 21–38. doi:10.1300/J017v22n04_02

Fleming, M. J., Greentree, S., Cocotti-Muller, D., Elias, K. A., & Morrison, S. (2006). Safety in cyberspace: Adolescents' safety and exposure online. *Youth & Society*, *38*(2), 135–154. doi:10.1177/0044118X06287858

Greenberg, K. R. (2003). *Group counseling in k-12 schools: A handbook for school counselors*. Boston: Allyn & Bacon.

Greenfield, P. M. (2004). Developmental considerations for determining appropriate Internet use guidelines for children and adolescents. *Journal of Applied Developmental Psychology*, *25*(6), 751–762. doi:10.1016/j.appdev.2004.09.008

Gross, E. F. (2004). Adolescent Internet use: What we expect, what teens report. *Journal of Applied Developmental Psychology*, *25*(6), 633–649. doi:10.1016/j.appdev.2004.09.005

Hawkins, J. D., Catalano, R. F., & Miller, J. Y. (1992). Risk and protective factors for alcohol and other drug problems in adolescence and early adulthood: Implications for substance abuse prevention. *Psychological Bulletin*, *112*(1), 64–105. doi:10.1037/0033-2909.112.1.64

Hinduja, S., Patchin, J., & Burgess-Proctor, A. (2006). *Cyberbullying: Parent/teenager scripts to promote dialogue and discussion*. Retrieved from http://www.cyberbullying.us/cyberbullying scripts.pdf

Hinduja, S., & Patchin, J. W. (2008). Personal information of adolescents on the Internet: A quantitative content analysis of MySpace. *Journal of Adolescence*, *31*, 125–146. doi:10.1016/j.adolescence.2007.05.004

Holz, J. (1998). *Measuring the child audience: Issues and implications for educational programming* (No. 3). Philadelphia, PA: The Annenberg Public Policy Center of the University of Pennsylvania. Jordan, A. B. (2002). A family systems approach to examining the role of the Internet in the home. In S. L. Calvert, A. B. Jordan, & R. R. Cocking (Eds.), *Children in the digital age* (pp. 231-248). Westport, CT: Praeger Publishers.

Lambie, G. W., & Rokutani, L. J. (2002). A systems approach to substance abuse identification and intervention for school counselors. *Professional School Counseling*, *5*(5), 353–360.

Leitenberg, H., & Saltzman, H. (2000). A statewide survey of age at first intercourse for adolescent females and age of their male partner: Relation to other risk behaviors and statutory rape implications. *Archives of Sexual Behavior*, *29*, 203–215. doi:10.1023/A:1001920212732

Leitenberg, H., & Saltzman, H. (2003). College women who had sexual intercourse when they were underage minors (13-15): Age of their male partners, relation to current adjustment, and statutory rape implications. *Sexual Abuse*, *15*, 135–147. doi:10.1177/107906320301500204

Lenhart, A., & Madden, M. (2007). *Teens, privacy & online social networks*. Washington, DC: Pew Internet & American Life Project.

Livingstone, S. (2007). Strategies of parental regulation in the media-rich home. *Computers in Human Behavior*, *23*(2), 920–941. doi:10.1016/j.chb.2005.08.002

Livingstone, S., & Bober, M. (2005). *UK children go online: Surveying the experiences of young people and their parents*. Retrieved from http://news.bbc.co.uk/1/shared/bsp/hi/pdfs/28_04_05_childrenonline.pdf

Livingstone, S., & Bober, M. (2006). Regulating the Internet at home: Contrasting the perspectives of children and parents. In D. Buckingham & R. Willet (Eds.), *Digital generations: Children, young people, and new media* (pp. 93-114). Mahwah, NJ: Lawrence Erlbaum Associates, Inc.

Malesky, L. A. (2007). Predatory online behavior: Modus operandi of convicted sex offender in identifying potential victims and contact minors over the Internet. *Journal of Child Sexual Abuse*, *16*(2), 23–32. doi:10.1300/J070v16n02_02

Manlove, J., Moore, K. A., Liechty, J., Ikramullah, E., & Cottinghman, S. (2005). *Sex between young teens and older individuals: A demographic portrait*. Washington, DC: Child Trends.

Mash, E. J., & Wolfe, D. A. (2005). *Abnormal child psychology* (3rd ed.). Pacific Grove, CA: Wadsworth.

McKenna, K. Y. A., Green, A. S., & Gleason, M. E. J. (2002). Relationship formation on the Internet: What's the big attraction? *The Journal of Social Issues, 58*, 9–31. doi:10.1111/1540-4560.00246

Mitchell, K. J., Finkelhor, D., & Wolak, J. (2001). Risk factors for and impact of online sexual solicitation of youth. *Journal of the American Medical Association, 285*(23), 3011–3014. doi:10.1001/jama.285.23.3011

Mitchell, K. J., Finkelhor, D., & Wolak, J. (2003). The exposure of youth to unwanted sexual material on the Internet: A national survey of risk, impact, and prevention. *Youth & Society, 34*(3), 330–358. doi:10.1177/0044118X02250123

Mitchell, K. J., Finkelhor, D., & Wolak, J. (2007a). Online requests for sexual pictures from youth: Risk factors and incident characteristics. *The Journal of Adolescent Health, 41*, 196–203. doi:10.1016/j.jadohealth.2007.03.013

Mitchell, K. J., Finkelhor, D., & Wolak, J. (2007b). Youth Internet users at risk for the most serious online sexual solicitations. *American Journal of Preventive Medicine, 32*(6), 532–537. doi:10.1016/j.amepre.2007.02.001

National Public Radio. (2000). *Survey shows widespread enthusiasm for high technology*. Retrieved from http://www.npr.org/programs/specials/poll/technology/index.html

ONDCP. (2008). *Parents. The anti-drug*. Retrieved from http://theantidrug.com

Patchin, J. W., & Hinduja, S. (2006). Bullies move beyond the schoolyard: A preliminary look at cyberbullying. *Youth Violence and Juvenile Justice, 4*(2), 148–169. doi:10.1177/1541204006286288

Ponton, L. E., & Judice, S. (2004). Typical adolescent sexual development. *Child and Adolescent Psychiatric Clinics of North America, 13*(3), 497–511. doi:10.1016/j.chc.2004.02.003

Reyna, V. F., & Farley, F. (2006). Risk and rationality in adolescent decision making: Implications for theory, practice, and public policy . *Psychological Science in the Public Interest, 7*(1), 1–44. doi:10.1111/j.1529-1006.2006.00026.x

Rogosch, F. A., Cicchetti, D., & Aber, J. L. (1995). The role of child maltreatment in early deviations in cognitive and affective processing abilities and later peer relationship problems. *Development and Psychopathology, 7*, 591–609. doi:10.1017/S0954579400006738

Rosen, L. D. (2007). *Me, MySpace, and I: Parenting the Net generation*. New York: Palgrave Macmillan.

SIECUS. (2008). *Families are talking*. Retrieved from http://www.siecus.org/

Storm, P. S., & Storm, R. D. (2005). Cyberbullying by adolescents: A preliminary assessment. *The Educational Forum, 70*, 21–32. doi:10.1080/00131720508984869

Turow, J. (2001). Family boundaries, commercialism, and the Internet: A framework for research. *Journal of Applied Developmental Psychology, 22*(1), 73–86. doi:10.1016/S0193-3973(00)00067-8

Turow, J., & Nir, L. (2000). The Internet and the family: The view from parents. In C. von Feilitzen & U. Carlsson (Eds.), *Children in the new media landscape* (pp. 331-348). Goteborg, Sweden: UNESCO International Clearing house on Children and Violence on the Screen.

Weinstein, E., & Rosenhaft, E. (1991). The development of adolescent sexual intimacy: Implications for counseling. *Adolescence, 26*, 331.

Wells, M., Mitchell, K., Finkelhor, D., & Becker-Blease, K. (2006). Mental health professionals' exposure to clients with problematic Internet experiences. *Journal of Technology in Human Services, 24*(4), 35–52. doi:10.1300/J017v24n04_03

Wells, M., & Mitchell, K. J. (2008). How do high-risk youth use the Internet? Characteristics and implications for prevention. *Child Maltreatment, 13*(3), 227–234. doi:10.1177/1077559507312962

Willard, N. E. (2007f). *Parents' Guide to cyberbullying and cyberthreats*. Retrieved from http://www.cyberbullying.org/cyberbully/docs/cbctparents.pdf

Wolak, J., Finkelhor, D., & Mitchell, K. (2004). Internet-initiated sex crimes against minors: Implications for prevention based on findings from a national study. *Journal of Adolescent Health, 35*(5), 424.e411-424.e420.

Wolak, J., Finkelhor, D., Mitchell, K. J., & Ybarra, M. L. (2008). Online "predators' and their victims: Myths, realities, and implications for prevention and treatment. *The American Psychologist, 63*(2), 111–128. doi:10.1037/0003-066X.63.2.111

Wolak, J., Mitchell, K., & Finkelhor, D. (2006). Online victimization of youth: Five years later. *National Center for Missing & Exploited Children Bulletin - #07-06-025*. Alexandria, VA.

Wolak, J., Mitchell, K. J., & Finkelhor, D. (2003a). *National juvenile online victimization study (N-JOV): Methodology report*. Crimes against Children Research Center. Retrieved from http://www.unh.edu/ccrc/pdf/jvq/CV72.pdf

Wolak, J., Mitchell, K. J., & Finkelhor, D. (2003b). Escaping or connecting? Characteristics of youth who form close online relationships. *Journal of Adolescence, 26*(1), 105–119. doi:10.1016/S0140-1971(02)00114-8

Ybarra, M. L., & Mitchell, K. J. (2004). Youth engaging in online harassment: Associations with caregiver-child relationships, Internet use, and personal characteristics. *Journal of Adolescence, 27*, 319–336. doi:10.1016/j.adolescence.2004.03.007

Ybarra, M. L., & Mitchell, K. J. (2005). Exposure to Internet pornography among children and adolescents: A national survey. *Cyberpsychology & Behavior, 8*(5), 473–486. doi:10.1089/cpb.2005.8.473

Ybarra, M. L., & Mitchell, K. J. (2008). How risky are social networking sites? A comparison of places online where youth sexual solicitation and harassment occurs. *Pediatrics, 121*(2), e350–e357. doi:10.1542/peds.2007-0693

Ybarra, M. L., Mitchell, K. J., Finkelhor, D., & Wolak, J. (2006). Examining characteristics and associated distress related to Internet harassment: Findings from the Second Youth Internet Safety Survey. *Pediatrics, 118*(4), e1169–e1177. doi:10.1542/peds.2006-0815

Ybarra, M. L., Mitchell, K. J., Finkelhor, D., & Wolak, J. (2007). Internet prevention messages: Targeting the right online behaviors. *Archives of Pediatrics & Adolescent Medicine, 161*, 138–145. doi:10.1001/archpedi.161.2.138

Chapter 11
Millenials, Social Networking and Social Responsibility

Sharmila Pixy Ferris
William Paterson University, USA

ABSTRACT

In this chapter the author explores Millenials' participation in the public good, investigating whether they use social networking for social responsibility. Millenials, the wired, connected generation for whom social networking is an essential aspect of life, are often criticized for their lack of social responsibility. Social networking, as new media uniquely a part of Millenials' wired and connected lifestyles, has the potential to "transform citizenship." To investigate Millenials' social networking and social responsibility, a Webnography was conducted. Findings go against conventional wisdom as the author found that Millenials use social networking to take social and political action, engage in social entrepreneurship, and conduct charitable solicitation and donation.

INTRODUCTION

Having grown up with the Internet and digital technologies, today's youth are the most wired and connected generation in human history. Members of this generation are constantly connected to each other—by cell phone, text messages, instant messaging (IM) and email—and continually plugged into the world of information on the Web, as will be demonstrated in the literature review. Although much has been written about this wired generation, most academic and popular writings about social networking focus on young people's personal and social use of social networking sites—sites such as MySpace, FaceBook, and YouTube. While academics are increasingly interested in the pedagogical potential of social networking sites, an area that remains neglected is the role of social networking in the public good. As Hamilton and Flanagan (2007) note, there is "little extant research on social responsibility within close peer relationships." Such research is, however, important as the country looks to Millenials for greater and more positive participation in the public good.

DOI: 10.4018/978-1-60566-926-7.ch011

BACKGROUND

The term "Millenial" (also spelled Millennial) denotes that generation of young people born after the advent of the Internet. Although variously called the Net Generation, Echo Boomers and the Digital Generation, among other names, this generation is *self-styled* "Millenials" after several thousand of them sent suggestions about what they want to be called to Peter Jennings at abcnews.com (Sweeney 2008). Millenials are unique in that their exposure to the Internet and digital technologies is lifelong, but also in the extent of their connectivity through the internet and digital technologies.

The Internet features prominently in Millenials' everyday lives (McMillan and Morrison 2006). For example, a recent Pew study found that 64% of adolescent (12 to 17 years old) were actively engaged in creating and sharing material on the Internet. Teenagers not only blogged, posted photos and posted videos but equally importantly "participated in conversations fueled by that content" (Lenhart, Madden, Rankin Macgill & Smith, 2007).

The phenomenal growth of social networking Web sites has promoted and stimulated adolescents' online lives. Social networking sites are screened sites where users build personal networks that connect them to other users. The most popular of these sites are Facebook and MySpace. A Pew study found that 75% of young adults (18-24 years old) use social networking sites (Lenhart, 2009), up from 55% of all adolescents (12 to 17 years old) (Lenhart, 2007). This makes it clear that Millenials' social lives revolve around the integration of the Internet.

Social networking has been intimately linked with social responsibility. Micromobilization research (Sherrod, 2006) finds that people's social ties can promote activism. Individuals with ties to social structures (that is, their social connections) will participate in the public good if their social ties engage them to do so. "Social network ties are critical determinants of social movement participation" (Sherrod, 2006, p. 597). Therefore the active social networking of adolescents offers them excellent opportunities to participate in socially responsible activities. Yet although social networking sites provide an effortless and convenient means for Millenials' communication and participation in social activities, they do not appear to have taken advantage of this opportune technology to participate in the public good. America's youth are charged with a lack of social responsibility.

The popular press abounds with criticism of Millenials' lack of involvement in the public good. Thomas Friedman, columnist for the *New York Times*, labeled Millenials the quiet generation or "Generation Q" as they are too quiet and lacking in what he calls "idealism, activism and outrage" (Friedman, 2007). A popular youth website supports Friedman's charge, noting that student "disengagement rates are at all-time highs, and costing billions in lost economic opportunities and crime" (www.tigweb.org). Although academic research on Millenial's involvement in the public good is scarce, some research supports the contentions of the popular press. For example, Robert Putnam (2000, cited in Arnett, 2007) says that 18–29 year-olds report less civic engagement than their parents or grandparents when they were the same age. Limber and Kaufman (2004) found that active community participation among youth was very low. They argue that participation by youth is important not just for young people, but for their communities and their countries. Malaney (2006) agrees, both on lack of youth participation and on the importance of social activism and civic engagement for students.

As Malaney (2006) noted, it is a necessity for youth to "bridge this apparent gap between our current world reality and our desire to teach civic responsibility, humanitarianism, equality, and social justice." Community participation, social responsibility and participation in the public good are essential for young people on both personal and social levels. On the personal level it develops self-confidence, builds important skills such as independence, interpersonal and relational skills, leadership and teamwork. Young people who participate in the public good grow and mature more successfully. Equally importantly, social responsibility is important for the maintenance of a healthy society as future leaders and workers learn to hear other's voices, to promote justice and equity, and to take responsibility for a stronger society.

Fortunately for the future of American society, although a strong body of opinion supports the lack of social responsibility by Millenials, some research contradicts this. A large national study on Millenials and corporate social responsibility found that an estimated 15.6 million Millenials (representing nearly 20% of Millenials surveyed, ages 13 – 25) volunteer at least once a week, while 81% of those surveyed had volunteered in the last year; and 61% of Millenials feel personally responsible for making a difference in the world and (Cone 2006 Millenial CAUSE Study). These findings are not isolated. Another survey released by the Corporation for National and Community Service (the federal agency that directs AmeriCorps) and based on data from the Current Population Survey (which began tracking volunteer rates for college students in 2002), found that 3.3 million college students, or 30 percent of all students ages 16 to 24 at American colleges, had donated their time to various causes in 2005, up from 2.7 million, or 28 percent of all students, in 2002 (Farrell, 2006).

Clearly Millenials today are *volunteering* in increasingly larger numbers, but this has not been acknowledged by the critics of this generation (perhaps because volunteering is not seen as socially responsible action when it is *required* by an educational institution rather than engaged in by choice). Whatever the explanation, it is clear that these contradictions call for an objective investigation of Millenials' actions for the public good. For the reasons discussed earlier I feel that

an examination of social responsibility should go with a study of social networking. While academic research connecting the issues of social networking and social responsibility is scarce, researchers and popular press writers alike agree that social networking provides an effective tool for "bridging the gap" between Millenials and the public good as it allows for "leverag(ing) the small efforts of the many with the large efforts of the few" (Brown, 2002, p. 4). Howard Rheingold, an authority on online communities, agrees, stating that students "need to use various Web 2.0 tools to be good citizens because those modes of communication are increasingly the way political discourse and activism take place" (Young, 2008). With this in mind, in this essay I explore Millenials' participation in the public good, investigating whether they use social networking for social responsibility.

CLARIFICATION OF TERMS

The literature utilizes a host of terms to discuss young people's participation in the public good including "civic engagement" "volunteering" "activism" and "philanthropy." Each of these terms has very specific connotations in the research - as a quick search of Wikipedia makes clear (see www. wikipedia.org). Volunteering is a term that has become associated with educational learning – a phenomenon that developed with requirements for service learning in the K-12 system for the Millenial generation. The term "activism" is often associated with political or civic participation, while the term "philanthropy" is frequently associated with large financial donations and/or corporate giving. Therefore in this essay I chose to use the term "social responsibility" as an inclusive term for all actions that contribute to the public good or make a positive difference in the world

It is important to note that this study did not examine *election-related* political or social activism. While both anecdotal evidence and preliminary data demonstrate that young people participated in an unprecedented rate in Barack Obama's election campaign, this is a unique phenomenon that may have skewed findings in an election year. However, this study did include other political activism as an important aspect of social responsibility.

METHODOLOGY

To investigate social networking and social responsibility among Millenials qualitative research methods were utilized, taking a phenomenological approach, following Kvale (1996). Here phenomenology is defined as an attempt to describe the details of the subject's consciousness in an attempt to make the invisible visible. Webnography or netnography is a participant-observation research method, where data are collected through online field research, based on the accepted qualitative method of ethnography. In ethnographic field research, the researcher immerses herself into the life of a social group or culture in order to collect data from within, understanding the culture from the perspectives of its members. Webnography or netnography is the use of the World Wide Web (or Internet) to collect data using the same methods. Because Millenials not only use social networking and the Internet to connect with their friends, but also to post their "most intimate thoughts, dreams, and worries" Tomaselli (2006), young people's communication on the Internet offers fertile grounds for study. Webnography/netnography is most commonly used in business research and anthropology, but it is ideal for our purposes, allowing us to gather the thick, rich data (Francis, 2004) that is the requirement for such research. For this study, webnography offered opportunities to learn the perspectives of young people "living the subject" (Francis, 2004) on their use of social networking and activism.

This study employed observational rather than participatory webnography. The author explored social networking websites, and read blogs and other postings by young people, rather than joining online communities. This use of webnography as a method of data collection is an accepted one, allowing for the unobtrusive collection of data and study of processes. Like many authors (for example, Dan & Forrest, 1997; Nelson & Otnes, 2005; Ryan, 2008) this author identified several sites which were actively used by young people for networking. A variety of sites was examined to provide more robust data, including the following:

- **Sites where content was created by young people**. Such sites typically include blogs and sites like Facebook. I specifically studied young people's responses on a popular blog – the NY times' columnist's Nicholas Kristof's "On the Ground" blog. I also examined the FaceBook, the most popular online social networking site

- **Social networking sites devoted to discussions about, and promotion of, social responsibility**. After a review of hundreds of sites on the Internet, I settled on an examination of two sites: TakingITGlobal (www.tigweb.org) and DoSomething (www.dosomething.org). TakingITGlobal is a social networking website devoted to "opportunities for learning, capacity-building, cross-cultural awareness, and self-development through the use of Information and Communication Technologies." This particular social networking site was selected because of its successful impact, with 10 million young people reached since it was started in 2007 (http://www.tigweb.org/about/). DoSomething is a different type of website, focusing more on real-world rather than online social responsibility. Its goal is "using the power of online to get teens to do good stuff online." The two sites represent a good sampling of young peoples' socially responsible actions.

- **Websites which were created by young people**. For example, Global Youth Connect (http://www.globalyouthconnect. org/) a social networking site formed by Millenials in 1997 to support community-based activists around the world
- **Websites devoted to charitable giving online.** Such sites include traditional and non-traditional charitable giving websites. One such site that bears noting is associated with Facebook—the Causes website.

FINDINGS: SOCIAL NETWORKING AND SOCIAL RESPONSIBILITY

Results were both surprising and heartening. Millenials are indeed using social networking for social responsibility, although they often do not participate in the public good in *traditional* ways. This can best be seen in their own words, as will be shown here from a variety of different web sources.

Social and Political Action

Excellent examples of the social networking utilized for social and political action are provided by Millenials on a blog - New York Times blog, by winners of this year's College Essay Contest (http://essay.blogs.nytimes.com/ tag/activism/?scp=2&sq=Youth%20and%20 activism&st=cse). The comments on social responsibility were provided by Millenials in response to an essay by Rick Perlstein (2008) in which he challenged college students to respond to his assertion that "college as America used to understand it is coming to an end." In response, Millenial student Will Cole (2008) from Chicago denies Perlstein's attack on his generation saying that at his own institution, Carleton College, "while some students are indeed apathetic, others work relentlessly to create change." Cole feels Millenials' social activism is not so different

from previous generations, and his generation is highly activistic and socially involved. In his own words:

Today's college students, by contrast, have responded to genocide. Hundreds of colleges across the country have founded Darfur activism groups, including the Genocide Intervention Fund, the Darfur Action Group, and Students Against Genocide. One group, "STAND: A Student Anti-Genocide Coalition," now includes several hundred college chapters. Their "adopt-a-camp" program works with other non-profit organizations to improve educational infrastructure in the refugee camps surrounding Sudan.

Like college students a generation before them, today's students have also launched massive protests in opposition to war. The student response to the invasion of Iraq was overwhelming, not only in the planning of worldwide protests which drew millions, but also on their own campuses. Take the "Books not Bombs" campaign, which organized strikes in over 360 high schools and colleges on the eve of the invasion. One student organizer of the event told CNN, "We don't want this [war] to be a cowboy fight. Every building we bomb in Baghdad will be another September 11. There will be innocent people dying in them." (2008)

Another young Millenial woman provides a different take on social responsibility, in another prize winning essay in the blog. Vandhana Rao (2008) from Holmdel, New Jersey and a student at the College of William and Mary, emphasizes Millenials' commitment to social change. She writes:

While it is true that many of my peers consider college to be a precursor to the "real world," it is a testament to the [sic] so many college students are eager to transform the stimulating yet isolated experiences of college into a tangible social revolution. Many of my peers, impatient for the opportunity to transform their passionate college debates into practical change, have chosen to forgo lucrative jobs in favor of grueling careers in social activism. Service corps such as Teach for America and the Peace Corp are aggressively competitive for college graduates. Harnessed by dogged perseverance and an almost arrogant belief in our ideals, college students believe that it has become a moral imperative to impress some sort of change upon the world. (2008)

These young people's comments are supported by some academic research. For example, in a series of focus groups with 386 students at 12 colleges and universities, Lopez and Marcello (2006) found that these students are more engaged than the generation before them (Gen-X). And Arnett (2007) notes that Millenials actions bear out their social responsibility: over 8,000 people a year serve in the Peace Corps and 70,000 a year serve in AmeriCorps, with the majority of the volunteers in both groups being Millenials.

Millenials are also actively involved in other online political activism. As Cole (2008) noted in his essay, it has been Millenials who raised awareness of the genocide in Darfur. It is Millenials who continue to rally against ongoing human rights violations around the world, working in online venues, from the personal to the global. An example of a smaller, more personal Darfur-related action by Millenials is Banaa.org, a website created by students at the George Washington University to give a full university scholarship to a qualified student from Darfur. An example at the more global level is a social networking site like Global Connect Youth.

Global Youth Connect (http://www.globalyouthconnect.org/) is a social networking site formed by Millenials in 1997 to support community-based activists around the world. As stated on the website, Global Youth Connect "is dedicated to empowering youth to advance human rights and create a more just world." Lombardo, Zakus and

Skinner (2002) tell us that Global Youth Connect (GYC) runs an e-mail listserv, with about 1,500 subscribers and has a "core group" of about 20 young activists from various countries, including Yugoslavia, Guatemala, Nigeria and the United States. A "real world" example of a recent GYC online-created project is a group of young people who volunteered to stay in Bhutanese refugee camps, and then used media to document their experiences. (Some of this media can be seen on the organization's website at www.globalyouthconnect.org/).

Other examples of Millenials' politically-oriented social responsibility are domestic rather than international. For example, a political network of teenagers, the International Student Activism Alliance (ISAA) was founded in 1996 by three Connecticut high school students: Ben Smilowitz, Jamie Rinaldi, and Abe Walker. The online network was quickly successful, growing to 160 chapters and 1,200 members in about a year. As its website proclaims, "ISAA is about students taking charge of their lives, using their voice and making a difference!" (http://orgs.takingitglobal.org/5570)

ISAA has indeed succeeded in helping students "make a difference" as can be seen in a story in the Nation three years after the founding of ISAA. When Galen Price, a high school student in North Carolina, contacted the ACLU regarding the Winston-Salem School Board's considering required drug tests for high school students participating in extracurricular activities, the ACLU connected him with ISAA and Ben Smilowitz. With Smilowitzes help, Price challenged the law. Although the drug test requirement was mandated, Price started his own ISAA chapter and did not give up the battle. In New Jersey, where a similar law was being considered, the Edison, New Jersey, ISAA chapter took up the challenge with a public education campaign on the constitutionality of random drug testing (Featherstone, 1999).

ISAA is not an isolated case of teen participation in the public good. Melber (2006) reports a

Figure 1.

> **Need suggestions on what i can do to help.**
>
> *Posted by: teenposter#1*
> *Date: Mon, 2008-04-07 15:57*
>
> *i really want to do a worthy cause with my friends but the problem is i can't drive yet and my parents are very busy and worn out. plus they are scared i'll get into trouble. i need a way to involve my friends and do something without my parents having to be involved. i live out in the country so i can't walk anywhere (plus it's out on a main highway,), and neither can my friends cause we live so far apart. im trying to get ideas like the cool ones for the BRICK nominees this year, like the guy who made the books and distributed them and the girl who handed out self-defense as well. any suggestions?*
>
> *ps. i need a way to get my friends interested. some are, but some aren't really into it. i get you cant force them but it would be really cool if they did.*

Figure 2.

> **Submitted by teenposter#2 on Wed, 2008-06-04 16:40.**
>
> *In your situation the only way I could see is getting involved over the internet, or wait until you can drive, and you could call your friends. For getting them interested try to make a project that would be fun for them, like if they like to color have them color posters for a project or other things. Hope this helped.*

high school movement in California in support of immigrants. On May 1, 2006, more than 100,000 students (a quarter of the total number of middle school and high school students in California's largest public school district) boycotted class on the "day without immigrants." As Melber notes, it is difficult for national organizations to find first-time student protesters let alone mobilize them, but this protest was undertaken by young people, many of whom learned of the issue and got involved through MySpace.

Teens without access to more "institutionalized" social actions seek arenas where they can act for the public good, as the dialogue below from DoSomething.org demonstrates. (Names changed to protect privacy*.)

As these posts demonstrate, participating in "worthy causes" is important enough to some young Millenials that they actively seek advice on ways for themselves (and their friends) to get involved in actions for the public good. Their own words speak more eloquently to their desires than does academic research on Millenials – conducted by members of previous generations!

One social networking site that links generations is Facebook. Any discussion of social participation and social networking would be incomplete without an examination of this popular site. Face-Book is the single most popular social networking site in the world, ranking ninth in overall Internet traffic in 2006 with 250 million hits daily in 2006 (Bugeja, 2006), while many high school students

Figure 3.

> **Submitted by teenposter#3 on Tue, 2008-06-24 16:00.**
>
> like _____ said, the only thing in your situation you can do is over the internet. its still doing something, i cant drive either so im in kinda the same situation. and about your friends, if their not willing, maybe after they see you getting involved they'll want to too. just by talking about it to them about something their familiar with they might become interested. also, the friends that are already into can persuade them. hope this helped.

Figure 4.

> **Students For Justice In Palestine**
> WPUNJ
>
> **Basic Info**
>
> Type: <u>Common Interest</u> - <u>Current Events</u>
>
> This group was created for the sole purpose of bringing justice where justice is long overdue.
>
> The people of Palestine AND Lebanon.
>
> *NOTE*
> THIS IS NOT AN ANTI-SEMITIC GROUP! This is only a group to show people that a politicide and genocide is currently being undertaken by the Israeli government toward all Palestinians and we, as HUMAN BEINGS,
> Description: should do everything in our will power to try and stop these atrocities.
>
> THE CORPORATE MEDIA HAS DONE A SUCCESSFUL JOB IN LYING TO THE MASSES BUT THE TRUTH WILL BE KNOWN.
>
> QUESTION, INVESTIGATE, SEE FOR YOURSELF, how far will the rabbit hole go?
>
> Irrational ignorance plagues society today and we should clear this problem once and for all, starting with this issue.

view Facebook as important enough to sign up for before they enter college (Market Wire, 2006). Facebook allows users to set up groups focused around users' individual interests. The nature of Facebook means that users must proactively use the networking system as they select what they want to look at. However, the software also allows users "to ping through hundreds of profiles in a matter of minutes" (Hirschorn, 2007) so that users interested in specific social issues can easily locate groups devoted to their interests.

Facebook thus offers a useful illustration of how young people use the site for socially responsible actions. Here are some groups from the authors' home university, reproduced verbatim:

These diverse examples of social networking sites used in ways that work towards the public good demonstrate the many ways in which Millenials *do* use social networking sites for social responsibility. In this one area, then, initial evidence goes against the conventional image of Millenials as apathetic and uninvolved.

Figure 5.

Kuddles for Kids drive *WPUNJ*	
Basic Info	
Type:	<u>*Organizations*</u> - <u>*Volunteer Organizations*</u>
Description:	*The William Paterson University Honors College Club is collecting any NEW stuffed animal to be donated to Robertwood Johnson Hospital in New Brunswick, NJ. The stuffed animals will be brought to the adolescent floor of the hospital*

Social Entrepreneurship

A different type of social responsibility that merits discussion is "social entrepreneurship." a term popularized by the founder of Ashoka (http://www.ashoka.org/fellows/social_entrepreneur.cfm). Social entrepreneurs are defined as "individuals with innovative solutions to society's most pressing social problems. ... social entrepreneurs act as the change agents for society." They are people who "neither hand out fish nor teach people to fish; their aim is to revolutionize the fishing industry" (Kristof, 2008). Although the concept of social entrepreneurship predates their generation, Millenials are uniquely drawn to this type of social responsibility. The wide range and scope of social entrepreneurship existing today can be seen in some postings by and about Millenials on the On the Ground Blog (n. d.). This particular blog was focused around an Op-Ed piece written by Nicholas Kristof of the New York Times on social entrepreneurs, whom he called "the 21st-century answer to the student protesters of the 1960s." Kristof, after profiling three Millenial social entrepreneurs, invited readers to respond and received 129 responses in two days. The responses are illuminating in terms of the range and magnitude of Millenials' impact on local and global communities. From social entrepreneurship organizations to work done by individuals, from international social networking sites (like microlending to the third world on kiva.com) to an individual Millenial who is working on starting a kids' microlending site, Millenials use social networking as a non-traditional means of action to work for the public good. Because hearing it in their own words is the most effective illustration, some postings are provided below, reproduced verbatim. (Names remain unchanged as these postings were in a public forum run by the online New York Times.)

As these comments demonstrate, Millenials are not only acting in innovative and socially responsible ways, but they availing of the power of the Internet and social networking to succeed, whether domestically or internationally.

Charitable Giving

The final type of social responsibility and social networking that involves Millenials is an adaptation of the conventional charity. Not only are many "traditional" charities redesigning their web sites for easier access and donation, but they are connecting with social networking sites like Facebook and MySpace to enable Millenials' involvement. One very successful application is Causes, founded by some of Facebook's early employees.

Figure 6.

> *January 27th, 2008 <u>10:06 am</u>*
>
> *Loved the article which just scratched the surface of what is going on. Check out the Omprakash Foundation, also started by a Harvard student and his friends. In addition to providing direct aid it also helps place students in volunteer opportunities. Dick Grace's foundation (successful businessman, winemaker turned social entrepreneur) is another. Close friends of ours, after successful careers in law and education, have opened a summer camp in Mississippi emphasizing the arts. They now live at the camp year round and seek out scholarship campers, seeking to change the lives of children from Louisiana, Mississippi and the South.*
>
> *— Posted by Cyndy*

Figure 7.

> *January 27th, 2008 <u>12:30 pm</u>*
>
> *Loved the column. My son is one who is pursuing this vision. His organization, love.futbol (www.lovefutbol.org), builds soccer fields for poor children in developing nations. (In fact, speaking of Harvard Business School, he is currently in Cambridge meeting with eleven Harvard Business School students who have chosen his organization to help develop it further.) His belief: providing poor children with a good place to play soccer will lead to all kinds of good things (as well as possibly preventing them doing bad thing).*
>
> *Hope does exist. — Posted by marc*

The Causes website is woven into Facebook and MySpace by enabling (and encouraging) members to solicit charitable donations through their pages. Members' profiles show the charities they've given money to, and the charities' Facebook pages list donors. Giving is thus very visible, and Millenials get "social credit" (Carroll, 2008) for their participation in the public good. About a year after its founding, Causes reports that 12 million people have signed up and have thus far donated $2.6 million to charity (Arrington, 2008).

While Causes is perhaps the most popular social networking charitable application, several others exist and enjoy a modest popularity. They include:

- **sixdegrees.org:** Founded by actor Kevin Bacon and the Network for Good, sixdegrees.org lets individuals solicit donations for a wide range of charities.
- **realitycharity.com:** The site lets people request donations either for charities or for individuals, such as a veteran of the Iraq war who lacks the money to pay all his medical bills.
- **chipin.com:** Users can create widgets that request and process donations for a cause and that can either be posted on an existing Web site or can be set up as a separate Web site.
- **firstgiving.com:** Users can set up Web pages on the site and steer friends there. The site provides tips on online fundraising.

Figure 8.

> *January 28th, 2008, <u>4:50 pm</u>*
>
> *Thank you for your timely and inspiring piece. The title 'Age of Ambition' is also significant in itself. As an educator, it is uplifting to see the young age at which our youth are demonstrating social entrepreneurial outlooks. In a new Global Kids program in partnership with Youth Venture, we are supporting teen residents of the virtual world Teen Second Life to launch their own social entrepreneurial ventures. These amazing young people, some as young as 13, are challenged to think about their community and work with teens across time zones and continents to bring change to issues that they collectively identify with. At such a young age, the youth that we've encountered are not only showing us that they can bring social change to the world as they see it, but are learning remarkable leadership and 21st century skills along the way. For more information about our Dream it. Do it. Initiative Initiative, please visit us at <u>http://globalkids.org/?id=69</u> —*
>
> *Posted by Amira Fouad*

Figure 9.

> *A splendid column. I nominate my daughter's website providing help for addicts: <u>www.thesecondroad.org.</u> She has spent well over a year of hard work and her own money on the universally applauded project.*
>
> *— Posted by william shore*

- **givemeaning.com:** Like firstgiving, givemeaning hosts Web pages where people can solicit donations. Unlike many sites, give meaning doesn't deduct credit-card fees or other processing fees from donations; advertisers and donors cover those costs.
- **justgive.org:** This site allows visitors to volunteer time and donate goods, as well as contribute cash. It suggests a different sort of wedding registry, where the couple can suggest that friends and family donate to a particular charity rather than buy wedding gifts. (Carroll, 2008).

These charitable social networking sites have had a measurable impact. Online giving has risen strongly with participation from a group who hadn't significantly donated in the past – young people. As well, because of the personal and social nature of social networking, some nontraditional charities have begun to benefit as Millenials promote their own causes. One example is a relatively unknown charity called Love Without Borders which provides heart surgery to orphans in China. It recently raised $150,000 through Causes (Carroll, 2008).

This success is understandable given that socially-connected giving and public acknowledgement works well with Millenials. Far more than previous generations, Millenials want to "work together with others on social issues" (Lopez & Marcello 2006, p. 4). That online charitable participation has already become part of Millenial culture can be seen by visiting Facebook or MySpace. For instance, the Facebook profile of one undergraduate student (who gave the author permission to profile her) showed her membership in the following groups: *International Rescue Committee (official)* and *International Red Cross and Red Crescent Movement*. The profile also showed groups of she was a fan, such as *Save the Children* and *Action Against Hunger*. For these "fan" groups the number of members was listed, as well as the date she joined.

These examples illustrate how online charitable giving has quickly become an established part of social networking.

DISCUSSION

The webnography findings presented above show that Millenials utilize social networking in many different ways: for social change through entrepreneurship, for political and social action, and for charitable solicitation and donation. Why then the conventional wisdom that Millenials do not take social responsibility, nor participate in the public good? This perception is pervasive enough that it is accepted even among Millenials. For example, Zachary Townsend, a Brown University student from Kansas wrote in a prizewinning New York Times Magazine essay posted online that "Students from most universities like mine retreat from the big issues of society and the world and our time into "the pygmy world of private piety…They have no idea how to do the real work entailed in activism" (Townsend, 2008).

When this opinion continues to be held by talented Millenials like Zachary Townsend and prominent writers like Thomas Friedman, they must be considered. An examination of the webnography findings revealed patterns that could explain the perception of Millenials as "quiet" and uninvolved. Some noteworthy themes emerged: Millenials' social responsibility takes a different form than that of their parents or grandparents. It is small-group oriented or personal, rather than public and protest-oriented. It craves social

recognition and reward. It is self-directed and it utilizes digital technologies. The face of social responsibility has changed.

These observations are supported by sociological research by Hustinx and Lammertyn (2003). They provide extensive research to show that the nature of participation in the public good has changed as a result of "broad social transformations" (p. 167). The changes are sweeping and radical as participation in volunteer efforts becomes individualized and "self-organized rather than institutionalized", as well as "sporadic, temporary and non-committal" (p. 168). Hustinx and Lammertyn's comments on modern day social responsibility bear quoting:

Nowadays, willingness to participate in volunteering seems to be more dependent on personal interests and needs than on service ethic and a sense of obligation to the community. Motivated by a search for self-realization, volunteers demand great freedom of choice and clearly limited assignments with tangible outcomes. Volunteer activities have to be spectacular and entertaining to keep volunteers involved. Instead of caring for older or disabled persons, volunteers nowadays opt for "trendy" problems such as HIV/AIDS, refugees, animal rights, and other modern "hot issues" (p. 168)

This quote aptly describes Millenials' actions for the public good and articulates the differences between their style of public participation and that of Boomers and GenXers. It validates the observations made based on the limited research conducted in this study.

FUTURE DIRECTIONS

This study is a start in helping clarify the relationship between social networking and social responsibility, but bears expansion through future research. Millenials do demonstrate social responsibility, although they may not do so in ways recognized by their parents or grandparents. They also avail of social networking to the extent they feel necessary, when they act for the public good. One fruitful direction for future research, therefore, would be to investigate further the ways in which Millenials act for the public good both online (through social networking and other online venues) and face-to-face. The world of the Web is immense, and this research has but touched the surface. Other researchers can fruitfully continue this investigation, particularly through the use of different methods of data collection. Particularly useful could be self-report data collected from Millenials through questionnaires and interviews.

This leads to a second fruitful area of future research: extending methods from the qualitative to the quantitative. While qualitative and ethnographic methods were ideal in the exploratory phases of research into this important area, quantitative methods could provide rich additional data. Qualitative methods here allowed the unobtrusive collection of data, in order to understand the perspectives and motivations of Millenials, and to view patterns among Millenials' actions and communications. Quantitative methods could usefully develop this initial study, investigating further the patterns found here, and adding validity and reliability that are lacking in webnographic research.

A third area that encourages future research is an investigation of the relative amounts of time Millenials spend on online activities related to the public good, compared to time spent online or real-time spent engaging in socially responsible actions; as well as satisfaction garnered from both types of social responsibility. Although this was beyond the scope of this study, results would be useful in that they could expand understanding of Millenials' styles of social responsibility, and provide us with strategies and knowledge we could use to better engage them.

CONCLUSION

A lesson this study offers the GenXers and Boomers is that we must accept and reward Millenials' efforts rather than judging them by our standards. As Rebecca, a Millenial, states, "I am tired of my generation being berated as apathetic simply because we don't choose to repeat the tactics of our parents in advocating for social change. One cannot measure the impact of a generation merely by the number of signs in the streets." (On the Ground Blog, January 28, 2008, 11:06 am).

This young Millenial gives us advice we should heed. And as the generations that oversee civic, educational, social and political life, GenXers and Boomers must go one step further and take responsibility for initiating and maintaining opportunities for social responsibility. Educators, as much as civic and industrial leaders, must actively work to create initiatives that focus on social action driven by Millenials. As Boyd (2007) notes, "Educators have a very powerful role to play in helping smooth the cultural transition that is taking place" (p. 1). The author agrees with Lombardo, Zakus and Skinner's (2002) observation that such initiatives will help Millenials build character "through the promotion of values such as individual responsibility and community service" (p. 364) among other strengths.

REFERENCES

Arnett, J. J. (2007). Suffering, selfish slackers? Myths and realities about emerging adults. *Journal of Youth and Adolescence, 36*(1), 23–29. doi:10.1007/s10964-006-9157-z

Arrington, M. (2008, May 28). Causes reports on its first year: 2.5 million for 20,000 charities and nonprofits. *Techcrunch*. Retrieved September 30, 2008 from http://www.techcrunch.com/2008/05/28/causes-reports-on-its-first-year/

Boyd, D. (2007, May 13). Social network sites: Public, private, or what? *Knowledge Tree*. Retrieved October 13, 2008, from http://kt.flexiblelearning.net.au/tkt2007/?page_id=28

Brown, J. S. (2002). Growing up digital. *US-DLA Journal, 16*(2). Retrieved September 30, 2008, from http://www.usdla.org/html/journal/FEB02_Issue/article01.html

Bugeja, M. J. (2006, January 27). Facing the FaceBook. *Chronicle of Higher Education*. Retrieved from http://chronicle.com/jobs/2006/01/2006012301c.htm

Carroll, P. B. (2008, July 14). Charity cases: Social networking sites make it easy for donors to promote their favorite causes online. *Wall Street Journal*, R11.

Cole, W. (2008, January 27). Full of passion, dressed as tomatoes. *New York Times*. Retrieved September 30, 2008 from http://essay.blogs.nytimes.com/tag/activism/?scp=2&sq=Youth%20activism&st=cse

Cone 2006 Millenial CAUSE Study. (2006, October 24). *Civic minded Millenials prepared to reward or punish companies based on commitment to social causes*. Retrieved September 30, 2008 from, http://www.causemarketingforum.com/page.asp?ID=473

Dann, S., & Forrest, E. J. (1997, Dec). Webnography: Developing unobtrusive online research. In *Proceedings of the Australia New Zealand Marketing Educators' Conference*, Melbourne, Australia (Vol. II, pp. 783-784). Retrieved February 9, 2009, from http://www.cbpp.uaa.alaska.edu/afef/webnography.htm

Farrell, E. F. (2006, Oct 27). More college students are volunteering. *The Chronicle of Higher Education, 53*(10), A40.

Featherstone, L. (1999). Hot wiring schools - Student activists across the country experiment with organizing by Internet. *Nation (New York, N.Y.), 268*(23), 15.

Francis, D. (2004). Learning from participants in field based research. *Cambridge Journal of Education, 34*(3), 265–277. doi:10.1080/0305764042000289910

Friedman, T. (2007, October 10). Generation Q. *New York Times*. Retrieved September 30, 2008 from http://www.nytimes.com/2007/10/10/opinion/10friedman.html?_r=4&oref=slogin&ref=opinion&pagewanted=print

Hamilton, C., & Flanagan, C. (2007). Reforming social responsibility within a technology-based youth activist program. *The American Behavioral Scientist, 51*(444).

Hirschorn, M. (2007, April). The Web 2.0 bubble: Why the social-media revolution will go out with a whimper. *Atlantic Monthly, 299*(3), 134.

Hustinx, L., & Lammertyn, F. (2003). Collective and reflexive styles of volunteering: A sociological modernization perspective. *Voluntas: International Journal of Voluntary and Nonprofit Organizations, 14*(2), 167–187. doi:10.1023/A:1023948027200

Kristof, N. (2008, January 27). The age of ambition. *New York Times*. Retrieved September 30, 2008, from http://www.nytimes.com/2008/01/27/opinion/27kristof.html?_r=1&oref=slogin

Kvale, S. (1996). *InterViews: An introduction to qualitative research interviewing*. Thousand Oaks, CA: Sage Publications.

Lenhart, A. (2007, January 3). Social networking websites and teens: An overview. *Pew Report on Family, Friends and Community*. Retrieved February 11, 2009, from http://www.pewinternet.org/pdfs/PIP_SNS_Data_Memo_Jan_2007.pdf

Lenhart, A. (2009, Jan 14). Adults and social network websites 1/14/2009. *Pew Report on Online Activities and Pursuits.* Retrieved February 11, 2009, from http://www.pewinternet.org/PPF/r/272/report_display.asp

Lenhart, A., Madden, M., Rankin Macgill, A., & Smith, A. (2007, Dec 19). The use of social media gains a greater foothold in teen life as they embrace the conversational nature of interactive online media. *Pew Report.* Retrieved February 11, 2009, from http://www.pewinternet.org/pdfs/PIP_Teens_Social_Media_Final.pdf

Lombardo, C., Zakus, D., & Skinner, H. (2002). Youth social action: Building a global latticework through information and communication technologies. *Health Promotion International, 17*(4), 363–371. doi:10.1093/heapro/17.4.363

Lopez, M. H., & Marcelo, K. B. (2006, November). *CIRCLE fact sheet: Youth demographics.* College Park, MD: The Center for Information Research on Civic Learning and Engagement.

Malaney, G. D. (2006). Educating for civic engagement, social activism, and political dissent: Adding the study of neoliberalism and imperialism to the student affairs curriculum. *Journal of College & Character, 7*(4). Retrieved September 30, 2008, from http://collegevalues.org/pdfs/Educating.pdf

Market Wire. (2006, February 8). *Online social networking soars on college campuses: eMarketer goes back to school to learn about social interactions.* Retrieved from http://findarticles.com/p/articles/mi_pwwi/is_/ai_n16048688

McMillan, S. J., & Morrison, M. (2000). Coming of age with the Internet: A qualitative online exploration of how the Internet has become an integral part of young people's lives. *New Media & Society, 8*(1), 73–95. doi:10.1177/1461444806059871

Melber, A. (2006, May 30). MySpace, My-Politics. *The Nation.* Retrieved September 30, 2008, from http://www.thenation.com/docprint.mhtml?i=20060612&s=melber

Nelson, M. R., & Otnes, C. C. (2005). Exploring cross-cultural ambivalence: A netnography of intercultural wedding message boards. *Journal of Business Research, 58*(1), 89–95. doi:10.1016/S0148-2963(02)00477-0

On the Ground Blog. (2008, Jan 27 & 28). Readers comments to Nicholas Kristof's "The Age of Ambition." *New York Times.* Retrieved September 30, 2008, from http://kristof.blogs.nytimes.com/2008/01/26/your-comments-on-my-social-entrepreneur-column/

Rao, V. (2008, January 27). Why college matters. *New York Times.* Retrieved September 30, 2008, from http://essay.blogs.nytimes.com/tag/activism/?scp=2&sq=Youth%20activism&st=cse'

Ryan, J. (2008). *The virtual campfire: An ethnography of online social networking.* Unpublished thesis, Wesleyan University. Retrieved February 7, 2009, from http://www.thevirtualcampfire.org/

Sherrod, L. R. (2006). *Youth activism: An international encyclopedia.* Westport, CT: Greenwood Press.

Sweeney, R. (2008, September 3). *The Millenial generation goes to college: A focus group.* Presentation at William Paterson University.

Tomaselli, K. P. (2006). Social software: Too much information? Is "online privacy" an oxymoron? *Virginia.edu, X*(1). Retrieved September 30, 2008, from http://www.itc.virginia.edu/virginia.edu/spring06/social.htm

Townsend, Z. (2008, January 27). The modern college: Cultivating students and its own reputation: Waning activism, becoming "the man" and moving up in the rankings game. *New York Times*. Retrieved September 30, 2008, from http://essay.blogs.nytimes.com/tag/activism/?scp=2&sq=Youth%20 activism&st=cse

Young, J. R. (2008, April 11). Why professors ought to teach blogging and podcasting. *The Chronicle of Higher Education*, *54*(31), A22.

Chapter 12
Cyberbullying Internationally Increasing:
New Challenges in the Technology Generation

Ikuko Aoyama
Baylor University, USA

Tony L. Talbert
Baylor University, USA

ABSTRACT

Cyberbullying is a growing phenomenon among adolescents, teens, and young adults who either perpetrate and/or are the recipients of harassing and threatening behaviors through the use of technologies such as emails, Internet communities and social networking Web sites, chat rooms, and cell phones. The incidences of cyberbullying have increased predominantly among students who are residents of technologically advanced countries throughout North America, Europe, and Asia (Anderson & Sturm, 2007; Li, 2006). Several studies have shown that as many as 57% of school age students in the U.S. have experienced some types of cyber harassment (Cook, Williams, Guera & Tuthill, 2007; Hinduja & Patchin, 2005; Lenhart, 2007; Li, 2004). However, many schools and teachers may not fully be aware of the increase of cyberbullying and the psycho-emotional and physical problems that arise from both the perpetuation and the receipt of cyberbullying. The purpose of this chapter is to present the characteristics and theoretical frameworks that define and contextualize cyberbullying including the international prevalence and related statistics, backgrounds and profiles of perpetrators, and adults' roles (Campbell, 2005; Cook, et al., 2007; Kennedy, 2005; Lenhart, 2007; Willard, 2005). This chapter will also provide educators and parents with prevention and intervention strategies to address cyberbullying among youth. Useful Web resources and additional readings are listed as well.

DOI: 10.4018/978-1-60566-926-7.ch012

INTRODUCTION

Internationally, school bullying has been one of the major concerns since the 1980s and various studies have been conducted by researchers with regard to the prevalence, the nature, the short/long-term consequences, perceptions of parents'/teachers', measures of prevention/intervention, and the cultural differences that define and distinguish traditional bullying (Bradshaw, Sawyer, & O-Brennan, 2007; Kanetsuna, Smith, & Morita, 2006; Holt, Finkelhor, & Kantor, 2007). In most western societies, traditional bullying is characterized by physical behaviors such as hitting, punching and spitting, or nonphysical aggression such as verbal assault, teasing, ridicule, sarcasm, and scapegoating (Campbell, 2005; Kanetsuna, et al., 2006; Smorti, Menesini, & Smith, 2003). It involves not only the perpetrator(s) and the victim(s), but also a large number of bystanders who witness the bullying events but do not interfere due to the fear of being the next victim (Akiba, 2005; Campbell, 2005; Talbert, 2004; Talbert & Glanzer, 2006; Talbert & White, 2003). The scientific definition of bullying is complex because it has to refer not only to a single act of aggression but also to situation, power-relation, and bullies' intent to harm (Carey, 2003; Eslea, et al., 2003; Smorti, et al., 2003).

The difficulty of establishing a definitive operational concept of bullying is further exacerbated by the cultural and linguistic derivations of the concept in non-western cultures. Oftentimes there is no equivalent word to describe exactly the same meaning of the English term, *bullying*, in other languages (Eslea, et al., 2003; Smorti, et al., 2003). For example, in Japanese, a word, *Ijime,* is a close linguistic cousin to the western notion of bullying. However, the concept of *ijime* has a more nuanced application and intent than is ascribed to traditional bullying in western society. Unlike the western definition of bullying, which is "aggressive behaviour characterized by repetition of action and asymmetric power relationship"

(Kanetsuna, et al., 2006, p. 570), *ijime* often takes psychological and indirect forms, such as ostracism/exclusion and systematic ignorance from a peer group, (Akiba, 2005; Kanetsuna, et al., 2006; Smorti, et al., 2003; Treml, 2001), and multiple perpetrators, often a whole class, target one victim (Akiba, 2005; Maeda, 1999; Smorti, et al., 2003). In fact, over 90% of Japanese students believed that only group-to-one harassments are *ijime* and they clearly distinguish *ijime* and fighting (Maeda, 1999). In a collective culture like Japan, it can be a serious threat to become an *ijime* victim because Japanese form their identity based on their roles in a community (Akiba, 2005; Nesdale & Naito, 2007). Japanese students think social isolation is the most dreadful thing that could happen (Akiba, 2005). Victims are often blamed and considered to be worthy of bullying because their behaviors are "Selfish", "Noisy", "Inappropriate", "Not following school rules", or "Different"(Akiba, 2005; Treml, 2001). In a collective society, being different can threaten to disturb the harmony within the group (Nesdale & Naito, 2007; Treml, 2001). The Japanese saying: "The nail that sticks up gets hammered down" reflects the concept well.

As described, there are many studies to demonstrate the distinctions that comprise traditional bullying between cultures and countries; however, little research on cyberbullying has been conducted. Analysis of several studies demonstrated a consistent description of the characteristics of cyberbullying as "the willful use of computers or computerized mechanics as tools to intentionally and repeatedly causes harm or discomfort through verbal or relational aggression that targets a specific person or group of persons" (Cook, et al., 2007, p. 4) and can be categorized into two distinct types: the use of computer technology or cell phones to bully others in the real world and the use of cyber space to bully others in the virtual world. More teachers, school administrators, and parents seem to be interested in cyberbullying; however, they may not be fully aware of the various ways that students use technology and how these technologies are being used by some students as a means of harassing other students. As Storm and Storm (2005) point out, teachers, administrators, and parents are not well-prepared to handle cyberbullying. When it comes to technology, it is possible that younger generations are much better versed than adults. Therefore, we have to know what is actually happening and develop appropriate preventions/interventions before things get worse.

A Technology Generation

Megan Meier was thrilled when her parents gave her permission to open her first MySpace account. Like most 13 year old girls Megan was eager to chat with her friends online about school, the latest gossip, and of course boys. Not long after Megan had established her identity using MySpace she began to send and receive her first messages to people who she knew and a few who she didn't know.

One evening Megan received a message from a boy named Josh. She didn't recognize the name but after taking a peek at Josh's information on his MySpace page Megan immediately became interested in the cute boy who was sending her messages. Unfortunately Megan's story is not one of young love being found using technology that is the 21ˢᵗ century's equivalent of the school romance. Instead, Megan's story is one of cyberbullying that splashed across the headlines of newspapers, appeared on the blogs of citizen journalists, and shocked the world when this 13-year old girl named Megan committed suicide in her bedroom inside her parent's home (Maag, 2007). Court records reveal the sordid tale of Megan's death caused by stress of being the target of a callous cyberbullying incident.

Instead of Megan developing a friendship and love interest on MySpace with who she thought was a new boy in the area named Josh, Megan had been targeted as a victim of cyberbullying by Lori Drews, the mother of one of Megan's 13-year

old former friends, with whom Megan had gotten into a fight with, and an 18-year-old temporary office worker who worked for Drews (Korman, 2008). Ms. Drews and her 18 year old accomplice orchestrated an elaborate hoax to convince Megan that she had a developing relationship with a boy named Josh and even went so far as to suddenly end the fake relationship by sending a final message to Megan that stated, *The world would be a better place without you…*(Maag, 2007; Shariff, 2008). When the hoax was finally revealed it spread like wildfire across the Internet for all to see. Sadly, Megan's emotional state was unable to deal with the humiliation and she took her own life.

While the outcome of Megan's story is not typical it is certainly endemic to the growing global phenomenon of cyberbullying. Moreover, there are few laws, policies, and established protocol that societies and schools have in place to address the incidences of cyberbullying that are all too common among today's adolescents and teenagers. As an example, in Megan's case the state of Missouri had no cyberbullying laws at the time of her suicide and while Lori Drews was convicted of misdemeanor offenses as a violation of the Consumer Fraud and Abuse Act for violating the terms and conditions of her MySpace account the full penalty of laws that would govern traditional physical and psychological bullying offenses did not readily apply in this tragic case.

Over the past few years, both major and minor cyberbullying incidences have been getting more attention in technologically advanced countries such as the United States, Great Britain, Canada, and Japan. In the U.K, a group of teens filmed themselves slapping and beating up the targeted victim and posted it on YouTube with the title of "Happy Slapping" (Shariff, 2008). In South Korea, two celebrities, who were severely attacked by numerous anonymous people on the Internet, killed themselves, too (Mckenna, 2007). In Japan, a sixth grade girl had slashed the throat of a girl in her class at school because she was angry at what the girl posted about her on her Website

(Watanabe, 2008). It maybe hard to imagine for adults to have a motive to kill someone based on a comment posted on the Internet, but maintaining a personal Web site can be time consuming. Thus, it "can also promote an increased focus on the self and a heightened, and perhaps exaggerated, sense that others are watching [it] with interest" (Wallace, 1999, p. 34). In fact, the Web site was an important place for self-expression for the girl who was awkward in communication in real life (Shimoda, 2008). Negative remarks on the personal Web page were possibly unbearable to the girl due to egocentrism in adolescence. Incidents such as these may only represent the tip of the iceberg. Similar episodes are reported in Australia, New Zealand, India and Thailand, as well (Shariff, 2008).

While societies and schools have been slow to respond to the increased incidences of cyberbullying, scholars studying the phenomenon have actively investigated and defined this new type of bullying in which perpetrators use technologies such as emails, cell phones, Internet Web sites, social networking sites (SNS), and/or chat rooms (Campbell, 2005; Cook, et al., 2007; Shariff, 2008; Storm & Storm, 2005) to harass, threaten, and even conspire to do harm. Studies have revealed that deliberate acts of cyberbullying include sending threatening or aggressive emails, text messages, and/or instant messages. Other acts also include spreading malicious rumors, posting embarrassing pictures and/or videos online without permission, setting up a derogatory Web site targeting the victim, breaking into someone's e-mail or SNS account to damage the person's reputation or relationships, excluding the victim from an online group, disclosing personal information, and attacking anonymously by using *avatars* (Campbell, 2005; Cook, et al., 2007; Lenhart, 2007; Shariff, 2008).

Some educators and parents may think cyberbullying is an unusual behavior in which only students with problems are engaged. However, considering the fact that new information technol-

ogy hardware, software, and application innovations are part of the lives of today's adolescents and teens, it is not surprising that the way students bully their peers has adapted with this technology. The prevalence of cyberbullying varies depending on the definition and the participants' age and gender; however, several studies have shown that approximately 15% to 57% of school age students in the U.S. have experienced some types of cyber harassment (Cook, et al., 2007; Hinduja & Patchin, 2005; Lenhart, 2007; Li, 2004). In Canada, it is revealed that 34% of students in grades 7 to 11 have been bullied through the Internet (Media Awareness Network). In England, it was reported that about 25% of youth aged 11 to 19 had been cyberbullied, and sixteen children committed suicide due to cyberbullying each year (Anderson & Sturm, 2007; Li, 2006). Another study on British youths also demonstrated that "31 percent of youth ages 9 to 19 had received that unwanted sexual comments and that 33 percent had received nasty comments sent via email, chat, instant message, or text message" (Willard, 2007, p. 32). In Japan, 45% of high school students, 67% of middle school students and 10% of elementary school students have experienced cyberbullying (Yomiuri Online). A study conducted by Li (2005) demonstrated that over 60% of students in China have experienced cyberbullying, as well.

As for the Internet use among American children age 5 to 17, 90% of them use computers, and 59% have access to the Internet (Cook, et al., 2007). A different survey revealed that 22% of teens ages 12 to 17 reported they were keeping a personal Web site (Willard, 2007). In Canada, 94% of students grades 4 to 11 (N=5000+) have the Internet access at home and by 11th grade, half of them have thier own Internet-connected computer. 28% of 4th graders use instant messenger (IM), and that figure rises to 86% among 11th graders (Media Awareness Network). In the U.K, about 70% of students have access to the Internet at home, and 75% of them carry cell phones (Shariff, 2008). In China, over 40% of high school students have their own computer with the Internet and 63% of them have cell phones (Watanabe, 2008). In Japan, the survey results (N= 25,800) demonstrated that 95% of high school students, 40% of middle school students, and 21% of elementary school children have cell phones with the Internet access (Yomiuri Online). The Internet space is a perfect playground for many adolescents which provides many like-minded friends and where self-expression is made easy (Shimoda, 2008). It is predicted that the number of students who have access to the Internet and cell phones will increase each year. Technological equipment is getting smaller, faster, more interactive, and more ubiquitous (Willard, 2007). As a result, the number of cyberbullying incidents may also rise worldwide; thus, it is essential for educators and parents to understand the diverse aspects of cyberbullying and prepare for strategies to prevent the problems.

Many of the studies on traditional bullying have focused on school-age children because school bullying incidents peak at middle school and then rapidly drop by the end of high school (Chapell et al., 2004; Chapell, Hasselman, Kitchin, Lomon, MacIver, & Sarullo, 2006). However, this drop may not be the case for cyberbullying because older students are more likely to have their own cell phones and computers. In fact, more eighth graders reported their cyberbullying experiences than sixth graders (Kowalski, et al., 2008), and cyberbullying is prevalent even among college students. A survey conducted by Aoyama (2009) revealed that about 30% of university students (N=421) reported that they have heard of cyberbullying taking place in a circle of friends, and about 46% of them have seen material posted online that denigrates or puts down a school staff member. In addition, 13% of students have received mean and nasty messages from someone. These findings suggest that not only middle and high school but also university administrators are facing new challenges.

The high prevalene of cyberbullying among collge students is not surprising because the ages between 18 and 24 had the highest rate of the Internet use of all age groups (Gordon, Juang, & Syed, 2007). Problematic Internet usage such as Internet addiction, among college students is often reported (Ceyhan & Ceyhan, 2007; Gordon, et al., 2007). The perfect example would be one Website called *juicycampus.com* in which rumors and gossips relating to the college/university are posted anonymously. On such a Website, some users discuss physical attributes, personal aesthetic, and intimacy relationships of faculty and students, and some posts even contain racist and sexist remarks (Hostin, 2008).

Gender differences also need to be mentioned. Because it is said girls are more likely to engage in indirect/psychological bullying than boys, researchers point out cyberbullying is more prevalent among girls (Willard, 2007). However, as will be described in the following discussion, there are several different forms of cyberbullying; thus, it is probable that boys and girls equally engage in cyberbullying, but in different ways and types. In fact, it is reported that boys' most popular activity online is gaming, and girls' favorite online activity is communication; therefore, *flaming* and *exclusion* types can be seen more among boys, and denigration and *outing/tricky* types can be seen more among girls (Willard, 2007). Another study demonstrates that males are "more likely to be bullies and cyber-bullies than their female counterparts" (Shariff, 2008, p. 84). Li (2006) also shows that more male students reported being cyberbullied than female students, but females are more likely to inform their victimized experiences to adults.

CATEGORICAL APPLICATIONS AND TYPOLOGICAL CHARACTERISTICS OF CYBERBULLYING

Research on cyberbullying has provided operational definitions that articulate both the applications and typologies of the phenomenon. Researchers outlined distinct categorical applications

Table. 1. Statistics on international cyberbullying and technology usage among youth

	Cyberbullying prevalence	**Teen's accessibility to technology**	**Cases**
U.S	15-57% of students have experienced some type of cyber-harassment	90% children ages 5 to 17 use computers & 59% have access to the Internet	13-year-old girl who was attacked on MySpace by her online boyfriend who turned out to be a mother of her friend killed herself
U.K	31% of youth ages 9 to 19 have experienced cyberbullying and cyber-harassment	70% of students have access to the Internet at home, and 75% of them carry a cell phone	"Happy Slapping": a group of teens beat up the targeted victim and film the actions, then uploaded it on YouTube
Canada	34% of students in grades 7 to 11 have been cyberbullied	94% of students grades 4 to 11 have Internet access at home	"Star Wars Kid": a boy who dressed like a Star Wars character was filmed by his peer who uploaded the video for fun. It was one of the most downloaded video of the year on YouTube. He was so embarrassed that he dropped out of high school
Japan	45% of high school, 67% of middle school & 10% of elementary students have been cyberbullied	95% of high school, 40% middle school students have a cell phone.	A 6th grade girl killed her classmate who left negative comments on the girl's Web site
China	60% of students have been cyberbullied	32% high school students use Internet	School teacher sued against his student who modified pictures of teacher's face with naked body and monkey and posted them online

and unique typologies of persons who engage in cyberbullying behaviors. As previously discussed, cyberbullying is most often perpetrated through the use of computer technology or cell phones to bully others in the real world (e.g., "Happy Slapping") and the use of cyber space to bully others in the virtual world (Cook, et al., 2007). For example, an online character such as one in *Second Life*, can attack or intentionally exclude other online characters.

Types of Cyberbullying

Willard (2007) identified seven applied categories which characterize cyberbullying.

Yasukawa (2008) also recognized four patterns of cyberbullying as follows.

Profiles of Perpetrators

Shariff (2008) also notes two types of cyberbullying in terms of target and intention of perpetrators.

The latter type of cyberbullying provides evidence to the fact that teachers and school staff, not simply youthful peers, can be victimized by cyberbullying as well. For example, a teacher who tried to stop cyberbullying and posted a warning message on the "unofficial" school Web-page ended up receiving many threatening emails (Yasukawa, 2008).

The characteristics of cyberbullying perpetrators also emerge in four distinct typologies that best articulate the phenomenon (Kennedy, 2005; Kowalski, Limber & Agaston, 2008).

However, the four categories listed above are not conclusive. Students may engage in cyberbullying without believing they do. Students believe it is okay to write anything on these Websites because nobody seems to be reproached for posting negative comments or rumors (Shimoda, 2008).

Table 2.

Flaming	Angry or rude messages sent directly to a victim or to an online group. Generally, *flaming* occurs in public communication such as chat room, game, and blog. According to Wallace (1999), group polarization can be quite high in the Internet community because it is so easy to find someone with similar opinions in the virtual settings. As a result, people may hold biased discussion and believe different opinions or attitudes deserve attacking.
Harassment	Bullies repeatedly sending a victim offensive messages. Contrary to *flaming, harassing* messages are generally sent though emails, instant messages, and text messages.
Cyberstalking	Threats of harm are made though emails, instant messages, and text messages. It is often linked to the termination of sexual relationship.
Denigration (Put down)	Harmful or cruel statements about a person are conveyed others by forwarding emails and posting misleading information about the victim on the Web sites. In this case, the intended recipient is not the target, but the public who read the email or watch the Web site.
Masquerading	It refers to someone who pretends to be somebody else and tries to make a victim look bad by sending or posting negative messages or comments. It can happen because the exchange of passwords is believed to be evidence of true friendship among teens, especially girls.
Outing and trickery	It refers to sensitive, private or embarrassing information disclosed by forwarding emails or posting information online. *Outing and trickery* can occur in the context of a failed relationship in which one party distributes private information acquired while the relationship was still mutual.
Exclusion	It means exclusion from online groups such as games.

Table 3.

Deception emails	It is similar to Willard's (2007) identified *masquerading* types; however, an exchange of the password is not necessary. There are Websites to make up deception emails. Users just type someone's email address and create messages. The Web-based email services send messages which seem to be sent by someone who uses the email address. For example, students receive emails from their own email addresses which often contain death notice. Perpetrators can use multiple peers' email address to harass the targeted victim, too. The victim student easily believes s/he is completely rejected.
Chain emails/texts	This is an electronic type of chain letter which attempts to induce the recipient to forward a number of messages and then pass them on to as many recipients as possible. For instance, it is reported the perpetrator took private pictures of his peer at the rest room and attached the picture with a chain email by using anonymous email address. The message said "If you do not forward the email, it is your turn to be the victim." (Yasukawa, 2008, p. 39) It did not take time that the picture was spread throughout the students at the school.
Masqueraded profile on SNS	It is also similar to Willard's (2007)*masquerading* and d*enigration (Put down)* types. A perpetrator sets up a SNS account and creates someone's profile which often describes the victim as a sex addict, a shoplifter etc. The profile looks so real that even teachers believe it. The victimized high school girl was suspected to prostitute and left the school (Yasukawa, 2008).
Unofficial School Web-sites	This is like a *juicycampus.com* where negative remarks or rumors about someone are posted, but students or alumni opened the "*unofficial*" school Web-page as a students' secrete place where they hang out without adult supervision because these Web-sites are often inaccessible without ID and password. In face-to-face bullying, it maybe difficult for some children not to conform to bossy student who bully other peer. However, a study showed that the degree of conformity did not disappear in the computer-mediated communication environment (Wallace, 1999). Thus, it is possible that students feel silent pressures to conform to the group even in the Internet community.

RISK FACTORS

Strom and Strom (2005) also argue that jealousy is a common motive for cyberbullying. Unlike traditional bullying, popular students can be targeted.

Another interesting study conducted by Shariff (2008) has revealed that 71% of students indicated

Table 4.

Peer-to-peer cyberbullying	Malicious and defamatory remarks and rumors are posted about a party.	e.g., *JuicyCampus.com*
Anti-authority cyber-expressions	Vitriolic comments are invited when students are angry with teachers or professors for a variety of reasons.	e.g.,*RateMyTeacher.com* and *RateMyProfessor.com*

Table 5.

Vengeful angels	Individuals who engage in cyberbullying to protect their friends and they do not see themselves as a bully.
Power hungry	Individuals who want to demonstrate their power in cyberspace. However, they are often the victim of traditional bullying and could not exert their power in real life situations.
Revenge of the nerds	Individuals who have high technology skills and use them to frighten or embarrass others. As in the power hungry typology, they may not be tough enough in real life. Anderson and Sturm (2007) point out "[cyber] bullies may have low self-esteem and act aggressively to overt compensate for their weakness." (p. 25) It is one of the characteristics of cyberbullying, which is seldom seen in traditional bullying, that cyberbullies can be physically smaller and younger than victims unlike traditional face-to-face bullying.
Mean girls	Individuals who are bored and engage in cyberbullying to look for some entertainment. These cyberbullies are often female (Kennedy, 2005).

they were less likely to bully others if they were happy at school. The study further reveals that stress can drive teens to misbehave online or cyberspace can be a stress outlet for them. In either case, students seem to engage in cyberbullying behaviors just for fun without thinking about the serious consequences. In fact, the *frustration-aggression theory*, first proposed by a group of researchers at Yale University in 1939, argues that frustration brings out anger and aggressive responses, and then anger triggers a hostile action (Berkowitz, 1989). Perpetrators are often less restrained in their attacks on the victim because they cannot observe the consequences or pains the victim suffers. As a result, they believe they do not hurt anyone (Mckenna, 2007). This is the phenomenon of *disinhibition* in which "the anonymity afforded by the Internet can lead people to pursue behaviors further than they might otherwise be willing to do." (Kowalski et al., 2008, p. 64) In real life face-to-face settings, our behaviors are modulated by the emotional reactions of others; however, because perpetrators face no social/peer disapproval and the threat of punishment in cyber-space, their behaviors can be more extreme than they normally would be.

Profiles of Cyberbullying Victims/Targets

Just as there are organized profiles of individuals who are most inclined to engage in cyberbullying behaviors, there are also predictors of those individuals who are typically targeted as victims of cyberbullying. The cyberbullied victims/targets fall into two identifiable at-risk groups (Willard, 2007). The first group is *the wannabe crowd* who tries hard to fit in with the group of peers and intentionally involve themselves in Internet communication. Second, *lesbian, gay, bisexual, and transsexual (LGBT)* students, who are often the target of traditional bullying as well,are generally targeted for personal characteristics or through sexual forms of harassment (Shariff, 2008). A study shows that GLBT individuals are "twice as likely to experience cyberstalking or e-mail harassment from a stranger as were students who identified themselves as heterosexual" (Finn, 2004, p. 480).

It is important to recognize that both victim-prone groups are frequent users and active inhabitants of social networking sites (SNS), thereby exposing them to more opportunities to not only be victims but also the potential to replicate cyberbullying behaviors toward others. According to Shariff (2008), about 40% of students who use SNS have been cyberbullied compared to 22% of students who do not use SNS. However, as mentioned earlier, everyone, teachers, popular students, and ex-boy/girl friend, can be victims. This is another difference from traditional bullying which victims are often younger or physically smaller and weaker. It is also possible that the victimized students in traditional bullying can be cyberbullies. Watanabe (2008) discusses that the victims are 17 times more likely to be bullies than bullies to be victims. A child's status as a bully or victim could be easily interchanged.

Negative Effects of Cyberbullying

Many researchers on traditional bullying have argued various undesirable influences on victims including depression, anxiety, lower self-esteem, poor academic achievement, more physical health problems, school avoidance, and future social phobia (Kowalski, et al., 2008; O' Moore & Kirkham, 2001; Shariff, 2008). Although fewer studies have been conducted, cyberbullying can be more damaging than traditional face-to-face bullying to victims because the fluidity and frequency of the bullying behaviors using technology. In other words, cyberbullying can occur anytime and anywhere. Hence, negative effects such as depression, anxiety or low self-esteem can be more severe and longer lasting.

Adolescents cannot simply turn off the computers or mobiles as many adults would do because technology is a vital tool of communication. Even though victims change their email addresses, phone numbers, and screen names, it may give an only temporal solution because it is unreasonable that the victims would never use the Internet again, and they simply may not be mature enough to handle the virtual world and its anonymous attack (Anderson & Sturm, 2007; Maag, 2007).

In traditional bullying, a limited number of children are involved. Contrarily, in cyberbullying, "hurtful or humiliating content can be sent to a large number of people in a short period of time" (Hinduja & Patchin, 2009, p. 23). For example, in Canada, a high school boy dropped out of school after his classmates found an embarrassing video of him pretending to be a Star Wars character and posted it on the Internet as a joke which became the Internet's most downloaded video of 2006 (Mckenna, 2007). It can cause further cyber-harassment by those who are not originally related to the victim. The fact that thousands of audience/bystanders may be involved will make victims helpless. What is more, the materials posted online are difficult to delete completely. They are easily copied by or forwarded to many people. Proof of harassment will last almost forever (Yasukawa, 2008).

Finally, unlike traditional bullying, many victims often have no idea who are the cyberbullies. In fact, about half of the students who had been cyberbullied did not know who was bullying them (Media Awareness Network). Anonymity may amplify fear and negative effects on victims; as a result, victimized students may doubt all of their peers and fail to seek out help

WHAT CAN WE DO? THE ROLE OF TEACHERS, PARENTS, AND RESEARCHERS

In spite of the high prevalence of bullying/cyberbullying among adolescents, a number of studies suggest that adults underestimate the incidents (Holt & Keyes, 2004). In fact, the district-wide survey conducted in Japan revealed that only half of the parents whose children have been cyberbullied have acknowledged that their children have been victimized online (Yomiuri Online). Shariff (2008) also reports that 32% of parents in her survey thought online bullying could not hurt children because "it is just words in cyberspace." (p. 80) That is why many teens think that adults do not understand their new online world (Willard, 2007). Even for adults who are aware of danger, the majority of them are not confident to instruct appropriate use of mobiles and the Internet to their children (Shimoda, 2008)

As described, cyberbullying can cause more serious problems than traditional face-to-face bullying; however, intervention is not easy. What makes cyberbullying intervention difficult is its hidden nature. Unlike traditional classroom bullying, cyberbullying is more likely to happen outside of the school, and proofs of victimization are invisible because cyberspace is the major place for bullying. Many parents who respect their children's privacy are reluctant to check emails or text messages. On the other hand, as students become older, they are less likely to report their bullying incidents even though cyberbullying seems to be more prevalent among older students (Smith, Madsen & Moody, 1999). In addition, there could be a context in which a young person has provided sexually suggestive pictures to his/her ex who is now making threats or cyberstalking. In such case, the victim is hesitant to report because of shame or fear of punitive consequences (Willard, 2007).

Another factor to consider is rights of free speech. Many schools do not have general guidelines to regulate off-campus speech. In the U.S., the student who was suspended for setting up a Web site mocking a teacher sued the school in 1998, and the Federal court determined that the student's rights were violated and ordered the school district to pay $30,000 and apologize to the student (Sturgeon, 2006). Most schools do not have a policy to punish cyberbullying (Kennedy, 2005). Nevertheless, it is essential to teach children about the limit on their free speech rights (Willard, 2007).

Teacher/School Strategies

First, schools have to teach children how to use technology and behave ethically online. Children may believe only physical threats and violence are bullying (Media Awareness Network). However, it is vital to educate children that cyberbullying can cause serious psychological distress among victims. Various *netiquette* programs and useful Web resources are available for schools and children (in Appendix A). Teaching social skills, such as anger control and stress management, can also be effective. Willard (2005) points out that social skill training can "enhance predictive empathy skills and ethical decision-making and conflict resolution skills." (p.11) To deliver effective education on technology use and cyberbullying prevention, teachers should understand full behavioral aspects of cyberbullying (Willard, 2007). It is also essential to encourage students to report cyberbullying to adults.

Second, many cyberbullies think they won't be caught; thus, it is important to teach them that they leave cyber-footprints on the Internet wherever they go, and a PC can be located with an IP address (Willard, 2007). It is also necessary to instruct that cyberbullying is a crime. In 2006, the U.S. Congress passed a law making it a federal crime to "annoy, abuse, threaten or harass" another person through the Internet, and approximately 36 states have enacted similar legislation (McKenna, 2007, p. 60). There is a similar law in Canada, too. "It is a crime to communicate repeatedly with someone if your communication caused them to fear for their own safety or for the safety of others" (Media Awareness Network). It's also a crime to publish information which injures a person's reputation. As Wallace (1999) argues, defining harassment and threats in legal terms is difficult; thus, introducing real stories can be helpful for students to visualize what is actually a crime.

Even though many schools would handle cyberbullying cases without legal procedures, it would be effective to know those facts. It may be also a good opportunity to review school policies. As of 2008, 30 states have laws related to bullying and five state laws (Arkansas, Idaho, Iowa, South, Carolina, and Washington) include electronic communications (Kowalski, et al., 2008). In Missouri, cyberbullying law was signed in July, 2008, and it "covers harassment from computers, text message and other electronic devices" (Associated Press).

In addition, teachers' education and professional development of school staff and policymakers are critical. Raising awareness is the very first step for schools and teachers. The teachers' education needs to include legal literacy which prepares them to apply legal principles because, through discussion and analysis of case law, they are able to reflect their school situations (Shariff, 2008).

If schools already have anti-bullying programs, cyberbullying needs to be included. Defining it operationally in easy language for young students is also important because cyberbullying can occur in several forms. If schools already have rules on Internet activity, it is best to be conveyed to students in the context of discussion (Willard, 2007). Educating staff about the seriousness of cyberbullying is also essential for successful school-based intervention because adults often think indirect nonphysical bullying has less harmlful than direct physical bullying (Bradshaw et al., 2007).

With regard to monitoring, there are some computer programs/software that filter harmful Web sites, detect emails or instant massagers (IMs) that contain certain words, keep logs, and track all Web sites children visited (Kowalski, et al., 2008). However, no monitoring system is perfect forever. Students in the computer generation may be able to use methods which allow them to bypass the filtering programs; thus, again it is important to encourage students to report cyberbullying. It would be also a good idea to invite experts in digital literacy to help teachers develop resources of databases of useful Web sites (Shariff, 2008)

Finally, informing parents of the issue is also necessary because, as mentioned earlier, cyberbullying is more likely to occur outside of schools. Providing workshops, sending information in school newsletters, and having more extensive information available in counselor's office are suggested (Campbell, 2005).

Parents Strategies

While teachers must certainly be prepared to address issues and incidences of cyberbullying the reality is that home Internet access facilitates a 24/7 playground for predators to bully others (Campbell, 2005; i-SAFE America) leading to more incidences of cyberbullying taking place away from schools than in schools. However, the victims of cyberbullying are often reluctant to report the incident to parents because they fear overreaction by their parents who may take away Internet access or a cell phone which is a vital tool for teens' socialization (Campbell, 2005; Storm & Storm, 2005). These facts make it more difficult for adults to identify cyberbullying. Thus, the consequences of cyberbullying can be more serious than face-to face bullying (Campbell, 2005).

Parents are primary sources to teach moral values and social expectations to their children even though influential mass media transmits contradicting messages (Willard, 2007). Unlike mass media like TV, newspapers, and books, the Internet information is personal media which individual responsibility is important; thus, parents of children who misbehave online are responsible for the behaviors (Shimoda, 2008).

The very first thing parents can do is to increase monitoring regarding the Internet or other technology use. "Parents of bullies have been found to demonstrate lack of involvement, no limit setting, and model aggressive problem-solving" (Willard, 2005, p. 6). It is also reported that only 33% of teens think their parents monitor their online activity contrary to 62% of parents said they check on teens' activity on the Internet

(Lenhart, 2005). Asking what they are doing online or helping them find resources increases adolescents' online skills; however, parents have to be careful not to be too pushy about monitoring, restricting and controlling their children's online activities because teens are extremely protective of their privacy (Shariff, 2008). Setting rules on Internet use and installing filtering software will be an appropriate first step, but establishing trust is more important (Willard, 2007).

Simply keeping eyes on the screen may not be helpful because teens use net lingo and abbreviations among friends. For example, do you know what the following words mean?

1. PSOS
2. BB
3. CT
4. P911
5. JAM

The answers are

1. Parents Standing Over Shoulder
2. Be Back
3. Can't Talk
4. Parents Alert
5. Just a Minute

To become not simply familiar but perhaps proficient in speaking the language of cyber communities and cultures is essential if we wish to not only understand the catalysts of cyberbullying but also the means by which we can prevent these acts. To learn more about the language used in cyber communities and cultures adults may wish to access online information pages such as: *NetLingo Top 20 Internet Acronyms Every Parent Needs to Know*www.netlingo.com/top20teens.cfm; and, *Text Message Abbreviations*www.Webopedia.com/quick_ref/textmessageabbreviations.asp)

Second, they must teach their children how to handle personal information. It sounds so common sense to adults, but children may simply be cognitively immature and have no idea that mailing address, telephone number, password should never been given to others online. Knowing the locations where children post information is important. Even though children can be upset that it is invasion of privacy, material posted online is *public*. Once negative information is posted, it is difficult to delete it completely. In reality, a high school girl who posted her high school information and her address on SNS was stalked by a middle-age pedophile (Watanabe, 2008).

If parents find out their children are cyberbullied, *DO NOT PANIC* and never respond to cyberbullies directly. Instead, keep all emails, IMs, and text messages as evidence, then block some contacts (Willard, 2007). They can also contact Internet service providers (ISPs) or mobile companies to trace bullies. Because "cyberbullying is almost always a violation of the terms of use agreements of the Web sites, ISPs, and cell phone companies where it takes places. One advantage of filing a complaint in this way is that it is not necessary to identify an anonymous cyberbully" (Willard, 2007, p.152-153). Even though a child is not victimized, Googling a child's name regularly and visiting children's SNS page can help to identify cyberbullying cases.

Researchers' Missions

Because cyberbullying is relatively a new phenomenon, there is not enough literature as of this writing. Thus, researchers need to study various aspects on cyberbullying. As Storm and Storm (2005) discuss the implications for future study, researchers can pursue the following study.

First of all, it is necessary to know the extent in which the students exposed to cyberbullying behaviors. A larger student sample with various backgrounds would give a more accurate prevalence of cyberbullying among youth.

Second, it is important to explore the similarities and differences between traditional bullies and cyberbullies. Shariff (2008) says "background on traditional bullying is important because it lays the foundation for an improved understanding of emerging profiles of cyberbullying" (p. 9). The behavior patterns of traditional bullies are well documented and contrary to popular assumptions, bullies often are intelligent, receive good grades, and usually express self-confidence. Kowalski, et al. (2008) also point out a high correlation between traditional bullies and cyber-bullies, and traditional bullying victims and cyberbullying victims. 55% of cyberbullies reported their school-yard bullying behaviors, and 61% of victims of cyberbullying reported being victimized in traditional bullying as well.

Third, the long-term effects on adolescents who are involved with cyberbullying also need more research. In traditional bullying, student perpetrators record higher than average rates of alcoholism, more frequent personality disorders and require greater use of mental health services than their non-bully peers (Storm & Storm, 2005). Classic bullying study by Olweus has demonstrated that 60% of boys who engaged in bullying were convicted at least once in adulthood (Watanabe, 2008). Moreover, depression, anxiety and low self-esteem can last for a long time. Thus, longitudinal studies will be necessary to investigate if similar findings are obtained from cyberbullying contexts.

Fourth, it is essential to comprehend the family relationships and environment of cyberbullies. Parents of traditional bullies do not use even a fraction of the praise, encouragement, or good humor that other parents use in communicating with their children (Storm & Storm, 2005). In addition, students who mistreat others are often victims themselves within their own home (Holt, Finkerlhor, & Kantor, 2007). The bully students are twice less likely to have family communication (Watanabe, 2008). These findings suggest parental involvements can be the key for cyberbullying prevention.

Fifth, developing research-based intervention/prevention programs is critical. In traditional bullying, many schools have helped adolescents to overcome social skill deficiencies and emotional immaturity. School-wide anti-bullying curricula are available, too. For example, Dan Olweus, a researcher in Norway, is a pioneer in bullying study who conducted the country-wide intervention program in the 1980s. The effectiveness of his programs is also proven empirically (Olweus, 1993). The program is adapted to the U.S school system and proved to be successful as well. Therefore, researchers have to test if existing programs would work for cyberbullying. It is crucial for researchers to understand the new phenomena and replicate the well-documented area of traditional bullying with cyberbullying perspectives (Cook, et al., 2007; Hinduja & Patchin, 2005; Lenhart, 2007; Li, 2004).

Subsequently, it is important to understand definition/perceptions of cyberbullying between students and teachers/parents because, as Bradshaw, et al. (2007) suggest, there is a large discrepancy between students and teachers in terms of perception of bullying. About 50% of children reported being bullied by other students at school at least once during the past month whereas 71% of staff estimated that 15% or less of the students at their schools were frequently bullied. Staff members who reported bullying rates similar to those indicated by students were only less than 1%. Additionally, whereas half of the staff (45.6%) indicated that a student had reported being bullied to them during the past month, 21.3% of students reported telling school staff after having been bullied.

It is hypothesized that the discrepancy will be much bigger for cyberbullying because it is rare for teachers and adults to witness the incident due to its hidden nature (Bradshaw, et al., 2007). It is also possible that the definition from researchers can be different from the one from students. In that case, the research findings are least valid.

The definition/perceptions of cyberbullying would be different in different cultures. For example, in China, behaviors of online prank and the Internet slander are forms of cyberbullying, and under the Chinese law, it is considered criminal to "insulting others using force or other methods or fabrication stories to slander others (Shariff, 2008, p. 61). In Japan, many students interviewed referred to name calling on bush boards as cyberbullying. (Aoyama & Talbert, 2009). They also mentioned that unofficial school Web sites are often created by students for cyberbullying, and the use of cell phones to access the sites is common. Wallace (1999) points out that the Internet is a global environment with people from many cultures with different social rules. Hence, it is also necessary to be aware of cross-cultural aspects of cyberbullying.

Finally, the lack of a well-validated scale/instrument to measure cyberbullying is one of the problems for future study. Currently, researchers who have conducted studies on cyberbullying have created their own questionnaires/surveys, but they rarely provide information on reliability and validity (e.g., Li, 2006). Different measurements may lead to different results; thus, a measurement that have demonstrated technical adequacy will be needed.

ENDING WHERE WE BEGAN: A COMMITMENT TO INFORM, REFORM, & TRANSFORM

While Megan's story is certainly tragic it serves as a reminder to each of us the importance of actively seeking remedies to ending harassing and violent behaviors whether they be perpetuated in cyber-space or the play ground. The reality is that the lines between the terrestrial-world and the cyber-world are no longer evident. The boundaries that separated fantasize and realities have long been blurred in our highly adaptable and intuitive technology enriched 21st century society. As clearly seen in reports from popular press and academic research many students internationally have already experienced cyberbullying at varying levels of intensity as reported by both perpetuators and victims of this phenomenon. While many adults fail to embrace the importance and even the severity of cyberbullying incidents and while the hidden and even seemingly pecular nature of the acts of cyberbullying are difficult to fully fathom by a generation of adults not fully immersed in the lifestyle of information technology, the reality is that as technology advances so will the diverse applications and typologies of cyberbullying.

As educators, parents and researchers strive to keep pace with the new challenges of evolving information technology use and abuse it becomes more important to include students in the conversation and the research initiatives in order to overcome the generational and operational gap obstacles that serve as a veil to full disclosure and understanding of cyberbullying activities. Although there are still many obstacles before we can fully and effectively eliminate many of the incidences of cyberbullying, the simple act of increasing awareness of information technology use and behaviors among students, teachers, parents, and researcher is a significantly proactive first step in surmounting the obstacles that have allowed cyberbullying to thrive. Most important, these proactive efforts to educate and inform all stakeholders of both the overt and covert varieties of cyberbullying will serve as a catalyst to prevent future tragic incidences as detailed in Megan's story.

REFERENCES

Akiba, M. (2004). Nature and correlates of ijime-bullying in Japanese middle school. *International Journal of Educational Research, 41*, 216–236. doi:10.1016/j.ijer.2005.07.002

Anderson, T., & Sturm, B. (2007). Cyberbullying: From playground to computer. *Young Adult Library Services, 5*, 24–27.

Aoyama, I. (2009, August). *Cyberbullying among university students: Definition, prevalence and predictors*. Paper presented at the meeting of the World Society of Victimology's 13th International Symposium on Victimology, Mito, Japan.

Aoyama, I., & Talbert, L. T. (2009, April). *A cross-cultural study on cyber-bullying among high school students in the Unites States and Japan*. Paper presented at the meeting of the American Educational Research Association (AERA), San Diego, CA.

Associated Press. (2008, July, 1). Missouri: Cyberbullying law is signed. *New York Times*. Retrieved October 20, 2008, from http://www.nytimes.com/2008/07/01/us/01brfs-CYBERBULLYIN_BRF.html?_r=1&scp=3&sq=cyberbullying,%20missouri&st=cse

Berkowitz, L. (1989). Frustration-aggression hypothesis: Examination and reformulation. *Psychological Bulletin, 106*, 59–73. doi:10.1037/0033-2909.106.1.59

Bradshaw, C. P., & Sawyer, A.L., & O-Brennan, L. (2007). Bullying and peer victimization at school: Perceptual differences between students and school staff. *School Psychology Review, 36*, 361–382.

Campbell, M. A. (2005). Cyber bullying: An old problem in a new guise? *Australian Journal of Guidance & Counselling, 15*, 68–76. doi:10.1375/ajgc.15.1.68

Ceyhan, E., & Ceyhan, A. (2007). *An investigation of problematic Internet usage behaviors on Turkish university students*. (ERIC Document Reproduction Service No. ED500186) Retrieved July 11, 2008, from ERIC database.

Chapell, M., Casey, D., De la Cruz, C., Ferrell, J., Forman, J., & Lipkin, R. (2004). Bullying in college by students and teachers. *Adolescence, 39*, 53–64.

Chapell, M., Hasselman, S., Kitchin, T., Lomon, S., MacIver, K., & Sarullo, P. (2006). Bullying in elementary school, high school, and college. *Adolescence (San Diego): An international quarterly devoted to the physiological, psychological, psychiatric, sociological, and educational aspects of the second decade of human life, 41*,633-648.

Cook, C. R., Williams, K. R., Guerra, N. G., & Tuthill, L. (2007). Cyberbullying. What it is and what we can do about it. [The newspaper of the National Association of School Psychologists]. *Communiqué, 36*, 4–5.

Eslea, M., Menesini, E., Morita, Y., O'Moore, M., Mora-Merchán, J., & Pereira, B. (2004). Friendship and loneliness among bullies and victims: Data from seven countries. *Aggressive Behavior, 30*, 71–83. doi:10.1002/ab.20006

Finn, J. (2004). A survey of online harassment at a university campus. *Journal of Interpersonal Violence, 19*, 468–483. doi:10.1177/0886260503262083

Gordon, C., Juang, L., & Syed, M. (2007). Internet use and well-being among college students: Beyond frequency of use. *Journal of College Student Development, 48*, 674–688. doi:10.1353/csd.2007.0065

Hinduja, S., & Patchin, J. W. (2005). *Research summary: Cyberbullying victimization*. Retrieved October 5, 2007, from http://www.cyberbullying.us/research.php Hinduja, S., & Patchin, J. W. (2009). *Bullying beyond the schoolyard: Preventing and responding to cyberbullying*. Thousand Oaks, CA

Holt, M., Finkelhor, D., & Kantor, G. (2007). Hidden forms of victimization in elementary students involved in bullying. *School Psychology Review, 36*, 345–360.

Holt, M. K., & Keyes, A. M. (2004). Teachers' attitude toward bullying. In D. L. Esspelage & S. M. Swearer (Eds.), *Bullying in American schools*. (pp. 121-139). London: Lawrence Erlbaum Associates, Publishers.

Hostin, S. (2008, April 11). Online campus gossips won't show their faces. *CNN.com.*

i-SAFE America Inc. (2007). *National i-SAFE survey finds over half of students are being harassed online.* Retrieved October 5, 2007, from http://www.dbprescott.com/internetbullying6.04.pdf

Kanetsuna, T., Smith, P., & Morita, Y. (2006). Coping with bullying at school: Children's recommended strategies and attitudes to school-based interventions in England and Japan. *Aggressive Behavior, 32,* 570–580. doi:10.1002/ab.20156

Kennedy, A. (2005). Students fall victim to high-tech harassment. *Counseling Today,* 10-11.

Korman, R. (2008, November 26). The verdict: Lori Drews is guilty. *ZDNet Government.* Retrieved March 2, 2009, from http://government. zdnet.com/?p=4207

Kowalski, R., Limber, S., & Agaston, P. (2008). *Cyberbullying: Bullying in the digital age.*

Lenhart, A. (2007, June 27). Cyberbullying and online teens. *Pew Internet and American Life Project.* Retrieved October 5, 2007, from http://www.pewInternet.org/pdfs/PIP%20Cyberbullying%20Memo.pdf

Li, Q. (2004). *Cyber-bullying in schools: Nature and extent of adolescents' experiences.* Paper presented at Annual American Educational Research Association Conference. Retrieved October 5, 2007, from http://www.ucalgary.ca/~qinli/publication/cyberbully_aera05%20.html

Li, Q. (2005). *Cyber-bullying in schools: A comparison of Canadian and Chinese adolescents' experience.* Paper presented at World Conference on E-Learning in Corporate, Government, Healthcare, and Higher Education (ELEARN). Retrieved August 3, 2008, from http://www.editlib.org/index.cfm?fuseaction=Reader.ViewAbstract&paper_id=21291&from=NEWDL

Li, Q. (2006). Cyberbullying in schools: A research of gender differences. *School Psychology International, 27,* 157–170. doi:10.1177/0143034306064547

Maag, C. (2007, December 16). When bullies turned faceless. *New York Times.* Retrieved January 22, from http://www.nytimes.com/2007/12/16/fashion/16meangirls.html?_r=1&ex=1198558800&en=35f8e2e63c570aab&ei=5070&emc=eta1&oref=slogin

Malden, MA: Blackwell Publishing.

Mckenna, P. (2007). The rise of cyberbullying. *New Scientist, 195,* 60. doi:10.1016/S0262-4079(07)62856-5

Media Awareness Network. (n. d.). *Cyber bullying: Understanding and preventing online harassment and bullying.* Retrieved October 5, 2007, from http://www.mediaeducationweek.ca/press_articles_cb.htm

Nesdale, D., & Naito, M. (2005). Individualism-collectivism and the attitudes to school bullying of Japanese and Australian students. *Journal of Cross-Cultural Psychology, 36,* 537–556. doi:10.1177/0022022105278541

O'Moore, M., & Kirkham, C. (2001). Self-esteem and its relationship to bullying behaviour. *Aggressive Behavior, 27,* 269–283. doi:10.1002/ab.1010

Olweus, D. (1993). *Bullying at school. What we know and what we can do.* Malden, MA: Blackwell.

Retrieved July 11, 2008, from http://www.cnn.com/2008/CRIME/03/17/sunny.juicy/index.html

Shariff, S. (2008). *Cyber-bullying: Issues and solutions for the school, the classroom and the home.* New York: Routledge.

Shimoda, H. (2008). 学校裏サイト [Unofficial school Websites]. Tokyo: Toyo Keizai Inc. (In Japanese)

Smith, P. K., Madsen, K. C., & Moody, J. C. (1999). What causes the age decline in reports of being bullies at school? Towards a developmental analysis of risks of being bullied. *Educational Research, 41*, 267–285.

Smorti, A., Menesini, E., & Smith, P. (2003). Parents' definitions of children's bullying in a five-country comparison. *Journal of Cross-Cultural Psychology, 34*, 417–432. doi:10.1177/0022022103034004003

Storm, P. S., & Storm, R. D. (2005). Cyberbullying by adolescents: A preliminary assessment. *The Educational Forum, 70*, 21–32. doi:10.1080/00131720508984869

Sturgeon, J. (2006). Bullies in cyberspace. *School Security*, 43-47.

Talbert, T. (2004). Give peace a chance…in our social education textbooks. *Journal of Pedagogy, Pluralism, and Practice, 8*, 9–15.

Talbert, T., & White, C. (2003). Lives in the balance: Controversy, militarism, and social studies efficacy. In C. White (Ed.), *True confessions: Popular culture, social studies efficacy, and the struggle in schools* (pp. 41-56). Cresskill, NJ: Hampton Press.

Talbert, T. L., & Glanzer, P. L. (2006). Giving peace a chance in America's social education classrooms: Teaching alternatives to violence from secular and religious communities nonviolence. In K. Kottu (Ed.), *Religion, terrorism and globalization: Nonviolence - a new agenda* (pp. 265-277). Hauppauge, NY: Nova Science Publishers.

Treml, J. M. (2001). Bullying as a social malady in contemporary Japan. *International Social Work, 44*, 107–117. doi:10.1177/0020872280104400109

Wallace, P. (1999). *The Psychology of the Internet*. New York: Cambridge University Press.

Watanabe, M. (2008). ネットいじめの真実 [Truth of cyberbullying]. Kyoto, Japan: Minerva Publishing Company. (In Japanese).

Willard, N. (2005). *An educator's guide to cyberbullying and cyberthreats. Center for safe and responsible Internet use*. Retrieved October 5, 2007, from http://cyberbully.org/cyberbully/docs/cbcteducator.pdf

Willard, N. (2007). *Cyberbullying and cyberthreats: Responding to the challenge of online social aggression, threats, and distress*. Champaign, IL: Research Press.

Yasukawa, M. (2008). 学校裏サイトからわが子をまもる [How to protect children from unofficial school Websites]. Tokyo, Japan: Chukei Publishing Company. (In Japanese)

「ネットいじめ」県内公立校3割…兵庫県教委が昨年度分調査 ["Cyberbullying" 30% of public schools had problems-investigation from Hyogo Prefecture Board of Education]. (2007, Oct 06). *Yomiuri online*. Retrieved October 25, 2007, from http://osaka.yomiuri.co.jp/edu_news/20071006kk03.htm

APPENDIX A

Useful Resources

Books

- Hinduja, S., & Patchin, J. W. (2009). Bullying beyond the schoolyard: Preventing and responding to cyberbullying. Thousand Oaks, CA: Crown Press.
- Kowalski,R., Limber, S., & Agaston, P. (2008). Cyberbullying: Bullying in the digital age. Malden, MA: Blackwell Publishing.
- Shariff, S. (2008). Cyber-Bullying: Issues and solutions for the school, the classroom and the home. New York: Routledge.
- Willard, N. (2007). Cyberbullying and cyberthreats: responding to the challenge of online social aggression, threats, and distress. Champaign, IL: Research Press.
- Willard, N. (2007). Cyber-safe kids, Cyber-savory teens: Helping young people learn to use the Internet safely and responsibly. San Francisco: Jossey-Bass.

Websites

- The NetLingo Top 20 Internet Acronyms Every Parent Needs to Know www.netlingo.com/top-20teens.cfmwww.netlingo.com/top20teens.cfm
- Text Message Abbreviations www.Webopedia.com/quick_ref/textmessageabbreviations.aspwww.webopedia.com/quick_ref/textmessageabbreviations.asp

In the U.S.

- i-SAFE America inc. www.isafe.org (Offers Internet safety education program and cyberbullying educational curricula in schools for grade 4 through 8)
- The U.S Department of Justice www.cybercrime.gov (Offers guidelines on cyber ethics for students, parents, and teachers and identifies government contacts for reporting Internet crimes)

In Canada

- Media Awareness Network www.media-awareness.ca (Interactive online resources and educational program for students, and teacher education program are available)

In the U.K.

- Teacher net http://www.teachernet.gov.uk/wholeschool/behaviour/tacklingbullying/http://www.teachernet.gov.uk/wholeschool/behaviour/tacklingbullying/

Government Webpage for cyberbullying)

- Childnet's Kidsmart Website www.kidsmart.org.uk(Offers an Internet safety guide to youth)

In Australia / New Zealand

- Net Alert www.netalert.net.au (Offers parents' guide to Internet safety and Internet safety education for school students)
- Net Safe http://www.cyberbullying.co.nr/ (Offers parents, teacher, community information on computer security)

In Japan

- Netiquette http://www.net-manners.com/ (Offers information about "Netiquette" on email, chat, communication etc. Written in Japanese)
- Disney official Website in Japan http://www.disney.co.jp/netiquette/ (Offers information about "Netiquette" with Disney characters to young children. Written in Japanese)

International

- International cyber-bullying project http://www.cyberbullying.co.nr/ (Offers information on international laws and resources)

Chapter 13
Misconceptions About Being Digital

Maja Pivec
University of Applied Sciences, Austria

Paul Pivec
Deakin University, Australia

ABSTRACT

Many academics have stated that the perceived decline in education is attributed to the change in the students themselves; that students today think differently, process information differently, and get bored with traditional schooling techniques; they are the digital generation. While the authors agree that technology such as electronic games provide a wealth of opportunities and are strong advocates of the use of these methods, they do not think that the digital generation learns any differently than previous generations, or children who have never been exposed to computing of any kind. Within this chapter the authors will expose the myth about today's media spoiled students and suggest how the creative mind can be captivated in both traditional and digital teaching environments. They will document several surveys and experiments, and highlight the success of teaching role-play classes face-to-face and in a constructivist digital environment.

INTRODUCTION

Academics have long been promoting a change in education to include technology-rich programs in the teaching curriculum (Papert, 1996; Rushkoff, 1996; Smith, Curtin & Newman, 1997); but they suggest that many teachers are feeling technically inadequate when teaching digitally literate students. These students have been called "the computer generation" and referred to as "screenagers". Many academics use the term "Nintendo Generation" and suggest that teachers, along with parents, are dealing with a new breed of learner. Other researchers (Green, Reid & Bigum, 1998) suggest a new breed of learner and believe that these children look upon school as an interruption in their computer usage time (Prensky, 2001; Squire, 2003); time they used for playing computer games, and that teaching institutions must use electronic media to re-package

DOI: 10.4018/978-1-60566-926-7.ch013

their course content to reach today's "digitally literate" students.

Much of this belief has been spawned from the notion that today's teenagers are "Digital Natives", having grown up in a digital world. However, other literature resources support the application of technology as a learning tool and also Game-Based Learning (GBL), yet refute the belief that this is because children grow up in a digital world as suggested by Prensky (2001), Gee (2003), Squire (2003), Shaffer (2006), and others. Take for an example the "Hole in the wall" project (Mitra & Rana, 2001). Computers were setup across India in locations that have never seen any type of technology before. No training or tuition was provided, yet these children were surfing the Internet within hours, downloading movies, using drawing software, playing video games, and even taught themselves how to cut, paste, and save their files. They collaborated with each other and worked in groups, they formed social groupings, and became highly motivated to continue to use this new available technology, all without supervision - all of the attributes Prensky and others suggests are only present in children that they refer to as digital natives.

Another example is the poverty alleviation project in Peru, set up by Dr. Logan Muller (Muller, 2004). The task of this project was to install computers in remote locations high in the Andes to provide access to information. These locations had no electricity and had never seen technology of any kind. With the help of solar powered generators and satellite Internet, computer systems were distributed to remote villages for farmers to access potential markets for the products. However, the local children were quick to utilize the computers, and often were assisting the older generation on how to use them. They collaborated, preferred multimedia applications, appeared to be goal orientated, and thus displayed all the traits of children who should have grown up playing computer games.

So are today's teenagers any different from previous generations and do they utilise technology as much as we believe? In fact, we questioned if they even preferred technology or was it just another form of entertainment. Were computer games and surfing the Internet serious activities or just a past time or a new toy? Are today's students digitally literate or is it that technology appeals to creative learners?

Within the following sections we provide a brief overview of number of interesting questions. An alternative approach based on number of surveys, several of them carried out by authors, is presented in the subsequent sections. The aim of this chapter is to provide reflections of how to orchestrate a challenging, enjoyable and effective learning experience that profits from students creative potential – with or without technology.

IS IT JUST A GAME?

In a survey completed in 1999 by Time and CNN (1999), questions were asked of a random group of 402 children between the ages of 13 and 17 years. Many played videogames, but most stated that although their parents knew about the content in the games, over half had no rules about the playing of them. We repeated this survey 7 years later and found that children in the same age group believe that not only their parents have less knowledge about the games they are playing, but they also have fewer rules about playing them. Yet many parents still advocate that violent computer games create violent people.

Based on the Table 1 (Kearney & Pivec, 2007c, p. 494) that compares the CNN pool from 1999 with the results of the repeated pool in 2006, 36% of parents don't have any knowledge about the games their children play (as opposed to only 10% in the earlier pool), and 67% of parents don't have any rules regarding the computer games (as opposed to 57% in the year 1999). The amount of

Table 1. Teens and games

CNN.com Poll - May 1999			Kearney-Pivec Poll - September 2006
Have you ever played computer games?			
Yes No	81% 19%	95% 5%	Yes No
Have you ever played violent computer games?			
Yes No	48% 52%	59% 41%	Yes No
If you play computer games, how much do your parents know about the games you play?			
A lot A little Nothing	57% 33% 10%	33% 30% 36%	A lot A little Nothing
If you play computer games, do your parents have rules about the games you play?			
Yes, and I always follow them Yes, but I don't always follow them Parents have no rules	24% 18% 57%	15% 18% 67%	Yes, and I always follow them Yes, but I don't always follow them Parents have no rules

children that have ever played games increased from 81% to 95%, and the amount of those who never played violent games decreased from 52% to 41%. Hence there is a trend towards game playing, towards what are perceived as violent games, and towards fewer parental rules about playing them. The children polled by in 1999 are now in their early twenties and are today's university students.

Hence 225 students attending university classes were given a pre-course survey for their preference of computer game including violent computer games. Although many of them played what their parents would label as violent and unsuitable games, these students were adamant in their statement that "it is only a game" and did not take it seriously. Over 50% of the males surveyed preferred First Person Shooter (FPS) games and many of the females enjoyed car-racing games traditionally targeted at males. The overall motivation for playing games was for fun, or to just fill in time, and those who did not play computer games (40%), suggested that games were a waste of time and stated that they don't have any interest in games preferring real contact with people face-

to-face (f2f). Whereas 40% of the males indicated that competition and socializing was an important motivator for playing, 28% of the girls stated that they only played to 'waste time'; although 29% of the girls stated that they used computer games as a learning tool.

We identified gender-neutral elements and features like humour and personalization that are equally important and appreciated by males and females. By introducing these elements in the e-learning we can expect more participation and enthusiasm in the learning situations. (Pivec & Panko, 2008, p.389)

Wanting to analyze the motivation for playing 'games for males' and establish differences in females' preferences, thus projecting these into requirements for designing 'games for females', we inquired about the motivational momentum of designing a game in terms if they were more motivated and achieved better learning results, and if more use should be made of games in education. The results were surprising and showed that many students did not believe in computer games being used within the educational curriculum. They perceive games as an un-serious activity reaffirming what they felt about perceived violent games – "it is only a game". Nearly all of the students surveyed (95%) suggested that they would only play educational games if they believed that they would learn something. They also suggested a need for educational games to be more interesting, have better game-play and perhaps humor, and agreed that multiplayer games would be of more value within the curriculum, providing the social aspect needed for learning.

In a separate on-going survey (Kearney & Pivec, 2007a), we asked 150 information design students on their usage of Internet technologies, email, chat, forums, etc. The average age of the student was 23 years and their usage was not what would have been expected being labeled as the digital generation. In fact many (45%) answered that they would rather spend little, if any at all, time on the Internet and preferred interacting with real people, face-to-face. Most were new to Blogs (73%), and most had never used Podcasts (85%). They suggested that the Internet was suitable for distance learning but they preferred the social interaction of class. Other forms of electronic communication used on a regular basis by the students polled were as follows:

- **Email** – 100% of the students used email and averaged 6-8 hours per week, with less than 1 hour of this for communication related to their studies. They did not perceive this as Internet usage and related it similar to SMS messaging.
- **Forums** – 80% of students used discussion boards or forums of some kind on a daily basis. Of those who used this form of communication, they averaged slightly less than 5 hours per week on informal discussion boards, yet less than 1 hour per week on formal discussion forums for their study.

- **Chat systems** – 75% of the students polled utilized chat programs of some kind, averaging 10 hours per week. This was mostly for social communication as a precursor to f2f or when circumstances didn't allow. Only 10 of them suggested that some chat was study related.
- **Skype** – 65% of the students used skype video conferencing, but only two students noted that this was study related. On average, the students used this form of communication for 5 hours per week.
- **Blogs** - 60% of students used blogs (although only recently) for an average of 3 hours per week, and less than half of this time was study related.
- **News groups** – 15% of the students polled spent 4 hours per week on Internet news groups, mainly related to their course of study.
- **Podcasts** – 15% of the students used Podcasts on a weekly basis and averaged 3 hours per week using this technology. However, none of this time was related to their studies.

The results of this poll suggest that students will willingly participate in online forums, news groups, chat systems, and other Internet technologies, but only use this technology for their course work when they are directed to do so. Likewise with using blogs, this was only for study when the lecturer requested this form of journal. Skype is also becoming a popular form of Internet communication and although not asynchronous, video or sound recordings would be accepted by students in the form of podcasts posted to a discussion forum. In summary, many of the students suggested that they had no preference for this technology but used it because it was available and often were directed to use it for their study. The surveyed students were all attending face-to-face traditional classes where discussion forums and blogs were only used as a supplement to the curriculum.

CAN YOU TELL ME WHAT I FEEL?

Our interviews of 20 design students with an average age of 21, suggested that the younger generation appear to perceive to themselves as being inside the virtual world and not just controlling an avatar. This is in contrast to older people, specifically those involved in teaching and interested in using this technology to enhance the educational curriculum. Reflections from an online seminar held at Deakin University on Social Software and Virtual environments suggest that the older generation, specifically the teachers, do not relate to their avatar as themselves but as a separate character that they control and with a separate personality.

"I was trying to get Phoebe out of one virtual reality and into another. Seems she was stuck in a parallel universe until I added her as an attachment rather than trying to insert image or url link.... phoebe finally got the harajuku makeover she has been dying for, took years off her."

However, Universities worldwide have embraced virtual worlds such as Second Life, creating a replica campus and look-a-like avatars for their lecturers, with the view to enhance learning and to appeal to their students of the "Digital" generation. Yet one of the comments from a surveyed student suggested that we are a long way from surpassing face-to-face teaching.

"In a future virtual reality, combining the real and the computer world, the meaning of the avatar could change in some ways. ...But you could also bring a digital copy of yourself, as you are, to life in that world. You would have your own face, you would have to think about the clothes you wear, (once even) the perfume you use, the way your hair is done and so on. Like three-dimensional characters within computer games nowadays you would be transferred into the virtual world. Being

online would become a whole new experience", at the moment it is not.

But are Avatars affective agents for conveying knowledge and understanding? A research question worth further exploration focused on our perception of avatars, specifically how do we look at avatars? In an experiment carried out by authors, 20 students attempted to recognize and determine emotions in virtual world avatars.

A pilot study using eye-tracking technology was earlier carried out (Pivec, 2006) to ascertain how we perceive the avatar as a whole. Results showed that we tend to focus more in detail at the unusual parts of fictive characters as opposed to the human like, where we look more upon face. For the study detailed in this chapter, we followed the question if we could recognize emotions from avatars as efficient and in the same way we do from digital photos of people. Second focus of the study was to determine where and how on the face do we look to gather the information. If today's students were "digital natives", surely they would have no problems in being taught by an avatar and their would be no misunderstanding by the student through miscommunication.

For this study, a Tobii ET-1750 eye-tracking device was used to track gaze path and time of participants. The ET-1750 is integrated in a 17-inch TFT monitor that runs at a resolution of 1280 x 1024 and uses a pair of near infra-red light-emitting diodes (NIR-LEDs) and cameras for corneal reflection eye tracking. Being integrated in the monitor, the device is almost invisible to the test subject and does not distract their attention. It can be used for eye-tracking studies with stimuli that can be presented on a monitor, such as Web sites, slide shows, videos and text documents. The eye tracker software ran on a Windows XP PC, and communicated with the application via a TCP/IP connection.

Figure 1 and Figure 2 show samples of gaze plots (left picture) and hotspot analysis (right

Figure 1. Sample gaze plot

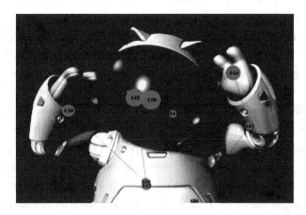

picture). Based on gaze plots one can see how participants explored the picture and follow their eye movements. Gaze plot also provides the information on gaze duration for each individual gaze, whereas hotspot analysis gives information at a glance, which spots on the displayed picture were of interest. With help of a color scheme, information on the intensity of observing different areas is provided.

A slideshow was created in a mixed order 20 pictures of headshots, 10 people and 10 avatars, mixed males and females, showing various facial emotions. A control group successfully verified the suggested emotions. In the experiment, participants were asked to note on a questionnaire which emotion they perceived while viewing digital images of people, human avatars, and non-human avatars. In conjunction with this, the gaze path of the participants was tracked using eye-tracking technology, to ascertain what features of each image were viewed.

The results (see Table 2 in appendix) showed that we correctly identify specific emotions in the images of people by viewing the eyes and sometimes the mouth, but struggled with the images of avatars. Based on the results, the female participants chose the correct emotion for human subjects 74% of the time, yet only scored 37% for the avatars. Where as the male participants chose correctly 83% of the time for human subjects and only 39% for avatars. In total, 79% of both male and female participants ascertained the correct emotion for human pictures and only 39% for avatars. This was further compounded by the

Figure 2. Sample hotspot analysis

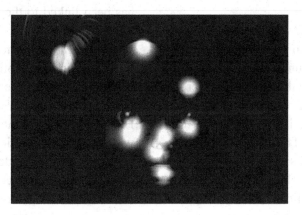

introduction of non-human avatars. However, the eye tracking data showed that all participants struggled to ascertain any emotional perception from avatars, human or non-human. While the majority of human subjects were viewed by looking at the eyes only, or the eyes and then the mouth, the avatars were scanned for other facial and explicable features. When an object such as a hand or jewelry was introduced into the foreground, this was ignored in human images but always viewed in the images of avatars. In the appendix of this chapter detailed results, separately for female and male, including the description of viewing for each picture, are presented.

The viewing of the eyes to perceive emotion is consistent with other research. In a study by the University of Oklahoma Health Sciences Center (American Academy of Neurology, 2000), researchers suggested that while we may focus on a person's mouth for speech comprehension, the upper areas of the face and specifically the eyes assist us to read emotional states. Ekman, Friesen, & Tomkins (1971) developed a scoring system to measure which areas of the face contribute the most to the emotional expression of a person. They found that although the mouth contributes to the perception of happiness and anger, sadness is only seen in the eyes. Hence the majority of us appear to be conditioned to view the eyes to perceive emotion, and the mouth for speech comprehension or as a confirmation of what the eyes are suggesting. Unfortunately, today's avatars do not yet assist the viewer with neither emotional nor verbal comprehension.

Our behavior in the real world does not appear to equal to our behavior in the virtual world and vice versa. We often encounter misunderstanding of email messages due to the lack of non-verbal communication and these results suggests that it is no different when we utilize avatars in virtual worlds. The conclusions of this study suggest that we naturally view avatars differently than images of humans and the technology available for virtual world communications cannot yet replace face-to-face meetings, not even for the digitally literate student.

What then does this imply for the team work in the virtual world that has components of communicating, discussing, reaching decisions and consensus? Our results showed that we experience difficulties by determining emotions displayed in the avatars, which decreases the expected component of non-verbal communication in the 3D virtual worlds. In some virtual worlds, the technology allows for an image or static photograph of a persons face to be wrapped on one's avatar, giving a sense of realism or at least ownership. Research into the social interaction between people meeting in Collaborative Virtual Environments (CVEs) and techniques for the facial tracking of emotions is ongoing at Stanford's Virtual Human Interaction Lab (VHIL, 2007). As technology improves, future virtual worlds may allow a video image of a participants face to be wrapped on the avatar; an image taken directly from the built-in web cam. This may assist with the perception of emotions when viewed from a frontal perspective.

Virtual world developers could also learn from game developers and mimic games such as Sims2 from Electronic Arts. A mood meter, emotion icon, or aspiration indicator hovering above an avatar's head instead of the avatars name, may help with communication. These indicators could be triggered when the participant uses emoticons in their typing. This technique is being developed in the game-design virtual world (Gamedesign-campus, 2008), where the content of the text chat has been linked to the animated body language of the avatar.

The results of this study suggested that without the perception of emotions, the social skills and communication between avatars do not yet replace that of face-to-face or even video conferencing. Hence we suggest that the use of virtual worlds with avatars for teaching can be prone to misunderstanding by the student through miscommunication. The current technology of Virtual worlds such as Second Life does not impress our Digital

Teenagers. With many Universities insisting that students would prefer to interact in a Virtual world, our students stated,

"Many people are far more outgoing and relaxed in the anonymity that the masquerade-like quality of avatars offers. This can be an advantageous factor in e-learning when working with, for example, shy kids"

None of our surveyed students had ever visited *Second Life* and some suggested that it could not compare with online game worlds such as *World of Warcraft* – so why try to.

ROLE-PLAY COURSE ON GBL: FACE-TO-FACE AND DIGITAL

Today's society, as well as many of our students, are captivated by computer and console video games. In 2007 there were over three hundred million game players worldwide and with over thirty one billion Euros revenue, game industry exceeds the music and movie industry (NPD Market Research, 2008). Games have been part of the culture and interaction between people from the early days on, e.g. one can see scenes depicting kings and queens playing a game of Senet on the frescos of ancient Egypt. Indian game of Pachisi is believed to be bases of European game culture based on the Thomas Hyde's book "De Ludis Orientalibus" dated 1695 (Gloonnegger, 1999) and is in many variations one of the most spread games worldwide. Humans have always used playful interaction and games of all types for learning – from interacting and playing with blocks in an early age to acquire counting skills and ability to compare and align in certain order, to flight simulators for perfecting skills of a more complex and specialized nature.

Although the skills involved when playing games differ dramatically from those needed to create one, players exhibit the same addictive nature seen in a person that is driven to succeed. A computer game can take anywhere between 3 months and 3 years to create. From the initial concept, the design, the coding, testing and error correction, through to the artwork, the music, packaging, promotion, and distribution, developers must stay focused and committed to the project throughout this entire time, often doing tedious tasks but always learning new and innovative techniques to do their craft. These people are usually young creative adults and have been avid game players themselves, and are often motivated by instant feedback and reward of success.

Commercial computer games are known for creating social environments and cult followings surrounding the gameplay, the character attributes, and player's abilities; this is where affective learning occurs. Garris et al., (2002) describes affective learning as including "feelings of confidence, self-efficacy, attitudes, preferences, and dispositions" (p.457). Figure 3 not only shows how player ability and experience affects the challenge element and the level of learning (ZPD), but also how the level of cognitive challenge can be appropriate for the learner's current abilities. This model shows the inclusion of instructional design and game characteristics as critical elements of a game or role-play to enable the achievement of the learning outcomes, as well as the additional factor of player abilities. Game-Based Learning occurs in a recursive loop and as such when the player skills are acquired, or incremented, the player moves on to the next level of the game. This is true for both educational and commercial recreational games and role-plays. The scaffolded level of skill requirement is what creates the immersion and the desire to play the game. If the game or role-play is done in a group, inputs such as player abilities are multiplied and hence so are the learning outcomes generated from the social environment.

To introduce the topic of educational game design and to create awareness of this discipline to the coming generation of potential game designers

Figure 3. Recursive loops of Game-Based Learning (GBL)

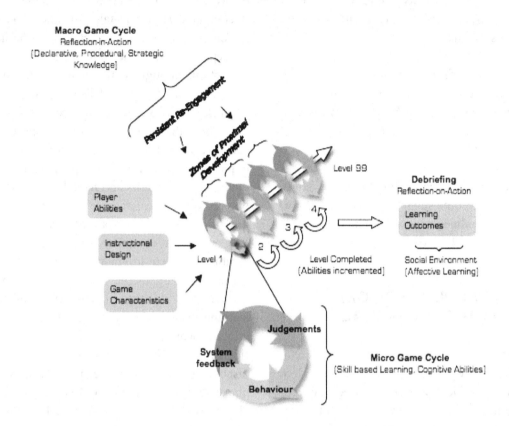

the authors designed a course that could be simply described as playing a game about educational game design. The challenge for students was to create a concept proposal for a publisher of educational games. Based on the pre- and post course surveys, the course work and results, we analyzed how students perceived the area of educational games for the use of teaching and as a career path. In the course post survey, 66% of the students agreed that designing educational games was a highly motivational topic and suggested that they now felt competent enough to write a professional educational game concept document. They also agreed the designing educational games could provide future career opportunities, however only 35% of them would consider this for their own career. The majority of the students found the course to be successful with 70% of the students enjoying the topic despite not considering themselves to be game players. Those

who did play computer games only did so for recreation and had not involved games with any of their schooling. However, upon completion of the course, 60% of the students suggested a preference for using games to learn.

This section outlines the educational game design course concept and documents the results of the course over two semesters with total of 150 Information Design students at the University of Applied Sciences Joanneum in Austria. The class was a role-play itself i.e. game about designing a game, where students had to work in teams, create a game design company and take a specific role and responsibilities within the team e.g. game producer, game developer, programmer, etc. to contribute to the task accomplishment. The progress of the work along with the problems they encountered were documented within the company blogs (see as examples http://legalaliengames.

blogspot.com/, blog of "the best in show" group 2006 or http://clownbox.blogger.de/, "the best in show" group 2007)

The course covered topics including the process of commercial game design, taking into consideration the pedagogical design required to achieve the desired learning outcomes. When we design games for learning both the target audience and the learning outcomes have to be considered at the initial conception of the game. In this way teachers can easily recognize the value of this resource and the possibilities to include such games in the curriculum.

The game concepts differ in excellence from the innovative use of technology, various topics (e.g. art epochs, art supplies, journalism, medicine, physics, history, etc.) to their possible market potential. The appearance of the new game console from Nintendo, the Wii, was reflected in some of the game concepts of the 2007. The game concept "Dare to Cook" by Clownbox is combination of simulation, role-play and strategy game genres, where players can learn about nourishment, spices, and try out various recipes, adding an educational focus to similar games on the commercial market. The possibilities of the Wii are also explored in addition with many mini games, where body movement influences the game play. Cassandra Syndrome is a game focused on touch-typing, and differs from existing similar games in the motivation component. The gameplay is based on the communication with non-player characters, which is supported by repetition of sequence of the letters. And when this is done successfully, the responses and instructions are translated in the understandable language of the player. The game concept was presented also to a group of K12 teachers and received excellent feedback. Each semester the class concludes with the presentation of the Golden Pineapple award ceremony (Golden Pineapple Award: 2006, 2007). In 2007 awarded concepts may be seen at the home page of Information Design (http://ind.fh-joanneum.at/node/493).

ROLE PLAY COURSE OUTLINE

'Instruction' is mostly focused on training and learning by repetition, whereas 'Design' stands for creativity and appropriate shaping i.e. creating for a purpose. Thus Instructional Design can be viewed as process of designing the learning experiences for learners as well as a system of procedures for developing educational and teaching programs in a consistent and reliable fashion for target audience (Reiser & Dempsy, 2001).

There are specific educational domains where learning in isolation is not effective and only interdisciplinary practice oriented learning brings results. With the course of Game-based learning designed in form of role-playing the computer game industry we wanted to provide an environment for problem-based interaction and application of topics from variety of disciplines e.g. game industry, game design, instructional design, programming, user-centered development, usability in games, game flow, user generated content, collaborative and pear learning, marketing concept, marketing material, etc..

The course is distributed throughout the semester and divided into 15 units made of 45-minute kick off lectures followed by 90-minute practical work. Lecture slides, work sheets, additional information, sample documents, links and readings related to the course are provided by means of an e-learning platform. Ongoing tuition in f2f practical sessions and in the form of blog comments is part of the learning process. During the course, students carry out the practical work in groups of 4 students that for a game-development company, to design an educational video game i.e. provide game concept design, related professional design documents and documented the semester work progress and results in the development log.

Targeted learning outcomes of the course are as follows:

- Educational (and) game design
- Pedagogical terminology

- Professional proposal requirements
- Digital Game Industry awareness
- Self-reflection of learning process (blog)
- Improvement of written and conversational English

Groups are assessed based on innovation, quality and completeness of their submissions. For the assessment, students have to provide professionally formatted completed game design document that includes all topics addressed in the lectures and practical work sessions. Students are encouraged to apply a creative and professional design. Development blogs showing group progress accessible throughout the semester and commented on by the tutors, are also part of the submission.

The course is developed for information design students and as such it has additional requirement to provide opportunities for creative work. Therefore as part of the assignment students have to produce a poster of the game and packaging samples for game. These topics are previously addressed at other classes earlier in the curriculum and the knowledge and skills should be applied within the task of the Game-based learning class.

The role-play course is structured in five major steps, as follows:

- Define your team:

Based on the input on video game industry roles, define your game design company, assign roles within the company team, outline project phases, reflect about resource requirements, and adequate time line.

- Define your game:

Conduct research on existing commercial games and game genres for leisure and for education. Brainstorm for game title, genre, and platform for your game concept document. Specify your target audience.

- Define your concept:

Use design guidelines for successful games and information on game-based learning to form an abstract, define gameplay, game elements and learning outcomes of your game idea.

- Test your concept:

Use iterative development approach and gameflow analysis to verify your concept with your target audience. Conduct prototype usability testing.

- Create your presentation:

Think about marketing, packaging, and promotion to create innovative, informative and professional presentation of your game concept.

At the end of semester, groups present in 10-minute presentations their game concepts and other results from their work. Many of the groups are so enthusiastic that they create small movie trailers for this presentation or think of some other way of non-conventional presentation approach to distinguish themselves from others, even though this is beyond requirements of the course (but clearly demonstrate their motivation and positive attitude to the topic).

WAS IT AN EFFECTIVE LEARNING OPPORTUNITY?

Research shows that games are appealing even if we only talk about them in a social environment (Kearney & Pivec, 2007b). For our course we wanted to use the momentum of games and (role) play to create more engaging and effective learning opportunity. However, when can we talk about an effective learning opportunity? Below we listed seven requirements suggested by Norman (1993) and used later by Kasvi (2000) for defining an effective learning environment. By mapping each of the requirements to the Game-Based Learning course we wanted to see if and to what extent we meet these requirements.

1. Provide a high intensity of interaction and feedback.

In the course elements of mentoring in the kick off and during practical sessions are included, as well as additional feedback via development blog after each of the practical sessions is provided.

2. Have specific goals and established procedures.

The goal is elaboration of a professional educational game design document, including insights into the commercial game industry. The stepwise work procedures presented in the kick offs are clearly outlined in the worksheets of the course.

3. Be motivational.

Motivating and relevant topics of games and educational games stand in the foreground, which allows for the interests of the students. In addition, public momentum with online blogs and established competition throughout the course foster motivation to produce outstanding concepts by means of yearly Golden Pineapple Awards.

4. Provide a continual feeling of challenge, not too difficult to be frustrating or too easy to create boredom.

The class is equally distributed throughout semester. Well-paced work sessions are providing enough scope for creativity and are requiring professional output. Each work session is focused on achieving outlined sub goals that help students to measure their progress.

5. Provide a sense of direct engagement on the task involved.

The class is based on relevant tasks, where input of each individual group member matters. Without good collaboration and work distribution the group can not deliver in expected time and quality.

6. Provide the appropriate tools that fit the task.

Set of resources i.e. readings, sample documents, lecture slides, work specifications and ongoing mentoring are essential to be able to carry out the work. The lecture resources are made available via the institutional e-learning environment. In addition, computers with basic office and graphic programs, as well as Internet access are provided at the location and are necessary for the practical sessions.

7. Avoid distractions and disruptions that destroy the subjective experience.

Students are confronted with a problem and related and clearly specified set of goals. Each of the sessions provides one step further to the solution. By working, students apply brainstorm and group discussions to achieve synergy, good results and to learn from peers. In addition, academic and industry feedback on their work is provided.

Kasvi (2000) suggests that computer games fulfill all of these requirements and believes that they "satisfy them better than most other learning mediums" (p.6). However, it is very difficult to find a game that includes a learning curriculum that is appropriate for different schooling levels. Even more difficult is to find an educational game that is really fun to play. Most educational games are low budget games and their look and feel can not compete with recreational games. But take a constructivists point of view and ask the same student to design an educational game, and the response would be quite different, as described further in the section.

NEXT STEP – TRANSFERRING F2F TO AN ONLINE EXPERIENCE

To transfer the f2f role-playing course for game-based learning to the online learning situation, we used The Training Room (2008) platform, that is based on the concept of the successful EC funded concept of UniGame (Dziabenko, Pivec, Bouras, et al., 2003). *"The Training Room"* platform provides an on-line role playing environment where teachers can define various topics, and develop learning situations for their specific lecture topics (Pivec, & Pivec, 2008). Communication and collaboration in "The Training Room" role-play game environment is based upon video conferencing that bridges the gap between real and virtual and still assures the visible and recognizable presence of emotions and non-verbal communication. It provides additional modes of communicating with other players via text, voice, and video, to ensure that the game objectives are achieved.

The pilot trial started with the fictive (though real life like) situation of Ministry of Education opening the "Call for innovative educational game concepts" in various learning disciplines. There are different categories of learning games: (a) additional learning opportunity, (b) interdisciplinary learning and (c) innovative use of technology. The bids from young startup companies will be presented to the Ministry upon the deadline and have to be structured and cover topics as outlined in the call (game concept document). For needs of communication and answering questions from the companies, Ministry also opened a forum for FAQ. All the accompanying documentation e.g. more detailed explanation of the call and background readings about educational games and learning resources and similar, has been provided in the Content Library.

The f2f kick off meetings can be replaced with uploaded annotated slides and additional documentation, relevant pod or video casts and forum discussions. By means of the news blog, teachers can provide paced motivation and additional guidance for the teams.

For introducing the additional dimension and time related competition into the game, start up companies can apply for a place in the business incubator, which will help them by means of mentoring. For a successful application they need to provide a company description including logo, background, competences and skills of their members, and outline of their game idea by the certain date. Four to five exceptional applications (out of 16) will be rewarded with the excellence points (that might also contribute to getting the contract from Ministry)

To foster participation of all team members in the team, each member of the team takes a subject that he/she is responsible for; similar to the class situation, where this is necessary, if the team wants to meat the deadline. Because each team has to address all proposed subjects in the concept document, within the team each player is responsible for at least one subject that is tightly coupled to the role – e.g. being in the role of game programmer, one has to cover game features and related development tools. This player will provide and upload the necessary background research in the team content library, prepare a short summary of information and argument the choice and then initiate a team discussion online with the intent to agree upon decision. Discussions can be either via synchronous or asynchronous tools, depending on the group dynamics of the team. The decisions are documented in the company blogs.

At the presentation date, teams submit their work and present their concepts at the public presentation via the main Video Conference, where all teams are present. There is opportunity to answer three questions from the public (coming from competing teams) and thee questions from the jury (ministry representative, educational representative and game company representative). Based on the marks gained from the presentation, provided answers, and bonus points, winning concepts are selected and announced at the end.

To prepare the role-play, teacher has to create the adequate skeleton e.g. creating amount of teams that will become companies with 4 different roles in each of the teams, to be later expanded by the players; Script the initial situation that sets the role-play and explains the goal; Upload the basic documentation into the Common Library; Open the Ministry FAQ Forum; Create the area of the Business Incubator, with the request for application and deadlines; Adopt the learning material to the online requirement and set the appropriate schedule for meetings (could be also in form of events, which is easier in an online environment) and milestones.

The entire role-play digital environment gives more opportunity to introduce a variety of game elements into the role-play that have positive influence on the player immersion as well as on the learning outcome. Although this concept has proved successful and the uptake of knowledge by the student was adequate, initial users of the original product found that video conferencing was an essential aspect of the game needed to elicit emotions, and to successfully discuss and communicate with other players, team members, and subject speakers. Without the perception of emotions, reaching decisions and maintaining positive team spirit would be difficult. When asked if 3D graphics, avatars, virtual worlds, etc., would enhance The Training Room platform, they stated that it would not. It would make it less serious.

We often believe that an e-learning platform is not appealing to today's students, as they do not include the extensive graphical environment that the digital generation has come to expect. This is a misconception. Jenkins (2007) argues that most game players see past the eye candy of

modern games and look for the affordances that allow them to progress through the objectives. Our participants were immersed in the role-play and we suggest that this can be achieved with or without technology.

CONCLUSIONS - IS BEING DIGITAL A SERIOUS ACTIVITY?

Oblinger (2004) named Prensky's digital natives as "Millennials" and listed their traits to include a tendency towards group activities and a fascination with technology. She argues that their strengths include collaboration, goal orientation, and multi-tasking, and claims that computer games provide an environment in which students can excel. While we agree that electronic games provide a wealth of opportunities and we are strong advocates of using this technology, we do not believe that the computer generation learns any different than previous generations, or children who have never been exposed to technology.

Many of younger generation, despite being game players themselves, still insisted that games were not a "serious activity" and hence could not be used for learning. The eye tracking study of the depiction of real people and 3D avatars showed that students have difficulties eliciting correct emotions from synthetic characters and therefore the role of 3D virtual worlds for learning is in question; due to potential of misinterpretation and lack of gestures amongst others. An option to avoid miscommunication in the digital environment is to provide multiple modes of communication for the participant.

Learning by means of a role-play of digital game industry has proven to be successful approach fostering interdisciplinary learning in a constructivist way. A game about creating an educational game sparks students' motivation and brings their creativity into the foreground thus the results that they produce are exceptional. Students' active participation in the learning process, acquisition of knowledge and problem solving skills are high. We also suggest that learning by means of a role-play scenario of any other industry would also prove to be successful.

Initial testing with the scenario based online role-play platform, The Training Room (2008), showed that all students enjoyed the experience and the ability to interact with geographically dispersed players through public and private chat, multimedia forums and multi-user whiteboards, and audio/video conferencing. This is reinforced by Jenkins view that young people enjoy the participation in the *"creation and circulation of media content within social networks that extend from their circle of face-to-face friends to a larger virtual community around the world"* (2007, p1.). Technology allows them to do this; they do not do it because of technology.

Immersive learning environments such as The Training Room can be provided without the eye-candy and the digital representation of oneself through an avatar in a highly graphical 3 dimensional world. One can achieve the desired learning outcomes for today's "digital" generation only if the activities are designed appropriately to enable and support learning. Therefore we have to focus on creating effective learning opportunities by means of appropriate instructional design, either for f2f or a digital learning setting. For a start one could explore, how good practice from the real classes can be adopted and transferred successfully into the constructivist digital experience. Today's students do not learn any differently than those of yesterday, but the environment we teach them in can be very different.

FUTURE TRENDS

The surveys conducted for this chapter are ongoing. Each semester, new students complete pre and post course questionnaires, and their changes in attitudes towards technology and preferences in teaching environments, can be observed. The role-play course detailed above is continually revised to take account for new technology and student reactions to the past semester. Work is also currently underway to modify the online platform, The Training Room, to allow for single player scenarios, and student experiences will be documented and reported on. Dissemination of these results, and new trends in student preferences, will be via the EC funded project, European Network for Growing Activity in Game-based learning in Education (ENGAGE) and highlighted on their web site: http://www.engagelearning.eu. Recent collaboration between the European Schoolnet (EUN) and the Interactive Software Federation of Europe (ISFE) also indicates that educators and developers are working together to develop further solutions based on the current state analysis published in the "Games in Schools" (Pivec & Pivec, 2008) report.

REFERENCES

American Academy of Neurology. (2000). Often missed facial displays give clues to true emotion, deceit. *ScienceDaily*. Retrieved December 3, 2007, from http://www.sciencedaily.com/releases/2000/05/000503181624.htm

CNN. (1999). *Parents aren't watching Internet surfing teens*. Retrieved November 28, 2008, from http://edition.cnn.com/US/9905/01/teen.poll/

Dziabenko, O., Pivec, M., Bouras, C., Igglesis, V., Kapoulas, V., & Misedakis, I. (2003). A Web-based game for supporting game-based learning. In *Proceedings of the 4th Annual European GAME-ON Conference (GAME-ON 2003)*, London (pp. 111-118).

Ekman, P., Friesen, W. V., & Tomkins, S. S. (1971). Facial affect scoring technique: A first validity study. *Semiotica, 3*, 37–58.

GA: Longstreet.

Gamedesigncampus. (2008). Retrieved February 29, 2008, from http://gamedesigncampus.com/index.html

Garris, R., Ahlers, R., & Driskell, J. E. (2002). Games, motivation, and learning: A research and practice model. *Simulation & Gaming, 33*(4), 441–467. doi:10.1177/1046878102238607

Gee, J. (2003). *What video games have to teach us about learning and literacy.* New York: PalGrave-McMillan.

Gloonnegger, E. (1999). *Das spiele-buch. Brett- und legespielel aus aller welt*. Germany: Drei Magier Verlag.

Green, B., Reid, J. A., & Bigum, C. (1998). Teaching the Nintendo generation? Children, computer culture and popular technologies. In S. Howard (Ed.), *Wired up: Young people and the electronic media* (pp. 19-41). London: Taylor and Francis.

Jenkins, H. (2007). Keynote at game in action conference, Gothenburg, Sweden.

Kasvi, J. (2000). Not just fun and games - Internet games as a training medium. In *Cosiga - learning with computerised simulation games* (pp. 23-34). Retrieved June 27, 2003, from http://www.knowledge.hut.fi/people/jkasvi/NJFAG.PDF

Kearney, P., & Pivec, M. (2007a). *Informal discussion forums: Can we harness the same passion in class?* Paper presented at the AACE World Conference on Educational Multimedia, Hypermedia and Telecommunications (ED-MEDIA 2007), Vancouver, Canada.

Kearney, P., & Pivec, M. (2007b). Recursive loops of game-based learning. In C. Montgomerie & J. Seale (Eds.), *Proceedings of the ED-MEDIA '07*, Vancouver BC, Canada (pp. 2546-2553).

Kearney, P., & Pivec, M. (2007c). Sex, lies and videogames. *British Journal of Educational Technology, 38*(3).

Mitra, S., & Rana, V. (2001). Children and the Internet: Experiments with minimally invasive education in India. *British Journal of Educational Technology, 32*(2), 221–232. doi:10.1111/1467-8535.00192

Muller, L. (2004). *ICT accelerating change in society and economies.* Paper presented to the Pontifica Universidad de Sao Paulo, Sao Paulo, Brazil.

Norman, D. (1993). *Things that make us smarter: Defending human attributes in the age of the machine.* New York: Addison -Wesley

NPD market research. (2008). Retrieved September 12, 2008, from http://www.npd.com

Oblinger, D. (2004). The next generation of educational engagement. *Journal of Interactive Media in Education*, (8): 1–18.

Papert, S. (1996). *The connected family: Bridging the digital generation gap.* Atlanta

Pivec, M. (2006). *The secret life of virtual you.* Invited presentation at the Social Skills and Social Software conference, Salzburg, Austria.

Pivec, M., & Panko, M. (2008). Instructional design - sex driven? T. Kidd & I. Chen (Eds.), *Social information technology: Connecting society and cultural issues.* Hershey, PA: Idea Group Publishing.

Pivec, M., & Pivec, P. (2008). Playing to learn: Guidelines for designing educational games. In *Proceedings of World Conference on Educational Multimedia, Hypermedia and telecommunications 2008,* Vienna, Austria (pp. 3247-3252).

Pivec, P., & Pivec, M. (2008). *Games in schools. Commissioned report for Interactive Software Federation of Europe (ISFE) by the European Commission (EC).* Retrieved November 30, 2008, from http://www.isfe.eu/

Prensky, M. (2001a). Digital natives, digital immigrants. *Horizon*, 9(5), 1–10. doi:10.1108/10748120110424816

Reiser, R., & Dempsy, J. (Eds.). (2001). *Trends and issues in instruction design and technology*. Englewood Cliffs, NJ: Prentice Hall.

Rushkoff, D. (1996). *Playing the future: How kids' culture can teach us to thrive in an age of chaos*. New York: HarperCollins.

Shaffer, D. W. (2006). *How video games help children learn*. New York: Palgrave Macmillan.

Smith, R., Curtin, P., & Newman, L. (1997). *Kids in the kitchen: The educational implications of computer and computer games use by young children*. Paper presented at the Australian Association for Research in Education Annual Conference, Brisbane, Australia.

Squire, K. (2003). Video games in education. *International Journal of Intelligent Simulations and Gaming*, 2(1), 49–62.

The training room. (2008). Retrieved February 29, 2008, from http://www.gamedesigncampus.com

VHIL. (2007). Retrieved December 5, 2007, from http://vhil.stanford.edu/projects

APPENDIX

Detailed Results

The following table (Table 2) shows the results from 20 participants, 10 male and 10 female with an average age of 21 years.

Table 2. Eye tracking results

Picture 1:	Young girl semi-smiling, with mouth closed, suggesting **Happy emotion.**
Male Perception	Happy 100%
Female Perception	Happy 80% Don't Know 20%
Combined	**Happy 90%** Don't Know 10%
Eye tracking analysis	All participants viewed eyes first with 50% viewing eyes only. The remaining 50% then viewed the mouth. No other features were viewed.
Picture 2:	Young woman smiling, with mouth open, suggesting **Happy emotion.**
Male Perception	Happy 100%
Female Perception	Happy 100%
Combined	**Happy 100%**
Eye tracking analysis	All participants viewed eyes first with only 10% viewing eyes only. 80% viewed the woman's mouth. No other features were viewed.
Picture 3:	Male Avatar from Poser, frowning with sad eyes, suggesting **Sad emotion.**
Male Perception	Sad 80% Scared 10% Don't Know 10%
Female Perception	Sad 60% Scared 30% Angry 10%
Combined	**Sad 70%** Scared 20% Angry 5% D'Know 5%
Eye tracking analysis	40% of participants viewed eyes and mouth with only 10% viewing eyes only. The remaining 50% also viewed other features of the Avatar.
Picture 4:	Young woman looking nervous, perhaps frightened, suggesting **Scared emotion.**
Male Perception	Scared 80% Don't Know 20%
Female Perception	Scared 70% Sad 10% Don't Know 20%
Combined	**Scared 75%** Sad 5% Don't Know 20%
Eye tracking analysis	All participants viewed eyes first with 40% viewing eyes only. The remaining 60% then viewed the mouth. No other features were viewed.
Picture 5:	Male Avatar from Poser, looking angry and showing teeth, suggesting **Angry emotion.**
Male Perception	Angry 70% Scared 30%
Female Perception	Angry 90% Sad 10%
Combined	**Angry 80%** Sad 5% Scared 15%
Eye tracking analysis	All participants viewed eyes and mouth with 25% viewing mouth only. 65% of participants also viewed other features of the Avatar.
Picture 6:	Female Avatar from Poser in happy pose, with mouth smiling and closed, suggesting **Happy emotion.** Hands in picture.
Male Perception	Happy 90% Don't Know 10%
Female Perception	Happy 90% Don't Know 10%
Combined	**Happy 90%** Don't Know 10%

Eye tracking analysis	All participants viewed eyes and mouth with 20% viewing mouth only. 60% of participants also viewed other features of the Avatar with 10% looking at the avatar's hands.
Picture 7:	Young woman looking down with mouth closed, looking sad, almost angry, suggesting **Sad emotion.**
Male Perception	Sad 60% Angry 30% Don't Know 10%
Female Perception	Sad 60% Angry 30% Don't Know 10%
Combined	**Sad 60%** Angry 30% Don't Know 10%
Eye tracking analysis	All participants viewed eyes first with 50% viewing eyes only. The remaining 50% then viewed the mouth. No other features were viewed.
Picture 8:	Alien Avatar from Poser, with mouth frowning and pointing hand suggesting **Sad emotion.**
Male Perception	Don't Know 60% Angry 20% Scared 20%
Female Perception	Don't Know 50% Angry 30% Happy 20%
Combined	**D'Know 55%** Angry 25% Happy 10% Scared 10%
Eye tracking analysis	All participants viewed eyes and mouth with 20% viewing mouth only. 80% of participants also viewed other features of the Avatar with 40% looking at the avatar's hand.
Picture 9:	Male Avatar from Second Life with a solemn look, one eye obscured by hair, cigarette in mouth, showing **Sad emotion.**
Male Perception	Happy 40% Don't Know 60%
Female Perception	Happy 40% Sad 10% Don't Know 50%
Combined	**Don't Know 55%** Happy 40% Sad 5%
Eye tracking analysis	All participants viewed eyes and mouth with 5% viewing eyes only. 60% of participants also viewed other features of the Avatar with 50% looking at the cigarette.
Picture 10:	Woman looking sad but showing no expression with mouth, suggesting **Sad emotion.**
Male Perception	Sad 80% Scared 10% Don't Know 10%
Female Perception	Sad 80% Don't Know 20%
Combined	**Sad 80%** Scared 5% Don't Know 15%
Eye tracking analysis	All participants viewed eyes first with 20% viewing eyes only. The remaining 80% then viewed the mouth. No other features were viewed.
Picture 11:	Woman smiling, with mouth open, suggesting **Happy emotion.**
Male Perception	Happy 100%
Female Perception	Happy 100%
Combined	**Happy 100%**
Eye tracking analysis	All participants viewed eyes first with 10% viewing eyes only and 90% viewed the mouth. No other features were viewed.
Picture 12:	Robot (Poser) with face but circles for eyes and no mouth, placed in happy pose with hands showing, suggesting **Happy emotion.**
Male Perception	Happy 40% Angry 10% Don't Know 50%
Female Perception	Happy 30% Don't Know 70%
Combined	**Don't Know 60%** Angry 5% Happy 35%
Eye tracking analysis	All participants viewed eyes and where the mouth would be. 70% of participants also viewed other features of the Avatar with 30% looking at the avatar's hands.
Picture 13:	Young girl semi-smiling, with mouth closed, suggesting **Happy emotion.**
Male Perception	Happy 100%
Female Perception	Happy 80% Don't Know 20%

Combined	**Happy 90%** Don't Know 10%
Eye tracking analysis	All participants viewed eyes first with 50% viewing eyes only. The remaining 50% then viewed the mouth. No other features were viewed.
Picture 14:	Female Avatar (Poser) with eyebrows frowning and teeth showing, suggesting **Angry emotion.**
Male Perception	Scared 60% Angry 40%
Female Perception	Scared 50% Angry 50%
Combined	**Scared 55%** Angry 45%
Eye tracking analysis	All participants viewed eyes and mouth with 20% viewing the mouth only. 60% of participants also viewed other features of the Avatar.
Picture 15:	Female Avatar from Second Life with sad eyes, mouth closed and facial jewellery, suggesting **Sad emotion.**
Male Perception	D'Know 90% Sad 10%
Female Perception	D'Know 60% Angry 20% Happy 10% Sad 10%
Combined	**D'Know 75%** Angry 10% Happy 5% Sad 10%
Eye tracking analysis	All participants viewed eyes and mouth. 60% then viewed other features of the Avatar. 40% of participants also viewed the facial jewellery.
Picture 16:	Side view of young woman with slight sad face and mouth closed, suggesting **Sad emotion.**
Male Perception	Sad 90% Don't Know 10%
Female Perception	Sad 70% Don't Know 30%
Combined	**Sad 80%** Don't Know 20%
Eye tracking analysis	All participants viewed eyes first with 20% viewing eyes only. The remaining 80% then viewed the mouth. No other features were viewed.
Picture 17:	Male Avatar from Poser, sad expression with hand in foreground, suggesting **Sad emotion.**
Male Perception	Sad 60% Happy 10% Don't Know 30%
Female Perception	Sad 30% Happy 20% Scared 10% D'Know 40%
Combined	**Sad 45%** Happy 15% Scared 5% D'Know 35%
Eye tracking analysis	All participants viewed eyes and the mouth would be. 90% of participants also viewed other features of the Avatar with 55% looking at the avatar's hand.
Picture 18:	Young woman looking very solemn, mouth closed and hand showing in foreground, suggesting **Sad emotion.**
Male Perception	Sad 50% Happy 10% Don't Know 40%
Female Perception	Sad 50% Happy 20% Don't Know 30%
Combined	**Sad 50%** Happy 15% Don't Know 35%
Eye tracking analysis	All participants viewed eyes first with 65% then viewing the mouth. No other features were viewed. The Hand was not looked at.
Picture 19:	Female Avatar (Poser), with mouth open showing teeth and eyebrows frowned, suggesting **Angry emotion.**
Male Perception	Scared 100%
Female Perception	Scared 80% Don't Know 20%
Combined	**Scared 90%** Don't Know 10%
Eye tracking analysis	All participants viewed eyes and mouth with 50% also viewing other features of the Avatar.
Picture 20:	Young woman looking away, slightly sad expression with mouth partially open and hand in foreground, suggesting **Sad emotion.**
Male Perception	Don't Know 50% Sad 50%

Female Perception	Don't Know 60% Sad 40%
Combined	**Don't Know 55%** Sad 45%
Eye tracking analysis	All participants viewed eyes first with 70% viewing the mouth. 20% of participants looked at other facial features but did not view the hand.

Chapter 14
Language Learning and Social Communication Using Chat Rooms

Muhammet Demirbilek
Suleyman Demirel University, Turkey

Berna Mutlu
University of Florida, USA

ABSTRACT

Information and communication technologies (ICT) have become an inevitable part of adolescents' daily life and have caused macro and micro changes that are shaping the societies in which adolescents of the future will live. As a two-way real time communication tool, chat rooms are one of the most popular forms of ICT in adolescents' daily life. Adolescents use ICT for meaningful communication and social interaction with their peers and relatives. Following are some of the purposes for interacting through chat rooms: staying current in what matters to them, shopping, entertainment, creating personal web pages, and, yes, completing homework assignments. These activities can promote opportunities for purposeful communication that leads to increased language production and social interaction as well as promotes higher order thinking skills. The purpose of this chapter is to highlight issues on chat rooms as a two-way real time communication tools frequently used by adolescents with an emphasis on the effects of chat rooms on adolescents' second language development with a comprehensive review of literature.

INTRODUCTION

Uses of the Internet and the web for second language acquisition and second language instruction have been gaining ground since the early 1990s. A plethora of technologies such as different forms of

chat, distant learning opportunities, and various software packages have since been adopted for the purpose of language learning (Hamatr, 2008).

Today, the Internet is an important part of adolescents' leisure lives and therefore increasingly a vital part of their culture. Pacheco (2005) states that the Internet offers diverse sources of information for students to explore. Synchronous computer-

DOI: 10.4018/978-1-60566-926-7.ch014

mediated communication is one of these effective resources that take place in real-time networking communication. In other words, messages are received and sent instantly, as if individuals were having a telephone conversation. This interaction occurs on-line, and can be either written down in text form or can occur through audio and video. Such communication is also called chatting, and can happen in a one-to-one basis or many-to many, as in the Internet-based chat rooms. (Warschauer, Shetzer, & Meloni, 2002). Given the wide application of chat rooms in online communication, there is an imminent need to understand their social and educational roles as well as the implications for language development and higher order thinking skills. The current chapter therefore focuses on the use of chat rooms in language education by examining various technological functionalities of chat rooms associated with ESL/EFL language learning.

TYPES OF CHAT ROOMS FOR ESL/ EFL LANGUAGE DEVELOPMENT

The most popular form of ICT among adolescents is chat rooms. Chat is "a two-way form of computer-mediated communication (CMC), a dialogue in real time as we keyboard or speak our words, an online conversation between two or more people" (Almeida d'Eça, 2002). Following are the most widely used chat room formats that teachers of English language learners can use for designing collaborative online activities that are based on chat room technologies.

Voice Chats

Payne and Ross (2005) conducted an experiment using voice chat with the participants consisted of 24 volunteers, 2 males and 22 females ranging in age from 18-26. Based on the findings of the study, the researchers concluded that the chat may provide a unique form of support to certain

types of learners in L2 oral proficiency. Jepson (2005) states that voice chats are superior for the purpose of meaning negotiation than text chats, giving an edge for the use of voice chats in certain situations. From a constructivist point of view, the study suggests that voice chats are just as effective for language development as text-based chat environments since voice chats provide opportunities where learners are more likely to negotiate for meaning with increased language production (Jepson, 2005). Voice chats in this study initiated higher instances of negotiation of meaning in comparison to those in text chat. The negotiations involved pronunciation repair moves where the goal of the speakers was to attend to pronunciation breakdowns.

White Board

Another form of synchronous communication is the web whiteboard, which allows users to communicate and share ideas in graphical forms over the web in real time. Hampel and Hauck (2004) describe the use of such a tool which forms a part of a system called Lyceum that was used at the United Kingdom (UK) Open University and carried out online with a cohort of 15 volunteers. The authors called the system an 'audio-graphic' conferencing tool as it allows users to conduct voice chats while working on the web whiteboard. They also reported that the use of the system helps learning in the sense that, "Student feedback suggests that participating in intense interactions with fellow learners as well as collaborative tasks is the most exciting aspect of learning and practicing a language in a virtual learning environment (VLE) like Lyceum."(p.76)

Multi-User Dungeon

Warner (2004) presents an interesting although rare form of synchronous communication, the multi-user dungeon (MUD), with all the participants between the ages of 18 and 25 having a language course. The MUD is an open chat room with multiple users interacting at the same time. It has a beginning as a way to conduct fantasy role playing games. Naturally, it involves interactions between characters (users) in a textual or graphical world. In a way, MUDs are precursor to current Massively Multiplayer Online Role-Playing Game (MMORPG) like Ragnarok and World of Warcraft. Warner (2004) reports that the use of MUD has shown that the communication is mainly 'playful' (non-academic), not only "simply with the language" but also "within the language"; in fact, this is significant because such non-academic and informal form of communication has been neglected by past research in second language acquisition.

PROMOTING ACADEMIC DEVELOPMENT FOR ESL LEARNERS THROUGH CHAT ROOM TECHNOLOGIES

The use of information and communication technologies (ICT) in language learning has increasingly gained momentum during the last decade. Chat rooms known as one of the most used ICT tools among adolescents may hold great promise for second language learning. Computer technology has become an indispensable component in second and foreign language classrooms. Warschauer, Shetzer and Meloni (2002) have explained that computer technology helps ESL/EFL classrooms come ALIVE (Authenticity, Literacy, Interaction, Vitality, Empowerment):

1. Authenticity with vast amounts of real life materials used by the learner;
2. Literacy skills that students master in order to excel academically and linguistically such as reading, writing, communicating, researching and publishing for academic and occupational goals;

3. Interaction with meaningful communication opportunities among native and non-native speakers worldwide;
4. Vitality where ESL/EFL learners are boosted in their motivational needs to communicate with freedom, flexibility, and real time without engaging in memorization of grammar rules;
5. Empowerment where learners become autonomous collaborative learners, and teachers, coaches that teach how to learn/ how to construct new knowledge.

The new approach to computer-assisted language learning (CALL), Integrative CALL, can only reach its goal of providing authentic means of communication if learners are exposed to this technology responsibly through assigning tasks for critical thinking and purposeful communication. Learners will not achieve levels of communicative competence by just having them use a computer. As any language class, the use of networking processes for learning a second or foreign language should be well-planned taking into consideration many different variables: students' interests, student's individual styles and strategies of learning, students' needs, lacks, and wants as well as the goals of the lesson, the content, and the resources. Likewise, both the roles of the students and teachers will change with students becoming autonomous learners who are "learning how to learn" and teachers assuming the role of coaches who are "teaching how to learn".

Berge (2000) has highlighted the changing roles of teachers that emerge in online learning: teachers' role changing from lecturer and instructor to consultant, guide, coach and resource provider; teachers that become expert questioners, rather than providers of answers; teachers that provide structure to student work, encouraging self-direction; a shift from teachers' total control of the teaching environment to sharing with the student as fellow learner. In short, according to Berge, teacher-learner hierarchy is broken down.

Students have opportunities of negotiating, persuading, clarifying meaning, requesting for information, exchanging ideas, discussing, asking questions, and so forth.

Berge (2000) also described the changing roles of learners: a switch from students acting as passive receptacles to those who are constructing their own knowledge; a type of students who put hands into complex problem solving activities rather than just memorizing facts; an increased role of collaborative/cooperative group members and teamwork in online classrooms; a shifting role towards autonomous, independent, self-motivated managers of their time; a role that makes emphasis on knowledge use rather than only the observation of the teacher's expert performance. However, a well-designed course that involves tasks based on online communication can also help learners become good listeners and responders by incorporating in the assignments evaluation rubrics that classmates complete to promote peer evaluation, or providing handouts where students can take notes that will be included in tests or by requiring peers to synthesize the information heard (Egbert, 2005). Egbert has added that "these techniques, are related, in part, to the condition of autonomy, in that the more autonomous students become in their learning, the more they need to interact, consult, or negotiate with their team members and class" (p. 55), and all these opportunities for collaboration and interaction also promote language development as well as academic development. Egbert (2005) has explained that "creativity implies doing something original, adapting or changing "Working with others often facilitates creativity" (p. 74). Evidently, there are many advantages of the Internet from which language learning and teaching can benefit.

Sharing information can also help students become good listeners and responders with the help of assignments that involve evaluation rubrics for classmates to complete. In this way, students critically evaluate their peer's work. Teachers can trigger students' critical thinking skills by provid-

ing handouts where students can critique and plan their learning with their peers by synthesizing new knowledge collaboratively (Egbert, 2005). Egbert also asserts that "these techniques, are related, in part, to the condition of autonomy, in that the more choices (autonomy) the students have, the more they need to interact, consult, or negotiate with their team members and class" (p. 55). In this way, students can learn language and practice their communication skills without the teacher's presence, which can decrease dependability on direct instruction and direction.

In addition, authenticity through Web-Based Learning (WBL) is also accomplished through creativity and production. With the net students are able to create and produce. Such tasks lead to an increase in students' use of higher order thinking skills. Furthermore, ESL students can be prompted to acquire and use language that is necessary for participating in creative tasks. Egbert (2005) has explained that "creativity implies doing something original, adapting or changing working with others often facilitates creativity" (p. 74). He links it with production by stating that "productivity tools maximize and extend students' ability to create products and to problem-solve collectively; they also expand opportunities for expression which is an important principle for language learning" (p.74). He further explains that both productivity and creativity tools support second language learners when they are able to construct models, plan, publish, organize and generate materials, collect data and develop and present creative works. Ways of achieving creativity in a web-based course could be having students create a poster, birthday cards or invitations, advertisements, class or school newsletters, class announcements, cartoons, classroom diary of poems and stories, and more sophisticated assignments such as interactive webpages. Egbert has suggested many other types of tasks to enhance creativity and productivity such as mazes, catalogs, digital montages of student's country or other countries with digital cameras or video cameras of life or any other authentic task. To make it authentic materials taken from real world as they are without any adaptations for language level, students are directed to web-links and web-searches to enrich the information they bring to class.

Finally, the Internet helps students interact with other cultures, and it helps instructors provide access to authentic communication for English as Second Language (ESL) students in order to promote effective second language development. Students can also develop autonomy by taking the responsibility of one's own learning and a prerequisite for optimum development. Furthermore, independence and flexibility create low affective filter in a low anxiety environment necessary for learning with high motivation and confidence the Internet provides (Krashen, 1985). Furthermore, web-based language interaction provides exposure to authentic language for ESL/EFL (English as a Second Language/ English as a Foreign Language) learners. For instance, when web-based activities are structured through cooperative learning strategies where each individual has a role to fulfill, students use language in order to accomplish a task, which also activates their problem solving skills. To help students reach higher levels of learning as well as achieving increased language use and interaction, teachers can assign tasks where they share the information through the web and collaboratively create an end-product.

PROMOTING SECOND/ FOREIGN LANGUAGE DEVELOPMENT THROUGH CHAT ROOM TECHNOLOGIES

Lu, Chiou, Day, Ong, and Hsu (2006) treat chat as a means of synchronous, real-time interaction that can be used in an online language classroom to extend the learning process well beyond the traditional four walls, and thereby make the learning process more fascinating, exciting and enriching. The researchers list the following characteristics of online chat:

- Promotes learner autonomy by enabling the learner to be in charge of his own learning;
- Encourages collaborative learning and team work and helps develop group skills;
- Promotes communication skills by allowing learners carry on a conversation, interviewing, and negotiating meaning;
- Promotes social and socialization skills and proper etiquette such as greeting others, introducing oneself, leave talking, stating and reinforcing one's own ideas, interacting politely and appropriately, showing respect and being responsible, making choices, helping, coaching, etc.;
- Facilitates interaction and learning with and from people of different cultures who speak different native languages;
- Exposes students to speaking a language as it is used by native speakers and allows them to interact in an authentic context with those speakers;
- Promotes different types of interaction: student to student, student to teacher, student to expert, and student to online resource;
- Offers an appropriate way of fostering inter-peer communication in a real and meaningful environment;
- Balances and increases participation among students with less involvement by teachers;
- Reduces anxiety among students by lowering their affective filter that may prevent language production in high anxiety settings (Krashen, 1985);
- Provides useful transcripts for studying the language used or for further analysis of a conversation"

Chat not only uses a communication medium that generally appeals to students but also takes place in an innovative and exciting setting, namely, cyberspace or virtual reality. Consequently, it puts a strong emphasis on communication and authentic language just like face-to-face communication and generates intensive practice in language skills. As students are left on their own to a large extent, they have to continue the flow of conversation on their own. This gives them a greater sense of responsibility and a large degree of autonomy. Students have to support each other and involve themselves more intensely in the collective and collaborative construction of knowledge. Finally, the exchanges are about the 'real' world, with 'real' people, in 'real' time, and online chat can facilitate opportunities and motivation for authentic interactive conversations in a virtual environment.

Mynard (2002a and 2002b) not only indicates the advantages of chat rooms for language development, but also introduces some techniques such as interviewing a guest from another country, gathering information and comparing with a friend, interviewing a couple about a recent event, interviewing a couple about their future plans, and sample lesson plans. Having elaborated the possible applications, she lists the following benefits. Chat rooms allow learners to interact in an authentic context with native speakers (Skinner & Austin, 1999; Carey, 1999) without being restricted by location (Wilson & Whitelock, 1998), they allow communication to take place in real time, they promote active involvement (Bump, 1990; Sullivan & Pratt, 1996; Warshauer et al, 1996b; Carey, 1999). Online chatting can promote learner autonomy due mainly to the fact that the teacher role is minimized (Bump, 1990; Chun, 1994; Sullivan & Pratt, 1996; Warshauer et al, 1996). Transcripts can be generated which are useful for students to study their own language production as well as analyzing how the conversation flows (Carey, 1999), and they can also spot their own weaknesses, which would help them

monitor their own language learning and improve their interactive competence (Chun, 1994). Students also have the opportunity to notice language used by native speakers (Schmidt & Frota, 1986; Schmidt, 1990, Brett, 1998), so that students are given the opportunity for skills development and practice (Sullivan & Pratt, 1996, Pica & Doughty, 1986, Brett, 1998; Chun, 1994).

Chat rooms can also increase autonomy in language learning by helping ESL learners acquire skills to monitor and guide their own language learning process. Learner autonomy refers to a learner's capacity for critical self-evaluation and self-determination, an ability to take control over and responsibility for his/her learning (Schwienhorst, 2003). There are three major approaches concerning this issue. The first approach might be called the individual-cognitive perspective. This model has often been related to language and linguistic awareness. The second perspective on learner autonomy may be called social-interactive. A social-interactive component has long been an essential element in second language acquisition, and the importance of both comprehensible input (Krashen, 1985) and comprehensible output (Swain, 1985). Finally, learner autonomy can be viewed from an experimental-participatory perspective. All three approaches share a concern for reflection. Through reflective processes, the learner should become more aware of language, language learning and her own relationship to the learning process and identity in the target language. We can also see that social-interaction, first in providing comprehensible input; second in the production of comprehensible output, particularly in the form of "pushed output" (Swain, 1985), and third in the form of feedback and scaffolding plays a significant role in language learning. If we want learners to assume responsibility for their learning process, then they must be given control over it, supported by a rich learning environment, peers, and teachers. In this respect synchronous text-based communication (chat rooms) can be used effectively for language learning.

Another aspect of chat rooms is social interaction, which is essential to language learning, according to the arguments presented by studies based in the communicative approach to language teaching (Hall & Verplaetse, 2000; Long, 1983, 1996; Pica, 1994). Negotiation of meaning is a linguistic process that speakers use to better understand one another, that is, to increase the comprehensibility of language input. Furthermore, negotiation of meaning may result in modified interaction (Ellis, Tanaka, & Yamazaki, 1994; Pica, 1994; Smith, 2004), which ostensibly optimizes second language acquisition. Sotillo (2000) found that participants in synchronous text chat sessions used interactional modifications similar to those used in face-to-face sessions. A number of studies have noted that adolescents pay more attention to their lexical development than their grammatical development while negotiating for meaning in both networked and face-to-face environments (Blake, 2000).

Although grammar has outweighed the vocabulary in school curriculums, the latter has an important role in learning a language. The importance of vocabulary instruction has been disregarded because of the traditional understanding of vocabulary instruction where the students are passively exposed to the teacher's explanation for meaning, definition, pronunciation and spelling. In addition, they acquire new lexemes (words) solely by means of their textbooks during classroom lessons. For instance, they come across new vocabulary items in the text and they just ask their teacher to explain and clarify the word. Most of them are hesitant at using the vocabulary items they learnt. They may recognize the words in context, but that does not mean that they are able to use the new words in a new context. As Taylor (1990) points out, receptive and productive skills are both within the domain of vocabulary learning. In order for students to remember and retain vocabulary items, students have to be directed meaningful, task based activities. The Communicative Language Teaching Method

posits that "Language that is meaningful to the learner supports learning process" (Richards & Rodgers, 2001, p. 72). Chat rooms can provide opportunities for using new vocabulary items for real communication purposes by creating a need for using new words during the flow of the conversation. In this way, vocabulary knowledge of students can be enhanced through communicative language learning tasks where the goal is using language for interaction and communication.

Task based activities that teachers can assign learners in chat rooms allow learners to use the target language for a communicative purpose in order to achieve an outcome (Willis, 1996). In order to make students' vocabulary learning more challenging and intrinsically motivating, task based activities are necessary. Because "it is the challenge of achieving the outcome that makes task based learning a motivating procedure" (Willis, 1996, p. 24). Thus, chat rooms facilitate the goal for enhancing students' language learning.

SUGGESTIONS FOR EFFECTIVE INSTRUCTIONAL USE OF CHAT ROOMS

Blogs, chat rooms, text messaging and other forms of information and communication technologies have become an inevitable part of adolescents' daily life. Online communication technologies allow meaningful communication and social interaction, so they have great potential for second language development and academic development. When using synchronous computer mediated communication, teachers may need to take into account the structure of tasks, group sizes, moderating techniques, and other variables that increase the probability that the resultant discussions will entail educational value. Merely instructing students to discuss a topic is likely to result in short superficial conversations with little educational value. Good tasks supported by meaningful graphical environments and avatars can be highly effective. Similarly, groups of the right size that follow some simple discussion rules can produce good results.

Pacheco (2005) claims that, Internet based learning environments that are supported with collaborative online communication tasks can improve students' metacognitive strategies by allowing opportunities for trial and error, reflection, and personal involvement. This type of instruction also gives learner higher order thinking skills for discovery by questioning, reflecting, and researching necessary for inquiry and problem-solving. Learners can acquire problem-solving experiences where they make accurate observations, or find and organize information as well as predict, synthesize, and use other higher order thinking skills to find solution. Accomplishing these levels of learning help learners remember and understand better, as we learn from this famous Chinese proverb: "I hear and I forget. I see and I remember. I do and I understand". Thus, a chat augmented course can serve as the channel to promote language and content learning which activates critical-thinking skills by way of inquiry and problem-solving activities. By working on collaborative assignments, students negotiate over issues regarding distinguishing fact from opinion, assessing a reliable web-source, distinguishing relevant from irrelevant information. Egbert includes guidelines for designing activities that can increase the quality of collaborative activities based on chat-oriented communication and help students reach levels of knowledge (Egbert, 2005):

- Learners should be able to formulate a question (inquiry question) that has meaning, define the problem and investigate what needs to be investigated to answer it.
- They should also investigate by researching; that is, students should be able to organize the information gathered.
- Students should be engaged in the creation of new ideas or plans of action by applying strategies such as summarizing and interpreting.

- Participants should have sessions of discussion to get insights on the entire process and share and compare prior knowledge to new knowledge.
- Students should reach levels of reflection on the entire inquiry process, and think over the decisions and conclusions taken and determine if the results of the inquiry/problem-solving were the ones expected or if further research has to be done."

These guidelines are also necessary to promote successful academic learning that supports language learning. Authentic communication based on collective problem solving is paramount in designing instructions with chat room technologies. Vygotskyan Sociocultural Theory asserts that human cognition and knowledge constructed through social activity within the society (Vygotsky, 1978). Incorporating collaborative inquiry and problem solving activities that take place through synchronous online communication can help learners of all levels in their language development by allowing language learners to bridge the gap between content learning and language learning, and this is what makes the learning of a language academically more meaningful.

CONCLUSION

Online chat rooms are the Internet applications that are exciting and interesting for many teenagers, and they have a great potential for English language learning and social communication. In using this Internet application, adolescents have an opportunity to communicate with people from other countries in genuine contexts and to practice their English language skills at their own convenience, rather than communicating with peers or their teacher in simulated settings. These interactive synchronous environments can be a rewarding experience for adolescents who want to learn any language and interact with different cultures. Adolescents can meet other learners and peers online and can communicate with them through text or speech.

Students interact with their peers in meaningful communication to fulfill a task such as a project, group work, discuss a topic, solving a problem, etc. If these conversations are cleverly planned and directed, they are more likely to help students improve their language skills in the ways that may be unique to chats. Thus, without any need for external motivation exerted by the teacher and assignments, students communicate in the second language with the necessary motivation to use the language in social context. Such an environment provides students almost optimum conditions for language learning as they analyze and reconstruct when they make mistakes, which leads to purposeful and meaningful communication about real life topics and over real life problems.

ACKNOWLEDGMENT

I would like to thank Ihsan Marulcu for his help regarding the first draft of this chapter.

REFERENCES

Almeida d'Eça, T. (2002). *To chat or not to chat in the EFL classroom, that is the question!* Paper presented at the "Language - Communication - Culture" International Conference, University of Évora, Portugal. Retrieved from http://www.malhatlantica.pt/teresadeca/papers/evora2002/chat-and-efl.htm

Almeida d'Eça, T. (2003). The use of chat in EFL/ESL. *TESL-EJ, 7*(1). Retrieved October 23, 2008, from: http://www-writing.berkeley.edu/TESL-EJ/ej25/int.html

Berge, Z. (2000). New roles for learners and teachers in online higher education. In G. Heart (Ed.). *Readings & resources in global online education* (pp. 3-9). Melbourne, Australia: Whirligig Press.

Blake, R. (2000). Computer-mediated communication: A window on L2 Spanish interlanguage. *Language Learning & Technology, 4*(1), 120-136. Retrieved November 14, 2004, from http://llt.msu.edu/vol4num1/blake/

Brett, P. (1998). Using multi-media: A descriptive investigation of incidental language learning. *Computer Assisted Language Learning, 11*(2), 179–200. doi:10.1076/call.11.2.179.5684

Bump, J. (1990). Radical changes in classroom discussion using network computers. *Computers and the Humanities, 24*, 49–65. doi:10.1007/BF00115028

Carey, S. (1999). The use of WebCT for a highly interactive virtual graduate seminar. *Computer Assisted Language Learning, 12*(4), 371–380. doi:10.1076/call.12.4.371.5701

Chun, D. (1994). Using computer networking to facilitate the acquisition of interactive competence. *System, 22*(1), 17–31. doi:10.1016/0346-251X(94)90037-X

Egbert, J. (2005). *CALL essentials: Principles and practice in CALL classrooms*. Alexandra, VA: TESOL.

Ellis, R., Tanaka, Y., & Yamazaki, A. (1994). Classroom interaction, comprehension, and the acquisition of L2 word meanings. *Language Learning, 44*, 449–491. doi:10.1111/j.1467-1770.1994.tb01114.x

Hall, J. K., & Verplaetse, L. S. (2000). *Second and foreign language learning through classroom interaction*. Mahwah, NJ: Erlbaum.

Hamatr, A. (2008). Web technologies for language learning and implications for the design of CMS for language instruction. *International Journal of social Sciences, 3*(1), 61-65. Retrieved September 18, 2008, from http://www.waset.org/ijss/v3/v3-1-9.pdf

Hampel, R., & Hauck, M. (2004). Towards an effective use of audio conferencing in distance language courses. *Language Learning & Technology, 8*(1), 66–82.

Jepson, K. (2005). Conversations and negotiated interaction in text and voice chat rooms. *Language Learning & Technology, 9*(3), 79–98.

Krashen, S. (1985). *The input hypothesis: Issues and implications*. London: Longman.

Lewis, M. (1997*). Implementing the lexical approach: Putting theory into practice*. Hove, UK: Language Teaching Publications.

Long, M. H. (1983). Linguistic and conversational adjustments to non-native speakers. *Studies in Second Language Acquisition, 5*, 177–193. doi:10.1017/S0272263100004848

Long, M. H. (1996). The role of the linguistic environment in second language acquisition. In W. Ritchie & T. Bhatia (Eds.), *Handbook of research on second language acquisition* (pp. 413-469). New York: Academic Press.

Lu, C. H., Chiou, G. F., Day, M. Y., Ong, C. S., & Hsu, W. L. (2006). Using instant messaging to provide an intelligent learning environment. In *Conference Proceedings of Intelligent Tutoring Systems 8th International,* Jhongli, Taiwan. Retrieved July 1, 2008, from http://www.iis.sinica.edu.tw/IASL/webpdf/paper-2006-Using_Instant_Messaging_to_Provide_an_Intelligent_Learning_Environment.pdf

Moras, S. (2001). *Computer-assisted language learning (CALL) and the Internet. Cultura Inglesa de Sao Carlos*. Retrieved May 12, 2008, from http://www3.telus.net/linguisticsissues/CALL.html

Mynard, J. (2002a). Introducing EFL students to chat rooms. *The Internet TESL Journal, 8*(2). Retrieved February 17, 2004, from http://iteslj.org/Lessons/Mynard-Chat.html

Mynard, J. (2002b). Making chat activities with native speakers meaningful for EFL learners. *The Internet TESL Journal, 8*(3). Retrieved February 17, 2004, from http://iteslj.org/Techniques/Mynard-Chat2/

Pacheco, A. Q. (2005). Web-based learning (WBL): A challenge for foreign language teachers. *Revista Electrónica Actualidades Investigativas en Educación* 5 (2005) H. 2, S.1-25. Retrieved September 12, 2008, from http://revista.inie.ucr.ac.cr/articulos/2-2005/archivos/web.pdf

Payne, S., & Ross, B. (2005). Synchronous CMC, working memory, and L2 oral proficiency development. *Language Learning & Technology, 9*(3), 35–54.

Pica, T. (1994). Review article -- research on negotiation: What does it reveal about second-language learning conditions, processes, and outcomes? *Language Learning, 44*, 493–527. doi:10.1111/j.1467-1770.1994.tb01115.x

Pica, T., & Doughty, C. (1986). Making input comprehensible: do interactional modifications help? *ILT Review of Applied Linguistics, 72*, 1–25.

Quesada Pacheco, A. (2005). Web-based learning (WBL): A challenge for foreign language teachers. *Revista Electrónica Actualidades Investigativas en Educación, 5*(2), 1-25. Retrieved December 13, 2007, from http://revista.inie.ucr.ac.cr/articulos/2-2005/archivos/web.pdf

Richards, J., & Rodgers, T. (2001). *Approaches and methods in language teaching*. New York: Cambridge University Press.

Schmidt, R. (1990). The role of consciousness in second language learning. *Applied Linguistics, 11*, 129–158. doi:10.1093/applin/11.2.129

Schmidt, R., & Frota, S. (1986). Developing basic conversational ability in a second language: A case study of an adult learner of Portuguese. In R. Daly (Ed.), *Talking to learn: Conversation in second language acquisition* (pp. 93-107). Rowley, MA: Newbury House.

Schwienhorst, K. (2003). Learner autonomy and tandem learning: Putting principles into practice in synchronous and asynchronous telecommunications environments. *Computer Assisted Language Learning, 16*, 427–443. doi:10.1076/call.16.5.427.29484

Skinner, B., & Austin, R. (1999). Computer conferencing - does it motivate EFL students? *ELT Journal, 53*(4), 270–279. doi:10.1093/elt/53.4.270

Smith, B. (2004). Computer-mediated negotiated interaction and lexical acquisition. *Studies in Second Language Acquisition, 26*, 365–398. doi:10.1017/S027226310426301X

Sotillo, S. (2000). Discourse functions and syntactic complexity in synchronous and asynchronous communication. *Language Learning & Technology, 4*(1), 82-119. Retrieved November 10, 2001, from http://llt.msu.edu/vol4num1/sotillo/default.html

Sullivan, N., & Pratt, E. (1996). A comparative study of two ESL writing environments: A computer-assisted classroom and a traditional oral classroom. *System, 29*(4), 491–501. doi:10.1016/S0346-251X(96)00044-9

Swain, M. (1985). Communicative competence: Some roles of comprehensible input and comprehensible output in its development. In S. Gass & C. Madden (Eds.), *Input in second language acquisition* (pp. 235-256). Rowley, MA: Newbury House.

Taylor, L. (1990). *Teaching and learning vocabulary*. Upper Saddle River, NJ: Prentice Hall.

Vygotsky, L. (1978). *Mind and society: The development of higher psychological processes*. Cambridge, MA: Harvard University Press.

Warner, C. N. (2004). It's just a game, right? Types of play in foreign language CMC. *Language Learning & Technology, 8*(2), 69–87.

Warschauer, M., Meloni, C., & Shetzer, H. (2002). *Internet for English teaching*. Alexandria, VA: TESOL.

Willett, R., & Sefton-Green, J. (2003). Living and learning in chat rooms (or does informal learning have anything to teach us?). *Éducation et Sociétiés, 2*, 1–18.

Willis, J. (1996). *Framework for task based learning*. Italy: Longman.

Wilson, T., & Whitelock, D. (1998). What are the perceived benefits of participating in a computer-mediated communication (CMC) environment for distance learning computer science students? *Computers & Education, 30*(3/4), 259–269. doi:10.1016/S0360-1315(97)00069-9

KEY TERMS AND DEFINITIONS

Chat: Chat is a two-way form of computer-mediated communication, a dialogue in real time as we keyboard or speak our words, an online conversation between two or more people

Chat Room: Chat room is a place online where a group of people can get together and chat about a particular subject or just to chat.

Synchronous Communication: Synchronous communication is computer-mediated communication that takes place in real-time, where participants are all logged in to one network at the same time from a variety of remote locations, and where participants' input is immediately conveyed to other users for immediate response. The most well-known kinds of synchronous communication are real-time chat and multi user object oriented environments (MOOs)

Compilation of References

「ネットいじめ」県内公立校3割...兵庫県教委が昨年度分調査 ["Cyberbullying" 30% of public schools had problems-investigation from Hyogo Prefecture Board of Education]. (2007, Oct 06). *Yomiuri online*. Retrieved October 25, 2007, from http://osaka.yomiuri.co.jp/edu_news/20071006kk03.htm

Aalsma, M. C., Lapsley, D. K., & Flannery, D. L. (2006). Personal fables, narcissism, and adolescent adjustment. *Psychology in the Schools, 43*, 481–491. doi:10.1002/pits.20162

Abbey, A. (1993). *The effect of social support on emotional well-being*. Paper presented at the First International Symposium on Behavioral Health, Nags Head, North Carolina.

Abramson, L. Y., Metalsky, G. I., & Alloy, L. B. (1989). Hopelessness depression: A theory-based subtype of depression. *Psychological Review, 96*, 358–372. doi:10.1037/0033-295X.96.2.358

Akiba, M. (2004). Nature and correlates of ijime-bullying in Japanese middle school. *International Journal of Educational Research, 41*, 216–236. doi:10.1016/j.ijer.2005.07.002

Alberts, A., Elkind, D., & Ginsberg, S. (2007). The personal fable and risk-taking in early adolescence. *Journal of Youth and Adolescence, 36*, 71–76. doi:10.1007/s10964-006-9144-4

Almeida d'Eça, T. (2002). *To chat or not to chat in the EFL classroom, that is the question!* Paper presented at the "Language-Communication-Culture" International Conference, University of Évora, Portugal. Retrieved from http://www.malhatlantica.pt/teresadeca/papers/evora2002/chat-and-efl.htm

Almeida d'Eça, T. (2003). The use of chat in EFL/ESL. *TESL-EJ, 7*(1). Retrieved October 23, 2008, from: http://www-writing.berkeley.edu/TESL-EJ/ej25/int.html

Altheide, D. (2002). *Creating fear: News and the construction of crisis*. Chicago: Aldine.

American Academy of Neurology. (2000). Often missed facial displays give clues to true emotion, deceit. *ScienceDaily*. Retrieved December 3, 2007, from http://www.sciencedaily.com/releases/2000/05/000503181624.htm

American heritage dictionary of the English language. (1992). (CD-ROM). Redmond, WA: Microsoft Corporation.

Amichai-Hamburger, Y., & Ben Artzi, E. (2003). Loneliness and Internet use. *Computers in Human Behavior, 19*, 71–80. doi:10.1016/S0747-5632(02)00014-6

Amichai-Hamburger, Y., & McKenna, K. Y. A. (2006). The contact hypothesis revisited: Interacting via the Internet. *Journal of Computer-Mediated Communication, 11*, 825–843. doi:10.1111/j.1083-6101.2006.00037.x

Amichai-Hamburger, Y., Wainapel, Y. G., & Fox, S. (2002). On the Internet no one knows I'm an introvert: Extroversion, neuroticism, and Internet interaction. *Cyberpsychology & Behavior, 5*(2), 125–128. doi:10.1089/109493102753770507

Anderson, K. J. (1999, August). *Internet use among college students: Should we be concerned?* Paper presented at the annual meeting of the American Psychological Association, Boston.

Anderson, T., & Sturm, B. (2007). Cyberbullying: From playground to computer. *Young Adult Library Services*, *5*, 24–27.

Anolli, L., Villani, D., & Riva, G. (2005). Personality of people using chat: An online research. *Cyberpsychology & Behavior*, *8*(1), 89–95. doi:10.1089/cpb.2005.8.89

Aoyama, I. (2009, August). *Cyberbullying among university students: Definition, prevalence and predictors.* Paper presented at the meeting of the World Society of Victimology's 13th International Symposium on Victimology, Mito, Japan.

Aoyama, I., & Talbert, L. T. (2009, April). *A cross-cultural study on cyber-bullying among high school students in the Unites States and Japan.* Paper presented at the meeting of the American Educational Research Association (AERA), San Diego, CA.

Aristotle, A. (2008). *Politics. Book III, part XV.* (B. Jowett, Trans.). Retrieved September 28, 2008, from http://classics.mit.edu/Aristotle/politics.3.three.html

Aristotle, A. (2008). *Politics. Book III, Part XVI.* (B. Jowett, Trans.). Retrieved September 28, 2008, from http://classics.mit.edu/Aristotle/politics.3.three.html

Arnett, J. J. (2007). Suffering, selfish slackers? Myths and realities about emerging adults. *Journal of Youth and Adolescence*, *36*(1), 23–29. doi:10.1007/s10964-006-9157-z

Arrington, M. (2008, May 28). Causes reports on its first year: 2.5 million for 20,000 charities and non-profits. *Techcrunch*. Retrieved September 30, 2008 from http://www.techcrunch.com/2008/05/28/causes-reports-on-its-first-year/

Ashcroft v. American Civil Liberties Union, 542 U.S. 656 (2004).

Ashcroft v. Free Speech Coalition, 535 U.S. 234 (2002).

Aslanidou, S., & Menexes, G. (2008). Youth and the Internet: Uses and practices in the home. *Computers & Education*, *51*, 1375–1391. doi:10.1016/j.compedu.2007.12.003

Associated Press. (2008, July, 1). Missouri: Cyberbullying law is signed. *New York Times*. Retrieved October 20, 2008, from http://www.nytimes.com/2008/07/01/us/01brfs-CYBERBULLYIN_BRF.html?_r=1&scp=3&sq=cyberbullying,%20missouri&st=cse

Atkin, C. K. (1985). Informational utility and selective exposure to entertainment media. In D. Zillmann & J. Bryant (Eds.), *Selective exposure to communication* (pp. 63-92). Hillsdale, NJ: Lawrence Erlbaum.

Baker, S. T., Victor, J. B., & Chambers, A. L. (2004). Adolescent personality: A five-factor model construct validation. *Assessment*, *11*(4), 303–315. doi:10.1177/1073191104269871

Bandura, A. (1993). Perceived self-efficacy in cognitive development and functioning. *Educational Psychologist*, *28*, 117–148. doi:10.1207/s15326985ep2802_3

Barak, A., & Sadovsky, Y. (2008). Internet use and personal empowerment of hearing-impaired adolescents. *Computers in Human Behavior*, *24*, 1802–1815. doi:10.1016/j.chb.2008.02.007

Bargh, J. A., & McKenna, K. Y. A. (2004). The Internet and social life. *Annual Review of Psychology*, *55*, 573–590. doi:10.1146/annurev.psych.55.090902.141922

Bargh, J. A., McKenna, K. Y. A., & Fitzsimons, G. M. (2002). "Can you see the real me?" Activation and expression of the "true self" on the Internet. *The Journal of Social Issues*, *58*, 33–48. doi:10.1111/1540-4560.00247

Barnett, M. A., Vitaglione, G. D., Harper, K. K. G., & Quackenbush, S. W. (1997). Late adolescents' experiences with and attitudes toward videogames. *Journal of Applied Social Psychology*, *27*(15), 1316–1334. doi:10.1111/j.1559-1816.1997.tb01808.x

Becker, K., El-Faddagh, M., & Schmidt, M. H. (2004). Cybersuizid oder werther-effekt online: Suizidchatrooms und-foren im Internet. *Kindheit und Entwicklung*, *13*(1), 14–25. doi:10.1026/0942-5403.13.1.14

Beebe, T. J., Asche, S. E., Harrison, P. A., & Quinlan, K. B. (2004). Heightened vulnerability and increased risk-taking among adolescent chat room users: Results from a statewide school survey. *The Journal of Adolescent Health*, *35*, 116–123.

Benes, F. M. (1989). Myelination of cortical-hippocampal relays during late adoescence. *Schizophrenia Bulletin, 15*(4), 585–593.

Benes, F. M. (1998). Brain development, VII. Human brain growth spans decades. *The American Journal of Psychiatry, 155*(11), 1480.

Beraman, P. S., & Moody, J. (2004). Adolescents' suicidability. *American Journal of Public Health, 94,* 89–95. doi:10.2105/AJPH.94.1.89

Berge, Z. (2000). New roles for learners and teachers in online higher education. In G. Heart (Ed.). *Readings & resources in global online education* (pp. 3-9). Melbourne, Australia: Whirligig Press.

Berger, P., & Luckmann, T. (1966). *The social construction of reality: A treatise in the sociology of knowledge,* Garden City, NY: Doubleday.

Berkowitz, L. (1989). Frustration-aggression hypothesis: Examination and reformulation. *Psychological Bulletin, 106,* 59–73. doi:10.1037/0033-2909.106.1.59

Berliner, L., & Elliott, D. M. (2002). Sexual abuse of children. In *The APSAC handbook on child maltreatment* (2nd ed., pp. 55-78). Thousand Oaks, CA: Sage.

Berlyne, D. E. (1971). *Aesthetics and psychology.* New York: Appleton-Century-Crofts.

Berndt, T. J., & Savin-Williams, R. C. (1993). *Peer relations and friendships.* Oxford, UK: John Wiley & Sons.

Berson, I. R., & Berson, M. J. (2005). Challenging online behaviors of youth: Findings from a comparative analysis of young people in the United States and New Zealand. *Social Science Computer Review, 23,* 29–38. doi:10.1177/0894439304271532

Bethel School District No. 403 v. Fraser, 478 U.S. 675 (1986).

Beussink ex rel. Beussink v. Woodland R-IV School District, 30 F.Supp. 2d 1175 (E.D. Mo. 1998).

Bianchi, A., & Phillips, J. G. (2005). Psychological predictors of problem mobile phone use. *Cyberpsychology & Behavior, 8*(1), 39–51. doi:10.1089/cpb.2005.8.39

Blais, J. J., Craig, W. M., Pepler, D., & Connolly, J. (2008). Adolescents online: The importance of Internet activity choices to salient relationships. *Journal of Youth and Adolescence, 37,* 522–536. doi:. doi:10.1007/s10964-007-9262-7

Blais, J. J., Craig, W. M., Pepler, D., & Connolly, J. (2008). Adolescents online: The importance of Internet activity choices to salient relationships. *Journal of Youth and Adolescence, 37,* 522–536. doi:10.1007/s10964-007-9262-7

Blake, R. (2000). Computer-mediated communication: A window on L2 Spanish interlanguage. *Language Learning & Technology, 4*(1), 120-136. Retrieved November 14, 2004, from http://llt.msu.edu/vol4num1/blake/

Blakemore, S. J., & Choudhury, S. (2006). Development of the adolescent brain: Implications for executive function and social cognition. *Journal of Child Psychology and Psychiatry, and Allied Disciplines, 47*(3-4), 296–312. doi:10.1111/j.1469-7610.2006.01611.x

Blos, P. (1962). *On adolescence.* New York: The Free Press.

Blumer, J. G. (1985). The social character of media gratifications. In K. E. Rosengren, L. A. Wenner, & P. Palmgreen (Eds.), *Media gratifications research* (pp. 41-60). Beverly Hills, CA: Sage.

Blumler, J. G. (1979). The role of theory in uses and gratifications studies. *Communication Research, 6,* 9–36. doi:10.1177/009365027900600102

Boling, E., Castek, J., & Zawilinski, L. (2008). Collaborative literacy: Blogs and Internet projects. *The Reading Teacher, 61*(6), 504–506. doi:10.1598/RT.61.6.10

Boneva, B. A., Quinn, A., Kraut, R., Kiesler, S., & Shklovski, I. (2006). Examining the effect of Internet use on television viewing: Details make a difference. In R. Kraut, M. Brynin, & S. Kiesler (Eds.), *Computers, phones, and the Internet: Domesticating information technology: Oxford series in human-technology interaction* (pp. 70-83). New York: Oxford University Press.

Boucher v. School Board of the School District of Greenfield, 134 F.3d 821 (7th Cir. 1998).

Boyd, D. (2007, May 13). Social network sites: Public, private, or what? *Knowledge Tree.* Retrieved October 13, 2008, from http://kt.flexiblelearning.net.au/tkt2007/?page_id=28

Boyd, D. M., & Ellison, N. B. (2007). Social network sites: Definition, history, and scholarship. *Journal of Computer-Mediated Communication, 13*, article 11. Retrieved from http://jcmc.indiana.edu/vol13/issue1/boyd.ellison.html

Boyd, D. M., & Ellison, N. B. (2007). Social network sites: Definition, history, and scholarship. *Journal of Computer-Mediated Communication, 13*(1), article 11. Retrieved from http://jcmc.indiana.edu/vol13/issue1/boyd.ellison.html

Bradshaw, C. P., & Sawyer, A. L., & O-Brennan, L. (2007). Bullying and peer victimization at school: Perceptual differences between students and school staff. *School Psychology Review, 36*, 361–382.

Brandenburg v. Ohio, 395 U.S. 444 (1969).

Bremer, J., & Rauch, P. K. (1998). Children and computers: Risks and benefits. *Journal of the American Academy of Child and Adolescent Psychiatry, 37*(5), 559–560. doi:10.1097/00004583-199805000-00019

Brennan, P. F., Moore, S. M., & Smyth, K. (1995). The effects of a special computer network on caregivers of persons with Alzheimer's disease. *Nursing Research, 44*, 166–172. doi:10.1097/00006199-199505000-00007

Brennan, P. F., Ripich, S., & Moore, S. M. (1991). The use of home-based computers to support persons living with AIDS/ARC. *Journal of Community Health Nursing, 8*, 3–14. doi:10.1207/s15327655jchn0801_1

Brenner, V. (1997). Psychology of computer use: XLVII. Parameters of Internet use, abuse, and addiction: The first 90 days of the Internet Usage Survey. *Psychological Reports, 80*, 879–882.

Brett, P. (1998). Using multi-media: A descriptive investigation of incidental language learning. *Computer Assisted Language Learning, 11*(2), 179–200. doi:10.1076/call.11.2.179.5684

Brooks-Gunn, J. (1988). Antecedents and consequences of variations in girls' maturational timing. *Journal of Adolescent Health Care, 9*, 365–373. doi:10.1016/0197-0070(88)90030-7

Brooks-Gunn, J., & Paikoff, R. (1997). Sexuality and developmental transitions during adolescence. In J. Schulenberg, J. L. Maggs, & K. Hurrelmann (Eds.), *Health risks and developmental transitions during adolescence* (pp. 190-219). New York: Cambridge University Press.

Bross, D. C. (2005). Minimizing risks to children when they access the World Wide Web. *Child Abuse & Neglect, 29*, 749–752.

Brown, J. D. (2000). Adolescents' sexual media diets. *The Journal of Adolescent Health, 27*(2Supplement), 35–40. doi:10.1016/S1054-139X(00)00141-5

Brown, J. D., & L'Engle, K. L. (2009). X-rated sexual attitudes and behaviors associated with US early adolescents' exposure to sexually explicit media. *Communication Research, 36*(1), 129–151. doi:10.1177/0093650208326465

Brown, J. D., L'Engle, K. L., Pardun, C. J., Guo, G., Kenneavy, K., & Jackson, C. (2006). Sexy media matter: Exposure to sexual content in music, movies, television, and magazines predicts black and white adolescents' sexual behavior. *Pediatrics, 117*(4), 1018–1027. doi:10.1542/peds.2005-1406

Brown, J. S. (2002). Growing up digital. *USDLA Journal, 16*(2). Retrieved September 30, 2008, from http://www.usdla.org/html/journal/FEB02_Issue/article01.html

Buchholz, E. S., & Catton, R. (1999). Adolescents' perceptions of aloneness and loneliness. *Adolescence, 34*(133), 203.

Buchholz, E. S., & Chinlund, C. (1994). En route to a harmony of being: Viewing aloneness as a need in development and child analytic work. *Psychoanalytic Psychology, 4*, 354–374.

Buchholz, E. S., & Tomasi, S. (1994). *Differentiating aloneness from loneliness: The alone state in theory and research* (unpublished manuscript).

Buchman, D. D., & Funk, J. B. (1996). Video and computer games in the 90's: Children's time commitment and game preference. *Children Today, 24*(1), 12–15.

Buckingham, D. (2004). New media, new childhoods? Children's changing cultural environment in the age of digital technology. In M. J. Kehily (Ed.), *An introduction to childhood studies* (pp. 108-122). Maidenhead, UK: Open University Press.

Bugeja, M. J. (2006, January 27). Facing the FaceBook. *Chronicle of Higher Education*. Retrieved from http://chronicle.com/jobs/2006/01/2006012301c.htm

Bump, J. (1990). Radical changes in classroom discussion using network computers. *Computers and the Humanities, 24*, 49–65. doi:10.1007/BF00115028

Bushman, B. J., & Anderson, C. A. (2001). Media violence and the American public: Scientific fact versus media misinformation. *The American Psychologist, 56*, 477–489. doi:10.1037/0003-066X.56.6-7.477

Buzwell, S., & Rosenthal, D. (1996). Constructing a sexual self: Adolescents' sexual self-perceptions and sexual risk-taking. *Journal of Research on Adolescence, 6*, 489–513.

Calvert, C. (2001). Off-campus speech, on-campus punishment: Censorship of the emerging Internet underground. *Boston University Journal of Science and Technology Law, 7*, 244–245.

Calvert, S. L., & Kotler, J. A. (2003). Lessons from children's television: The impact of the Children's Television Act on children's learning. *Journal of Applied Developmental Psychology, 24*(3), 275–335. doi:10.1016/S0193-3973(03)00060-1

Calvert, S. L., Mahler, B. A., Zehnder, S. M., Jenkins, A., & Lee, M. S. (2003). Gender differences in preadolescent children's online interactions: Symbolic modes of self-presentation and self-expressions. *Applied Developmental Psychology, 24*, 627–644. doi:10.1016/j.appdev.2003.09.001

Campbell v. Acuff-Rose, 510 U.S. 569 (1994).

Campbell, M. A. (2005). Cyber bullying: An old problem in a new guise? *Australian Journal of Guidance & Counselling, 15*, 68–76. doi:10.1375/ajgc.15.1.68

Caplan, S. E. (2002). Problematic Internet use and psychosocial well-being: Development of a theory-based cognitive-behavioral measurement instrument. *Computers in Human Behavior, 18*, 553–575. doi:10.1016/S0747-5632(02)00004-3

Caplan, S. E. (2003). Preference for online social interaction: A theory of problematic Internet use and psychosocial well-being. *Communication Research, 30*, 625–648. doi:10.1177/0093650203257842

Cardwell v. Bechtol, 724 S.W. 2d 739 (Tenn. 1987).

Carey, S. (1999). The use of WebCT for a highly interactive virtual graduate seminar. *Computer Assisted Language Learning, 12*(4), 371–380. doi:10.1076/call.12.4.371.5701

Carroll, P. B. (2008, July 14). Charity cases: Social networking sites make it easy for donors to promote their favorite causes online. *Wall Street Journal*, R11.

Casey, B. J., Tottenham, N., Liston, C., & Durston, S. (2005). Imaging the developing brain: What have we learned about cognitive development? *Trends in Cognitive Sciences, 9*(3), 104–110. doi:10.1016/j.tics.2005.01.011

Cauffman, E., & Steinberg, L. (2000). (Im)maturity of judgment in adolescence: Why adolescents may be less culpable than adults. *Behavioral Sciences & the Law, 18*, 741–760. doi:10.1002/bsl.416

Ceyhan, E., & Ceyhan, A. (2007). *An investigation of problematic Internet usage behaviors on Turkish university students.* (ERIC Document Reproduction Service No. ED500186) Retrieved July 11, 2008, from ERIC database.

Chak, K., & Leung, L. (2004). Shyness and locus of control as predictors of Internet addiction and Internet use. *Cyberpsychology & Behavior, 7*(5), 559–570.

Chapell, M., Casey, D., De la Cruz, C., Ferrell, J., Forman, J., & Lipkin, R. (2004). Bullying in college by students and teachers. *Adolescence, 39*, 53–64.

Chapell, M., Hasselman, S., Kitchin, T., Lomon, S., MacIver, K., & Sarullo, P. (2006). Bullying in elementary school, high school, and college. *Adolescence (San Diego): An international quarterly devoted to the physiological, psychological, psychiatric, sociological, and educational aspects of the second decade of human life, 41,*633-648.

Chia, S. C., & Lee, W. P. (2008). Pluralistic ignorance about sex: The direct and the indirect effects of media consumption on college students misperception of sex-related peer norms. *International Journal of Public Opinion Research, 20*(1), 52–73. doi:10.1093/ijpor/edn005

Child On-Line Protection Act (COPA), 47 USC § 231 (1998).

Child Pornography Prevention Act (CPPA), 18 USC §§ 2256(8)(B) and 2256(8)(D) (1996).

Children's Internet Protection Act (CIPA), 17 USC 1701 et seq (2000).

Children's On-Line Privacy Protection Act (COPPA), 15 USC § 6501-6506 (1998).

Chilman, C. (1983). The development of adolescent sexuality. *Journal of Research and Development in Education, 16,* 16–25.

Chin-Chung, T., & Sunny, L. (2003). Internet addiction of adolescents in Taiwan: An interview study. *Cyberpsychology & Behavior, 6,* 649–652. doi:10.1089/109493103322725432

Chiou, W. B. (2008). Induced attitude change on online gaming among adolescents: An application of the less-leads-to-more effect. *Cyberpsychology & Behavior, 11*(2), 212–216. doi:10.1089/cpb.2007.0035

Chou, C. (2001). Internet heavy use and addiction among Taiwanese college students: An online interactive study. *Cyberpsychology & Behavior, 4,* 573–585. doi:10.1089/109493101753235160

Chun, D. (1994). Using computer networking to facilitate the acquisition of interactive competence. *System, 22*(1), 17–31. doi:10.1016/0346-251X(94)90037-X

Clemmitt, M. (2006). Cyber socializing. *CQ Researcher, 16*(27), 625–648.

CNN. (1999). *Parents aren't watching Internet surfing teens.* Retrieved November 28, 2008, from http://edition.cnn.com/US/9905/01/teen.poll/

Cobb, S. (1976). Social support as a moderator of life stress. *Psychosomatic Medicine, 38,* 301–314.

Coffey, S., & Stipp, H. (1997). The interactions between computer and television usage. *Journal of Advertising Research, 37*(2), 61–67.

Cohen, S., & Syme, L. (1985). *Social support and health.* Orlando, FL: Academic Press.

Cole, W. (2008, January 27). Full of passion, dressed as tomatoes. *New York Times.* Retrieved September 30, 2008 from http://essay.blogs.nytimes.com/tag/activism/?scp=2&sq=Youth%20activism&st=cse

Collins, L. H. (2007). A review of 'netaholism…' Another pseudodiagnosis. *PsycCRITIQUES, 52*(330), Article 3.

Collins, W. A., & Laursen, B. (1999). *Relationships as developmental contexts.* Mahwah, NJ: Lawrence Erlbaum Associates, Inc.

Communications Decency Act (CDA), 47 USC § 223 (1996).

Cone 2006 Millenial CAUSE Study. (2006, October 24). *Civic minded Millenials prepared to reward or punish companies based on commitment to social causes.* Retrieved September 30, 2008 from, http://www.causemarketingforum.com/page.asp?ID=473

Connolly, J., Furman, W., & Konarski, R. (2000). The role of peers in the emergence of heterosexual romantic relationships in adolescence. *Child Development, 71*(5), 1395–1408. doi:10.1111/1467-8624.00235

Cook, C. R., Williams, K. R., Guerra, N. G., & Tuthill, L. (2007). Cyberbullying. What it is and what we can do about it. [The newspaper of the National Association of School Psychologists]. *Communiqué, 36,* 4–5.

Corston, R., & Colman, A. M. (1996). Gender and social facilitation effects on computer competence and attitudes toward computers. *Journal of Educational Computing Research, 14*(2), 171–183.

Crosnoe, R. (2000). Friendships in childhood and adolescence: The life course and new directions. *Social Psychology Quarterly, 63,* 377–391. doi:10.2307/2695847

CSRIU. (2008). *Center for Safe and Responsible Internet Use.* Retrieved from http://www.csriu.org

Cuijpers, P. M. (2002). Effective ingredients of school-based drug prevention programs: A systematic review. *Addictive Behaviors, 27*(6), 1009–1023. doi:10.1016/S0306-4603(02)00295-2

Cummings, J. N., Butler, B., & Kraut, R. (2002). The quality of online social relationships. *Communications of the ACM, 45,* 103–108. doi:10.1145/514236.514242

Cummings, J. N., Sproull, L., & Kiesler, S. B. (2002). Beyond hearing, where real world and online support meets. *Group Dynamics, 5,* 78–88. doi:10.1037/1089-2699.6.1.78

Cunningham, L. (2006). A question of capacity: Towards a comprehensive and consistent vision of children and their status under law. *University of California at Davis Journal of Juvenile Law and Policy, 10,* 277.

D'Amico, M., Baron, L. J., & Sissons, M. E. (1995). Gender differences in attibutions about microcomputer learning in elementary school. *Sex Roles, 33*(5-6), 353–385. doi:10.1007/BF01954574

Dann, S., & Forrest, E. J. (1997, Dec). Webnography: Developing unobtrusive online research. In *Proceedings of the Australia New Zealand Marketing Educators' Conference,* Melbourne, Australia (Vol. II, pp. 783-784). Retrieved February 9, 2009, from http://www.cbpp.uaa.alaska.edu/afef/webnography.htm

Davis, R. (2001). A cognitive-behavioral model of pathological Internet use. *Computers in Human Behavior, 17,* 187–195. doi:10.1016/S0747-5632(00)00041-8

DeBell, M., & Chapman, C. (2006). *Computer and Internet use by students in 2003* (NCES 2006-065). U. S. Department of Education. Washington, DC: National Center for Educational Statistics.

Deci, E. L., & Ryan, R. M. (2000). The "what" and "why" of goal pursuits: Human needs and the self-determination of behavior. *Psychological Inquiry, 11,* 227–268. doi:10.1207/S15327965PLI1104_01

DeLamater, J. D., & Hyde, J. S. (1998). Essentialism vs. social constructionism in the study of human sexuality. *Journal of Sex Research, 35,* 10–18.

DeLamater, J., & Friedrich, W. N. (2002). Human sexual development. *Journal of Sex Research, 39,* 10–14.

Dempsey, J. X. (2007, November/December). The Internet at risk. *EDUCAUSE Review,* 72–82.

Diamanduros, T., Downs, E., & Jenkins, S. J. (2008). The role of school psychologists in the assessment, prevention and intervention of cyberbullying. *Psychology in the Schools, 45*(8), 693–704. doi:10.1002/pits.20335

Dietz-Uhler, B., & Bishop-Clark, C. (2005). Formation of and adherence to a self-disclosure norm in an online chat. *Cyberpsychology & Behavior, 8*(2), 114–120. doi:10.1089/cpb.2005.8.114

Donald, C. A., & Ware, J. E. (1984). The measurement of social support. In R. Greenley (Ed.), *Research in community and mental health* (Vol. 4, pp. 325-370). Greenwich, CT: JAI Press.

Donohew, L., Finn, S., & Christ, W. G. (1988). The nature of news' revisited: The roles of affect, schemas, and cognition. In L. Donohew, H. E. Sypher, & E. T. Higgins (Eds.), *Communication, social cognition, and affect* (pp. 195-218). Hillsdale, NJ: Lawrence Erlbaum.

Dorman, S. M. (1997). Video and computer games: Effect on children and implications for health education. *The Journal of School Health, 67*(4), 133–138. doi:10.1111/j.1746-1561.1997.tb03432.x

Durston, S., Thomas, K. M., Yang, Y. H., Ulug, A. M., Zimmerman, R. D., & Casey, B. J. (2002). A neural basis for the development of inhibitory control. *Developmental Science, 5*(4), F9–F16. doi:10.1111/1467-7687.00235

Dziabenko, O., Pivec, M., Bouras, C., Igglesis, V., Kapoulas, V., & Misedakis, I. (2003). A Web-based game for supporting game-based learning. In *Proceedings of the 4th Annual European GAME-ON Conference (GAME-ON 2003),* London (pp. 111-118).

Eastin, M. S. (2005). Teen Internet use: Relating social perceptions and cognitive models to behavior. *Cyberpsychology & Behavior, 8*(1), 62–75. doi:10.1089/cpb.2005.8.62

Eastin, M. S., Greenberg, B. S., & Hofschire, L. (2006). Parenting the Internet. *The Journal of Communication, 56*(3), 486–504. doi:10.1111/j.1460-2466.2006.00297.x

Egan, K. (2001).*The cognitive tools of children's imagination.* Paper presented at EECREA. Retrieved March 3, 2009, from http://www.educ.sfu.ca/kegan/Cognitive_tools_and_imagin.html

Egan, K. (n.d.). *Fantasy and reality in children's stories.* Retrieved March 3, 2009, from http://www.educ.sfu.ca/kegan/FantasyReality.html

Egan, K., & Gajdamaschko, N. (n.d.). *Some cognitive tools of literacy.* Retrieved March 3, 2009, from http://www.educ.sfu.ca/kegan/Vygotskycogandlit.pdf

Egbert, J. (2005).*CALL essentials: Principles and practice in CALL classrooms.* Alexandra, VA: TESOL.

Ekman, P., Friesen, W. V., & Tomkins, S. S. (1971). Facial affect scoring technique: A first validity study. *Semiotica, 3,* 37–58.

Elkind, D. (1967). Egocentrism in adolescence. *Child Development, 38,* 1025–1034. doi:10.2307/1127100

Elkind, D. (1984). *All grown up & no place to go: Teenagers in crisis.* Reading, MA: Addison-Wesley.

Elkind, D., & Bowen, R. (1979). Imaginary audience behavior in children and adolescents. *Developmental Psychology, 15,* 38–44. doi:10.1037/0012-1649.15.1.38

Ellis, H. C., & Moore, B. A. (1999). Mood and memory. In T. Dalgleish & M. J. Power (Eds.), *Handbook of cognition and emotion* (pp. 193-210). Chichester, UK: Wiley.

Ellis, R., Tanaka, Y., & Yamazaki, A. (1994). Classroom interaction, comprehension, and the acquisition of L2 word meanings. *Language Learning, 44,* 449–491. doi:10.1111/j.1467-1770.1994.tb01114.x

Ellison, N. B., Steinfield, C., & Lampe, C. (2007). The benefits of Facebook "friends": Social capital and college students' use of online social network sites. *Journal of Computer-Mediated Communication, 12*(4), article 1. Retrieved from http://jcmc.indiana.edu/vol12/issue4/ellison.html

Emmett v. Kent School District No. 415, 92 F.Supp 2d 1088 (W.D. Wash 2000).

Engel, Y., & Kasser, T. (2005). Why do adolescent girls idolize male celebrities? *Journal of Adolescent Research, 20,* 263–283. doi:10.1177/0743558404273117

Erhard, R. (1999). Peer-led and adult-led programs – student perceptions. *Journal of Drug Education, 29*(4), 295–308. doi:10.2190/DK18-4305-W7AB-PLPE

Erikson, E. (1950/1993). *Childhood and society.* New York: W. W. Norton.

Erikson, E. (1968). *Identity: Youth and crisis.* New York: Norton.

Escobar-Chaves, S. L., Tortolero, S. R., Markham, C. M., Low, B. J., Eitel, P., & Thickstun, P. (2005). Impact of the media on adolescent sexual attitudes and behaviors. *Pediatrics, 116,* 303–326. doi:10.1542/peds.2004-2541

Eslea, M., Menesini, E., Morita, Y., O'Moore, M., Mora-Merchán, J., & Pereira, B. (2004). Friendship and loneliness among bullies and victims: Data from seven countries. *Aggressive Behavior, 30,* 71–83. doi:10.1002/ab.20006

European Commision. (2006). *The appropriation of New Media.* Brussels, Belgium: Mediappro.

Eysenck, H. Y., & Eysenck, S. B. G. (1964). *Manual of the Eysenck personality inventory.* San Diego, CA: Educational and Industrial Testing Service.

Farrar, K. M. (2006). Sexual intercourse on television: Do safe sex messages matter? m*Journal of Broadcasting & Electronic Media, 50*(4), 635–650. doi:10.1207/s15506878jobem5004_4

Farrell, E. F. (2006, Oct 27). More college students are volunteering. *The Chronicle of Higher Education, 53*(10), A40.

Featherstone, L. (1999). Hot wiring schools - Student activists across the country experiment with organizing by Internet. *Nation (New York, N.Y.), 268*(23), 15.

Federal Bureau of Investigation. (n.d.). *A parent's guide to Internet safety.* U. S. Department of Justice, FBI, Cyber Division. Retrieved January 4, 2008, from http://www.fbi.gov/publications/pguide/pguidee.htm

Feinberg, T. (2003). *Bullying prevention and intervention.* Retrieved from http://www.nasponline.org/resources/principals/nassp bullying.aspx

Feld, S. (1981). The focused organization of social ties. *American Journal of Sociology, 86,* 1015–1035. doi:10.1086/227352

Fergusson, D. M., Boden, J. M., & Horwood, J. L. (2008). Exposure to childhood sexual and physical abuse and adjustment in early adulthood. *Child Abuse & Neglect, 32*(6), 607–619. doi:10.1016/j.chiabu.2006.12.018

Fine, G. A. (1988). Friends, impression management, and preadolescent behavior. In G. Handel (Ed.), *Childhood socialization.* New York: Aldine de Gruyter.

Finkelhor, D., & Dziuba-Leatherman, J. (1994). Children as victims of violence: A national survey. *Pediatrics, 94*(4), 413–420.

Finkelhor, D., Mitchell, K. J., & Wolak, J. (2000). *Online victimization: A report on the nation's youth.* Arlington, VA: National Center for Missing & Exploited Children.

Finkelhor, D., Omrod, R. K., & Turner, H. A. (2007). Re-victimization patterns in a national longitudinal sample of children and youth. *Child Abuse & Neglect, 31,* 479–502. doi:10.1016/j.chiabu.2006.03.012

Finkelhor, D., Omrod, R. K., Turner, H. A., & Hamby, S. L. (2005). The victimization of children and youth: A comprehensive, national survey. *Child Maltreatment, 10,* 5–25. doi:. doi:10.1177/1077559504271287

Finn, J. (2004). A survey of online harassment at a university campus. *Journal of Interpersonal Violence, 19,* 468–483. doi:10.1177/0886260503262083

Finn, J., & Kerman, B. (2004). Internet risks for foster families online. *Journal of Technology in Human Services, 22*(4), 21–38. doi:10.1300/J017v22n04_02

Flanagin, A. (2006). IM online: Instant messaging use among college students. *Communication Research Reports, 22*(3), 175–187. doi:10.1080/00036810500206966

Fleming, M. J., Greentree, S., Cocotti-Muller, D., Elias, K. A., & Morrison, S. (2006). Safety in cyberspace: Adolescents' safety and exposure online. *Youth & Society, 38*(2), 135–154. doi:10.1177/0044118X06287858

Flood, M. (2007). Exposure to pornography among youth in Australia. *Journal of Sociology (Melbourne, Vic.), 43*(1), 45–60. doi:10.1177/1440783307073934

Forgas, J. P., & Bower, G. H. (1987). Mood effects on person-perception judgments. *Journal of Personality and Social Psychology, 53,* 53–60. doi:10.1037/0022-3514.53.1.53

Francis, D. (2004). Learning from participants in field based research. *Cambridge Journal of Education, 34*(3), 265–277. doi:10.1080/0305764042000289910

Freeman, M. (1997). Electronic media and how kids (don't) think. *Education Digest, 63*(3), 22–27.

Friedman, T. (2007, October 10). Generation Q. *New York Times.* Retrieved September 30, 2008 from http://www.nytimes.com/2007/10/10/opinion/10friedman.html?_r=4&oref=slogin&ref=opinion&pagewanted=print

Funk, J. B., & Buchman, D. D. (1996). Playing violent video and computer games and adolescent self-concept. *The Journal of Communication, 46*(2), 19–32. doi:10.1111/j.1460-2466.1996.tb01472.x

Furedi, F. (2006). *Culture of fear revisited: Risk-taking and the morality of low expectation.* New York: Continuum.

Furger, R. (1998). *Does Jane compute?: Preserving our daughters' place in the cyber revolution.* New York: Warner Books.

GA: Longstreet.

Gagnon, J. H., & Simon, W. (1973). *Sexual conduct: The social sources of human sexuality.* Chicago: Aldine.

Gagnon, J. H., & Simon, W. (1987). Sexual scripts: Permanence and change. *Archives of Sexual Behavior, 15,* 97–120.

Galanaki, E. (2004). Are children able to distinguish among the concepts of aloneness, loneliness, and solitude? *International Journal of Behavioral Development, 28*(5), 435–443. doi:10.1080/01650250444000153

Galanaki, E. (2005). solitude in the school: a neglected facet of children's development and education. *Childhood Education, 81*(3), 128–133.

Gallienne, R. L., Moore, S. M., & Brennan, P. F. (1993). Alzheimer's caregivers: Psychosocial support via computer networks. *Journal of Gerontological Nursing, 19,* 15–22.

Gamedesigncampus. (2008). Retrieved February 29, 2008, from http://gamedesigncampus.com/index.html

Garris, R., Ahlers, R., & Driskell, J. E. (2002). Games, motivation, and learning: A research and practice model. *Simulation & Gaming, 33*(4), 441–467. doi:10.1177/1046878102238607

Garstka, T. A., Branscombe, N. R., & Hummert, M. L. (1997). *Age group identification across the life span* (unpublished manuscript).

Gee, J. (2003). *What video games have to teach us about learning and literacy.* New York: PalGrave-McMillan.

Gee, J. P. (2007). Learning by design. In P. Messaris & L. Humphreys (Eds.), *Digital media: Transformation in human communication* (pp. 173-186). New York: Peter Lang.

Gergen, K. J., Gergen, M. M., & Barton, W. H. (1973). Deviance in the dark. *Psychology Today, 7,* 129–130.

Giedd, J. N., Castellanos, F. X., Rajapakse, J. C., Vaituzis, A. C., & Rapoport, J. L. (1997). Sexual dimorphism of the developing human brain. *Progress in Neuro-Psychopharmacology & Biological Psychiatry, 21*(8), 1185–1201. doi:10.1016/S0278-5846(97)00158-9

Giordano, P. C. (2003). Relationships in adolescence. *Annual Review of Sociology, 29,* 257–281. doi:10.1146/annurev.soc.29.010202.100047

Glass, R., & Spiegelman, M. (2007-2008). Incorporating blogs into the syllabus: Making their space a learning space. *Journal of Educational Technology Systems, 36*(2), 145–155. doi:10.2190/ET.36.2.c

Glassner, B. (2000). *The culture of fear: Why Americans are afraid of the wrong things.* New York: Basic Books.

Gloonnegger, E. (1999). *Das spiele-buch. Brett-und legespielel aus aller welt.* Germany: Drei Magier Verlag.

Gogtay, N., Giedd, J. N., Lusk, L., Hayashi, K. M., Greenstein, D., & Vaituzis, A. C. (2004). Dynamic mapping of human cortical development during childhood through early adulthood. *Proceedings of the National Academy of Sciences of the United States of America, 101*(21), 8174–8179. doi:10.1073/pnas.0402680101

Gold, S. (1993). *Court acquits teenage hacker.* Retrieved March 27, 2002, from http://www.eff.org/pub/Net_culture/Hackers/uk_court_acquits_teenage_hacker.article

Gordon, C., Juang, L., & Syed, M. (2007). Internet use and well-being among college students: Beyond frequency of use. *Journal of College Student Development, 48,* 674–688. doi:10.1353/csd.2007.0065

Granovetter, M. (1973). The strength of weak ties. *American Journal of Sociology, 73,* 1361–1380.

Green, B., Reid, J. A., & Bigum, C. (1998). Teaching the Nintendo generation? Children, computer culture and popular technologies. In S. Howard (Ed.), *Wired up: Young people and the electronic media* (pp. 19-41). London: Taylor and Francis.

Green, K. C. (1996). The coming ubiquity of information technology. *Change, 28*(2), 24–28.

Greenberg, K. R. (2003). *Group counseling in k-12 schools: A handbook for school counselors*. Boston: Allyn & Bacon.

Greenfield, P. (2004). Developmental considerations for determining appropriate Internet use guidelines for children and adolescents. *Applied Developmental Psychology, 25*, 751–762. doi:10.1016/j.appdev.2004.09.008

Greenfield, P. M. (2004). Inadvertent exposure to pornography on the Internet: Implications of peer-to-peer file-sharing networks for child development and families. *Journal of Applied Developmental Psychology, 25*, 741–750. doi:10.1016/j.appdev.2004.09.009

Greenfield, P. M., & Yan, Z. (2006). Children, adolescents, and the Internet: A new field of inquiry in developmental psychology. *Developmental Psychology, 42*, 391–394. doi:10.1037/0012-1649.42.3.391

Greenfield, P., Pickwood, P., & Tran, H. H. (2001). *Effectiveness of Internet filtering software products*. Retrieved October 26, 2004, from http://www.aba.gov.au/internet/research/filtering/filtereffectiveness.pdf

Griffin, M. (2001). The phenomenology of the alone condition: More evidence for the role of aloneness in social facilitation. *The Journal of Psychology, 135*(1), 125–128.

Griffin, M., & Kent, M. V. (1998). The role of aloneness in social facilitation. *The Journal of Social Psychology, 138*(5), 667–669.

Griffiths, M. (1998). Internet addiction: Does it really exist? In J. Gackenbach (Ed.), *Psychology and the Internet: Intrapersonal, interpersonal and transpersonal applications* (pp. 61-75). New York: Academic Press.

Griffiths, M. D. (1995). Technological addictions. *Clinical Psychology Forum, 76*, 14–19.

Griffiths, M. D. (1996a). Internet addiction: An issue for clinical psychology? *Clinical Psychology Forum, 97*, 32–36.

Griffiths, M. D. (2000a). Internet addiction – time to be taken seriously? *Addiction Research, 8*(5), 413–418. doi:10.3109/16066350009005587

Griffiths, M. D. (2000b). Does Internet and computer "addiction" exist? Some case study evidence. *Cyberpsychology & Behavior, 3*, 211–218. doi:10.1089/109493100316067

Griffiths, M. D. (2001). Sex on the Internet: Observations and implications for sex addiction. *Journal of Sex Research, 38*, 333–342.

Griffiths, M. D. (2005). A "components" model of addiction within a biopsychosocial framework. *Journal of Substance Use, 10*, 191–197. doi:10.1080/14659890500114359

Griffiths, M. D. (2008). Internet and video-game addiction. In C. Essau (Ed.), *Adolescent addiction: Epidemiology, assessment and treatment* (pp. 231-267). San Diego, CA: Elselvier.

Grinter, R. E., & Palen, L. (2002). *Instant messaging in teen life*. Paper presented at the CSCW'02, New Orleans, Louisiana.

Grinter, R. E., Palen, L., & Eldridge, M. (2006). Chatting with teenagers: Considering the place of chat technologies in teen life. *ACM Transactions on Computer-Human Interaction, 13*(4), 423–447. doi:10.1145/1188816.1188817

Groebel, J. (2001). Media violence in cross-cultural perspective: A global study on children's media behavior and some educational implications. In D. G. Singer & J. L. Singer (Eds.), *Handbook of children and the media* (pp. 255-268). Thousand Oaks, CA: Sage.

Gross, E. F. (2004). Adolescent Internet use: What we expect, what teens report. *Journal of Applied Developmental Psychology, 25*(6), 633–649. doi:10.1016/j.appdev.2004.09.005

Gross, E. F., Juvonen, J., & Gable, S. L. (2002). Internet use and well being in adolescence. *The Journal of Social Issues, 58*, 75–90. doi:10.1111/1540-4560.00249

Hall, G. S. (1905). *Adolescence.* New York: Appleton and Co.

Hall, J. K., & Verplaetse, L. S. (2000). *Second and foreign language learning through classroom interaction.* Mahwah, NJ: Erlbaum.

Hallman, J. (2008). *Adolescent update: Keeping adolescents safe online.* St. Louis Children's Hospital. Retrieved December 30, 2008, from http://www.stlouischildrens.org/content/AdolescentUpdateKeepingAdolescentsSafeOnline.htm.

Hamatr, A. (2008). Web technologies for language learning and implications for the design of CMS for language instruction. *International Journal of social Sciences, 3*(1), 61-65. Retrieved September 18, 2008, from http://www.waset.org/ijss/v3/v3-1-9.pdf

Hamilton, C., & Flanagan, C. (2007). Reforming social responsibility within a technology-based youth activist program. *The American Behavioral Scientist, 51*(444).

Hamilton, K., & Kalb, C. (1995, December 18). They log on, but they can't log off. *Newsweek.*

Hampel, R., & Hauck, M. (2004). Towards an effective use of audio conferencing in distance language courses. *Language Learning & Technology, 8*(1), 66–82.

Harter, S. (1993). Causes and consequences of low self-esteem in children and adolescents. In R. Baumeister (Ed.), *Self-esteem: The puzzle of low self-regard* (pp. 87-116). New York: Plenum.

Hartup, W. W. (1997). The company they keep: Friendships and their developmental significance. *Annual Progress in Child Psychiatry and Child Development*, 63-78.

Harwood, J. (1999). Age identification, social identity gratifications, and television viewing. *Journal of Broadcasting & Electronic Media, 43*, 123–136.

Harwood, J. (1999). Age identity and television viewing preferences. *Communication Reports, 12*(2), 85.

Hawkins, J. D., Catalano, R. F., & Miller, J. Y. (1992). Risk and protective factors for alcohol and other drug problems in adolescence and early adulthood: Implications for substance abuse prevention. *Psychological Bulletin, 112*(1), 64–105. doi:10.1037/0033-2909.112.1.64

Haythornthwaite, C. (2002). Strong, weak, and latent ties and the impact of new media. *The Information Society, 18*, 385–402. doi:10.1080/01972240290108195

Hazelwood School District v. Kuhlmeier, 484 U.S. 260 (1988).

Hinduja, S., & Patchin, J. W. (2005). *Research summary: Cyberbullying victimization.* Retrieved October 5, 2007, from http://www.cyberbullying.us/research.php Hinduja, S., & Patchin, J. W. (2009). *Bullying beyond the schoolyard: Preventing and responding to cyberbullying.* Thousand Oaks, CA

Hinduja, S., & Patchin, J. W. (2008). Personal information of adolescents on the Internet: A quantitative content analysis of MySpace. *Journal of Adolescence, 31*, 125–146. doi:10.1016/j.adolescence.2007.05.004

Hinduja, S., & Patchin, J. W. (2008). Social networking and identity construction: Personal information of adolescents on the Internet: A quantitative content analysis of MySpace. *Journal of Adolescence, 31*(1), 125–146. doi:10.1016/j.adolescence.2007.05.004

Hinduja, S., Patchin, J., & Burgess-Proctor, A. (2006). *Cyberbullying: Parent/teenager scripts to promote dialogue and discussion.* Retrieved from http://www.cyberbullying.us/cyberbullying scripts.pdf

Hirschorn, M. (2007, April). The Web 2.0 bubble: Why the social-media revolution will go out with a whimper. *Atlantic Monthly, 299*(3), 134.

Hlebec, V., Manfreda, K. L., & Vehovar, V. (2006). The social support networks of Internet users. *New Media & Society, 8*(1), 9–32. doi:10.1177/1461444806058166

Hofer, B. K., & Pintrich, P. R. (1997). The development of epistemological theories: Beliefs about knowledge and knowing and their relation to learning. *Review of Educational Research, 67*, 88–140.

Hofer, B. K., & Pintrich, P. R. (2002). *Personal epistemology: The psychology of beliefs about knowledge and knowing*. Mahwah, NJ: Erlbaum.

Hoffer, C., & Cantor, J. (1991). Perceiving and responding to mass media characters. In J. Bryant & D. Zillmann (Eds.), *Responding to the screen: Reception and reaction processes* (pp. 63-102). Hillsdale, NJ: Erlbaum Associates.

Holt, M. K., & Keyes, A. M. (2004). Teachers' attitude toward bullying. In D. L. Esspelage & S. M. Swearer (Eds.), *Bullying in American schools.* (pp. 121-139). London: Lawrence Erlbaum Associates, Publishers.

Holt, M., Finkelhor, D., & Kantor, G. (2007). Hidden forms of victimization in elementary students involved in bullying. *School Psychology Review, 36,* 345–360.

Holz, J. (1998). *Measuring the child audience: Issues and implications for educational programming* (No. 3). Philadelphia, PA: The Annenberg Public Policy Center of the University of Pennsylvania. Jordan, A. B. (2002). A family systems approach to examining the role of the Internet in the home. In S. L. Calvert, A. B. Jordan, & R. R. Cocking (Eds.), *Children in the digital age* (pp. 231-248). Westport, CT: Praeger Publishers.

Hostin, S. (2008, April 11). Online campus gossips won't show their faces. *CNN.com.*

House, J. S. (1986). Social support and the quality and quantity of life. In F. M. Andrew (Ed.), *Research on the quality of life*. Ann Arbor, MI: Survey Research Center, Institute for Social Research, University of Michigan.

Houston, T. K., Cooper, S., & Ford, D. E. (2002). Internet support groups for depression: A 1-year prospective cohort study. *The American Journal of Psychiatry, 159*(12), 2062–2068. doi:10.1176/appi.ajp.159.12.2062

Hrastinski, S., & Keller, C. (2007). Computer-mediated communication in education: A review of recent research. *Educational Media International, 44,* 61–77. doi:10.1080/09523980600922746

Hu, Y., Wood, J. F., Smith, V., & Westbrook, N. (2004). Friendship through IM: Examining the relationship between instant messaging and intimacy. *Journal of Computer Mediated Communication, 10*(6). Retrieved from http://jcmc.indiana.edu/vol10/hu.html

Huffaker, D. A., & Calvert, S. L. (2005). Gender, identity, and language use in teenage blogs. *Journal of Computer-Mediated Communication, 10*(2), 26.

Hussain, Z., & Griffiths, M. D. (2008). Gender swapping and socialising in cyberspace: An exploratory study. *Cyberpsychology & Behavior, 11,* 47–53. doi:10.1089/cpb.2007.0020

Hustinx, L., & Lammertyn, F. (2003). Collective and reflexive styles of volunteering: A sociological modernization perspective. *Voluntas: International Journal of Voluntary and Nonprofit Organizations, 14*(2), 167–187. doi:10.1023/A:1023948027200

Hustler Magazine v. Falwell, 485 U.S. 46 (1988).

Huston, A. C., Wartella, E., Donnerstein, E., Scantlin, R., & Kotler, J. (1998). *Measuring the effects of sexual content in the media: A report to the Kaiser Family Foundation*. Oakland, CA: The Kaiser Family Foundation.

i-SAFE America Inc. (2007). *National i-SAFE survey finds over half of students are being harassed online*. Retrieved October 5, 2007, from http://www.dbprescott.com/internetbullying6.04.pdf

J.S. v. Bethlehem School District, 807 A.2d 847 (Pa. 2002).

Jackson, L. A. (2008). Adolescents and the Internet. In P. E. Jamieson & D. Romer (Eds.), *The changing portrayal of adolescents in the media since 1950* (pp. 377-411). New York: Oxford University Press.

Jenkins, H. (2007). Keynote at game in action conference, Gothenburg, Sweden.

Jepson, K. (2005). Conversations and negotiated interaction in text and voice chat rooms. *Language Learning & Technology, 9*(3), 79–98.

Joinson, A. (2004). Self-esteem, interpersonal risk, and preference for e-mail to face-to-face communication. *Cyberpsychology & Behavior*, *7*(4), 472–478. doi:10.1089/cpb.2004.7.472

Jordan, A. B. (2008). Childrens media policy. *The Future of Children*, *18*(1), 235–253. doi:10.1353/foc.0.0003

Jordan, A., Schmitt, K., & Woodard, E. (2001). The developmental implications of commercial broadcasters' educational offerings. *Journal of Applied Developmental Psychology*, *22*(1), 87–102. doi:10.1016/S0193-3973(00)00068-X

Juneau School District. (1985, January 8). *Policy manual: Policy 5850, social events and class trips.*

Juneau School District. (1998, February 17). *Policy manual: Policy 5520, disruption and demonstration.*

Kahn, R. L., & Antonucci, T. C. (1980). Convoys over the life course: Attachment, roles and social support. In P. B. Baltes & O. Brim (Eds.), *Life-span development and behavior* (Vol. 3). Boston: Lexington Press.

Kallen, D. J., Stephenson, J. J., & Doughty, A. (1983). The need to know – recalled adolescent sources of sexual and contraceptive information and sexual behavior. *Journal of Sex Research*, *19*, 137–159.

Kaltiala-Heino, R., Lintonen, T., & Rimpela, A. (2004). Internet addiction? Potentially problematic use of the Internet in a population of 12-18 year-old adolescents. *Addiction Research and Theory*, *12*, 89–96. doi:10.1080/1606635031000098796

Kanetsuna, T., Smith, P., & Morita, Y. (2006). Coping with bullying at school: Children's recommended strategies and attitudes to school-based interventions in England and Japan. *Aggressive Behavior*, *32*, 570–580. doi:10.1002/ab.20156

Kasvi, J. (2000). Not just fun and games - Internet games as a training medium. In *Cosiga - learning with computerised simulation games* (pp. 23-34). Retrieved June 27, 2003, from http://www.knowledge.hut.fi/people/jkasvi/NJFAG.PDF

Kavanagh, A. L., & Patterson, S. J. (2001). The impact of community computer networks on social capital and community involvement. *The American Behavioral Scientist*, *45*(3), 496–510. doi:10.1177/00027640121957312

Kearney, P., & Pivec, M. (2007a). *Informal discussion forums: Can we harness the same passion in class?* Paper presented at the AACE World Conference on Educational Multimedia, Hypermedia and Telecommunications (ED-MEDIA 2007), Vancouver, Canada.

Kearney, P., & Pivec, M. (2007b). Recursive loops of game-based learning. In C. Montgomerie & J. Seale (Eds.), *Proceedings of the ED-MEDIA'07*, Vancouver BC, Canada (pp. 2546-2553).

Kearney, P., & Pivec, M. (2007c). Sex, lies and videogames. *British Journal of Educational Technology*, *38*(3).

Kennedy, A. (2005). Students fall victim to high-tech harassment. *Counseling Today*, 10-11.

Kennedy-Souza, B. (1998). Internet addiction disorder. *Interpersonal Computing and Technology: An Electronic Journal for the 21st Century*, *6*(1-2). Retrieved December 10, 2003, from http://www.emoderators.com/ipct-j/1998/n1-2/kennedy-souza.html

Kiesler, S., Siegal, J., & McGuire, T. (1984). Social psychological aspects of computer-mediated communication. *The American Psychologist*, *39*(10), 1123–1134. doi:10.1037/0003-066X.39.10.1123

Kiesler, S., Zubrow, D., Moses, A., & Geller, V. (1985). Affect in computer-mediated communication: An experiment in synchronous terminal-to-terminal discussion. *Human-Computer Interaction*, *1*, 77–104. doi:10.1207/s15327051hci0101_3

Killion v. Franklin Regional School District, 136 F. Supp. 2d 446 (W.D. Pa. 2001).

Kinnear, A. (1995). Introduction of micocomputers: A case study of patterns of use and children's perceptions. *Journal of Educational Computing Research*, *13*(1), 27–40. doi:10.2190/NA0H-1RV6-LFLU-23H0

Knobloch, S. (2003). Mood adjustment via mass communication. *The Journal of Communication, 53*(2), 233–150. doi:10.1111/j.1460-2466.2003.tb02588.x

Knobloch, S., & Zillmann, D. (2002). Mood management via the digital jukebox. *The Journal of Communication, 52*, 351–366. doi:10.1111/j.1460-2466.2002.tb02549.x

Korman, R. (2008, November 26). The verdict: Lori Drews is guilty. *ZDNet Government.* Retrieved March 2, 2009, from http://government.zdnet.com/?p=4207

Kowalski, R., Limber, S., & Agaston, P. (2008). *Cyberbullying: Bullying in the digital age.*

Krashen, S. (1985). *The input hypothesis: Issues and implications.* London: Longman.

Kraus, S. W., & Russell, B. (2008). Early sexual experiences: The role of Internet access and sexually explicit material. *Cyberpsychology & Behavior, 11*(2), 162–168. doi:10.1089/cpb.2007.0054

Kraut, R., Kiesler, S., Boneva, B., Cummings, J., Helgeson, V., & Crawford, A. M. (2002). Internet paradox revisited. *The Journal of Social Issues, 58*(1), 49–74. doi:10.1111/1540-4560.00248

Kraut, R., Kiesler, S., Boneva, B., Cummings, J., Helgeson, V., & Crawford, A. (2002). Internet paradox revisited. *The Journal of Social Issues, 58*, 49–74. doi:10.1111/1540-4560.00248

Kraut, R., Patterson, M., Lundmark, V., Kiesler, S., Mukopadhyay, T., & Scherlis, W. (1998). Internet paradox: A social technology that reduces social involvement and psychological well-being? *The American Psychologist, 53*, 1017–1031. doi:10.1037/0003-066X.53.9.1017

Kraut, R., Patterson, M., Lundmark, V., Kiesler, S., Mukopadhyay, T., & Scherlis, W. (1998). Internet paradox: A social technology that reduces social involvement and psychological well-being? *The American Psychologist, 53*, 1017–1031. doi:10.1037/0003-066X.53.9.1017

Kraut, R., Patterson, M., Lundmark, V., Kiesler, S., Mukophadhyay, T., & Scherlis, W. (1998). Internet paradox: A social technology that reduces social involvement and psychological well being? *The American Psychologist, 53*, 1017–1031. doi:10.1037/0003-066X.53.9.1017

Kraut, R., Patterson, M., Lunmark, V., Kiesler, S., Mukopadyay, T., & Scherlis, W. (1998). A social technology that reduces social involvement and psychological well-being. *The American Psychologist, 53*, 1017–1031. doi:10.1037/0003-066X.53.9.1017

Kraut, R., Sherlis, W., Mukhopadhayay, T., Manning, J., & Kiesler, S. (1996). The HomeNet field trials of residential Internet services. *Communications of the Association for Computing Machinery . Inc., 39*(12), 55.

Kristof, N. (2008, January 27). The age of ambition. *New York Times.* Retrieved September 30, 2008, from http://www.nytimes.com/2008/01/27/opinion/27kristof.html?_r=1&oref=slogin

Kubey, R. W., Lavin, M. J., & Barrows, J. R. (2001). Internet use and collegiate academic performance decrements: Early findings. *The Journal of Communication, 51*, 366–382. doi:10.1111/j.1460-2466.2001.tb02885.x

Kuhlmeier v. Hazelwood School District, 795 F.2d 1368, 1372 (8th Cir. 1986), *rev'd*, 484 U.S. 260 (1988).

Kunkel, D., & Goette, U. (1997). Broadcasters' response to the Children's Television Act. *Communication Law and Policy, 2*, 289–308.

Kunkel, D., & Wilcox, B. L. (2001). Children and media policy. In D. G. Singer & J. L. Singer (Eds.), *Handbook of children and the media* (pp. 589-604). Thousand Oaks, CA: Sage.

Kupfer, A. (1995). Alone together: Will being wired set us free?. *Fortune, 131*(Mar. 20), 94-96.

Kutner, L. A., Olson, C. K., Warner, D. E., & Hertzog, S. M. (2008). Parents' and sons' perspectives on video game play: A qualitative study. *Journal of Adolescent Research, 23*, 76–96. doi:10.1177/0743558407310721

Kvale, S. (1996). *InterViews: An introduction to qualitative research interviewing.* Thousand Oaks, CA: Sage Publications.

L'Engle, K. L., Brown, J. D., & Kenneavy, K. (2006). The mass media are an important context for adolescents' sexual behavior. *The Journal of Adolescent Health, 38*(3), 186–192. doi:10.1016/j.jadohealth.2005.03.020

Lambie, G. W., & Rokutani, L. J. (2002). A systems approach to substance abuse identification and intervention for school counselors. *Professional School Counseling, 5*(5), 353–360.

LaRose, R., Mastro, D., & Eastin, M. S. (2001). Understanding Internet usage: A social-cognitive approach to uses and gratifications. *Social Science Computer Review, 19*(4), 395–414. doi:10.1177/089443930101900401

Larson, R. W. (1990). The solitary side of life: An examination of the time people spend alone from childhood to old age. *Developmental Review, 10*, 155–183. doi:10.1016/0273-2297(90)90008-R

Larson, R. W. (1997). The mergence of solitude as a constructive domain of experience in early adolescence. *Child Development, 68*, 80–93. doi:10.2307/1131927

Layshock v. Hermitage School District, 496 F.Supp.2d 587 (W.D. Pa. 2007).

Lee, S. J., & Chae, Y. G. (2007). Children's Internet use in a family context: Influence on family relationships and parental mediation. *Cyberpsychology & Behavior, 10*(5), 640–644. doi:10.1089/cpb.2007.9975

Leeds-Hurwitz, W. (1995). Introducing social approaches. In W. Leeds-Hurwitz (Ed.), *Social approaches to communication.* New York: The Guilford Press.

Lefkowitz, E. S., Boone, T. L., & Shearer, C. L. (2004). Communication with best friends about sex-related topics during emerging adulthood. *Journal of Youth and Adolescence, 33*, 339–351. doi:10.1023/B:JOYO.0000032642.27242.c1

Leitenberg, H., & Saltzman, H. (2000). A statewide survey of age at first intercourse for adolescent females and age of their male partner: Relation to other risk behaviors and statutory rape implications. *Archives of Sexual Behavior, 29*, 203–215. doi:10.1023/A:1001920212732

Leitenberg, H., & Saltzman, H. (2003). College women who had sexual intercourse when they were underage minors (13-15): Age of their male partners, relation to current adjustment, and statutory rape implications. *Sexual Abuse, 15*, 135–147. doi:10.1177/107906320301500204

Lenhart, A. (2007, January 3). Social networking websites and teens: An overview. *Pew Report on Family, Friends and Community.* Retrieved February 11, 2009, from http://www.pewinternet.org/pdfs/PIP_SNS_Data_Memo_Jan_2007.pdf

Lenhart, A. (2007, June 27). Cyberbullying and online teens. *Pew Internet and American Life Project.* Retrieved October 5, 2007, from http://www.pewInternet.org/pdfs/PIP%20Cyberbullying%20Memo.pdf

Lenhart, A. (2009, Jan 14). Adults and social network websites 1/14/2009. *Pew Report on Online Activities and Pursuits.* Retrieved February 11, 2009, from http://www.pewinternet.org/PPF/r/272/report_display.asp

Lenhart, A., & Madden, M. (2007). *Social networking sites and teens: An overview.* Washington, DC: Pew Internet and American Life Project.

Lenhart, A., & Madden, M. (2007). *Teens, privacy & online social networks.* Washington, DC: Pew Internet & American Life Project.

Lenhart, A., Madden, M., Rankin Macgill, A., & Smith, A. (2007, Dec 19). The use of social media gains a greater foothold in teen life as they embrace the conversational nature of interactive online media. *Pew Report.* Retrieved February 11, 2009, from http://www.pewinternet.org/pdfs/PIP_Teens_Social_Media_Final.pdf

Lenhart, A., Rainie, L., & Lewis, O. (2001). *Teenage life online. The rise of the instant-message generation and the Internet's impact on friendship and family relationships.* PEW Internet and American Life Project, Washington, DC. Retrieved September 9, 2008, from http://www.pewinternet.org/pdfs/PIP_Teens_Report.pdf

Leung, L. (2001). College student motives for chatting on "ICQ.". *New Media & Society, 3*(4), 483–500. doi:10.1177/14614440122226209

Leung, L. (2003). Impacts of Net-generation attributes, seductive properties of the Internet, and gratifications-obtained on Internet use. *Telematics and Informatics, 20*(2), 107–129. doi:10.1016/S0736-5853(02)00019-9

Leung, L., & Lee, P. S. N. (2005). Multiple determinants of life quality: The roles of Internet activities, use of new media, social support, and leisure activities. *Telematics and Informatics, 22*(3), 161–180. doi:10.1016/j. tele.2004.04.003

Lever, J. (1988). Sex differences in the complexity of children's play and games. In G. Handel (Ed.), *Childhood socialization*. New York: Aldine de Gruyter.

Lewis, M. (1997). *Implementing the lexical approach: Putting theory into practice*. Hove, UK: Language Teaching Publications.

Li, Q. (2004). *Cyber-bullying in schools: Nature and extent of adolescents' experiences*. Paper presented at Annual American Educational Research Association Conference. Retrieved October 5, 2007, from http://www.ucalgary.ca/~qinli/publication/cyberbully_aera05%20.html

Li, Q. (2005). *Cyber-bullying in schools: A comparison of Canadian and Chinese adolescents' experience*. Paper presented at World Conference on E-Learning in Corporate, Government, Healthcare, and Higher Education (ELEARN). Retrieved August 3, 2008, from http://www.editlib.org/index.cfm?fuseaction=Reader. ViewAbstract&paper_id=21291&from=NEWDL

Li, Q. (2006). Cyberbullying in schools: A research of gender differences. *School Psychology International, 27*, 157–170. doi:10.1177/0143034306064547

Lightfoot, C. (1997). *The culture of adolescent risk-taking*. New York: Guilford Press.

Lin, H. F. (2006). Understanding behavioral intention to participate in virtual communities. *Cyberpsychology & Behavior, 9*(5), 540–547. doi:10.1089/cpb.2006.9.540

Lin, M., Hummert, M. L., & Harwood, J. (2004). Representation of age identities in on-line discourse. *Journal of Aging Studies, 18*(3), 261. doi:10.1016/j. jaging.2004.03.006

Ling, R. (2004). *The mobile connection: The cell phone's impact on society*. San Francisco: Elsevier.

Ling, R., & Ytri, B. (2002). Hyper-coordination via mobile phone in Norway. In J. E. Katz & M. Aakhus (Eds.), *Perpetual contact: Mobile communication, private talk, public performance* (pp. 139-169). Cambridge, UK: Cambridge University Press.

Livingstone, S. (2002). *Young people and new media*. Thousand Oaks, CA: Sage.

Livingstone, S. (2003). Children's use of the Internet: Reflections on the emerging research agenda. *New Media & Society, 5*(2), 147–166. doi:10.1177/1461444803005002001

Livingstone, S. (2007). Strategies of parental regulation in the media-rich home. *Computers in Human Behavior, 23*(2), 920–941. doi:10.1016/j.chb.2005.08.002

Livingstone, S. (2008). Taking risky opportunities in youthful content creation: Teenagers' use of social networking sites for intimacy, privacy and self-expression. *New Media & Society, 10*(3), 393–411. doi:10.1177/1461444808089415

Livingstone, S., & Bober, M. (2005). *UK children go online: Surveying the experiences of young people and their parents*. Retrieved from http://news.bbc.co.uk/1/shared/bsp/hi/pdfs/28_04_05_childrenonline.pdf

Livingstone, S., & Bober, M. (2006). Regulating the Internet at home: Contrasting the perspectives of children and parents. In D. Buckingham & R. Willet (Eds.), *Digital generations: Children, young people, and new media* (pp. 93-114). Mahwah, NJ: Lawrence Erlbaum Associates, Inc.

Livingstone, S., Bober, M., & Helsper, E. J. (2005). Active participation or just more information? Young people's take-up of opportunities to act and interact on the Internet. *Information Communication and Society, 8*(3), 287–314. doi:10.1080/13691180500259103

Lloyd, B. T. (2002). A conceptual framework for examining adolescent identity, media influence, and social development. *Review of General Psychology, 6*, 73–91. doi:10.1037/1089-2680.6.1.73

Lo, V. H., & Wei, R. (2005). Exposure to Internet pornography and Taiwanese adolescents' sexual attitudes and behavior. *Journal of Broadcasting & Electronic Media, 49*(2), 221–237. doi:10.1207/s15506878jobem4902_5

Loader, B. D., Muncer, S., Burrows, R., Pleace, N., & Nettleton, S. (2002). Medicine on line? Computer mediated social support and advice for people with diabetes. *International Journal of Social Welfare, 11*, 53–65. doi:10.1111/1468-2397.00196

Lombardo, C., Zakus, D., & Skinner, H. (2002). Youth social action: Building a global latticework through information and communication technologies. *Health Promotion International, 17*(4), 363–371. doi:10.1093/heapro/17.4.363

Long, M. H. (1983). Linguistic and conversational adjustments to non-native speakers. *Studies in Second Language Acquisition, 5*, 177–193. doi:10.1017/S0272263100004848

Long, M. H. (1996). The role of the linguistic environment in second language acquisition. In W. Ritchie & T. Bhatia (Eds.), *Handbook of research on second language acquisition* (pp. 413-469). New York: Academic Press.

Lopez, M. H., & Marcelo, K. B. (2006, November). *CIRCLE fact sheet: Youth demographics.* College Park, MD: The Center for Information Research on Civic Learning and Engagement.

Lu, C. H., Chiou, G. F., Day, M. Y., Ong, C. S., & Hsu, W. L. (2006). Using instant messaging to provide an intelligent learning environment. In *Conference Proceedings of Intelligent Tutoring Systems 8th International*, Jhongli, Taiwan. Retrieved July 1, 2008, from http://www.iis.sinica.edu.tw/IASL/webpdf/paper-2006-Using_Instant_Messaging_to_Provide_an_Intelligent_Learning_Environment.pdf

Maag, C. (2007, December 16). When bullies turned faceless. *New York Times.* Retrieved January 22, from http://www.nytimes.com/2007/12/16/fashion/16meangirls.html?_r=1&ex=1198558800&en=35f8e2e63c570aab&ei=5070&emc=eta1&oref=slogin

Madell, D., & Muncer, S. J. (2006). Internet communication: An activity that appeals to shy and socially phobic people? *Cyberpsychology & Behavior, 9*(5), 618–622. doi:10.1089/cpb.2006.9.618

Madell, D., & Muncer, S. J. (2007). Control over social interactions: An important reason for young peoples use of the Internet and mobile phones for communication? *Cyberpsychology & Behavior, 10*(1), 137–140. doi:10.1089/cpb.2006.9980

Malaney, G. D. (2006). Educating for civic engagement, social activism, and political dissent: Adding the study of neoliberalism and imperialism to the student affairs curriculum. *Journal of College & Character, 7*(4). Retrieved September 30, 2008, from http://collegevalues.org/pdfs/Educating.pdf

Malden, MA: Blackwell Publishing.

Malesky, L. A. (2007). Predatory online behavior: Modus operandi of convicted sex offender in identifying potential victims and contact minors over the Internet. *Journal of Child Sexual Abuse, 16*(2), 23–32. doi:10.1300/J070v16n02_02

Manlove, J., Moore, K. A., Liechty, J., Ikramullah, E., & Cottinghman, S. (2005). *Sex between young teens and older individuals: A demographic portrait.* Washington, DC: Child Trends.

Mardsen, P., & Campbell, K. E. (1984). Measuring tie strength. *Social Forces, 63*, 482–494. doi:10.2307/2579058

Market Wire. (2006, February 8). *Online social networking soars on college campuses: eMarketer goes back to school to learn about social interactions.* Retrieved from http://findarticles.com/p/articles/mi_pwwi/is_/ai_n16048688

Marks, I. (1990). Non-chemical (behaviourial) addictions. *British Journal of Addiction, 85*, 1389–1394. doi:10.1111/j.1360-0443.1990.tb01618.x

Martino, S. C., Collins, R. L., Kanouse, D. E., Elliott, M., & Berry, S. H. (2005). Social cognitive processes mediating the relationship between exposure to television's sexual content and adolescents' sexual behavior. *Journal of Personality and Social Psychology, 89*(6), 914–924. doi:10.1037/0022-3514.89.6.914

Mash, E. J., & Wolfe, D. A. (2005). *Abnormal child psychology* (3rd ed.). Pacific Grove, CA: Wadsworth.

Matters, L. (n. d.). *Ensuring safety*. Retrieved January 4, 2008, from http://www.literacymatters.org/content/research/ensure.htm

Mazalin, D., & Moore, S. (2004). Internet use, identity development and social anxiety among young adults. *Behaviour Change*, *21*(2), 90–102. doi:10.1375/bech.21.2.90.55425

McCann, R. M., Kellermann, K., Giles, H., Gallois, C., & Viladot, M. A. (2004). Cultural and gender influences on age identification. *Communication Studies*, *55*(1), 88.

McCrae, S. (1996). Coming apart at the seams: Sex, text and the virtual body. In L. Cherry & E. Reba Weise (Eds.), *Wired women: Gender and new realities in cyberspace*. Seattle, WA: Seal Press.

McKay, H. G., Glasgow, R. E., Feil, E. G., Boles, S. M., & Barreta, M. (2002). Internet-based diabetes self-management and support: Initial outcomes from the diabetes network project. *Rehabilitation Psychology*, *47*, 31–48. doi:10.1037/0090-5550.47.1.31

McKenna, K. Y. A., & Bargh, J. A. (2000). Plan 9 from cyberspace: The implications of the Internet for personality and social psychology. *Personality and Social Psychology Review*, *4*, 57–75. doi:10.1207/S15327957PSPR0401_6

McKenna, K. Y. A., Green, A. S., & Gleason, M. E. J. (2002). Relationship formation on the Internet: What's the big attraction? *The Journal of Social Issues*, *58*, 9–31. doi:10.1111/1540-4560.00246

McKenna, K. Y., & Bargh, J. A. (1998). Coming out in the age of the Internet: Identity "de-marginalization" through virtual group participation. *Journal of Personality and Social Psychology*, *75*, 681–694. doi:10.1037/0022-3514.75.3.681

McKenna, K. Y., & Bargh, J. A. (2000). Plan 9 from cyberspace: The implications of the Internet for personality and social psychology. *Personality and Social Psychology Review*, *4*(1), 57–75. doi:10.1207/S15327957PSPR0401_6

McKenna, K., Green, A. S., & Gleason, M. E. (2002). Relationship formation on the Internet: Whats the big attraction? *The Journal of Social Issues*, *58*(1), 9–31. doi:10.1111/1540-4560.00246

Mckenna, P. (2007). The rise of cyberbullying. *New Scientist*, *195*, 60. doi:10.1016/S0262-4079(07)62856-5

McMillan, S. J., & Morrison, M. (2000). Coming of age with the Internet: A qualitative online exploration of how the Internet has become an integral part of young people's lives. *New Media & Society*, *8*(1), 73–95. doi:10.1177/1461444806059871

McPherson, M., Smith-Lovin, L., & Cook, J. M. (2002). Birds of a feather: Homophily in social networks. *Annual Review of Sociology*, *27*, 415–444. doi:10.1146/annurev.soc.27.1.415

Media Awareness Group. (2005). *Young Canadians in a wired world*. Canada: Erin Research Inc.

Media Awareness Network. (n. d.). *Cyber bullying: Understanding and preventing online harassment and bullying*. Retrieved October 5, 2007, from http://www.mediaeducationweek.ca/press_articles_cb.htm

Melber, A. (2006, May 30). MySpace, MyPolitics. *The Nation*. Retrieved September 30, 2008, from http://www.thenation.com/docprint.mhtml?i=20060612&s=melber

Memling, M., & Buchholz, E. S. (1994). *Psychoanalytic reflections on the need for aloneness in children's literature* (unpublished manuscript).

Mesch, G. (2006). Online communities. In R. Cnaan & C. Milofsky (Eds.), *Handbook of community and community organization*. New York: Springer.

Mesch, G. S. (2001). Social relationships and Internet use among adolescents in Israel. *Social Science Quarterly*, *82*(2), 329–339. doi:10.1111/0038-4941.00026

Mesch, G. S. (2006). Family relations and the Internet: Exploring a family boundaries approach. *Journal of Family Communication*, *6*(2), 119–138. doi:10.1207/s15327698jfc0602_2

Mesch, G. S. (2007) Social diversification: A perspective for the study of social networks of adolescents offline and online. In N. Kutscher & H. U. Otto (Eds.), *Grenzenlose cyberwelt* (pp. 105-121). Heidelberg, Germany: Verlag für Sozialwiseenschaften.

Mesch, G. S., & Talmud, I. (2006). The quality of online and offline relationships, the role of multiplexity and duration. *The Information Society, 22*(3), 137–149. doi:10.1080/01972240600677805

Mesch, G. S., & Talmud, I. (2007). Similarity and the quality of online and offline social relationships among adolescents in Israel. *Journal of Research on Adolescence, 17*(2), 455–466. doi:10.1111/j.1532-7795.2007.00529.x

Mesch, G., & Talmud, I. (2006). The quality of online and offline relationships: The role of multiplexity and duration of social relationships. *The Information Society, 22*, 137–148. doi:10.1080/01972240600677805

Miller, N. L. (1993). Are computers dangerous to children's health? *Education Digest, 58*(5), 24.

Mitchell, K. J., & Ybarra, M. L. (2007). Online behavior of youth who engage in self-harm provides clues for preventive intervention. *Preventive Medicine, 45*, 392–396. doi:10.1016/j.ypmed.2007.05.008

Mitchell, K. J., Finkelhor, D., & Becker-Blease, K. A. (2007). Linking youth Internet and conventional problems: Findings from a clinical perspective. *Journal of Aggression, Maltreatment & Trauma, 15*(2), 39–58. doi:10.1300/J146v15n02_03

Mitchell, K. J., Finkelhor, D., & Wolak, J. (2001). Risk factors for and impact of online sexual solicitation of youth. *Journal of the American Medical Association, 285*(23), 3011–3014. doi:10.1001/jama.285.23.3011

Mitchell, K. J., Finkelhor, D., & Wolak, J. (2003). The exposure of youth to unwanted sexual material on the Internet: A national survey of risk, impact, and prevention. *Youth & Society, 34*(3), 330–358. doi:10.1177/0044118X02250123

Mitchell, K. J., Finkelhor, D., & Wolak, J. (2005). Protecting youth online: Family use of filtering and blocking software. *Child Abuse & Neglect, 29*, 753–765.

Mitchell, K. J., Finkelhor, D., & Wolak, J. (2007). Youth Internet users at risk for the most serious online sexual solicitations. *American Journal of Preventive Medicine, 32*(6), 532–537. doi:10.1016/j.amepre.2007.02.001

Mitchell, K. J., Finkelhor, D., & Wolak, J. (2007a). Online requests for sexual pictures from youth: Risk factors and incident characteristics. *The Journal of Adolescent Health, 41*, 196–203. doi:10.1016/j.jadohealth.2007.03.013

Mitchell, K. J., Wolak, J., & Finkelhor, D. (2007). Trends in youth reports of sexual solicitations, harassment and unwanted exposure to pornography on the Internet. *The Journal of Adolescent Health, 40*, 116–126. doi:10.1016/j.jadohealth.2006.05.021

Mitchell, K. J., Wolak, J., & Finkelhor, D. (2008). Are blogs putting youth at risk for online sexual solicitation or harassment? *Child Abuse & Neglect, 32*, 277–294. doi:10.1016/j.chiabu.2007.04.015

Mitra, S., & Rana, V. (2001). Children and the Internet: Experiments with minimally invasive education in India. *British Journal of Educational Technology, 32*(2), 221–232. doi:10.1111/1467-8535.00192

Moore, D. (1995). *The emperor's virtual clothes: The naked truth about the Internet culture.* Chapel Hill, NC: Alogonquin.

Moore, S., & Rosenthal, D. (2006). *Sexuality in adolescence: Current trends.* New York: Routledge/Taylor & Francis Group.

Morahan-Martin, J. (2005). Internet abuse: Addiction? Disorder? Symptom? Alternative explanations? *Social Science Computer Review, 23*(1), 39–48. doi:10.1177/0894439304271533

Morahan-Martin, J., & Schumaker, P. (1997). *Incidence and correlates of pathological Internet use.* Paper presented at the 105th Annual Convention of the American Psychological Association, Chicago, IL.

Moras, S. (2001). *Computer-assisted language learning (CALL) and the Internet. Cultura Inglesa de Sao Carlos.* Retrieved May 12, 2008, from http://www3.telus.net/linguisticsissues/CALL.html

Morse v. Frederic, 127 S.Ct. 2618 (2007).

Moustakas, C. E. (1989). *Loneliness.* New York: Prentice Hall.

Muller, L. (2004). *ICT accelerating change in society and economies.* Paper presented to the Pontifica Universidad de Sao Paulo, Sao Paulo, Brazil.

Mynard, J. (2002a). Introducing EFL students to chat rooms. *The Internet TESL Journal, 8*(2). Retrieved February 17, 2004, from http://iteslj.org/Lessons/Mynard-Chat.html

Mynard, J. (2002b). Making chat activities with native speakers meaningful for EFL learners. *The Internet TESL Journal, 8*(3). Retrieved February 17, 2004, from http://iteslj.org/Techniques/Mynard-Chat2/

Nalwa, K., & Anand, A. P. (2003). Internet addiction in students: A cause of concern. *Cyberpsychology & Behavior, 6*(6), 653–656. doi:10.1089/109493103322725441

National Public Radio. (2000). *Survey shows widespread enthusiasm for high technology.* Retrieved from http://www.npr.org/programs/specials/poll/technology/index.html

Nelson, M. R., & Otnes, C. C. (2005). Exploring cross-cultural ambivalence: A netnography of intercultural wedding message boards. *Journal of Business Research, 58*(1), 89–95. doi:10.1016/S0148-2963(02)00477-0

Neman, D. (2007, June 18). Uneven 4th: 'Live Free or Die Hard' / Willis does a bang-up job, but film implodes at the end. *Richmond Times-Dispatch*, p. 15.

Nesdale, D., & Naito, M. (2005). Individualism-collectivism and the attitudes to school bullying of Japanese and Australian students. *Journal of Cross-Cultural Psychology, 36*, 537–556. doi:10.1177/0022022105278541

Nie, N. Hillygus. S. D., & Erbring, L. (2002). Internet use, interpersonal relations and sociability: A time diary study. In B. Wellman & C. Haythornthwaite (Eds.), *The Internet in everyday life.* Hoboken, NJ: Wiley-Blackwell.

Niemz, K., Griffiths, M. D., & Banyard, P. (2005). Prevalence of pathological Internet use among university students and correlations with self-esteem, GHQ and disinhibition. *Cyberpsychology & Behavior, 8*, 562–570. doi:10.1089/cpb.2005.8.562

Norman, D. (1993). *Things that make us smarter: Defending human attributes in the age of the machine.* New York: Addison-Wesley

NPD market research. (2008). Retrieved September 12, 2008, from http://www.npd.com

O'Moore, M., & Kirkham, C. (2001). Self-esteem and its relationship to bullying behaviour. *Aggressive Behavior, 27*, 269–283. doi:10.1002/ab.1010

O'Neill, M. (1995, March 8). The lure and addiction of life on-line. *The New York Times.*

Oblinger, D. (2004). The next generation of educational engagement. *Journal of Interactive Media in Education,* (8): 1–18.

Olson, C. K., Kutner, L. A., & Warner, D. E. (2008). The role of violent video game content in adolescent development: Boys' perspectives. *Journal of Adolescent Research, 23*, 55–75. doi:10.1177/0743558407310713

Olweus, D. (1993). *Bullying at school. What we know and what we can do.* Malden, MA: Blackwell.

On the Ground Blog. (2008, Jan 27 & 28). Readers comments to Nicholas Kristof's "The Age of Ambition." *New York Times.* Retrieved September 30, 2008, from http://kristof.blogs.nytimes.com/2008/01/26/your-comments-on-my-social-entrepreneur-column/

ONDCP. (2008). *Parents. The anti-drug.* Retrieved from http://theantidrug.com

Orleans, M. (1991). Phenomenological sociology. In H. Etzkowitz & R. M. Glassman (Eds.), *The renascence of sociological theory: Classical and contemporary.* Itasca, IL: F.E. Peacock Publishers.

Orleans, M. (1997). Caught in the Web: The phenomenon of cyberaddiction. In J. Behar (Ed.), *Sociological studies of telecommunications, computerization and cyberspace.* Oakdale, NY: Dowling College Press.

Orleans, M., & Laney, M. C. (2000). Children's use of computers in the home: Isolation or sociation? *Social Science Computer Review, 18*(1), 56–72. doi:10.1177/089443930001800104

Orleans, M., & Walters, G. (1996). Human-computer enmeshment: Identity diffusion through mastery. *Social Science Computer Review, 14*(2), 144–156. doi:10.1177/089443939601400202

Pacheco, A. Q. (2005). Web-based learning (WBL): A challenge for foreign language teachers. *Revista Electrónica Actualidades Investigativas en Educación* 5 (2005) H. 2, S.1-25. Retrieved September 12, 2008, from http://revista.inie.ucr.ac.cr/articulos/2-2005/archivos/web.pdf

Padilla-Walker, L. M. (2006). "Peers I can monitor, It's media that really worries me!": Parental cognitions as predictors of proactive parental strategy choice. *Journal of Adolescent Research, 21,* 56–82. doi:10.1177/0743558405282723

Papacharissi, Z., & Rubin, A. M. (2000). Predictors of Internet use. *Journal of Broadcasting & Electronic Media, 44*(2), 175–196. doi:10.1207/s15506878jobem4402_2

Papert, S. (1996). *The connected family: Bridging the digital generation gap.* Atlanta

Parks, M. R., & Roberts, L. D. (1998). "Making MOOsic": The development of personal relationships on line and a comparison to their off-line counterparts. *Journal of Social and Personal Relationships, 15,* 517–537. doi:10.1177/0265407598154005

Parsad, B., & Jones, J. (2005). *Internet access in U.S. public schools and classrooms: 1994–2003* (NCES 2005–015). U.S. Department of Education. Washington, DC: National Center for Education Statistics.

Patchin, J. W., & Hinduja, S. (2006). Bullies move beyond the schoolyard: A preliminary look at cyberbullying. *Youth Violence and Juvenile Justice, 4*(2), 148–169. doi:10.1177/1541204006286288

Payne, S., & Ross, B. (2005). Synchronous CMC, working memory, and L2 oral proficiency development. *Language Learning & Technology, 9*(3), 35–54.

Pearce, W. B. (1994). *Interpersonal communication: Making social worlds.* New York: HarperCollins.

Peter, J., & Valkenburg, P. M. (2006). Adolescents' exposure to sexually explicit material on the Internet. *Communication Research, 33*(2), 178–204. doi:10.1177/0093650205285369

Peter, J., & Valkenburg, P. M. (2008). Adolescents' identity experiments on the Internet - consequences for social competence and self-concept unity. *Communication Research, 35*(2), 208–231. doi:10.1177/0093650207313164

Peter, J., Valkenburg, P. M., & Schouten, A. P. (2005). Development a model of adolescent friendship formation on the Internet. *Cyberpsychology & Behavior, 8,* 423–430. doi:10.1089/cpb.2005.8.423

Peter, J., Valkenburg, P. M., & Schouten, A. P. (2006). Characteristics and motives of adolescents talking with strangers on the Internet. *Cyberpsychology & Behavior, 9,* 526–530. doi:10.1089/cpb.2006.9.526

Peter, J., Valkenburg, P., & Schouten, A. P. (2005). Developing a model of adolescent friendship formation on the Internet. *Cyberpsychology & Behavior, 8*(5), 423–430. doi:10.1089/cpb.2005.8.423

Peter, J., Valkenburg, P., & Schouten, A. P. (2006). Characteristics and motives of adolescents talking with strangers on the Internet. *Cyberpsychology & Behavior, 9*(5), 526–530. doi:10.1089/cpb.2006.9.526

Petersen, A., Silbereisen, R. K., & Sorenson, S. (1996). Adolescent development: A global perspective. In K. Hurrelmann & S. F. Hamiliton (Eds.), *Social problems and social contexts in adolescence* (pp. 3-38). Edison, NJ: Aldine Transaction.

Pew Internet & American Life Project. (2005). *Teens and technology: Youth are leading the transition to a fully wired and mobile nation.* Retrieved June 30, 2008, from http://www.pewinternet.org/pdfs/PIP_Teens_Tech_July2005web.pdf

Pew Internet & American Life Project. (2007). *Social networking websites and teens: An overview.* Retrieved June 30, 2008, from http://www.pewinternet.org/pdfs/PIP_Teens_Social_Media_Final.pdf

Piaget, J. (1967). *Six psychological studies.* New York: Random House.

Pica, T. (1994). Review article -- research on negotiation: What does it reveal about second-language learning conditions, processes, and outcomes? *Language Learning, 44*, 493–527. doi:10.1111/j.1467-1770.1994.tb01115.x

Pica, T., & Doughty, C. (1986). Making input comprehensible: do interactional modifications help? *ILT Review of Applied Linguistics, 72*, 1–25.

Pierce, L. L., Wilkinson, L. K., & Anderson, J. (2003). Analysis of the concept of aloneness as applied to older women being treated for depression. *Journal of Gerontological Nursing, 29*(7), 20.

Pivec, M. (2006). *The secret life of virtual you*. Invited presentation at the Social Skills and Social Software conference, Salzburg, Austria.

Pivec, M., & Panko, M. (2008). Instructional design - sex driven? T. Kidd & I. Chen (Eds.), *Social information technology: Connecting society and cultural issues*. Hershey, PA: Idea Group Publishing.

Pivec, M., & Pivec, P. (2008). Playing to learn: Guidelines for designing educational games. In *Proceedings of World Conference on Educational Multimedia, Hypermedia and telecommunications 2008*, Vienna, Austria (pp. 3247-3252).

Pivec, P., & Pivec, M. (2008). *Games in schools. Commissioned report for Interactive Software Federation of Europe (ISFE) by the European Commission (EC)*. Retrieved November 30, 2008, from http://www.isfe.eu/

Ponton, L. E., & Judice, S. (2004). Typical adolescent sexual development. *Child and Adolescent Psychiatric Clinics of North America, 13*(3), 497–511. doi:10.1016/j.chc.2004.02.003

Porter, P. B. (1993). Fostering collaborative word processing with writing disabled adolescents (Doctoral dissertation, University of Toronto, Canada). *Dissertation Abstracts International, 55-03A*, 0460.

Preece, J. J., & Ghozati, K. (2001). Observations and explorations in empathy online. In R. Rice & J. E. Katz (Eds.), *The Internet and health communication: Experience and expectations* (pp. 237-260). Thousand Oaks, CA: Sage.

Prensky, M. (2001a). Digital natives, digital immigrants. *Horizon, 9*(5), 1–10. doi:10.1108/10748120110424816

Prentice-Dunn, S., & Rogers, R. (1982). Effects of public and private self-awareness on deindividuation and aggression. *Journal of Personality and Social Psychology, 43*, 503–513. doi:10.1037/0022-3514.43.3.503

Quesada Pacheco, A. (2005). Web-based learning (WBL): A challenge for foreign language teachers. *Revista Electrónica Actualidades Investigativas en Educación, 5*(2), 1-25. Retrieved December 13, 2007, from http://revista.inie.ucr.ac.cr/articulos/2-2005/archivos/web.pdf

Raacke, J., & Bonds-Raacke, J. (2008). MySpace and facebook: Applying the uses and gratifications theory to exploring friend-networking sites. *Cyberpsychology & Behavior, 11*(2), 169–174. doi:10.1089/cpb.2007.0056

Rao, V. (2008, January 27). Why college matters. *New York Times*. Retrieved September 30, 2008, from http://essay.blogs.nytimes.com/tag/activism/?scp=2&sq=Youth%20activism&st=cse'

Reid, E. (1998). The self and the Internet: Variations on the illusion of one self. In J. Gackenbach (Ed.), *Psychology and the Internet: Intrapersonal, interpersonal and transpersonal applications*. New York: Academic Press.

Reiser, R., & Dempsy, J. (Eds.). (2001). *Trends and issues in instruction design and technology*. Englewood Cliffs, NJ: Prentice Hall.

Reno v. American Civil Liberties Union, 521 U.S. 844 (1997).

Requa v. Kent School Dist. No. 415, 492 F.Supp.2d 1272, (W.D.Wash. 2007).

Retrieved July 11, 2008, from http://www.cnn.com/2008/CRIME/03/17/sunny.juicy/index.html

Reyna, V. F., & Farley, F. (2006). Risk and rationality in adolescent decision making: Implications for theory, practice, and public policy . *Psychological Science in the Public Interest, 7*(1), 1–44. doi:10.1111/j.1529-1006.2006.00026.x

Rhodes, J. E., & Jason, L. A. (1990). A social stress of substance abuse. *Journal of Consulting and Clinical Psychology, 58,* 395–401. doi:10.1037/0022-006X.58.4.395

Richards, J., & Rodgers, T. (2001). *Approaches and methods in language teaching.* New York: Cambridge University Press.

Rideout, V., Richardson, C., & Resnick, P. (2002). *See no evil: How Internet filters affect the search for online health information.* Retrieved October 26, 2004, from http://www.kff.org/entmedia/20021210a-index.cfm

Roberts, D. F., Foehr, U., & Rideout, V. (2005). *Kids and media in America.* New York: Cambridge University Press.

Rogers, P., Sandler, B., Duffy, T., Salcines, M., & Duignan-Cabrera, A. (1997, August 11). Snared by the net: Lured to the Internet by fun and friends, some teens get caught in a web of trouble. *People,* 48.

Rogosch, F. A., Cicchetti, D., & Aber, J. L. (1995). The role of child maltreatment in early deviations in cognitive and affective processing abilities and later peer relationship problems. *Development and Psychopathology, 7,* 591–609. doi:10.1017/S0954579400006738

Rosen, L. D. (2007). *Me, MySpace, and I: Parenting the Net generation.* New York: Palgrave Macmillan.

Rosen, L. D., & Carrier, M. L. (2008). The association of parenting style and child age with parental limit setting and adolescent MySpace behavior. *Journal of Applied Developmental Psychology, 29,* 459–471. doi:10.1016/j.appdev.2008.07.005

Rosengren, K. E., & Windahl, S. (1989). *Media matters: TV use in childhood and adolescence.* Norwood, NJ: Ablex.

Rosser, R. (1994). *Cognitive development: Psychological and biological perspectives.* Boston: Allyn and Bacon.

Rossi, P. H. (1988). On sociological data. In N. J. Smelser (Ed.), *Handbook of sociology.* Newbury Park, CA: Sage Publications.

Rubenstein, C. M. (1996). Internet dangers. *Parents' Magazine (Bergenfield, N.J.), 71*(3), 145.

Rubin, A. M. (2002). The uses-and-gratifications perspectives of media effects, In J. Bryant & D. Zillmann (Eds.), *Media effects: Advances in theory and research* (pp. 525-548). Mahwah, NJ: Laurence Erlbaum.

Rubin, K. H., Bukowski, W. M., & Parker, J. G. (1998). Peer interactions, relationships and groups. In N. Eisenberg (Ed.), *Handbook of child psychology: Social, emotional and personality development* (pp. 619-700). New York: Wiley.

Ruble, D. N. (1994). A phase model of transitions: Cognitive and motivational consequences. In M.P. Zanna (Ed.), *Advances in experimental social psychology* (Vol. 26, pp. 163-214). New York: Academic.

Rushkoff, D. (1996). *Playing the future: How kids' culture can teach us to thrive in an age of chaos.* New York: HarperCollins.

Ryan, J. (2008). *The virtual campfire: An ethnography of online social networking.* Unpublished thesis, Wesleyan University. Retrieved February 7, 2009, from http://www.thevirtualcampfire.org/

Sanders, C. E., Field, T. M., Diego, M., & Kaplan, M. (2000). The relationship of Internet use to depression and social isolation among adolescents. *Adolescence, 35*(138), 237–242.

Santrock, J. W. (2009). *Child development* (12th ed.). Boston: McGraw-Hill.

Schall, P. L., & Skeele, R. (1995). Creating a home-school partnership for learning: Exploiting the home computer. *The Educational Forum, 59*(3), 244–249. doi:10.1080/00131729509336399

Scherer, K. (1997). College life on-line: Healthy and unhealthy Internet use. *Journal of College Student Development, 38,* 655–665.

Schmidt, R. (1990). The role of consciousness in second language learning. *Applied Linguistics, 11,* 129–158. doi:10.1093/applin/11.2.129

Schmidt, R., & Frota, S. (1986). Developing basic conversational ability in a second language: A case study of an adult learner of Portuguese. In R. Daly (Ed.), *Talking to learn: Conversation in second language acquisition* (pp. 93-107). Rowley, MA: Newbury House.

Schmmer, M. (1993). Epistemological development and academic performance among secondary students. *Journal of Educational Psychology, 85,* 1–6.

Schouten, A. P., Valenburg, P. M., & Peter, J. (2007). Precursors and underlying processes of adolescents' online self-disclosure: Developing and testing an "Internet-attribute-perception" model. *Media Psychology, 10,* 292–315. doi:.doi:10.1080/15213260701375686

Schwartz, M. (2008, August 3). The trolls among us. *New York Times Magazine,* 27-30.

Schwienhorst, K. (2003). Learner autonomy and tandem learning: Putting principles into practice in synchronous and asynchronous telecommunications environments. *Computer Assisted Language Learning, 16,* 427–443. doi:10.1076/call.16.5.427.29484

Seiter, E. (2005). *The Internet playground: Children's access, entertainment and mis-education.* New York: Peter Lang.

Shadish, W., Cook, T., & Campbell, D. T. (2002). *Experimental and quasi-experimental designs for generalized causal inference.* Boston: Houghton Mifflin.

Shaffer, D. W. (2006). *How video games help children learn.* New York: Palgrave Macmillan.

Shariff, S. (2008). *Cyber-bullying: Issues and solutions for the school, the classroom and the home.* New York: Routledge.

Shea, V. (1994). *Netiquette.* San Francisco, CA: Albion

Sheeks, M. S., & Birchmeier, Z. P. (2007). Shyness, sociability, and the use of computer-mediated communication in relationship development. *Cyberpsychology & Behavior, 10*(1), 64–70. doi:10.1089/cpb.2006.9991

Sherbourne, C. D., & Stewart, A. (1991). The MOS social support survey. *Social Science & Medicine, 32,* 705–714. doi:10.1016/0277-9536(91)90150-B

Sherrod, L. R. (2006). *Youth activism: An international encyclopedia.* Westport, CT: Greenwood Press.

Shimoda, H. (2008). 学校裏サイト [Unofficial school Websites]. Tokyo: Toyo Keizai Inc. (In Japanese)

Shulman, M. (1996, May 9). Are we creating Internet introverts? Culture: Our children need to be in the real world. *Los Angeles Times,* p. 9.

SIECUS. (2008). *Families are talking.* Retrieved from http://www.siecus.org/

Simon, M. (2008). *Online student-teacher friendships can be tricky.* Retrieved August 13, 2008, from http://www.cnn.com/2008/TECH/08/12/studentsteachers.online/index.html20080813

Simon, W., & Gagnon, J. H. (1986). Sexual scripts: Permanence and change. *Archives of Sexual Behavior, 15,* 97–120. doi:10.1007/BF01542219

Sisk, C. (2006). New insights into the neurobiology of sexual maturation. *Sexual and Relationship Therapy, 21,* 5–14. doi:10.1080/14681990500470009

Skinner, B., & Austin, R. (1999). Computer conferencing - does it motivate EFL students? *ELT Journal, 53*(4), 270–279. doi:10.1093/elt/53.4.270

Smahel, D. (2003). Communication of adolescents in the Internet environment. *Československá Psychologie, 47,* 144–156.

Smith, B. (2004). Computer-mediated negotiated interaction and lexical acquisition. *Studies in Second Language Acquisition, 26,* 365–398. doi:10.1017/S027226310426301X

Smith, J. (1955). *Understanding the media: A sociology of mass communication.* Creekskill, NJ: Hapmpton Press, Inc.

Smith, L. (2007). Online networkers who click to 1000 friends. *The Times.* Retrieved September 20, from http://www.thetimes.co.uk/tol/news/science/article2416229

Smith, P. K., Madsen, K. C., & Moody, J. C. (1999). What causes the age decline in reports of being bullies at school? Towards a developmental analysis of risks of being bullied. *Educational Research, 41,* 267–285.

Smith, R., Curtin, P., & Newman, L. (1997). *Kids in the kitchen: The educational implications of computer and computer games use by young children.* Paper presented at the Australian Association for Research in Education Annual Conference, Brisbane, Australia.

Smorti, A., Menesini, E., & Smith, P. (2003). Parents' definitions of children's bullying in a five-country comparison. *Journal of Cross-Cultural Psychology, 34,* 417–432. doi:10.1177/0022022103034004003

Sotillo, S. (2000). Discourse functions and syntactic complexity in synchronous and asynchronous communication. *Language Learning & Technology, 4*(1), 82-119. Retrieved November 10, 2001, from http://llt.msu.edu/vol4num1/sotillo/default.html

Sowell, E. R., Thompson, P. M., Leonard, C. M., Welcome, S. E., Kan, E., & Toga, A. W. (2004). Longitudinal mapping of cortical thickness and brain growth in normal children. *The Journal of Neuroscience, 24*(38), 8223–8231. doi:10.1523/JNEUROSCI.1798-04.2004

Spanierman v. Hughes, --- F.Supp.2d ----, 2008 WL 4224483 (D. Conn. 2008).

Spears, R., & Lea, M. (1992). Social influences and the influence of the "social" in computer-mediated communication. In M. Lee (Ed.), *Contexts in computer-mediated communication* (pp. 30-65). London: Harvester Wheatsheaf.

Sproull, L., & Kiesler, S. (1986). Reducing social context cues: Electronic mail in organizational communication. *Management Science, 32,* 1492–1512. doi:10.1287/mnsc.32.11.1492

Sproull, L., & Kiesler, S. (1986). Reducing social context cues: Electronic email in organizational communications. *Management Science, 32,* 1492–1512. doi:10.1287/mnsc.32.11.1492

Sproull, L., & Kiesler, S. (1991). *Connections: New ways of working in the networked organization.* Cambridge, MA: MIT Press.

Squire, K. (2003). Video games in education. *International Journal of Intelligent Simulations and Gaming, 2*(1), 49–62.

Stafford, T. F., & Gonier, D. (2004). What Americans like about being online. *Communications of the ACM, 47*(11), 107–112. doi:10.1145/1029496.1029502

Staub, E., & Pearlman, L. (2002). *Understanding basic psychological needs.* Retrieved August 20, 2008, from http://www.heal-reconcile-rwanda.org/lec_needs.htm

Stearns, P. N. (2006). *American fear: The causes and consequences of high anxiety.* New York: Routledge.

Stein, G. quoted in Shapiro, F.S. (2006). *The Yale book of quotations.* New Haven, CT: Yale University Press.

Stoeltje, M. (1996). Human costs in the computer age – commentary. *Journal of Systems Management, 47*(1), 57.

Stone, S. (1991). Will the real body please stand up? Boundary stories about virtual culture. In M. Benedikt (Ed.), *Cyberspace: First steps.* Cambridge, MA: MIT Press.

Storm, P. S., & Storm, R. D. (2005). Cyberbullying by adolescents: A preliminary assessment. *The Educational Forum, 70,* 21–32. doi:10.1080/00131720508984869

Storr, A. (1988). *Solitude: A return to the self.* New York: The Free Press.

Sturgeon, J. (2006). Bullies in cyberspace. *School Security,* 43-47.

Subrahmanyam, K., & Greenfield, P. (2008). Online communication and adolescent relationships. *The Future of Children, 18*(1), 119–146. doi:10.1353/foc.0.0006

Subrahmanyam, K., & Lin, G. (2007). Adolescents on the Net: Internet use and well-being. *Adolescence, 42*(168), 659–677.

Subrahmanyam, K., Greenfield, P. M., & Tynes, B. (2004). Constructing sexuality and identity in an online teen chat room. *Journal of Applied Developmental Psychology, 25,* 651–666. doi:10.1016/j.appdev.2004.09.007

Subrahmanyam, K., Greenfield, P., & Tynes, B. (2007). Constructing sexuality and identity in an online teen chat room. *Applied Developmental Psychology, 25,* 651–666. doi:10.1016/j.appdev.2004.09.007

Subrahmanyam, K., Greenfield, P., Kraut, R., & Gross, E. (2001). The impact of computer use on children's and adolescents' development. *Applied Developmental Psychology, 22,* 7–30. doi:10.1016/S0193-3973(00)00063-0

Subrahmanyam, K., Smahel, D., & Greenfield, P. (2006). Connecting developmental constructions to the Internet: Identity presentation and sexual exploration in online teen chat rooms. *Developmental Psychology, 42,* 395–406. doi:10.1037/0012-1649.42.3.395

Subrahmanyan, S., Kraut, R. E., Greenfield, P. M., & Gross, E. F. (2000). The impact of home computer use on children's activities and development. *The Future of Children, 10,* 123–144. doi:10.2307/1602692

Subrahmanyan, K., Smahel, D., & Greenfield, P. (2006). Connecting developmental constructions to the Internet: Identity presentation and sexual exploration on online teen chatrooms. *Developmental Psychology, 42,* 395–406. doi:10.1037/0012-1649.42.3.395

Suler, J. R. (2002). Identity management in cyberspace. *Journal of Applied Psychoanalytic Studies, 4,* 455–460. doi:10.1023/A:1020392231924

Sullivan, N., & Pratt, E. (1996). A comparative study of two ESL writing environments: A computer-assisted classroom and a traditional oral classroom. *System, 29*(4), 491–501. doi:10.1016/S0346-251X(96)00044-9

Sun, M. P. (1995). Effects of new media use on adolescents' family lives: Time use and relationships with family members in Taiwan (Doctoral dissertation, Ohio University). *Dissertation Abstracts International, 56-12A,* 4598.

Suoninen, A. (2001). The role of media in peer group relations, In S. Livingstone & M. Bovill (Eds.), *Children and their changing media environment* (pp. 201-219). Mahwah, NJ: Laurence Erlbaum.

Suratt, C. G. (2006). *The psychology of netaholics.* New York: Novinka Books.

Surratt, C. G. (1999). *Netaholics: The creation of a pathology.* New York: Nova Science Publishers.

Suzuki, L. K., & Calzo, J. P. (2004). The search for peer advice in cyberspace: An examination of online teen bulletin boards about health and sexuality. *Journal of Applied Developmental Psychology, 25*(6), 685–698. doi:10.1016/j.appdev.2004.09.002

Suzuki, L., & Calzo, J. (2004). The search for peer advice in cyberspace: An examination of online teen bulletin boards about health and sexuality. *Journal of Applied Developmental Psychology, 25,* 685–698. doi:10.1016/j.appdev.2004.09.002

Swain, M. (1985). Communicative competence: Some roles of comprehensible input and comprehensible output in its development. In S. Gass & C. Madden (Eds.), *Input in second language acquisition* (pp. 235-256). Rowley, MA: Newbury House.

Sweeney, R. (2008, September 3). *The Millenial generation goes to college: A focus group.* Presentation at William Paterson University.

Tajfel, H. (1978). Social categorization, social identity, and social comparison. In H. Tajfel (Ed.), *Differentiation between social groups: Studies in the social psychology of inter-group relations* (pp. 61-76). London: Academic Press.

Tajfel, H., & Turner, J. C. (1986). The social identity theory of intergroup behavior. In S. Worschel & W. C. Austin (Eds.), *Psychology of intergroup relations* (pp. 7-24). Chicago: Nelson-Hall.

Talbert, T. (2004). Give peace a chance…in our social education textbooks. *Journal of Pedagogy, Pluralism, and Practice, 8,* 9–15.

Talbert, T. L., & Glanzer, P. L. (2006). Giving peace a chance in America's social education classrooms: Teaching alternatives to violence from secular and religious communities nonviolence. In K. Kottu (Ed.), *Religion, terrorism and globalization: Nonviolence - a new agenda* (pp. 265-277). Hauppauge, NY: Nova Science Publishers.

Talbert, T., & White, C. (2003). Lives in the balance: Controversy, militarism, and social studies efficacy. In C. White (Ed.), *True confessions: Popular culture, social studies efficacy, and the struggle in schools* (pp. 41-56). Cresskill, NJ: Hampton Press.

Talbott, S. (1995). *The future does not compute.* Sebastopol, CA: O'Reilly and Associates.

Taylor, A. S., & Harper, R. (2003). The gift of the gab? A design oriented sociology of young people's use of mobiles. *Computer Supported Cooperative Work . International Journal (Toronto, Ont.), 12*(4), 267–296.

Taylor, L. (1990). *Teaching and learning vocabulary.* Upper Saddle River, NJ: Prentice Hall.

Taylor, L. D. (2005). Effects of visual and verbal sexual television content and perceived realism on attitudes and beliefs. *Journal of Sex Research, 42*(2), 130–137.

The training room. (2008). Retrieved February 29, 2008, from http://www.gamedesigncampus.com

Thomas, S. G. (1996). Great games for girls. *U.S. News and World Report, 121*(Nov. 25), 108.

Thornburgh, D., & Lin, H. S. (Eds.). (2002). *Youth, pornography, and the Internet.* Washington, DC: National Academic Press.

Tinker v. Des Moines Independent Community School District, 393 U.S. 503 (1969).

Toga, A. W., Thompson, P. M., & Sowell, E. R. (2006). Mapping brain maturation. *Trends in Neurosciences, 29*(3), 148–159. doi:10.1016/j.tins.2006.01.007

Tomaselli, K. P. (2006). Social software: Too much information? Is "online privacy" an oxymoron? *Virginia. edu, X*(1). Retrieved September 30, 2008, from http://www.itc.virginia.edu/virginia.edu/spring06/social.htm

Townsend, Z. (2008, January 27). The modern college: Cultivating students and its own reputation: Waning activism, becoming "the man" and moving up in the rankings game. *New York Times.* Retrieved September 30, 2008, from http://essay.blogs.nytimes.com/tag/activism/?scp=2&sq=Youth%20activism&st=cse

Trebilock, B. (1997). Child molesters on the Internet: Are they in your home. *Redbook Magazine, 188*(April), 100–103.

Treml, J. M. (2001). Bullying as a social malady in contemporary Japan. *International Social Work, 44,* 107–117. doi:10.1177/002087280104400109

Tsai, C.-C., & Lin, S. S. J. (2003). Internet addiction of adolescents in Taiwan: An interview study. *Cyberpsychology & Behavior, 6,* 649–652. doi:10.1089/109493103322725432

Turkle, S. (1995). *Life on the screen: Identity in the age of the Internet.* New York: Simon and Schuster.

Turkle, S. (2001). Who am we? In D. Trend (Ed.), *Reading digital culture* (pp. 236-250). Malden, MA: Blackwell Publishers.

Turner, J. W., Grube, J. A., & Meyers, J. (2001). Developing an optimal match within online communities: An exploration of CMC support communities and traditional support. *The Journal of Communication,* 231–251. doi:10.1111/j.1460-2466.2001.tb02879.x

Turow, J. (2001). Family boundaries, commercialism, and the Internet: A framework for research. *Journal of Applied Developmental Psychology, 22*(1), 73–86. doi:10.1016/S0193-3973(00)00067-8

Turow, J., & Nir, L. (2000). The Internet and the family: The view from parents. In C. von Feilitzen & U. Carlsson (Eds.), *Children in the new media landscape* (pp. 331-348). Goteborg, Sweden: UNESCO International Clearing house on Children and Violence on the Screen.

Tynes, B. M. (2007). Internet safety gone wild? Sacrificing the educational and psychosocial benefits of online social environments. *Journal of Adolescent Research, 22,* 575–584. doi:10.1177/0743558407303979

Tynes, B. M., Giang, M. T., & Thompson, G. N. (2005). Ethnic identity, intergroup contact and outgroup orientation among diverse groups of adolescents on the Internet. *Cyberpsychology & Behavior, 11*(4), 459–465. doi:10.1089/cpb.2007.0085

Tynes, B., Reynolds, L., & Greenfield, P. M. (2004). Adolescence, race, and ethnicity on the Internet: A comparison of discourse in monitored vs. unmonitored chat rooms. *Applied Developmental Psychology, 25,* 667–684. doi:10.1016/j.appdev.2004.09.003

United States v. American Library Association, 539 U.S. 194 (2003). Virginia Department of Education. (n.d.). *Acceptable use policies: A handbook.* Retrieved September 29, 2008, from http://www.doe.virginia.gov/VDOE/Technology/AUP/home.shtml

Vail, K. (1997). Electronic school: Girlware. *The American School Board Journal, 184*(6), A18–A21.

Valkenburg, P. M., & Peter, J. (2007). Preadolescents and adolescents online communication and their closeness to friends. *Developmental Psychology, 43,* 267–277. doi:10.1037/0012-1649.43.2.267

Valkenburg, P. M., Jochen, P., & Schouten, A. P. (2006). Friend networking sites and their relationship to adolescents' well-being and social self-esteem. *Cyberpsychology & Behavior, 9*(5), 584–590. doi:10.1089/cpb.2006.9.584

Valkenburg, P., Peter, J., & Schouten, A. P. (2006). Friend networking sites and their relationship to adolescents well-being and social self-esteem. *Cyberpsychology & Behavior, 9*(5), 584–590. doi:10.1089/cpb.2006.9.584

Valkenburg, P., Schoutten, A., & Peter, J. (2005). Adolescents' identity experiments on the Internet. *New Media & Society, 7*(3), 383–401. doi:10.1177/1461444805052282

van Aken, M. A. G., van Lieshout, C. F. M., & Scholte, R. H. J. (1998). *The social relationships and adjustment of the various personality types and subtypes.* Paper presented at the 7th Biennial Meeting of the Society for Research on Adolescence, San Diego, CA.

van den Eijnden, R., Meerkerk, G. J., Vermulst, A. A., Spijkerman, R., & Engels, R. (2008). Online communication, compulsive Internet use, and psychosocial well-being among adolescents: A longitudinal study. *Developmental Psychology, 44*(3), 655–665. doi:10.1037/0012-1649.44.3.655

VHIL. (2007). Retrieved December 5, 2007, from http://vhil.stanford.edu/projects

Vivian, J. (2008). *The media of mass communication.* New York: Pearson.

Vygotsky, L. (1978). *Mind and society: The development of higher psychological processes.* Cambridge, MA: Harvard University Press.

Wallace, P. (1999). *The Psychology of the Internet.* New York: Cambridge University Press.

Walther, J. B. (1996). Computer-mediated communication: Impersonal, interpersonal, and hyperpersonal interactions, *Communication Research, 23*(1), 3-43. Retrieved from http://crx.sagepub.com/cgi/content/abstract/23/1/3

Walther, J. B., & Boyd, S. (2002). Attraction to computer-mediated social support. In C.A. Lin & D. Atkin (Eds.), *Communication technology and society: Audience adoption and uses* (pp. 153-188). Cresskill, NJ: Hampton Press.

Wan, C., & Chiou, B. (2006). Why are adolescents addicted to online gaming? An interview study in Taiwan. *Cyberpsychology & Behavior, 9,* 762–766. doi:10.1089/cpb.2006.9.762

Ward, L. M. (2003). Understanding the role of entertainment media in the sexual socialization of American youth: A review of empirical research. *Developmental Review, 23,* 347–388. doi:10.1016/S0273-2297(03)00013-3

Warner, C. N. (2004). It's just a game, right? Types of play in foreign language CMC. *Language Learning & Technology, 8*(2), 69–87.

Warschauer, M., Meloni, C., & Shetzer, H. (2002). *Internet for English teaching.* Alexandria, VA: TESOL.

Watanabe, M. (2008). ネットいじめの真実 [Truth of cyberbullying]. Kyoto, Japan: Minerva Publishing Company. (In Japanese).

Waterman, A. S., & Archer, S. L. (1990). A life-span perspective on identity formation: Developments in form, function, and process. In P. B. Baltes, D. L. Featherman, & R. M. Lerner (Eds.), *Life-span development and behavior* (pp. 29-57). Hillsdale, NJ: Laurence Erlbaum.

Weinstein, E., & Rosenhaft, E. (1991). The development of adolescent sexual intimacy: Implications for counseling. *Adolescence, 26,* 331.

Welch, A. (1995, May 25-29). *The role of book, television, computers and video games in children's day to day lives.* Paper presented at the Annual Meeting of the International Communication Association, Albuquerque, NM.

Wellman, B., Salaff, J., & Dimitrova, D. (1996). Computer networks as social networks: Collaborative work, telework, and virtual community. *Annual Review of Sociology, 22,* 213–238. doi:10.1146/annurev. soc.22.1.213

Wells, J., & Lewis, L. (2006). *Internet access in U.S. public schools and classrooms: 1994–2005* (NCES 2007-020). U.S. Department of Education. Washington, DC: National Center for Education Statistics.

Wells, M., & Mitchell, K. J. (2008). How do high-risk youth use the Internet? Characteristics and implications for prevention. *Child Maltreatment, 13*(3), 227–234. doi:10.1177/1077559507312962

Wells, M., Mitchell, K., Finkelhor, D., & Becker-Blease, K. (2006). Mental health professionals' exposure to clients with problematic Internet experiences. *Journal of Technology in Human Services, 24*(4), 35–52. doi:10.1300/J017v24n04_03

West Virginia State Board of Education v. Barnett, 319 U.S. 624 (1943).

Westerhof, G. J., & Barrett, A. E. (2005). Age identity and subjective well-being: A comparison of the United States and Germany. *Journal of Gerontology, 60B*(3), S129.

Whitely, B. E. (1997). Gender differences in computer-related attitudes and behavior: A meta-analysis. *Computers and Behavior, 13*(1), 1–22. doi:10.1016/S0747-5632(96)00026-X

Whitlock, J. L., Powers, J. L., & Eckenrode, J. (2006). The virtual cutting edge: The Internet and adolescent self-injury. *Developmental Psychology, 42,* 407–417. doi:10.1037/0012-1649.42.3.407

Wickstrom, A. (1996). Hackers (videotape review). *Video, 19*(April), 75.

Widyanto, L. (2007). *Internet addiction: Assessment and the online and offline selves.* Unpublished doctoral dissertation, Nottingham Trent University, UK.

Widyanto, L., & McMurran, M. (2004). The psychological properties of the Internet addiction test. *Cyberpsychology & Behavior, 7*(4), 443–450. doi:10.1089/cpb.2004.7.443 Widyanto, L., Griffiths, M. D., Brunsden, V., & McMurran, M. (2008). The psychometric properties of the Internet related problem scale: A pilot study. *International Journal of Mental Health and Addiction, 6,* 205–213. doi:10.1007/s11469-007-9120-6

Willard, N. (2005). *An educator's guide to cyberbullying and cyberthreats. Center for safe and responsible Internet use.* Retrieved October 5, 2007, from http://cyberbully.org/cyberbully/docs/cbcteducator.pdf

Willard, N. (2007). *Cyberbullying and cyberthreats: Responding to the challenge of online social aggression, threats, and distress.* Champaign, IL: Research Press.

Willard, N. E. (2007f). *Parents' Guide to cyberbullying and cyberthreats.* Retrieved from http://www.cyberbullying.org/cyberbully/docs/cbctparents.pdf

Willett, R., & Sefton-Green, J. (2003). Living and learning in chat rooms (or does informal learning have anything to teach us?). *Éducation et Sociétiés, 2,* 1–18.

Williams, A. L., & Merten, M. J. (2008). A review of online social networking profiles by adolescents: Implications for future research and intervention. *Adolescence, 43,* 253–273.

Williams, G. III. (1994). Plugging kids into computers. *The American Legion, 136*(6), 23.

Willis, J. (1996). *Framework for task based learning.* Italy: Longman.

Willoughby, T. (2008). A short-term longitudinal study of Internet and computer games use by boys and girls: Prevalence, frequency of use and psychosocial predictors. *Developmental Psychology, 44*, 195–204. doi:10.1037/0012-1649.44.1.195

Wilson, T., & Whitelock, D. (1998). What are the perceived benefits of participating in a computer-mediated communication (CMC) environment for distance learning computer science students? *Computers & Education, 30*(3/4), 259–269. doi:10.1016/S0360-1315(97)00069-9

Winkel, S., Groen, G., & Petermann, F. (2005). Soziale unterstutzung in suizidforen. *Praxis der Kinderpsychologie und Kinderpsychiatrie, 54*(9), 714–727.

Winnicott, D. W. (1965). *The maturational processes and the facilitating environment: Studies in the theory of emotional development.* New York: International University Process.

Wolak, J., Finkelhor, D., & Mitchell, K. (2004). Internet-initiated sex crimes against minors: Implications for prevention based on findings from a national study. *Journal of Adolescent Health, 35*(5), 424.e411-424.e420.

Wolak, J., Finkelhor, D., & Mitchell, K. (2008). Is talking online to unknown people always risky? Distinguishing online interaction styles in a national sample of youth Internet users. *Cyberpsychology & Behavior, 11*, 340–343. doi:. doi:10.1089/cpb.2007.0044

Wolak, J., Finkelhor, D., Mitchell, K. J., & Ybarra, M. L. (2008). Online "predators' and their victims: Myths, realities, and implications for prevention and treatment. *The American Psychologist, 63*(2), 111–128. doi:10.1037/0003-066X.63.2.111

Wolak, J., Finkelhor, D., Mitchell, K. J., & Ybarra, M. L. (2008). Online 'predators' and their victims: Myths, realities, and implications for prevention and treatment. *The American Psychologist, 63*(2), 111–128. doi:10.1037/0003-066X.63.2.111

Wolak, J., Mitchell, K. J., & Finkelhor, D. (2002). Close online relationships in a national sample of adolescence. *Adolescence, 37*, 441–455.

Wolak, J., Mitchell, K. J., & Finkelhor, D. (2003). Escaping or connecting? Characteristics of youth who form close online relationships. *Journal of Adolescence, 26*, 105–119. doi:10.1016/S0140-1971(02)00114-8

Wolak, J., Mitchell, K. J., & Finkelhor, D. (2003a). *National juvenile online victimization study (N-JOV): Methodology report.* Crimes against Children Research Center. Retrieved from http://www.unh.edu/ccrc/pdf/jvq/CV72.pdf

Wolak, J., Mitchell, K., & Finkelhor, D. (2006). Online victimization of youth: Five years later. *National Center for Missing & Exploited Children Bulletin - #07-06-025.* Alexandria, VA.

Wolak, J., Mitchell, K., & Finkelhor, D. (2007). Unwanted and wanted exposure to online pornography in a national sample of youth Internet users. *Pediatrics, 119*(2), 247–257. doi:10.1542/peds.2006-1891

Wolak, K. J., Mitchell, K. J., & Finkelhor, D. (2003). Escaping or connecting? Characteristics of youth who form close online relationships. Journal of Adolescence, 26(1), 105–119. doi:10.1016/S0140-1971(02)00114-8

Wolf, M. J. P. (2007). On the future of video games. In P. Messaris & L. Humphreys (Eds.), *Digital media: Transformation in human communication* (pp. 187-195). New York: Peter Lang.

Wright, K. (2000). Computer-mediated social support, older adults, and coping. *The Journal of Communication, 50*(3), 100–118. doi:10.1111/j.1460-2466.2000.tb02855.x

Yan, Z. (2005). Age differences in children's understanding of complexity of the Internet. *Journal of Applied Developmental Psychology, 26*, 385–396. doi:10.1016/j.appdev.2005.04.001

Yan, Z. (2006). What influences children's and adolescents' understanding of the complexity of the Internet? *Developmental Psychology, 42*, 418–428. doi:10.1037/0012-1649.42.3.418

Yan, Z. (in press). Useful resources, important messages: The explosion of parenting books on adolescents and social networking sites. *Journal of Applied Developmental Psychology.*

Yasukawa, M. (2008). 学校裏サイトからわが子をまもる [How to protect children from unofficial school Websites]. Tokyo, Japan: Chukei Publishing Company. (In Japanese)

Ybarra, M. L., & Mitchell, K. J. (2004). Youth engaging in online harassment: Associations with caregiver-child relationships, Internet use, and personal characteristics. *Journal of Adolescence*, *27*, 319–336. doi:10.1016/j.adolescence.2004.03.007

Ybarra, M. L., & Mitchell, K. J. (2005). Exposure to Internet pornography among children and adolescents: A national survey. *Cyberpsychology & Behavior*, *8*(5), 473–486. doi:10.1089/cpb.2005.8.473

Ybarra, M. L., & Mitchell, K. J. (2008). How risky are social networking sites? A comparison of places online where youth sexual solicitation and harassment occurs. *Pediatrics*, *121*(2), e350–e357. doi:10.1542/peds.2007-0693

Ybarra, M. L., Mitchell, K. J., Finkelhor, D., & Wolak, J. (2006). Examining characteristics and associated distress related to Internet harassment: Findings from the Second Youth Internet Safety Survey. *Pediatrics*, *118*(4), e1169–e1177. doi:10.1542/peds.2006-0815

Ybarra, M. L., Mitchell, K. J., Finkelhor, D., & Wolak, J. (2007). Internet prevention messages: Targeting the right online behaviors. *Archives of Pediatrics & Adolescent Medicine*, *161*, 138–145. doi:10.1001/archpedi.161.2.138

Yee, N. (2006). The demographics, motivations and derived experiences of users of massively-multiuser online graphical environments. *Presence (Cambridge, Mass.)*, *15*, 309–329. doi:10.1162/pres.15.3.309

Yellowlees, P. M., & Marks, S. (2007). Problematic Internet use or Internet addiction? *Computers in Human Behavior*, *23*(3), 1447–1453. doi:10.1016/j.chb.2005.05.004

Youn, S. (2007). Teenagers' perceptions of online privacy and coping behaviors: A risk–benefit appraisal approach. *Journal of Broadcasting & Electronic Media*, *49*(1), 86–110. doi:10.1207/s15506878jobem4901_6

Young, J. R. (2008, April 11). Why professors ought to teach blogging and podcasting. *The Chronicle of Higher Education*, *54*(31), A22.

Young, K. (1996). Internet addiction: The emergence of a new clinical disorder. *Cyberpsychology & Behavior*, *3*(1), 237–244.

Young, K. (1998). *Caught in the Net*. New York: John Wiley & Sons.

Young, K. (1999). Internet addiction: Evaluation and treatment. *Student British Medical Journal*, *7*, 351–352.

Young, K. S. (1996). Psychology of computer use: XL. Addictive use of the Internet: A case that breaks the stereotype. *Psychological Reports*, *79*(3), 251–270.

Young, K., & Rodgers, R. (1998). *Internet addiction: Personality traits associated with its development.* Paper presented at the 69th annual meeting of the Eastern Psychological Association.

Zenhausen, B. (1995, February 26). *Preliminary draft of the DSM-V committee in cyberdisorders.*

Zillmann, D. (1982). Television viewing and arousal. In D. Pearl, L. Bouthilet, & J. Lazar (Eds.), *Television and behavior: Ten years of scientific progress and implications for the eighties (Vol. 2): Technical reviews* (pp. 53-67). Washington, DC: Government Printing Office.

Zillmann, D. (1985). The experimental exploration of gratifications from media entertainment. In K. E. Rosengren, et al. (Eds.), *Media gratifications research: Current perspectives*. Newbury Park, CA: Sage.

Zillmann, D. (1988a). Mood management through communication choices. *The American Behavioral Scientist*, *31*, 327–340. doi:10.1177/000276488031003005

Zillmann, D. (1988b). Mood management: Using entertainment to full advantage. In L. Donohew, H. E. Sypher, & E. T. Higgins (Eds.), *Communication social cognition, and effect* (pp. 147-171). Hillsdale, NJ: Lawrence Erlbaum.

Zillmann, D., & Bryant, J. (Eds.). (2002). *Media effects: Advances in theory and research* (2nd ed.). Mahwah, NJ: Erlbaum.

Zillmann, D., Schweitzer, J. J., & Mundorf, N. (1994). Menstrual cycle variation of women's interest in erotica.

Archives of Sexual Behavior, 23, 579–597. doi:10.1007/BF01541499

Zimbardo, P. (1977). *Shyness: What is it and what to do about it.* London: Pan Books.

About the Contributors

Robert Z. Zheng is Assistant Professor of Instructional Design and Educational Technology in the Educational Psychology Department at the University of Utah. His research agenda includes online learning and pedagogy, multimedia and cognition, and educational technology and assessment. He edited and co-edited several books including *Understanding Online Instructional Modeling: Theories and Practices (2007), Cognitive Effects of Multimedia Learning (2008),* and *Adolescent Online Social Communication and Behavior: Relationship Formation on the Internet (2009).* He is the author of numerous book chapters and peer-reviewed journal papers on the topics of cognitive load, multimedia, Web-based instruction, and problem solving in multimedia learning.

Jason J. Burrow-Sanchez, PhD, is Associate Professor of Counseling Psychology in the Educational Psychology Department at the University of Utah. His research interest is in the area of at-risk adolescents with a specific focus on the prevention and treatment of substance abuse problems in school and community settings. He is also a licensed psychologist and his clinical experience includes working with adolescents experiencing substance abuse and other problem behavior.

Clifford J. Drew is Associate Dean for Research and Outreach in the College of Education at the University of Utah. He is also a professor in the Special Education and Educational Psychology Departments. Dr. Drew came to the University of Utah in 1971 after serving on the faculties of the University of Texas at Austin and Kent State University. He received his master's degree from the University of Illinois and his Ph.D. from the University of Oregon. He has published numerous articles in education and related areas including intellectual disabilities, research design, statistics, diagnostic assessment, cognition, evaluation related to the law and information technology. His most recent book, *Designing and Conducting Research in Education* (Sage, 2008) is Dr. Drew's 30th text. His professional interests include research methods in education and psychology, human development and disabilities, applications of information technology, and outreach in higher education.

* * *

Christine Allison has undergraduate and master's degrees in Special Education and Transition to Work for Students with Special Needs. She is currently pursuing a doctoral degree in Educational Psychology at Kent State University with a research focus on the use of use massive multiplayer online gaming environments as support for students with special needs.

Ikuko Aoyama is a doctoral student in Educational Psychology program at Baylor University. She is also involved in the federally funded program, called GEAR UP (Gaining Early Awareness and Readiness for Undergraduate Programs) as a research assistant. Her research interests are bullying/cyberbullying including cross-cultural study and development of valid/reliable instrument to measure cyberbullying.

Larry L. Burriss (Ph.D., J.D.) is a professor of journalism in the College of Mass Communication at Middle Tennessee State University where he teaches Media Law and Mass Media & National Security. He has served as dean of the College of Mass Communication and as director of the School of Journalism. He received his doctorate from Ohio University and his law degree from Concord Law School. Dr. Burriss has made numerous presentations at national and international conferences on the subject of children's safety on the Internet, and has written extensively for both popular and academic publications.

Megan E. Call, MS, is a graduate student in the Counseling Psychology program in the Educational Psychology Department at the University of Utah. Her research interest is in developing and evaluation school-based prevention programming for adolescents at risk for substance abuse problems. Her clinical experience includes working with adolescents and adults experiencing substance abuse problems.

Muhammet Demirbilek (Ph.D.) is a visiting Post Doctoral Researcher at Games, Learning, and Society (GLS) group in the Educational Communications and Technology division of Curriculum and Instruction at the University of Wisconsin-Madison and an Assistant Professor of Educational Technology at Suleyman Demirel University, Turkey. Demirbilek was the partner and IT expert of Implementing Learning Game Resources Based on Educational Content project (ILGRECO: Grundtvig 1: European Union Cooperation Project). He is a team member of European Union Lifelong Learning program project titled Increased Mainstreaming of Games in Learning Policies (IMAGINE: Multilateral project. EU Lifelong Learning Program). Demirbilek earned his PhD and masters degree in Educational Technology program from University of Florida. He also holds B.S. and MS degrees in electronics engineering. He worked on the PT3 project and served as a graduate assistant in the School of Teaching and Learning at the University of Florida.

Stephanie Donnelly earned a BS in Psychology from Brigham Young University and a M.Ed in Counseling Psychology from the University of Utah. She is currently a doctoral student in the Counseling Psychology program at the University of Miami. Her research interests include the development of culturally adapted mental health treatments for underserved populations and the impact of immigration and acculturation issues on women's decision to seek assistance for dealing with domestic violence.

Sharmila Pixy Ferris (PhD 1995, Pennsylvania State University) is Professor in the Department of Communication at William Paterson University of New Jersey. Her research brings an interdisciplinary focus to the study of computer-mediated communication, and her work can be seen in both online journals (such as *The Journal of Electronic Publishing, Innovate, The Electronic Journal of Communication, Interpersonal Computing and Technology* and *First Monday)* and print journals (such as *Qualitative Research Reports,* and *The New Jersey Journal of Communication*). She has co-edited several books in the area of CMC for IGI/Idea Group including *Teaching and learning with virtual teams* (2005) and

Virtual and collaborative teams: Theory, process and practice (2004), with Sue Godar, and *Online Instructional Modeling: Theories and Practices* (2007), with Robert Zheng. She is also an experienced consultant (with clients like State Farm, AAA, RTP Environmental and BAE Engineering, among others) and dedicated teacher with a co-authored book in the area of faculty development: *Beyond survival in the academy: A practical guide for beginning academics* (2003, Hampton Press).

Mark Griffiths (Ph.D.) is a Chartered Psychologist and Professor of Gambling Studies at the Nottingham Trent University, and Director of the International Gaming Research Unit. He has spent over two decades in the field is internationally known for his work into gambling and gaming. He has published over 210 refereed research papers, three books, over 55 book chapters and over 600 other articles. He has served on numerous national and international committees and gambling charities (e.g. National Chair of GamCare, Society for the Study of Gambling, Gamblers Anonymous General Services Board, National Council on Gambling etc.). He has won eight national and international awards for his work including the John Rosecrance Prize (1994), the CELEJ Prize (1998) and the Joseph Lister Prize (2004). He also does a lot of freelance journalism and has appeared on over 1800 radio and television programmes.

Louis Leung (Ph.D.) is Associate Professor in the School of Journalism & Communication at the Chinese University of Hong Kong and was Assistant Professor at the University of Hawaii at Manoa. He currently serves as Director of Center for Communication Research conducting public opinion polls on issues related to media and society. His research interests focus on the uses and impact of new communication technologies. He is co-editor of *Embedding into Our Lives: New Opportunities and Challenges of the Internet* (HK: Chinese University Press, 2008) and *Impact and Issues in New Media: Toward Intelligent Societies* (NJ: Hampton Press, 2004). Some of his recent publications appear in *Journal of Broadcasting & Electronic Media, Journalism and Mass Communication Quarterly, CyberPsychology & Society, New Media & Society, Telematics and Informatics, Telecommunications Policy, Asian Journal of Communication, and Gazette*. He holds a PhD in communication from the University of Texas at Austin.

Gustavo S. Mesch holds a PhD from the Ohio State University and is an Associate Professor of Sociology at the University of Haifa. He is currently the Chair of the Communication and Information Technologies section of the American Sociological Association. He had studied the effects of information and communication technologies on youth social networks, contextual factors affecting communication channel choice and parent-adolescent conflicts over Internet use. Currently he is conducting two major studies. The first is a 4 year longitudinal study on social inequalities in access to the Internet, focusing on the consequences of different Internet uses on the access to social capital in Israel. The second is a longitudinal study of the Internet population investigating the determinants of social networking sites drop-outs.

Kenneth L. Miller (Ph.D.) is Associate Professor in the counseling program in Youngstown University, USA. He earned his B.A. in Sociology (Social Work) from Purdue University, M.S. Ed. in Counseling from Purdue University Calumet, and Ph.D. in Counselor Education from Purdue University. Prior to joining the faculty at Youngstown State University, Dr. Miller held tenure-track positions at The University of Hawaii at Manoa, The Citadel, and California State University, San Bernardino. Dr. Miller's teaching interests include appraisal techniques in counseling, counseling practicum/internship, and clinical supervision. His research interests include: the effectiveness of Internet communication tools on relationship development, particularly in the delivery of clinical supervision; prevention and treatment of child abuse and neglect; the impact of Home Outreach Programs on autistic children's attainment of communication and functional goals; and, measurement of cultural bias and discrimination.

Susan Miller (Ph.D.) earned a bachelor's degree at the University of Chicago and master's and doctoral degrees (educational psychology) at Purdue University. Prior to joining the faculty in educational psychology and instructional technology at Kent State University, Dr. Miller held a tenure-track position at Temple University and a tenured position at Texas A & M University-Commerce. Dr. Miller's teaching includes the areas of development, educational psychology, cognition, and educational technology. Her research interests focus on the use of advance technologies, simulations, and gaming in academic settings. She has been awarded several federal and state grants in the area of technology and learning. Dr. Miller has published extensively regarding the use of technology for learning as well as the measurement of cultural bias and discrimination in higher education.

Berna Mutlu is a Ph.D. candidate at the University of Florida in ESOL/Bilingual Education program. She currently teaches courses on ESOL methods and strategies for pre-service teachers at the same institution. Her research interests include innovative instructional strategies for successful second language development and computer assisted language learning.

Myron Orleans (Ph.D.) is a retired professor who continues to teach sociology and criminology online courses for different universities. He travels frequently to Asia and Brazil while maintaining his Internet connections. His publications have been in the area of social theory, computer use, communications, deviance and aging. He founded and co-edited a now non-operational online journal that remains accessible on the Internet: The Journal of Mundane Behavior: http://www.mundanebehavior.org. He is active in fitness activities, enjoys cultural learning with a particular emphasis on spicy foods. His post-adolescent children survived the usual cyber challenges and are engaged in productive early adulthood pursuits. Currently, Orleans is striving to attain the proper balance between enjoying the fruits of a long professorial career while remaining an engaged scholar.

Bryant Paul (Ph.D. in Communication [2003]: University of California, Santa Barbara) is an Assistant Professor in the Department of Telecommunications at Indiana University. His research and teaching interests include the social and psychological effects of mediated sexual depictions and evolutionary psychological explanations for media effects.

Maja Pivec is Professor of Game-Based Learning and e-Learning at the University of Applied Sciences FH JOANNEUM in Graz, Austria. For her research achievements, Maja Pivec received in the year 2001 Herta Firnberg Award (Austria) in the field of computer science. In the 2003 she was awarded by European Science Foundation in form of a grant for an interdisciplinary workshop organisation in the field of affective and emotional aspects of human-computer interaction, with emphasis on game-based learning and innovative learning approaches. Maja's full academic resume can be viewed on http://www.majapivec.com.

Paul Pivec has worked in computing for over 30 years in all aspects of the industry. He has consulted to both game development and publishing companies, and teaches game development at tertiary level. He has a Masters degree in Computer Technology with specific emphasis on digital games. His thesis showed that multitasking skills are enhanced from player immersive computer games. He also has a graduate diploma in higher education and is currently working on his PhD in Game-Based Learning at Deakin University in Melbourne, Australia. Paul's academic history can be seen at http://www.paupivec.com.

Lelia Samson is a PhD student at Indiana University, Department of Telecommunications. Her research focuses on processing arousing media messages, media content analysis, dynamic systems and developmental psychology.

Dr. Tony L. Talbert, Associate Professor in the School of Education at Baylor University, is a qualitative and ethnographic researcher whose teaching and research areas of expertise include: qualitative research design and analysis; social studies education; democracy education; peace education; and, social justice education. Dr. Talbert's refers to his field of research as Education As Democracy which integrates democracy, peace, social studies, and social justice education into a focused discipline of qualitative and ethnographic inquiry examining teacher and student empowerment through activist engagement in political, economic, and social issues confronting education.

Laura Widyanto (Ph.D.) is a psychologist who recently completed her doctoral thesis on Internet addiction at the Nottingham Trent University. Dr Widyanto has published her research into online identity and Internet addiction in a number of journals including *CyberPsychology and Behavior* and the *International Journal of Mental Health and Addiction*.

Zheng Yan received a doctoral degree in Human Development and Psychology from Harvard University Graduate School of Education and currently is Associate Professor of Educational and Developmental Psychology at State University of New York, Albany with primary research interest in Internet and child development and longitudinal research methodology.

Index